CIVIC CENTER
PROPOSED FOR THE CITY OF
LOS ANGELES
CALIFORNIA
LEGEND
PARKS AND PARKED WAYS
BUILDINGS
PUBLIC BUILDINGS
RAIL ROADS
LLOYD WRIGHT
ARCHITECT
LOS ANGELES CALIFORNIA
BOULEVARD TO ELYSIAN PARK
NORMAL
WELFARE
COURT
COUNTY BLDS
CITY HALL
UPPER TERRACE
RAPID TRANSIT
STATION PLAZA
CHAMBER OF COMM
FEDERAL POST
TEMPLE ST
OLD PLAZA
NEW PLAZA
BROAD WAY
FIRST STREET
SECOND
THIRD STREET
HILL STREET
FORUM
UPPER TERRACE GARDENS
GALLERIES (OVER)
TECHNICAL & MECHANICAL ARTS BLDS
FINE ARTS BUILDINGS
ELEVATORS FROM LOWER LEVEL STREETS & RAPID TRANSIT SUBWAYS
AIR-PLANE LANDING
FLOWER STREET
PRESENT LIBRARY SITE
PERSHING SQUARE
OLIVE STREET
CW01558755

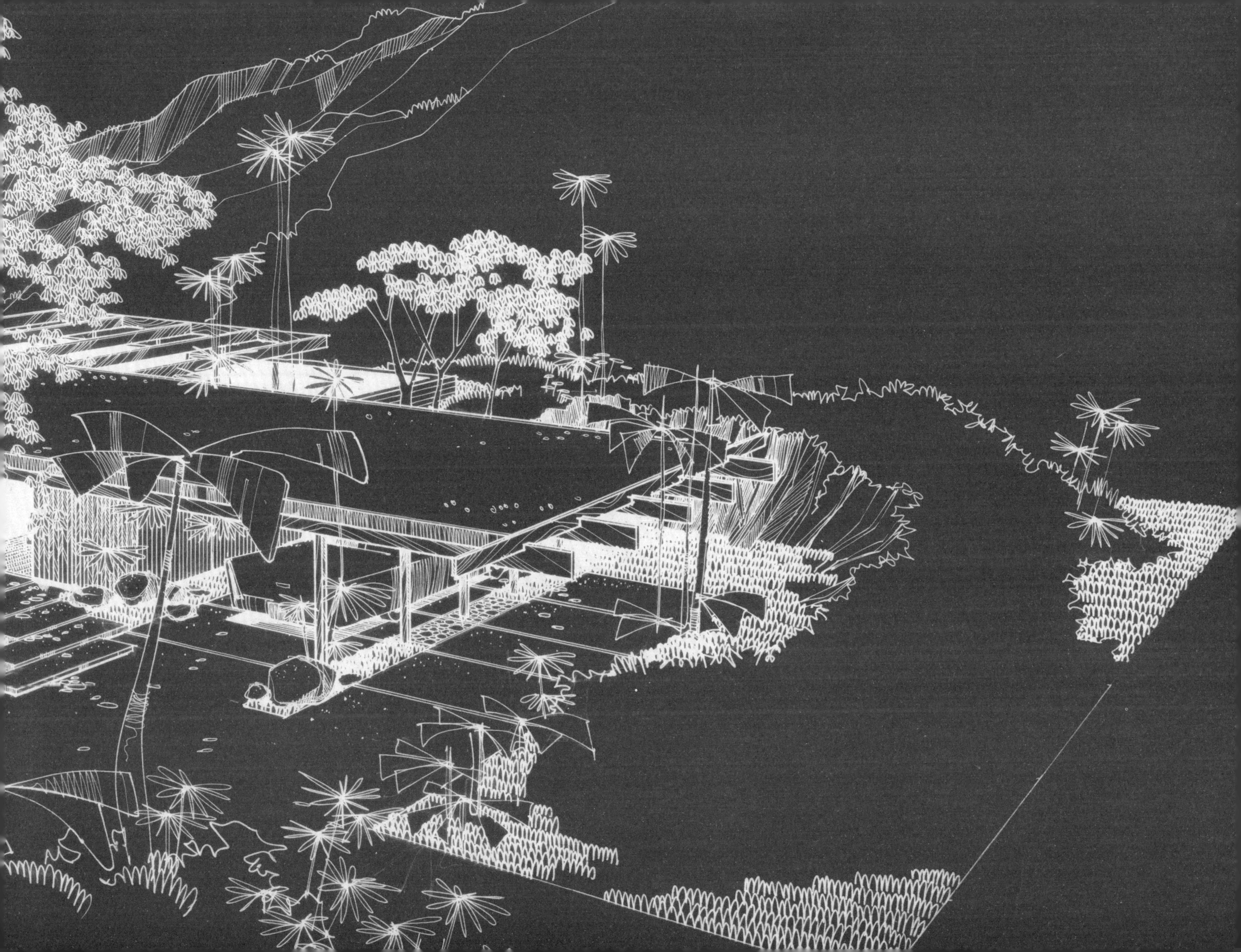

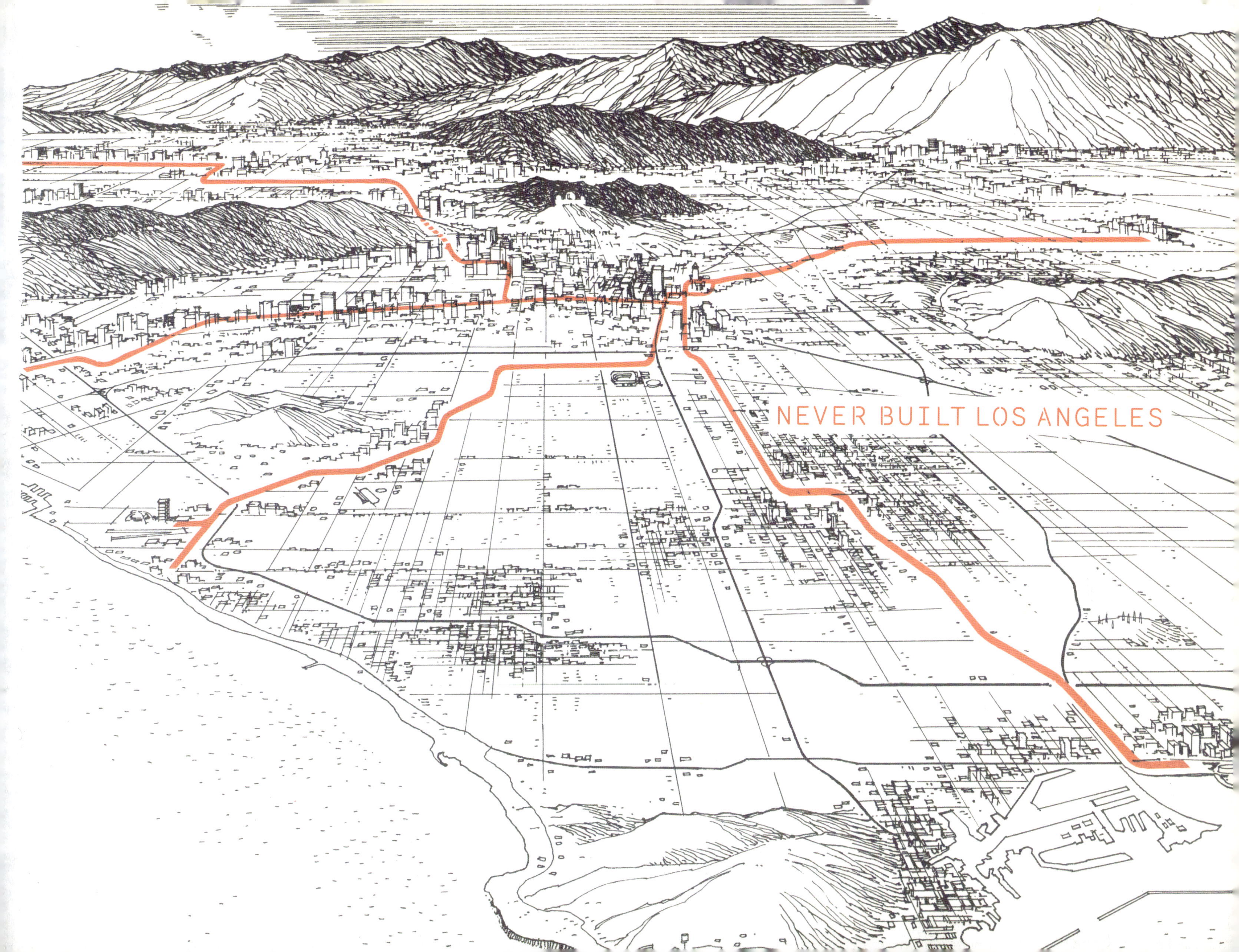
NEVER BUILT LOS ANGELES

MARKETLAND

Bullocks
Bullocks
NEW

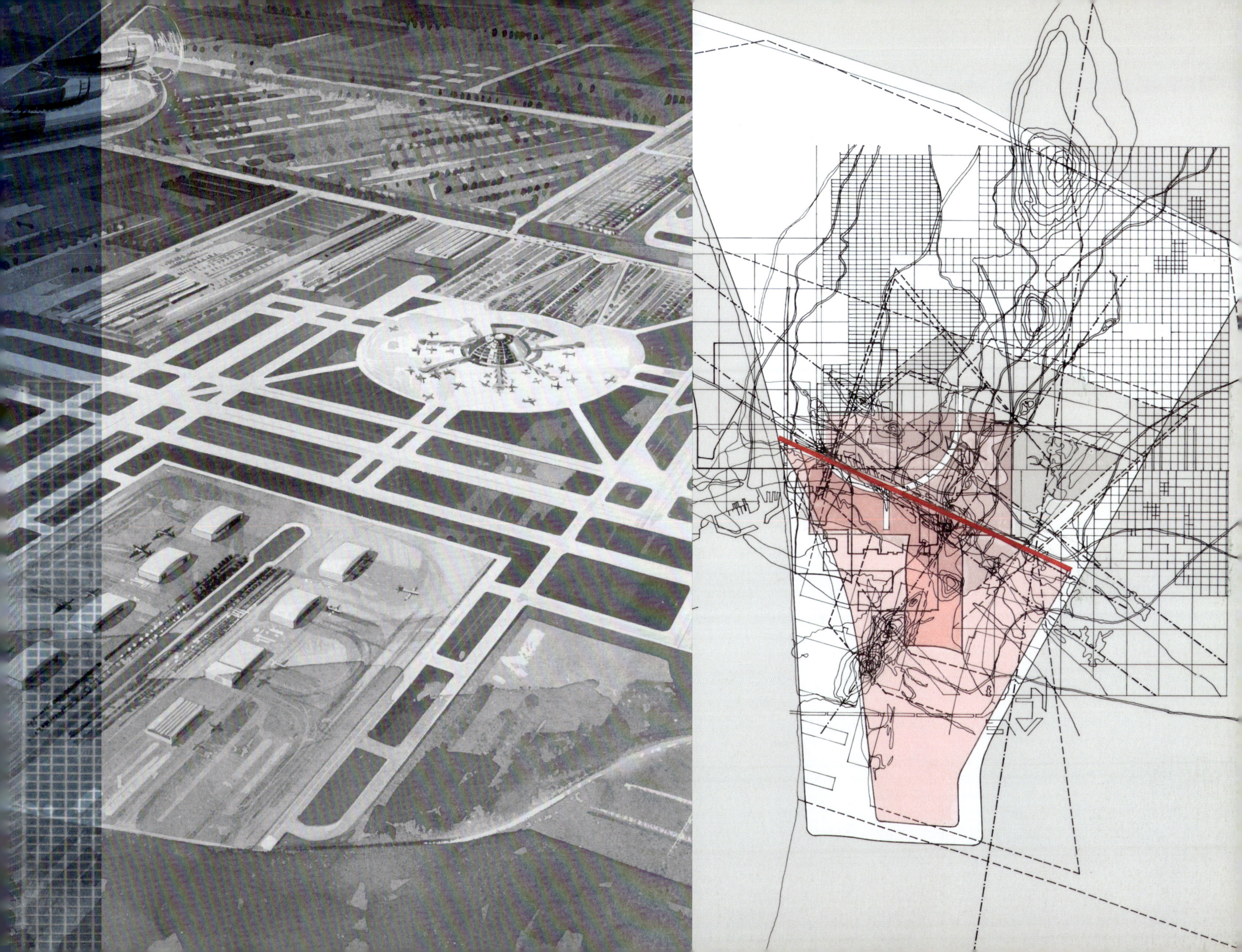

NEVER BUILT

LOS ANGELES

GREG GOLDIN SAM LUBELL

foreword by THOM MAYNE

METROPOLIS BOOKS

HOLLYWOOD
UCLA
SANTA MONICA
DODGER STADIUM
STAPLES
USC
MONTEREY PARK
SOUTH BAY
LOS ANGELES
CALABASAS
BEVERLY HILLS
WEST HOLLYWOOD
CULVER CITY
INGLEWOOD
HAWTHORNE
GARDENA
TORRANCE
CARSON
COMPTON
LYNWOOD
SOUTH GATE
HUNTINGTON PARK
VERNON
MAYWOOD
BELL
DOWNEY
PARAMOUNT
BELLFLOWER
LAKEWOOD
LONG BEACH
SIGNAL HILL
NORWALK
CERRITOS
ARTESIA
LA PALMA
CYPRESS
LOS ALAMITOS
SANTA FE SPRINGS
PICO RIVERA
MONTEBELLO
ROSEMEAD
ALHAMBRA
SAN GABRIEL
SAN MARINO
SOUTH PASADENA
PASADENA
TEMPLE CITY
SOUTH EL MONTE
LOMITA
ROLLING HILLS ESTATES
ROLLING HILLS
RANCHO PALOS VERDES

DUARTE
GLENDORA
AZUSA
IRWINDALE
LA VERNE
CLAREMONT
UPLAND
RANCHO
CUCAMONGA
RIALTO
BALDWIN
PARK
COVINA
SAN
DIMAS
MONTCLAIR
FONTANA
COLTON
BLOOMINGTON
WEST
COVINA
LA
PUENTE
WALNUT
POMONA
DIAMOND
BAR
INDUSTRY
ONTARIO
CHINO
ROWLAND
HEIGHTS
LA HABRA
HEIGHTS
CHINO HILLS
LA
HABRA
BREA
CHINO HILLS
STATE PARK
RIVERSIDE
NORCO
YORBA
LINDA
PLACENTIA
FULLERTON
CORONA
ANAHEIM
ORANGE
VILLA
PARK
ANAHEIM
STANTON
GARDEN GROVE
ESTMINSTER
LAKE
MATHEWS
IRVINE
LAKE
CLEVELAND
NATIONAL
FOREST
WEIR CANYON
WILDERNESS PARK
IRVINE
REGIONAL
PARK
SAN BERNARDINO CO.
RIVERSIDE CO.
LOS ANGELES CO.
ORANGE CO.

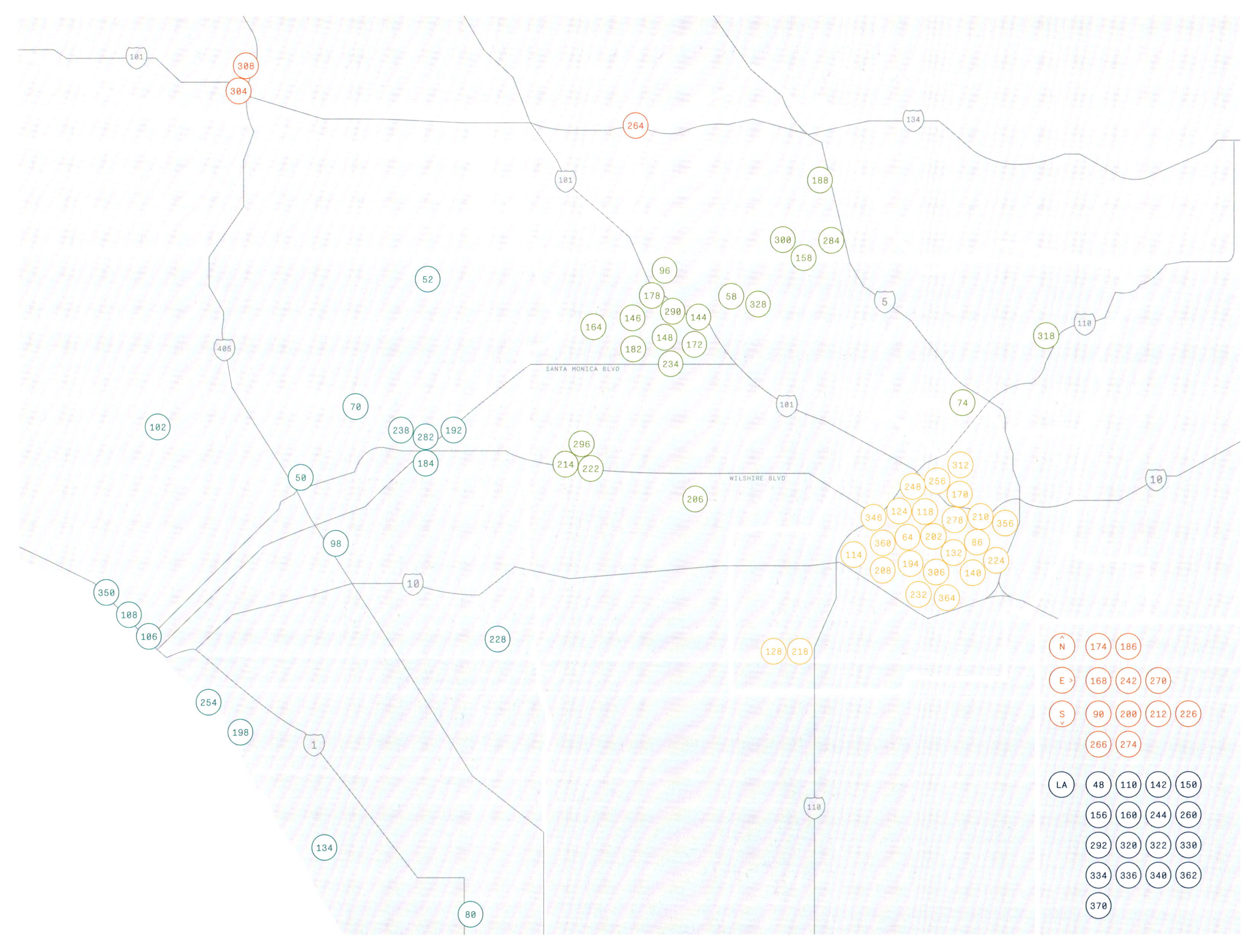

101
308
304
264
134
101
188
300
284
158
96
52
178
290
144
58
328
5
110
164
146
148
172
318
182
234
405
SANTA MONICA BLVD
101
74
70
102
238
282
192
296
312
214
222
256
50
184
WILSHIRE BLVD
248
170
10
206
346
124
118
278
210
356
98
360
64
202
86
114
132
208
194
306
140
224
10
232
364
350
108
106
228
128
218
N
174
186
E
168
242
270
S
90
200
212
226
266
274
254
198
1
LA
48
110
142
150
156
160
244
260
110
292
320
322
330
134
334
336
340
362
80
370

CONTENTS

LA CITYWIDE

WS WEST SIDE

MC MID-CITY

DT DOWNTOWN

SB SUBURBS

MISSED OPPORTUNITIES: LOS ANGELES

2013

LA

THOM MAYNE

The built environment of Los Angeles has always exhibited a split personality of presence and potential. Branded as a tabula rasa on an urban scale, L.A. is a heterogeneous city of immigrants governed by a dispersed, fluctuating center of authority. It has an open-ended culture that constantly emerges to overturn its own past and future. During the past 100 years, the city has cultivated an architectural practice parallel to this identity of flexibility and reinvention, in which designers have found themselves united by an understanding of innovation as an engine of transformation. Yet this conversation—which has evolved as Los Angeles itself has grown—is often out of sync, projecting to an international audience while remaining inaudible on a local level.

Los Angeles's relationship to its architecture is unique among major American metropolitan centers, characterized by a laissez-faire environment that has afforded incredible experimentation in the private sector. Commissions have largely come at the behest of a small group of idiosyncratic clients—quirky but not necessarily wealthy—who have supported provocative projects on a domestic scale. Public architecture, with a few exceptions, has been similarly dependent upon individual donors and their personal agendas rather than being generated out of the interconnected institutional framework that supports civic architecture in New York and other established American cities.

The radical practice that has grown here has seen four major iterations, but its origins are quintessentially L.A. in their eclecticism, launched from a dialogue between two native Austrians—Rudolph M. Schindler and Richard Neutra—in a foreign city. Modernist architect Adolph Loos had advised Schindler, then a student, to pursue work outside Vienna, which at the time was pervaded by a growing conservatism. In 1914, Schindler came to the United States to work with Frank Lloyd Wright, who brought him to Los Angeles to oversee construction on the Barnsdall House. Neutra and his wife, Dione, followed in 1923 and joined Schindler and his wife, Pauline, in the Kings Road House, which Schindler designed as an experiment in communal living. The mild climate and radicalized underground made Los Angeles an ideal laboratory for ideas that these architects transplanted from the intellectual avant-gardes in their home country. Both came with very European, modernist aspirations; and while these concepts were tolerated in residential construction, they proved too strange and too foreign to catch on in the public imagination of a still relatively provincial city. For instance, Neutra's Lovell House (1927–29), with its unprecedented reconsideration of domestic space, predates Le Corbusier's game-changing Villa Savoye (1928–31) yet remained relatively unsung and never led to bigger public commissions.

With the launch of John Entenza's Case Study House program in 1945, architects started to expand the residential-scale experiments of a few iconoclastic individuals into a coherent program aimed at transforming the realities of everyday living. Supported by a revamped magazine, *Arts & Architecture*, a current

↗ Morphosis's plan for LACMA, 2001

→ Morphosis's 101 Pedestrian Bridge, a connector between the Civic Center and the Los Angeles Plaza, over the 101 Freeway, 1998

THE PLAZA PROPOSED LOS ANGELES TERMINAL

PLAZA

TERMINAL STATION

ALISO STREET

MAIN STREET

ALAMEDA

CASE NO 970, ET SEQ. EXHIBIT NO 2 OF CENTRAL DEVELOPMENT ASSO-CIATION, FILED JULY 26, 1917

Exhibit No. 3 Central Development Association

FIG. 107. PERSPECTIVE OF UNION TERMINAL AT THE PLAZA

↖
Proposal by the Central Development Association for Los Angeles's Union Station, 1918

←←
Richard Neutra's proposal for a Museum of Contemporary Art, Westwood, 1936

←
Fred Lyman's vision of a Malibu Monorail

was developing in Los Angeles that linked the city with the broader modernist project, despite the lag in civic support.

By the 1960s, young architects of my generation perceived an exhaustion of the problems of modernism and challenged the reductionist agenda through new questions advancing complexity and hybridization. With the founding of UCLA's architecture program in 1968 and SCI-Arc in 1972, the architectural discourse in Los Angeles experienced an enormous acceleration, corresponding with the city's growth from a provincial town into a major metropolis of international influence. As the city still lacked an ongoing public dialogue about architecture and urbanism, schools now became the main forum for exchanging ideas, facilitating a powerful conceptual camaraderie that allowed up-and-comers to break from their intellectual predecessors in a major way.

As possibilities shifted in the nineties with the advance of digital work environments, Los Angeles continued to play host to vanguard ideas, with a new wave of designers exploring nonlinear progressions in form and knowledge through more fluid approaches to site and context. On the international stage, Los Angeles gained a reputation as an inexhaustible source of breakthroughs in design and urban planning. As an architectural culture, our identity was evolving; we were no longer mere experimenters on a domestic scale but now major exporters of creative capital. And, continuing the tradition of important ideas being implemented outside the local public arena, architectural practice in Los Angeles expanded to large-scale civic work, though not in our own backyard.

People love to portray the freedom of L.A.'s pluralism as a strength; in reality, it goes hand in hand with the city's distinct failure to collectively embrace communal projects. That pluralism, combined with the lack of an ordering center, has prevented the cohesion necessary for rigorous architecture to take root in the civic sphere. Instead, the huge amount of talent in this city is being put to use on architectural projects globally and, except in rare instances, has played little role in shaping our public environment.

The real missed opportunity of Los Angeles, then, lies in the loss or displacement of intellectual creative capital that has occurred as our architects move on to other cities, other countries, other opportunities. The treasure trove of innovation contained in this book attests to a history of latent, untapped potential, yet the message of these unrealized projects is one of not only regret but also optimism. In considering *Never Built Los Angeles*, we see that our city clearly still holds its original promise—that there remains unfinished space here to transform and build.

LA

CITY OF ILLUSIONS

GREG GOLDIN
SAM LUBELL

2013

A city is but the shadow cast by men's thoughts.

H. M. Tomlinson

Cities boom and then they bust. But when they're flush, they're alive with architectural and urban bluster—even greatness. Think of Tikal's towers and Chicago's skyscrapers. Think of the vertical city of the Anasazi and the vertical city of Manhattan. Think of St. Paul's Cathedral in London, the Eiffel Tower in Paris, and Angkor Wat in Cambodia. Even cities on the periphery of global power produce civic masterpieces that embody and embolden the spirit of the place. Seattle commissioned Rem Koolhaas to build its main library. Redding, California, got Santiago Calatrava to build the Sundial Bridge. Seville had Jürgen Mayer erect Metropol Parasol. And Bilbao changed the very idea of a building when it put up Frank Gehry's Guggenheim. Great cities rise around ambitions, often written in sticks and stone, and steel and glass.

And then there is Los Angeles, always the exception.

The city is a mecca for architects, home to two Pritzker Prize winners (Gehry and Thom Mayne) and a roll call of modern architecture's most famous talents. The entertainment hub of the United States, if not the world, it is a magnet for ingenuity, individuality, and imaginative ideas. Yet Los Angeles lacks the grand gestures of urban innovation. Several of the best houses of the twentieth century were conceived and built here, but the same cannot be said of civic buildings or parks or plazas or monuments. With a few notable exceptions—Los Angeles City Hall, Disney Hall, the Bradbury Building, the Department of Water and Power building, Griffith Park Observatory, and Griffith Park itself—a gift for public architecture and planning is missing. These scattered, almost accidental urban triumphs are so singular that they underscore how little has been done, and how little they alone can do, to piece the city together into a compelling whole. The urban historian Robert M. Fogelson aptly titled his book about Los Angeles *The Fragmented Metropolis*. Essayist William Alexander McClung described the city as "landscapes of desire," implying someplace transient, fickle, rewritable.

The gap between Los Angeles's genius for design and its public output reveals a reluctant city whose institutions, citizens, politics, and infrastructure, not to mention its sheer size, have often undermined inspired urban schemes. The result: an enormous, 100-year backlog of unbuilt proposals, many of them relegated to dusky archives, dank newspaper morgues, and disorderly stacks of ephemera. These marvels include the energetic, the audacious, and the ludicrous. They consist of wholesale master plans; buildings of all types; parks, civic squares, green spaces, and public gathering points; monuments and follies, including some hilariously farcical amusement parks; and transit designs stretching in all directions over land and sea, adopting every foreseeable technology from monorail to flying bus. A few of these—and certainly all of them combined—would have transformed both the reality and the collective perception of the metropolis. Perhaps Los Angeles's befuddling illegibility would have yielded to a comprehensible, citylike clarity.

→ Big projects destined to fail

GRIFFITH TRAM BATTLE LOOMING

Meeting Unveils Plans

By JIM NEWSOM

HOLLYWOOD — A bomb was lighted during a Hollywood premiere-like press conference which promises to explode into a bitter public and political controversy today. The gunpowder—a 6.5 million dollar, privately financed installation for the top of Mount Hollywood, deep in Griffith Park.

As Councilman Arthur Snider stood at the corner of Hollywood and Vine to protest, two giant filmland industrial

---

Los Angeles Times

In Three Parts — PART II

...IDAY MORNING, AUGUST 16, 1929.

CITY NEWS—EDITORIAL—SOC...

"HOW TO LIVE" TOLD BY COLE ON 103rd BIRTHDAY

[P. & A. Photo]

Young Man Offers Congratulations

...usha Cole, left, being congratulated on the occasion of his 103rd birthday by C. R. Hodges, 73 years of age, of Alhambra.

Galusha Cole, who celebrated ...s one hundred and third ...rthday over in Pasadena yes...rday, gave out his recipe on ...w to live to be 100 or more ...ars old.

Here it is:

Just live!

In short, Mr. Cole does not ...lieve there is any recipe or ...ogram of living that will ...ing one to a life of 100 years ... more.

"Why," he hesitated and ...oked around for a moment as ... sought an answer to such a ...ly question, "there isn't any ...le to follow if you want to ...e to be 100. You just live. If ...u are to live to be 100 you will ...e to be 100; and that's all ...ere is to it."

NO DAILY DOZEN

"You never went through any ...ally dozen or followed an ...ghteen-day diet, did you?"

He let out a snort of ridicule ... such nonsensical stunts.

"Land sakes, no!" he ex...aimed.

The outstanding feature about ...r. Cole is the fine state of ...eservation that the world ...nds him in at 103 years of age ...physically and mentally. The ...sitor upon meeting him would ...ver guess that he is 103 years ... age. In the first place, his ...atures do not tell the story of ... years of life. He is really ...ing, not just existing. He ... up every day after a regular ...ght's sleep of about eight ...ours. He has a breakfast of ...real, fruit once in a while, ...ffee, perhaps a doughnut, pan...kes occasionally and if there

...wears glasses. He sits in his rocking chair and reads.

Once in a while Mr. Cole takes a short walk. He is not walking in the past year as much as he used to. It will be recalled that on his ninety-fifth birthday he walked up to the top of Mt. Wilson.

"It was a crazy thing to do," said Miss Irene Wilbur, who has kept house for Mr. Cole ever since his wife, Susan, died eight years ago. Mr. Cole laughed at that comment, although somewhat sheepishly.

"Do you credit your long life to any particular program of living that you followed?" he was asked yesterday.

"Not a bit of it," he came right back. "I have just lived, that's all. I have lived a perfectly normal life. I guess I was meant to live a long life and that's all there is to it. I never have taken over a few spoonfuls of medicine in my whole life. I never was really ill."

WORKED ON FARM

"It's just like this," broke in Miss Wilbur, "when the Lord is ready to take him He will take him."

"Certainly!" agreed Mr. Cole, "that's it."

"Do you smoke?" he was asked.

No, he has not smoked since he was married, many, many years ago. His wife bet him he could not quit and he just showed her he could.

Mr. Cole has done various types of work in his day, from hard work on the farm to teaching singing lessons. He went out in the back yard yesterday and took a few swings at the corn patch with his hoe just

STEEL LEADERS VISIT TORRANCE

New York Men Inspect Plant of Columbia Company

Coast Manager Denies Plan to Make Purchase

Rumored Building Site Deal Steel Persists

Two vice-presidents of the United States Steel Corporation of New York, I. L. Hughes and John Hulst, are in Los Angeles and yesterday inspected the Torrance plant of the Columbia Steel Company which was reported earlier in the month to have given the larger corporation a ninety-day option on its plants.

The two vice-presidents were accompanied by A. T. De Forrest of San Francisco, who has charge of the corporation's western activities. Mr. De Forrest yesterday denied rumors current that the official visit here is for the purpose of selecting a site for the erection of a plant.

"Mr. Hughes and Mr. Hulst are in Los Angeles to look over our property here. This is their first visit to the Coast and I am just showing them about a bit," De Forrest declared. "As to the purchase of the Columbia plant I know nothing of it. Such matters are decided in New York. Nor do I know anything of the building of a factory here."

Recent purchase by the Columbia Steel Company of thirty-four acres of land adjoining its Torrance plant gave rise to the report the company planned the erection of tube mills on the property. The plant at present consists of a three-unit rolling mill, sheet mill and foundry. Products include angles, channels, reinforcing bars, sheet and blue annealed steel and castings.

The visit to Los Angeles of the corporation officials was intimated by J. D. Grant, San Francisco, president of the Columbia company, recently when he verified the report that United States Steel had been given a ninety-day option on the Columbia properties and that officials of the larger concern would inspect the Torrance property.

The Columbia Steel Company operates four plants in the West, the others being at Provo, Utah, Pittsburg, Cal., and Portland.

SKYSCRAPER HOTEL SKETCHED

Forty Stories to Tower Over Wilshire

Architect's Drawing of $5,000,000 Structure That Will Adorn Boulevard

THE first photograph of the sketch of the proposed $5,000,000 forty-

PHONE CHARGES CUT CONTESTED

State Railway Board Hears Schedules on Rates

Engineer and Werner Vary on Extent of Slash

Company's Counsel Combats Reduction Programs

What is a fair earning rate for a telephone company servicing Los Angeles.

At yesterday's investigation by the State Railroad Commission into Los Angeles telephone rates there developed a wide diversity of opinion.

Lester S. Ready, consulting engineer for the commission, declared on the witness stand that 7½ per cent is an adequate rate for the Southern California Telephone Company to earn

City Attorney Werner told the commission that 6½ per cent will be sufficient.

Oscar Lawler, attorney for the telephone company, declared that the company cannot operate successfully for less than an 8 per cent return.

BOARD TO CONSIDER

There was only one point of agreement, and that developed at the afternoon session when Dion Holm representing the City Attorney's office of San Francisco, interposed and asked permission to file briefs with the commission to prove San Francisco's contention that the rate of 6½ per cent, as proposed by City Attorney Werner, is an adequate rate of return. The commission took all recommendations under advisement.

The hearing, launched in June on the commission's own motion to investigate the rates and practices of various public utilities companies operating in California, was resumed yesterday when the commission's engineer submitted a report recommending that the Southern California Telephone Company's rates be reduced $2,200,000 a year. At a former hearing he testified that the company is earning better than 9 per cent, and that 7½ per cent will be a fair rate of return.

Ready's schedule, submitted yes-

PARRISH TO

...URBANK DAILY REVIEW

Established 1908

...Oldest Daily Newspaper In The San Fernando Valley

and Burbank News combined with Magnolia Park News and Sun Valley News.

Associated Press United Press Associated Press Wirephoto

WEATHER

More warm weather is in prospect for Burbank today and tomorrow with the weatherman calling for fair, warm days with a bit of smog and some very high thin clouds. High today near 80. High yesterday 79. Low this morning 51. Noon humidity 25 percent.

...8-220 East Orange Grove BURBANK, CALIF., THURSDAY, MARCH 27, 1952 Phone CHarleston 6-7111 and ROckwell 9-1475 TWO SECTIONS SECTION

Walt Disney Make-Believe Land Project Planned Here

$1,500,000 Dreamland to Rise On Site in Burbank

"Disneyland," a spectacular world of make-believe made reality by the genius of famed cartoon producer Walt Disney is being planned as a $1,500,000 development on Disney Studio property at Riverside and Buena Vista.

Tentative approval has been given by the City Board of Parks and Recreation for use of land leased by the city lying adjacent to the studio property as a picnic and parking site.

"Disneyland will be something of a fair, an exhibition, a playground, a community center, a museum of living facts and a showplace of beauty and magic," according to a description by its creator.

Various scenes of Americana, rides in a "Space Ship" and submarine, zoo of miniature animals and exhibit halls

Transamerica Must Break Up

Reserve Board Votes

...e High State Budget Okayed

The Citizen-News

5¢

...., Hollywood 28, Calif. TUESDAY, JUNE 16, 1959 Phone HOllywood 9-1234 22 Pa...

FILM MUSEUM PLAN OKAYED

ASSEMBLYMEN FIND:

Hollywood...

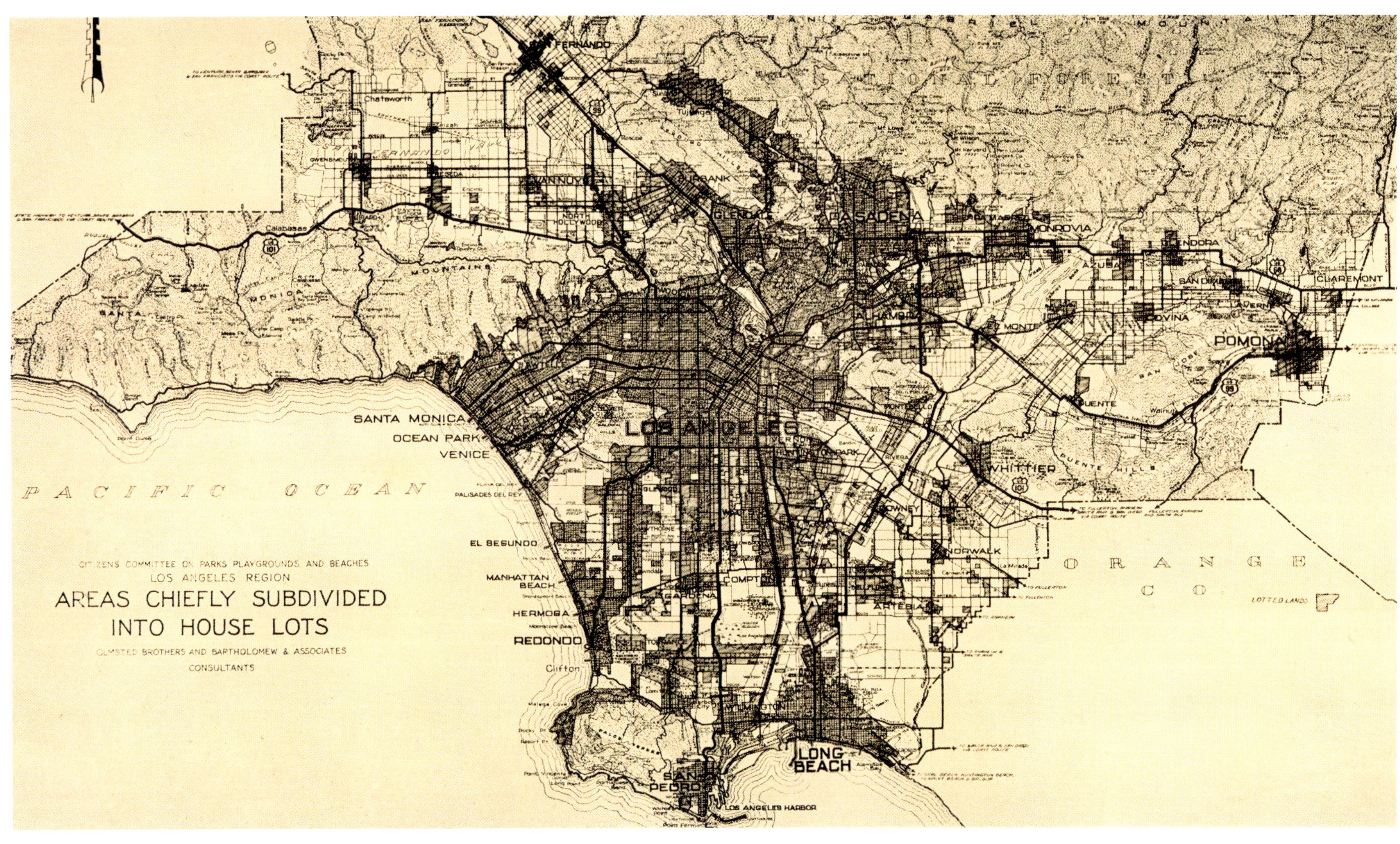

←
Olmsted and Bartholomew's map showing Los Angeles before population boom

→
Los Angeles Times 1913 editorial illustration "Advanced Plan for Relief of Overcrowded Streets"

The stories surrounding these projects tell us what it is about Los Angeles that causes bold architectural efforts to founder. They also shed light on the frustrations of building in general, in which turning dreams into reality requires an almost impossible mixture of civic will, financial luck, and boundless perseverance. Rising out of this narrative of thwarted goals is a catalogue of virtuoso drawings and renderings that, on a visceral level, ignite the imagination, painting an unmistakable picture of a city that might have been—and still could be.

***

DREAMS OF BEAUTY, AMBITION, AND FOLLY

The deepest irony of never-built Los Angeles is that of all the cities in the world, this is one of the richest in architectural, not to mention wider, creativity. Originality, chutzpah, and alternative thinking are its building blocks. Since the early twentieth century, millions have flocked here to escape the rigidity of their surroundings and carry out their unobstructed California fantasies. You came to Los Angeles to fix, or perhaps sully, your lungs or your reputation, but it didn't really matter which, because if all went well, you'd start a movie studio or an aviation corporation or, like Howard Hughes, both.

There's space here for that brand of reckless self-invention, the kind that made Hollywood—the imaginary landscape, not the physical one—the global hub of illusion and delusory place-making. And despite its conservative political machinations and decidedly regressive land use and transportation patterns, Los Angeles is still an outpost of the counterculture and of movie-star liberalism. It's also a center for individuality, where two buildings rarely look alike. "Mexican ranch houses, Samoan huts, Mediterranean villas, Egyptian and Japanese temples, Swiss chalets, Tudor cottages, and every possible combination of these styles," burned satirist Nathanael West in his novel *The Day of the Locust*, peevishly suggesting that "only dynamite would be of any use" against the hodgepodge of frenzied self-expression. Los Angeles, in short, is a pool of unchecked ambition, where waitresses become paparazzi-chased goddesses and parking lot attendants become art barons. If ever a place catered to the immortal ego and its wanton subconscious, this was it.

Something about the innate beauty of the hills, the ocean, and the pellucid air combined with an uneasy feeling of upheaval—fed by earthquakes, drenching rains, and scourging fires—aroused architects' daring impulses in this caldera of ceaseless striving. Fed, too, by what was once an endless supply of money, land, technology, and visionaries, Los Angeles became the capital of single-family residential architectural invention, nurturing some of the greatest talents the country has seen. Irving Gill, Frank Lloyd Wright, Rudolph M. Schindler, Richard Neutra, Wallace Neff, Paul Williams, Rafael Soriano, John Lautner, A. Quincy Jones, Ray Kappe, and Craig Ellwood helped establish Los Angeles—despite its dystopian stereotypes—as the nation's locus for revolutionary home design. John Entenza, in the pages of *Arts & Architecture* magazine, exported the ideals of many of these architects, who found champions among influential critics including Reyner Banham, David Gebhard, and Esther McCoy, and the savvy, indefatigable photographer Julius Shulman.

In contrast, the public realm—with its intimidating blockades of bureaucratic fiat, nervous neighbors, conservative developers, and elusive financing—proved unyielding, particularly when these innovators tried to push the boundaries of convention. Yes, idealists were welcome in Los Angeles, as long as they didn't venture far beyond the ground floor.

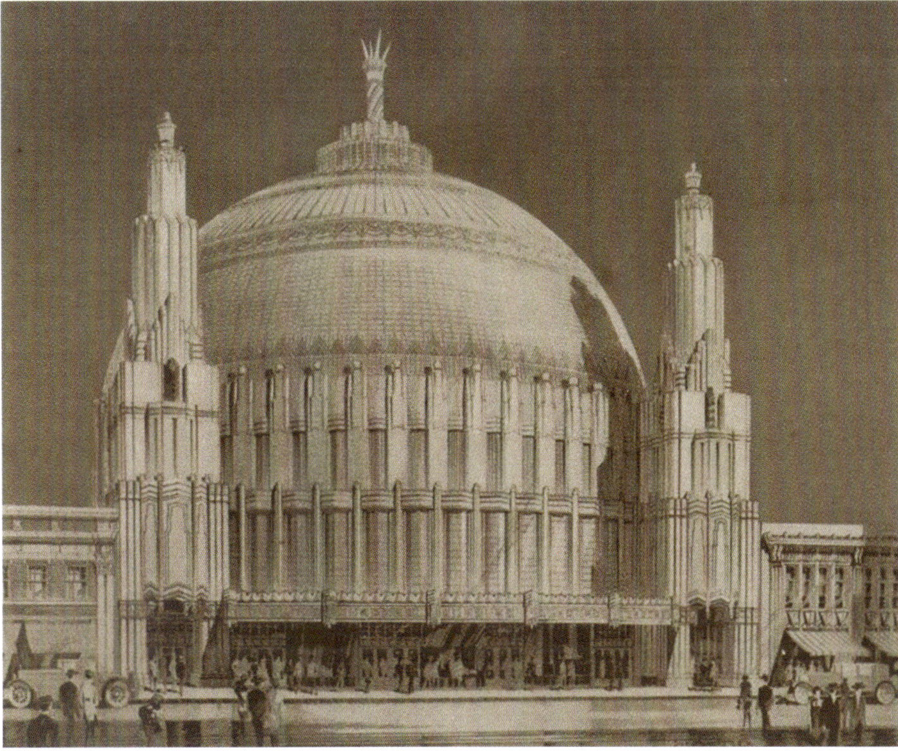

←
George A. Howard Jr., Aqueduct Memorial Fountain for Rose Garden at Exposition Park, 1913

↗
Hollywood Boulevard planetarium and department store proposed by businessman Charles E. Toberman, 1930

↗↗
Rudolph M. Schindler's Photoplay building, 1921

Still, such obstacles did not stem the flow of ultimately frustrated ideas—hopeful, earnest, often arrogant—filling a staggering library of reverie and nerve. Over the last century and into the current one, architects, engineers, landscape designers, planners, and con artists have used Los Angeles as a blank canvas for their hopes, no matter how outlandish. These include a 150-story tower, a hybrid helicopter-bus airlift from Union Station to Los Angeles International Airport (LAX), and plans for more than 100 miles of subway tunnels, as outlined by famed transit planners Kelker, De Leuw and Company back in 1925. There was also John Lautner's Alto Capistrano, which would have launched a series of spaceshiplike apartments to hover above a hillside on the road to San Diego.

The list goes on, decade after decade, bringing to light the lost works of many of the most famous architects in the city and uncovering the work of those once prominent but now obscure, such as Samuel Lunden, Anthony Lumsden, and partners William Allen and William George Lutzi. More than just dynamic in scope (and imagery), many of these ideas were prescriptions to remedy the obvious failures of the city. They proposed knitting together the scattered metropolis or inserting much-needed green space, or decreasing sprawl and dependence on the automobile, or giving purpose and definition to neighborhoods that seemed eternally consigned to the outskirts.

Olmsted Brothers and Harland Bartholomew and Associates' groundbreaking 1930 Plan for the Los Angeles Region, if it hadn't been upended by business groups, would have shaped the southland into an urban pastoral. Frank Lloyd Wright's Doheny Ranch, pitched to the distracted ears of a 1920s oil magnate, would have replaced a monotonous, and destructive, suburban housing model with a single encompassing tapestry of stone, glass, tile, and willowy foliage.

For every urban recipe that stood on its own, there were repeat candidates that showed up with the regularity and force of the temblors that shake the city. Some sort of Hollywood motion-picture museum has been on the drawing boards since the 1920s and

is still in the works, despite the outpouring of renderings from such notable architects as William Pereira, Charles Luckman, Christian de Portzamparc, and now Renzo Piano. Versions of a monorail, a transportation system we now associate with airports and Disney resorts, were proposed in Los Angeles nearly a dozen times in 50 years. At least three aerial tramways leading to revolving restaurants were supposed to grace the top of Mount Hollywood, overlooking Griffith Observatory. A Los Angeles world's fair, proposed repeatedly by political leaders in the first half of the twentieth century, always found the treasury doors sealed shut. It is impossible to accurately count the number of freeways that were mapped, beginning as early as 1930, only to be remanded to the archives.

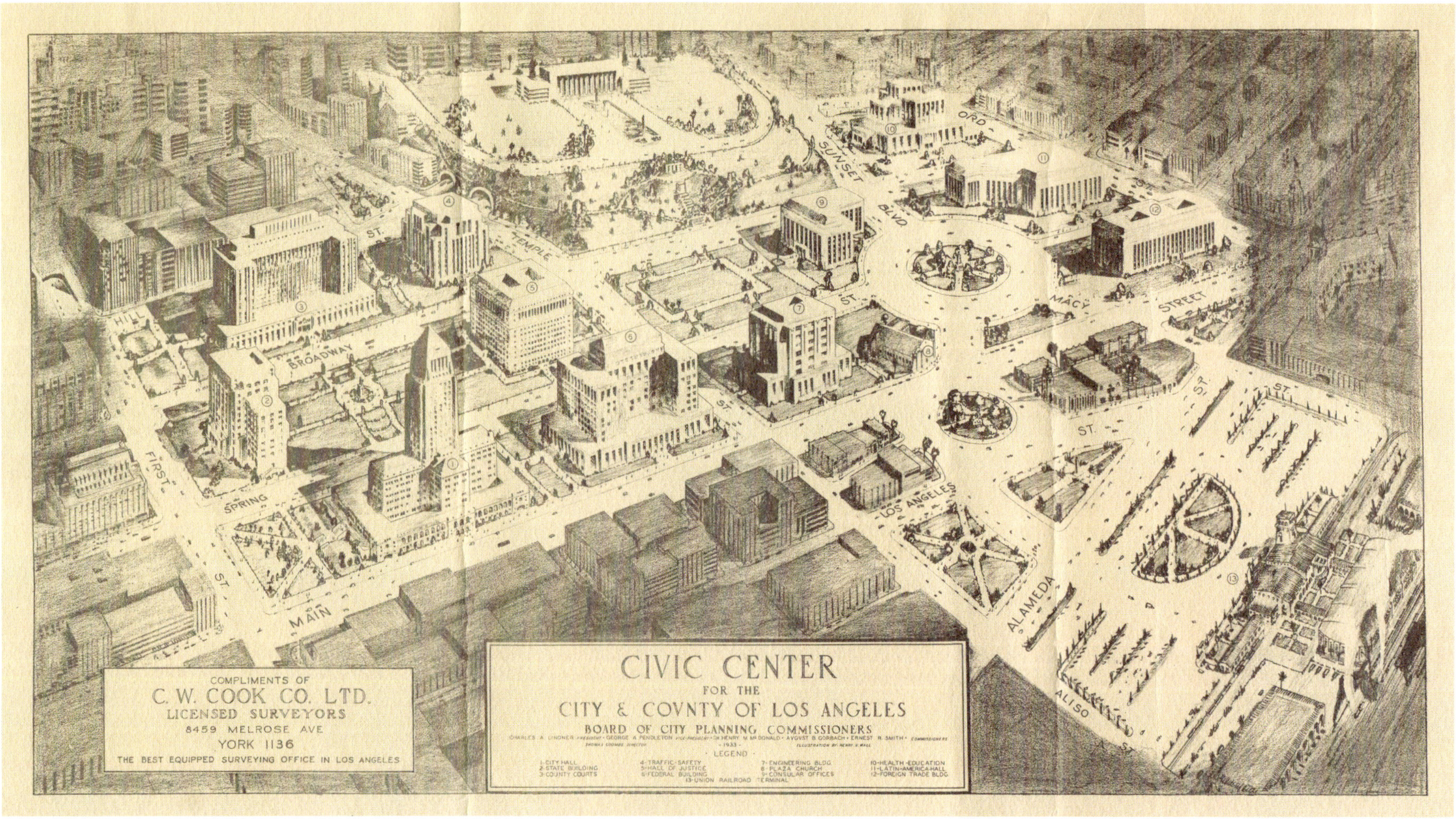

A survey of such unrealized projects reveals a metropolis deeply divided by competing visions, between those who favored a "city beautiful" and those who favored a "city practical." Would Los Angeles be a horizontal or vertical city? A lush Arcadia or a steel labyrinth? Would it be a place of civic grandeur or one of bustling commerce? Would it have a central, crowning downtown or become a landscape strewn with multiple civic outposts? Many cities have figured out the answers to these issues, but Los Angeles has struggled with them and continues to do so today.

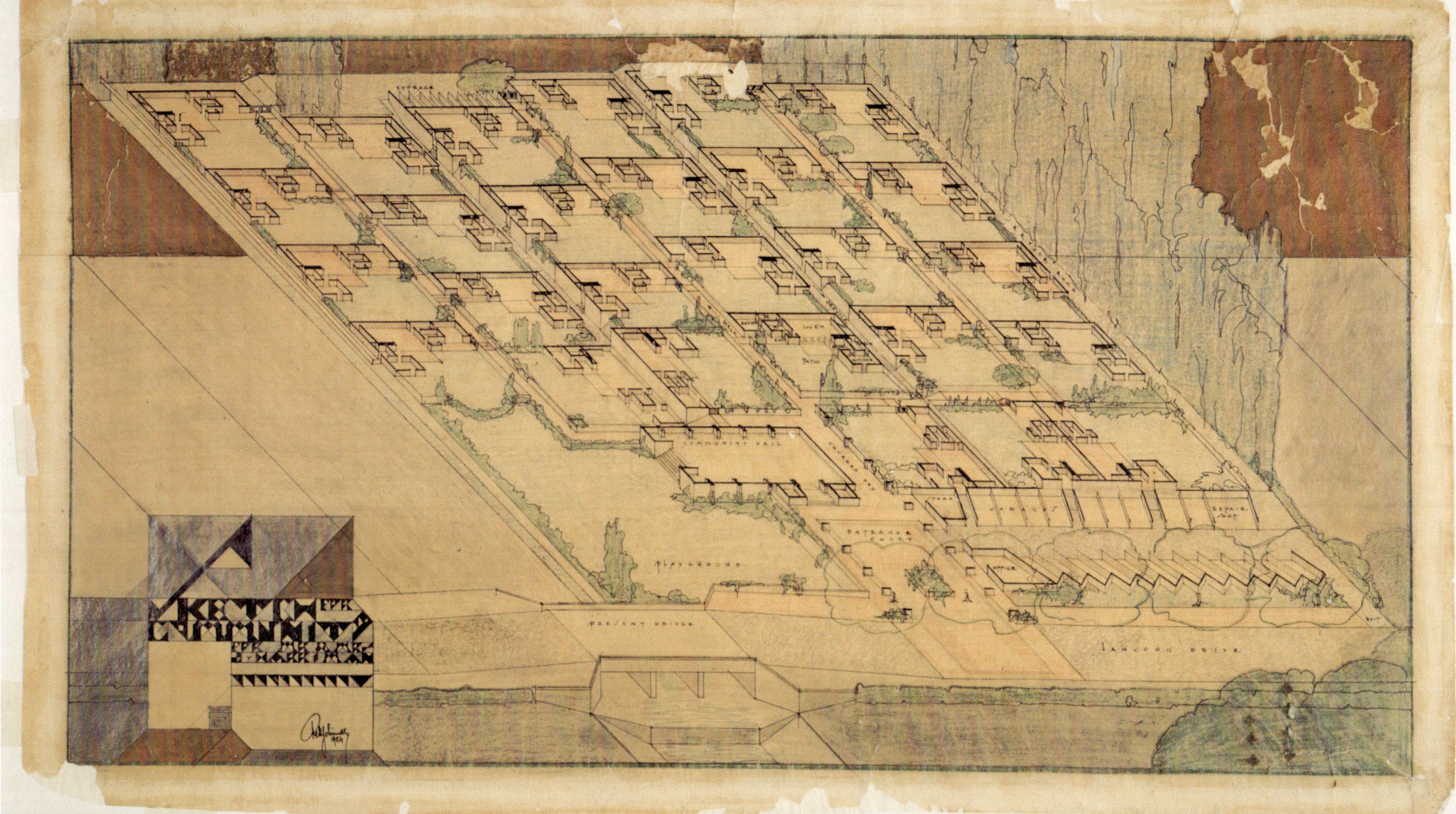

←←
"Wilshire Boulevard of the Future," 1928

←
Official plan for civic center, 1933

→
Rudolph M. Schindler, drawing of labor leader Job Harriman's Mojave Desert utopian colony, 1924

Harlan Georgescu's Skylots, a reaction to the city's sprawl, would have stretched more than 100 "vertical villages" along the 405 Freeway from Westwood to beyond Long Beach. At the very same time, planners were insisting on elevated sidewalks to lift pedestrians high above the downtown streetscape, planting them in a bubble safe from the grittiness of the street grid. Some proposed replacing the car altogether, while others, like S. Charles Lee, wanted to make the car—and its drivers on the highway—a focus for design, merging building and billboard into a seamless, singular composition. All these interpretations orbited around an eternal conflict: Was Los Angeles a paradise that must not be despoiled or should its natural beauty be understood merely as a backdrop to human enterprise?

As with any creative process, the mutations that emerged in the urban realm were sometimes malignant. Rejected or not, such troubled projects reveal a city often ready to succumb to its baser instincts. For every park or subway the city foolishly dismissed, it fortunately dodged an albatross. The construction of a grid of endless freeways, more than double the size of the existing system, was never carried out. A City of Angels Monument, a 350-foot-tall sword-wielding bronze angel mounted atop a 750-foot Tower of Babel-like pedestal at the edge of downtown, never found backing. The imposition of superblocks in

the center of downtown—patches of development so outsized they required their own internal road systems linked to even larger freeway ramps and superhighways—never got past the early stages. Often, the more detached a concept was from reality, the more seductive it became. An entire generation of midcentury engineers, architects, and planners, for example, was mesmerized by the possibility of an offshore freeway that would run along a series of man-made islands from Santa Monica to Malibu.

MARCHING THROUGH TIME

The city, like any living organism, has had its growth spurts, each accompanied by a spirit that, with hindsight, seemed to suit its age. So each of Los Angeles's never-built concepts can be understood as a product—and amplification—of its particular epoch. Within the dim silhouette of completed buildings from every era can be perceived the halos of equally, if not far more, remarkable unrealized doppelgängers.

The first big leap into cityhood happened between the world wars. Vacant land was plentiful, and Los Angeles presented a utopian clean slate onto which anyone could write as he wished. The city went up with alarming briskness, and a vast if skeletal civic framework started to come into focus. "Speculation is in the air," stated one banker, "because people think of Los Angeles as the land of easy money, and because for so many it has proved these things."

Amid this rollicking gilded age, a whirl of architectural inventions emerged. And so along what would become Wilshire Boulevard, on terrain not yet even within city limits, lawyer-powerbroker Henry O'Melveny practically commanded the construction of a roadway wider than the Santa Monica Freeway that, in his musings, one day would be adorned with stelae, fountains, obelisks, and similar Napoleonic landmarks. Spanning the Los Angeles River, if C. E. Noerenberg had had his way, would have been a railway station requiring a dam's worth of earth and concrete, and an Empire State Building's dose of structural steel.

The age also encouraged Lloyd Wright, whose brilliant but unrealized conceptions for the city perhaps more than any other architect's work summed up the sweeping, almost galactic drive that infused nearly every noteworthy, if not exactly

↖
A. C. Martin's Egyptian Swim Club, 1926

→
John Lautner's 335 West Sixth Street building, 1962

→→
Richard Neutra's megascale Rush City Reformed, 1928

notable, project to come after the initial bursts of the 1920s. Somehow, it was not improbable for a Mayan ziggurat to rise at a major Hollywood intersection, or for a concrete-block Catholic cathedral, soaring 50 stories, to draw inspiration from the stone carvings of pagan Mesoamerica.

The Great Depression and World War II ushered in the end of this fanciful era. Suddenly, Los Angeles was engaged in a makeover, from cow town to self-proclaimed international prototype and destination. The raw fantasies of the prior decades were replaced by a cosmopolitan, technologically advanced modernism meant to transform the life of the everyman. The imported languages of elsewhere—Central America, England, or Japan—gave way to a flair for experimentation with the materials at hand, such as aluminum and steel borrowed from the aircraft industry, which

←
Carlos Diniz, silkscreen rendering of Ladd and Kelsey's International Exposition, 1966

→
Entrance to Duckett and Jenkins's Chavez Ravine Los Angeles Zoo, 1957

→→
Culver City Sky Slope by Hoops, Borbals, 1966

boomed during the war. What might have been is perhaps best expressed by one magnificent drawing, devised by William Pereira, for the airfield that would become LAX. He envisioned an expansive, soaring passenger terminal under a single glass lid, as dramatic an enclosed space as the great train stations of Europe.

Alas, the idealism that spurred such confident residential innovation as Entenza's Case Study Houses also engendered a period of destructive overreach in the public sphere. Architects and planners working on a civic scale believed their ideas could do no wrong and, largely because of such arrogance, did the most wrong of all.

Entrance Opens Into New Animal World

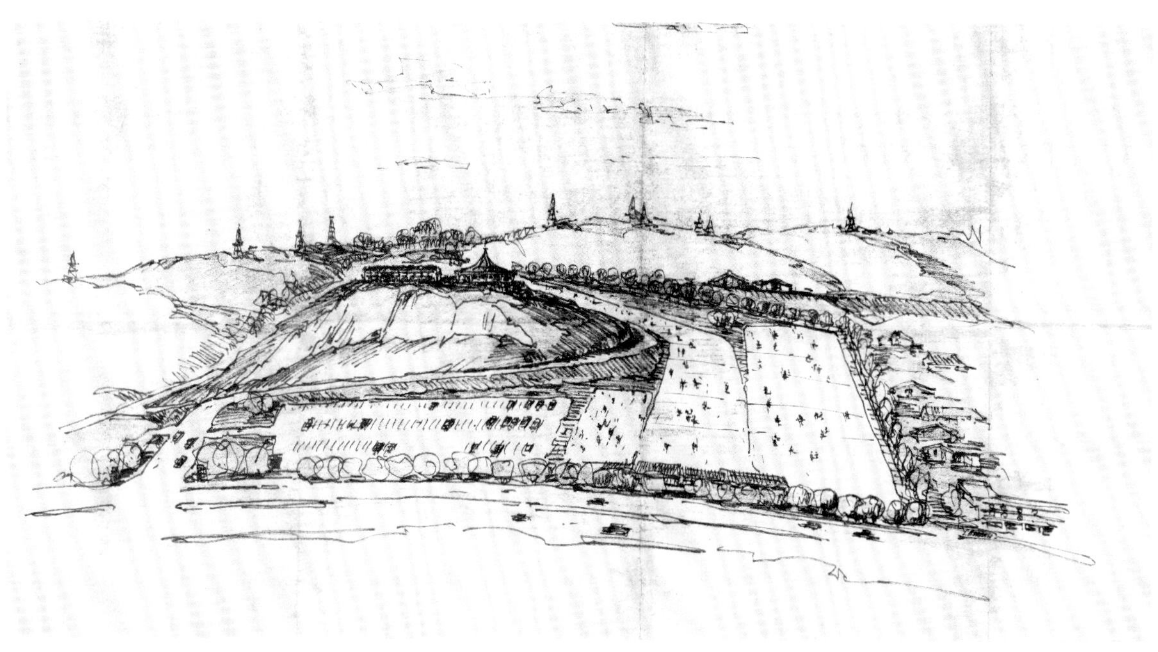

The urban facelift—per the all-or-nothing dictums of modernist planning—was designed as radical surgery. Herculean, seemingly unstoppable machines like the city's Community Redevelopment Agency and the state's highway bureau tapped bottomless sources of federal and local taxpayer dollars to gut much of the city's texture.

Hope, hubris, naiveté, and a free hand fueled many of the never builts of this future-obsessed era. Neutra and Alexander's Elysian Park Heights; Pereira and Luckman's original plans for Bunker Hill; Calvin Hamilton's City Centers strategy; and a dense grid of freeways that left no driver more than a few minutes from an entry ramp—all would scrub the grime from urban life, replacing slums and chaotic streets with environments that were groomed, orderly, safe, and clean. What emerged in drawings (and occasionally, in reality) were gargantuan superblocks, multiple "cities within cities," elevated sidewalks, and a loose skein of jammed expressways. The truly Olympian dream documented in these lost plans has a haunting beauty; a newly conceived city almost floats above the wasteland.

Then, like a chronicle of events foretold, riots erupted in Watts, the Vietnam War imploded, and the sparkling American Century turned matte. A backlash against the city-defining freeways congealed into a forceful lobby, helping to dash more than half of the engineers' concrete dreams. Even the alternatives lost their magic: Maglev trains, monorails, subways, and bus lanes appeared on paper and nowhere else.

←
Los Angeles Department of Water and Power's Bolsa Chica desalinization and nuclear-power plant, 1967

→
Helmut Jahn, sketches of Ninth and Figueroa Tower, 1987

→→
Harry Wolf's 747 South Flower Street building, 1990

And so we approach the present. Burdened by the brutal dreams of high modernism, knee-jerk futurism became knee-jerk corporatism and Nimbyism. In some ways, the city reverted to the fundamentalist culture of individualism that Nathanael West despised. In the wake of Proposition 13—a 1978 state ballot initiative that slashed corporate property taxes in the name of relief to homeowners—municipal wealth and power all but collapsed. With local governments drained of free-flowing tax dollars, elected officials started wooing and kowtowing to boardrooms.

In a city where developers had always had first dibs, these powerbrokers became the new Medicis, summoning starchitects and global design firms alike to do their bidding. A parade of boldface names came to town flourishing inky sketches—Michael Graves, Steven Holl, Helmut Jahn, Daniel Libeskind, I. M. Pei, Cesar Pelli—only to be met by the anvil of frustration that had stopped so many of their predecessors. Perhaps most famous for its premature demise is the Maguire Partners' 1979–80 plan for Grand Avenue, an animated and cacophonous symphony of buildings designed by a roomful of luminaries from Pelli to Gehry. The idea consisted of nine projects loosely connected by a variety of

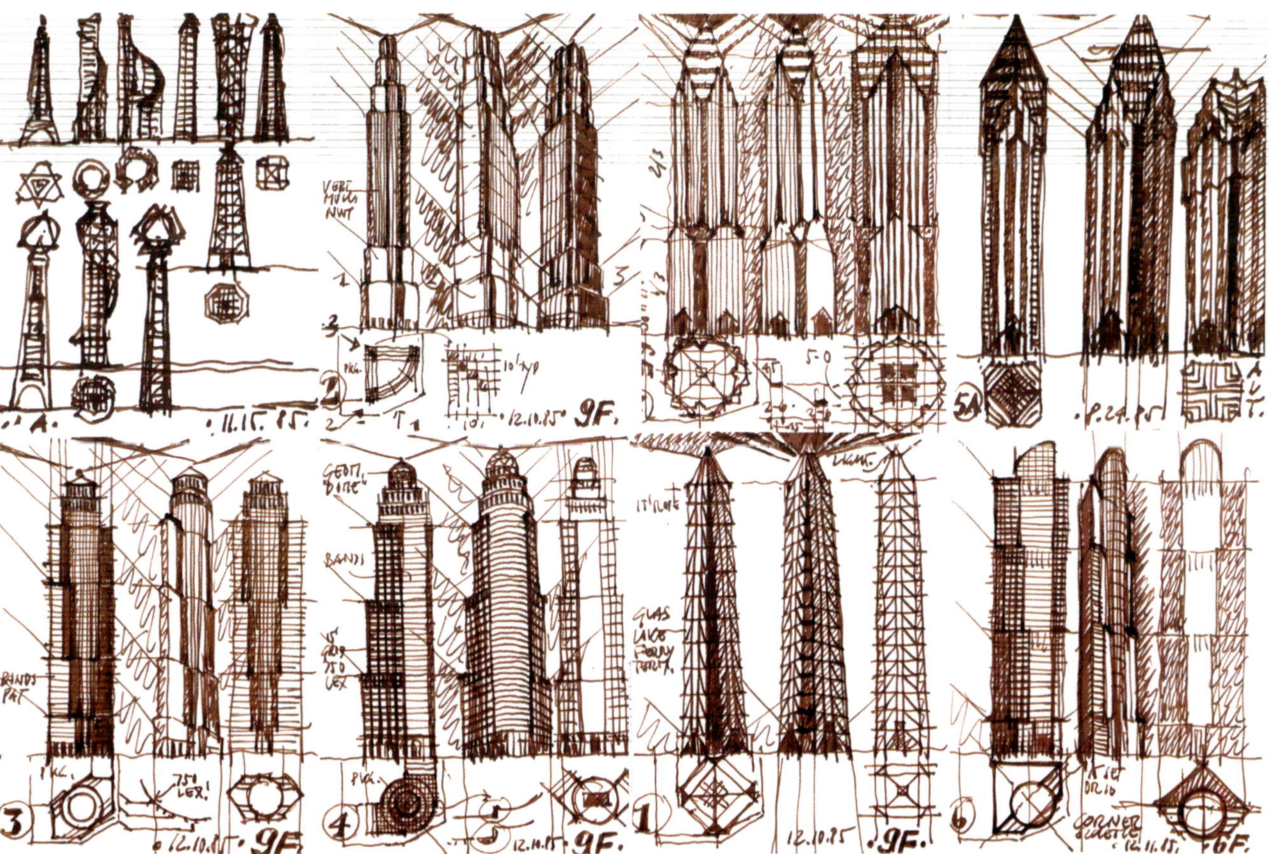

parks, plazas, and promenades—"an urban room [built to convert] a prototypical 'megablock' development [into]...a richer, denser environment." But Maguire's "exquisite corpse" was too messy for the Community Redevelopment Agency, which, in an international competition, chose the bland towers of Arthur Erickson.

Los Angeles officials endorsed corporate "altruism," abandoning the city's design to deep-pocketed developers who were encouraged—in theory, at least—to embrace urban richness and density. In reality, projects like Doug Suisman's Ten Minute Diamond, meant to animate downtown's wide sidewalks, Holl's greensward Natural History Museum in Exposition Park, or B+U's office building in Downey withered and fell to budget cuts. In their place grew corny, prepackaged "destinations" like LA Live and Hollywood & Highland. Risk-averse corporate spreadsheets became the blueprints for the built environment.

LOS ANGELES, THE GREAT EXCEPTION

So what is it about Los Angeles that fosters so many imaginative, potentially transformative public-realm projects—good and bad—yet simultaneously quashes them? The reasons for this failure are as plentiful as the failed proposals themselves.

For one, since political power in Los Angeles is concentrated in unelected and usually invisible commissions, from the airport to parks to public works, the best ideas don't have the kind of single, design-conscious, czarlike champion they need and deserve. No Robert Moses could ever hold sway here; even the mayor is far too weak under the city charter to do much more than hold press conferences. Power is further diluted among innumerable elected officials, from unimaginative county supervisors to part-time community college trustees.

A famous example: The Los Angeles County Museum of Art's fractured board chose William Pereira over modernist luminaries Ludwig Mies van der Rohe and Edward Durell Stone to design the institution's decidedly restrained new quarters. A few decades later, museum leaders picked Hardy Holzman Pfeiffer as the architects of the Robert O. Anderson building, a hulking warehouse that dismantled any coherence Pereira had achieved. More recently, the directors decided not to follow through with Rem Koolhaas's scorched-earth proposal to unify the complex by basically starting over from scratch.

The list goes on. Gehry's proposal for a riotous new home for the Rapid Transit District headquarters was trumped by a blanched—literally, beige—tower by corporate Orange County architects McLarend Vasquez. AECOM's police headquarters, directly across from City Hall, scuttled a civic plaza dedicated to political, social, and cultural events. Barton Myers's ziggurat-like park topping a new wing for the Central Library was beat out by, again, Hardy Holzman Pfeiffer, with an Art Deco-Babylonian stylistic mash-up. The Los Angeles Unified School District squandered billions of dollars on public schools in the city's neediest neighborhoods designed more like malls than beacons of lifelong inquisitiveness and participatory citizenship.

In many instances, the city's legions of engineers, not its architects or planners, conferred upon Los Angeles some of its most beloved architecture. These pioneers often dictated the

↖↖
A. C. Martin's Shuwa Gas Company building, 1986

↖
Kisho Kurokawa's 40-story Gateway Center at Figueroa and Temple streets, 1987

→
Michael Lehrer's Campanile at Barnsdall Park, 1995

←
OMA's runner-up scheme for The Broad, 2010

→
XTEN's downtown Los Angeles hotel, 2012

→→
Escher GuneWardena's Linc.LA, Clean Tech Corridor research center, 2010

form of L.A. itself—and sometimes stole the show. The city's greatest engineering feat remains the Los Angeles Aqueduct, William Mulholland's siphon bringing Owens River water from the eastern slopes of the Sierras to the northern end of the San Fernando Valley. No one can deny the spellbinding enchantment of watching the cascades at Sylmar. Engineers also created the now-historic spans across the Los Angeles River. The unquestionable scenic beauty of those 13 bridges is largely the gift of an unassuming civil engineer named Merrill Butler and his tireless, enterprising boss, Lloyd Aldrich.

Ostensibly unimaginative engineers were responsible, as well, for the Santa Monica-San Diego freeway flyover, about which historian and critic Reyner Banham rhapsodized in *Los Angeles: The Architecture of Four Ecologies*: "The wide-swinging curved ramps of the intersection...immediately persuaded me

that the Los Angeles freeway system is indeed one of the greater works of Man."

Banham, like the rest of the city's inhabitants, was enthralled by what historian Perry Miller called the "technological sublime." Huge concrete structures conjured reverence with the sheer force of their scale and the American prowess they seemed to enfold. This concrete aesthetic played perfectly into the hands of engineers, who understood that time abides; the bigger the enterprise, the more incrementally it progresses, the more likely it is to be built.

Yet while engineers historically have had the advantage of money, Los Angeles has been notoriously parsimonious with its purse when it comes to public buildings and plans. It almost doesn't matter which epoch you examine—the script reads much the same. The money dries up when it comes to civic undertakings.

The enormous scale of the region also discourages consensus around any canon. How do you get the 88 cities in Los Angeles County to agree on anything? This territorial antagonism is reinforced by an underlying failure of legitimacy for downtown Los Angeles. Despite its wealth and strength, the city's civic center has never been the defining capital of the region and therefore has never held moral, political, or geographic sway, leading to a power vacuum filled by back-benchers governing minor city-states scattered throughout the southern stretches of California.

For all of its liberal glitter and largesse, much of the city's power base is notoriously apathetic to the needs of the general public. Tinseltown wears its progressive ideals proudly at awards dinners, but most of its members are sequestered in the hills or by the shore, far from the fight, secure in their architect-designed gated fortresses and unplugged from the

process of shaping the city. Conspicuous consumption is still the controlling modus operandi of the beau monde. Disney Hall, so essential to L.A.'s self-image today, was almost never built; 22 years passed from the time Gehry submitted his design to the day the concert hall opened.

In Los Angeles more than almost anywhere, once you pull back the curtain of civic leadership and artistic energy you see the puppetmaster: The fates of potential dream projects are controlled by developers, not citizens or officials. And most developers, by the nature of their occupation, are conservative. They don't want to lose their shirts because an architect insists on travertine when plaster will do.

The city faces ideological as well as systemic impediments. Part of Los Angeles's problems involve the siphoning of ingenuity and drive into the creative machinery of Hollywood, where ideas and riches are closely held and rarely converted into public gestures or endowments. The vast opportunities for architects and developers in the residential realm also starve the public realm. Talent gets comfortable rolling out individual homes and doesn't want to mess with the thorny public stuff. Another hiccup resides in the legendary rivalry between L.A.'s historical elites and its nouveaux-riches, groups that could never hammer out a mutual path for the city. Maybe, in the end, it's just that Los Angeles thrives on inscrutable messiness, and any effort to impose beauty or order is doomed.

↖
Altoon + Porter, Frank Gehry, Laurie Olin, Arata Isozaki, and Rafael Moneo, Grand Avenue Urban Design Plan, 2000

←
Jerde Partnership's Grand Avenue concept, 2004

→
Ehrenkrantz Eckstut and Kuhn and UNStudio's Union Station Vision Plan, 2012

UNION STATION MASTER PLAN

UNION STATION MAIN ENTRANCE

'Meet me at Union Station'
In the design of the LA Union Station Master Plan, the transit experience will be integrated with aspirations for an expanded civic space. The historic Union Station is already a valued and appreciated place. The next steps for the development of the station are to ensure a robust transit plan that enhances the historic building and grounds by creating a new destination within downtown LA. City and regional transit will be given the stage, with a focus on increased ridership and transit connections.
Within this new transit oriented place, a uniquely programmed urban park, extending the ideas of the existing courtyards, will be integrated into the transit experience and provide a new public amenity. New development opportunities will be provided for residential and hotel accommodations, business, retail, and entertainment functions. Weekend markets, shops, and viable entertainment clusters will serve the vibrant community around the Station and act as an important attraction for the City and region. There is a special opportunity to add tremendous value to the transit experience, the City, and the region.
MAIN STATION HALL
China Town
EE&K
A PERKINS EASTMAN
COMPANY
IN ASSOCIATION WITH UNSTUDIO

CAFE

← Frank Gehry's skyscraper across from Disney Hall, 2006

→ 101 Freeway cap parks: (top) Meyer and Allen, 1991; (bottom) AECOM, 2010

MOCK-UP CITY: ARCHITECTURE AS DREAMCRUSHER

Of course, Los Angeles is in many ways like every other city. Completing any building, park, or master plan takes a degree of cooperation that makes other creative endeavors seem simple by comparison. It depends on so many factors: If the money doesn't evaporate, and costs don't wildly escalate, and political fortunes don't shift, and land barons don't become distracted by more enticing pursuits, and apparatchiks don't shred the drawings, a building might go up.

There is a worldwide backlog of never-built splendors, from a mile-deep underground skyscraper in Mexico City to a mile-high tower in Saudi Arabia. Often, these visions are more effective than the work itself could ever be. As in the eighteenth-century etchings by Giovanni Piranesi, even imaginary edifices that are unmoored and unachievable become sources of power, beauty, and revelatory insight.

Thinking about never-built Los Angeles deepens one's appreciation for the degree to which architecture has always been unbuilt. The discipline involves taking up a pencil or pen—or today, a mouse—and drawing. Lines and gum erasures, gouache and wash are part of the language of architecture; every building starts with these, and most proceed no further. The magic of a city exists as much on vellum and blueprint as it does in soil and sky. It is invariably true that no rendering is worse than the completed structure. The drawing, then, is the Platonic

←
Koning Eizenberg's 180-unit AMP Lofts, downtown Arts District, 2007

→
Mia Lehrer's Los Angeles River Revitalization Master Plan, 2007

ideal: pure absolute beauty, novelty, or seductiveness in two dimensions. We learn as much, maybe more, about the city by looking closely at these scraps of ephemera. For this alone, architectural drawings deserve their place in the catalogue raisonné of international artwork: The potential bound up in lost projects contains the spark of city-building, past and future.

The range of never-built projects also teaches us about the nature of drawing itself, how the human hand expresses the mind's aspirations—a connection that, with the increasing dominance of technology, is becoming increasingly lost. Thumbing through countless architectural renderings and sketches affirms how closely the life of the hand is tied to the life of the building. In a time, too, when a drafting board is as quaint as a typewriter, examining the skill with which artists rendered the imagined Los Angeles can be like taking communion. A dream-filled new city can form in your mind just by glancing at a sketch.

WHAT'S NEXT?

Back in reality, we remain trapped in an era of timorousness, with a long lineup of stalled projects frightfully close to being added to the Los Angeles roster of the never built. Once again, dreamers envision beauty and change, and as bland pre-scriptions for the cityscape rise, imaginative ideas sit idle on the boards. Mia Lehrer's Los Angeles River Revitalization

←
Lawrence Scarpa and Lorcan O'Herlihy's headquarters of MGA Entertainment, Chatsworth, 2009

→
(fer) Studio's plan for Market Street, Inglewood, 2010

Master Plan, which calls for greening the river's concrete banks and reshaping a wasted area into a several-mile-long recreational expanse, languishes in limbo. We can only wonder, with abiding skepticism, about the fate of Frank Gehry and Related Companies' Grand Avenue Plan for a rush of retail, office, and entertainment spaces (including wavy metallic skyscrapers) on the ever-suffering top of Bunker Hill. Calls for parks sprouting from concrete decks over freeways near downtown, Hollywood, and Santa Monica still remain expensive question marks. Progress on Richard Meier's glassy condominiums next to the former Robinsons-May building in Beverly Hills has stalled, but the firm insists the project is still happening. With the city's redevelopment agency recently abolished by the California legislature, we hold our breath as the future of its proposed Clean Tech Corridor—a center for green jobs south of downtown—lies in the balance. Even adventurous proposals to reweave Union Station into the fabric of the city are stillborn: The Los Angeles Metropolitan Transportation Authority, in spring 2012, asked for "vision plans" for the area but never intended to carry out any of them.

If there was an inkling of financial and civic will, we might feel optimistic. But in a state billions of dollars in debt and in a city equally upside down financially, with the regional transit agency the only vaguely solvent engine of urban design, it might be some time before the city taps its poetic impulse. We know that visionary ideas will continue to be produced in Los Angeles, even if hopes for their realization have dimmed. What we don't know is when or whether the great wall that has for so long divided the city's dreams from reality will begin to yield or crack.

In the end, cities are never complete, even when they perish. Ghosts of cities past inhabit the ruins and affect us across the ages. Crumbling Mayan temples made converts of Robert Stacy-Judd and Frank Lloyd Wright. The frayed and faded notions of countless others who have sketched and doodled may, in turn, stir new generations to toy with the boundaries of artistic and urban expression and to rethink a place that, to this day, is trying to solve the riddle of what it wants to become. Los Angeles's future dwells in the reinterpretation of its unfulfilled past. We hope these dredged-up never-built schemes—remnants of an alternate L.A. reality—will intensify the appetite for making new ones.

101
134
101
405
5
110
SANTA MONICA BLVD
101
WILSHIRE BLVD
10
10
1
110
52
96
58
70
102
74
50
124
118
64
86
132
114
98
108
106
128
N
E
S
90
LA
48
110
134
80

MP

MASTER PLANS

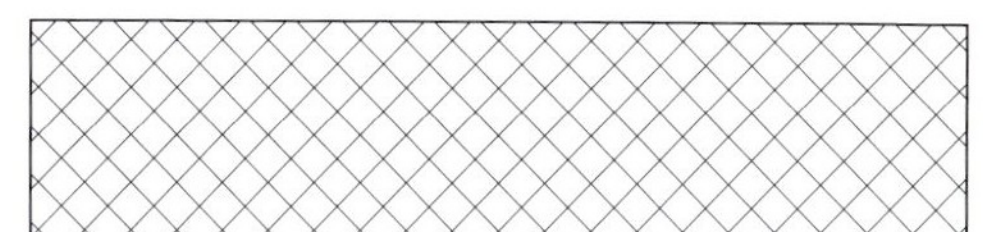

LA

CHARLES MULFORD ROBINSON
CITY BEAUTIFUL PLAN

1907

I know of no city in the United States which has so much to gain by making itself civically attractive.

Charles Mulford Robinson

Charles Mulford Robinson, one of the founders of the City Beautiful Movement—the Beaux-Arts planning crusade that captivated the imagination of cities across the country at the turn of the century—called for wide avenues, broad vistas, and open spaces for the increasingly cramped and unplanned Los Angeles metropolis. "You simply cannot afford to stand still—or rather, with your increasing population, to go from bad to worse, as you would, in congestion, in...discomfort and ugliness, and in paucity of municipal effectiveness," he wrote in a 1907 report entitled "Los Angeles, California: The City Beautiful."

The urban-planning pioneer told the Municipal Art Commission that his scheme would make the city "better planned and more beautiful....I know of no city in the United States which has so much to gain by making itself civically attractive." His report, calling for $50 million in improvements ($2 billion in today's money), was also published in the *Los Angeles Times*.

This unabashed amalgam of Daniel Burnham's plan for Chicago and Baron von Haussmann's for Paris foresaw, among other things, new "permanent" roads, including curving residential streets, and streets and river banks lined on either side with 14-foot-wide gardens. It suggested a mile-long, 200-foot-wide "grand concourse"—edged with flowering trees, electric lights, and trolley poles of "artistic design"—that would connect the "heart of the city to a central railroad station." The plan also specified a "boulevard system" of improved, widened streets linking residential and business areas and reaching all major parks, "so as to give a sense of unity."

Robinson's vision included a new "administrative center," containing an eclectic mix of public buildings inspired by the Beaux-Arts, Victorian, and Renaissance periods and centering on large plazas and terraced gardens. He also wanted to add several new parks, from small plots scattered throughout the city to a mall connecting "Central Park"—today's Pershing Square—with the rest of Los Angeles.

A few elements of the scheme were taken up decades later, such as building the city's Union Station, its Central Library, and a (significantly altered) civic center. But the overall plan, marginalized for years as a divided City Planning Commission continually lost battles with early-twentieth-century NIMBYs, was dealt its final blow under a 1925 charter reform. Voters stripped the commission of its power to initiate civic design, making it instead a rubber stamp for advancing real estate interests. Robinson's hope that "the city was big enough and rich enough and brave enough, and had enough confidence in itself, to do what was necessary and worth while" proved false.

→
One of Robinson's grand boulevards, and a grouping of civic buildings

PEARLY GATES.

GRAND CONCOURSE DOMINANT IDEA IN RARE VISION OF CITY BEAUTIFUL.

Artistic Grouping of Public Buildings and Extension of Boulevards and Parks Also Are Recommended.

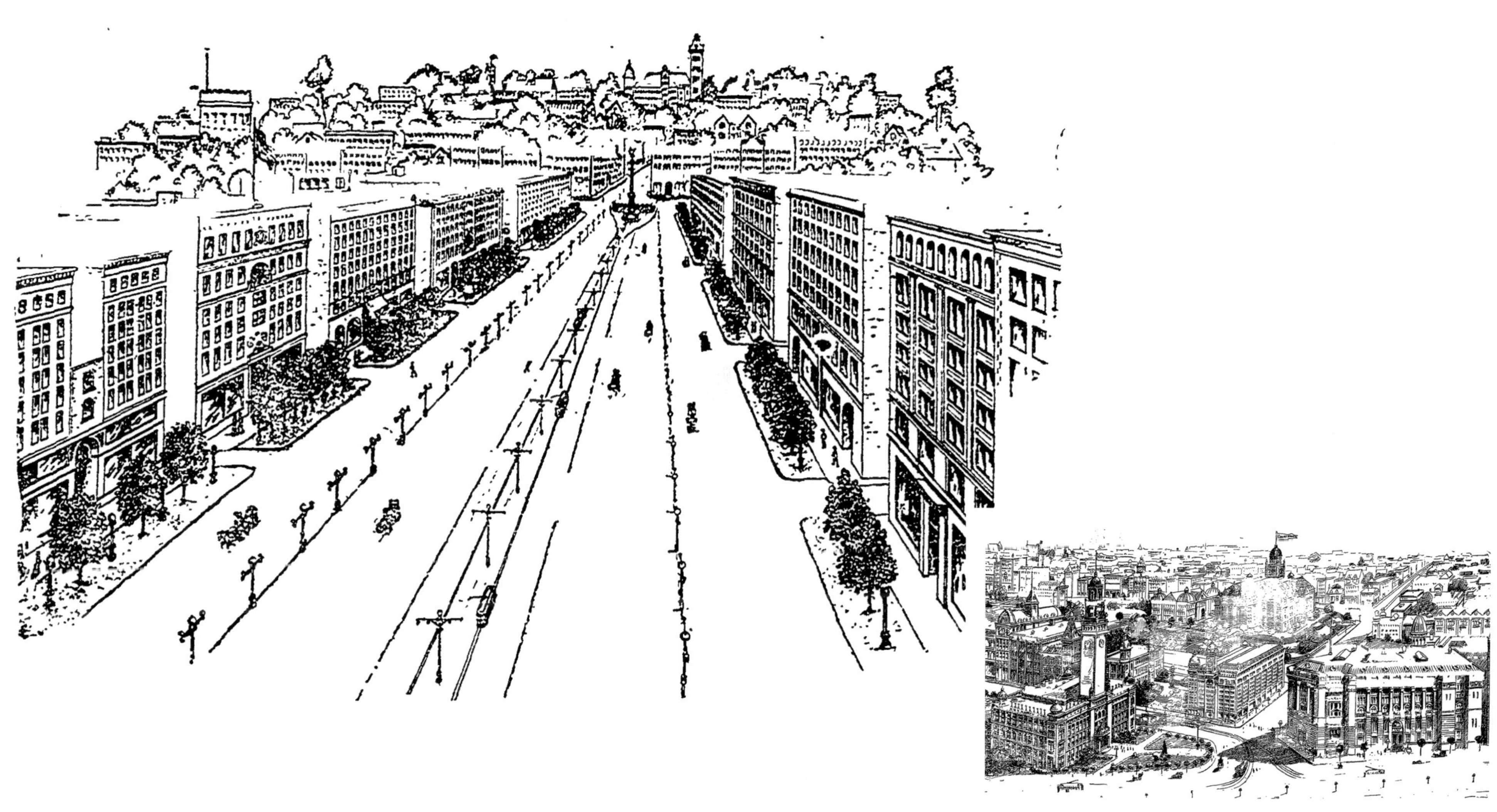

MP

WS

AURELE VERMEULEN
ARCHWAY PLAN

1922

Aurele Vermeulen, the landscape architect of the Westside's lush private enclave, Bel Air, developed a bombastic plan to make Wilshire Boulevard a paean to civic pride. Proponents pronounced it the Champs-Elysées of Los Angeles, a claim that would echo down through the decades. The main players behind the scheme were lawyer-potentate Henry O'Melveny and newspaper heir Harry Chandler, the same team that later built the Los Angeles Coliseum and brought the 1932 Olympics to the city.

The duo envisioned a street flanked by statues and fountains in homage to the romanticized history of California and the nation. The plan, conceived before the city had actually annexed the Wilshire Corridor, would extend Wilshire Boulevard from Westlake Park (now McArthur Park) to the future home of the Veterans Administration Hospital, just west of what is now the 405 Freeway. It would then jog north and proceed through Santa Monica Canyon to the coast.

The average width of the tree-and-shrub-lined boulevard was to be tremendous—240 feet and between seven and eight lanes. To speed the flow of traffic, intersecting streets would pass beneath the boulevard. Pedestrians, too, would be funneled into underground passageways to allow for unimpeded crossing.

Wilshire would be a strand of arches, fountains, and monuments, which historian Matthew Roth called "imperial gestures." Eleven triumphal arches housing police stations were to be placed at the major north-south corners, with the names of heroes of California—Vasco Nuñez de Balboa, Juan Rodriguez Cabrillo, John C. Frémont, Junipero Serra, and John Sutter—engraved in stone. O'Melveny and Chandler proposed fountains celebrating their personal values: the Fountain of Western Spirit, the Fountain of Progress, the Fountain of Work and Play, and the Fountain of Youth. The monuments promoted the virtues of self-cultivation: the National Educators Monument, the National Artists Monument, and the National Poets Monument.

Ten-story arches adorned with neoclassical cornices and Spanish Colonial Revival balconies were planned at the eastern and western portals—one at Westlake Park, the other at the edge of the Pacific.

Brimming with Napoleonic ambition, the seemingly unstoppable magnates couldn't be bothered to describe a funding arrangement. They expected the city to rubber-stamp the plan, then open the treasury to execute it. Chandler's *Los Angeles Times* scripted the outcome, proclaiming the boulevard approved before the city had acted.

But the roadway was politically doomed because it required the approvals of Beverly Hills and Santa Monica and depended upon legislation in an unwilling Sacramento. The coup de grâce: The real estate speculators along the route, seeing it as a region for vast commercial growth, outfoxed the city's most powerful men by proposing a narrower business thoroughfare devoted to commerce. Their ballot proposition, rezoning Wilshire from residential to commercial, won in 1926, sinking the Archway Plan.

→ Wilshire Boulevard as Los Angeles's Grand Concourse

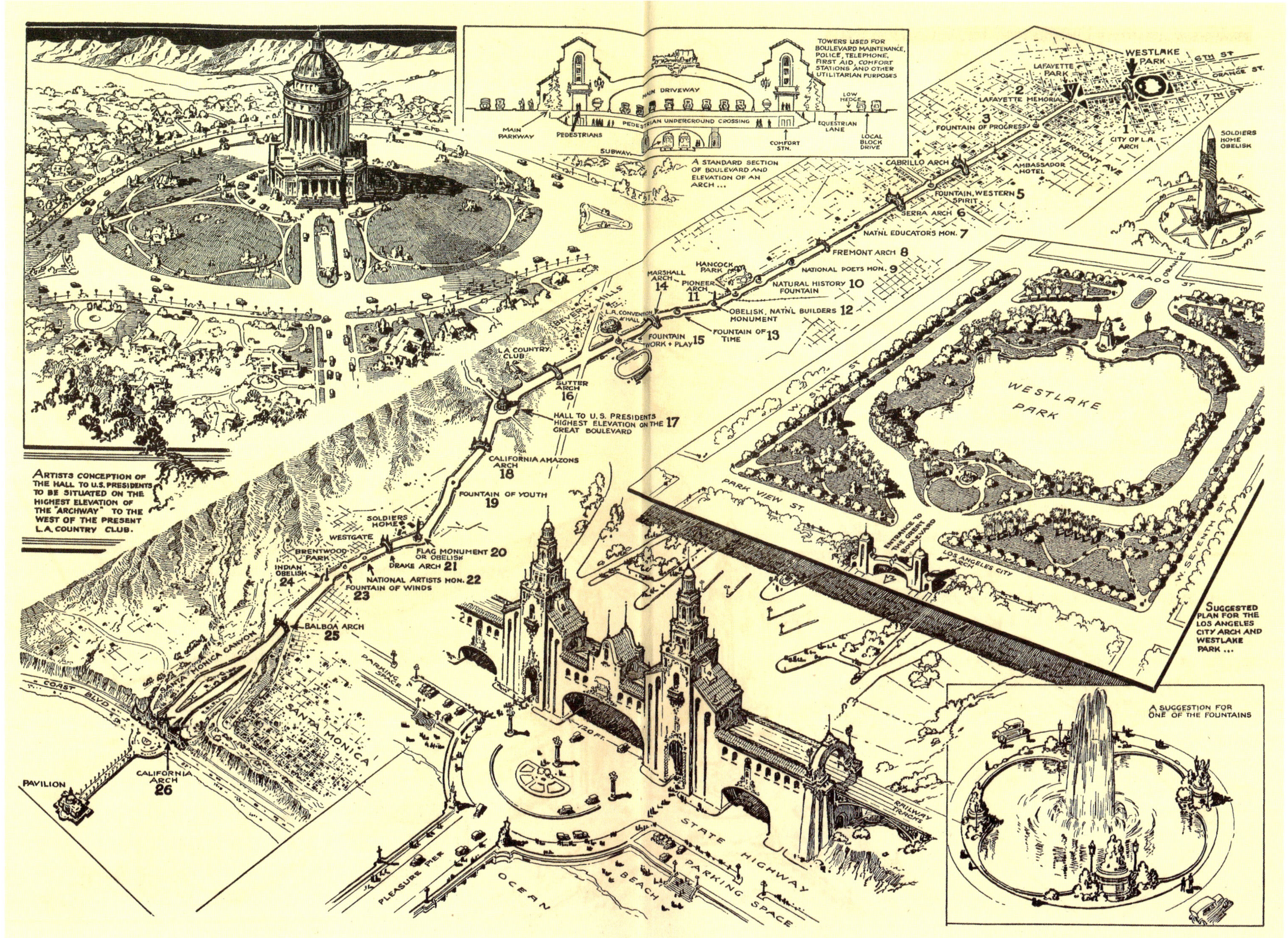

Artists conception of the Hall to U.S. Presidents to be situated on the highest elevation of the "Archway" to the west of the present L.A. Country Club.
Towers used for boulevard maintenance, police, telephone, first aid, comfort stations and other utilitarian purposes
Main driveway
Main parkway
Pedestrians
Pedestrian underground crossing
Subway
Comfort stn.
Low hedge
Equestrian lane
Local block drive
A standard section of boulevard and elevation of an arch ...
Westlake Park
6th St
Orange St.
7th St
Lafayette Park
2 Lafayette Memorial
3 Fountain of Progress
1 City of L.A. Arch
Soldiers Home Obelisk
4 Cabrillo Arch
Vermont Ave
Ambassador Hotel
Fountain, Western Spirit 5
Serra Arch 6
Nat'l Educators Mon. 7
Fremont Arch 8
National Poets Mon. 9
Natural History Fountain 10
Hancock Park
Pioneer Arch 11
Marshall Arch 14
Obelisk, Nat'l Builders Monument 12
Fountain of Time 13
Fountain Work + Play 15
Beverly Hills
L.A. Country Club
Sutter Arch 16
Hall to U.S. Presidents highest elevation on the great boulevard 17
California Amazons Arch 18
Fountain of Youth 19
Soldiers Home
Westgate
Flag Monument or Obelisk 20
Drake Arch 21
Brentwood Park
Indian Obelisk 24
National Artists Mon. 22
Fountain of Winds 23
Balboa Arch 25
Santa Monica Canyon
Santa Monica
Coast Blvd
Pavilion
California Arch 26
Parking space
Pleasure Pier
Ocean
Beach
Parking space
State Highway
Railway tracks
120 ft.
Alvarado St
W. Sixth St
Westlake Park
Park View St.
Entrance to the Great Boulevard
Los Angeles City Arch
W. Seventh St
Suggested plan for the Los Angeles City Arch and Westlake Park ...
A suggestion for one of the fountains

WS

FRANK LLOYD WRIGHT AND LLOYD WRIGHT

DOHENY RANCH

1923

A residential development of truly Wrightean scale and ambition, Doheny Ranch would have been embedded into the valuable canyons above what is now Beverly Hills, on land owned by the city's richest resident, oilman Edward Laurence Doheny. The site is now part of the Greystone Mansion property.

Frank Lloyd Wright (whose son Lloyd assisted him on the project) sketched a prototype for a new kind of American suburb, composed of variously sized and shaped homes. The residences would be made of patterned concrete textile blocks, like those he used for his Ennis and Millard houses that same year. The architecture was knitted into an intricate network of terraced slopes, ravines, and rugged landscapes. The buildings, roadways, bridges, plantings, and retaining walls, all hugging the contours of the land, were conceived as an integrated whole, each designed by Wright as if it were furniture in one of his houses.

Wright described this work as "Earth-architectures: gigantic masses of masonry raised up on great stone-paved terrain, all planned as one mountain, one vast plateau lying there or made into the great mountain ranges themselves; those vast areas of paved earth walled by stone construction."

An antidote to the monotonous tracts and bulldozed hillsides already starting to overwhelm California, the free-flowing, 411-acre site would have contained between 200 and 300 houses with floor plans in the shapes of triangles, octagons, hexagons, and trapezoids. In essence, Wright was playing with geometry; adding asymmetry and diagonals to bring his buildings to life and gain needed variety.

The composition evoked, as historian Thomas Hines put it, "pre-Columbian cities, poetically kneaded into exotic landscapes." Wright's plan, which he proposed with real estate developer John B. Van Winkle, was wishful thinking: Doheny rejected their pitch. All that remains are the evocative, almost mythical drawings that conjure the ancient gardens of Babylon.

→ Overall view of Wright's hillside development

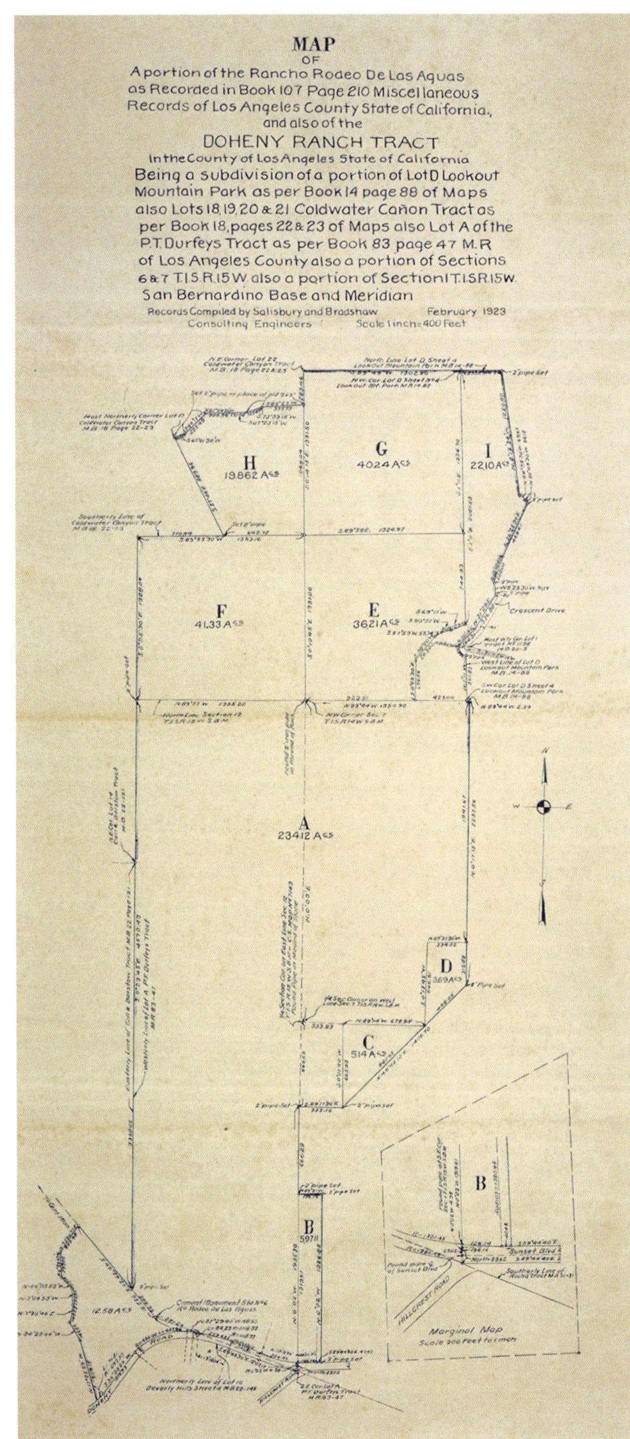

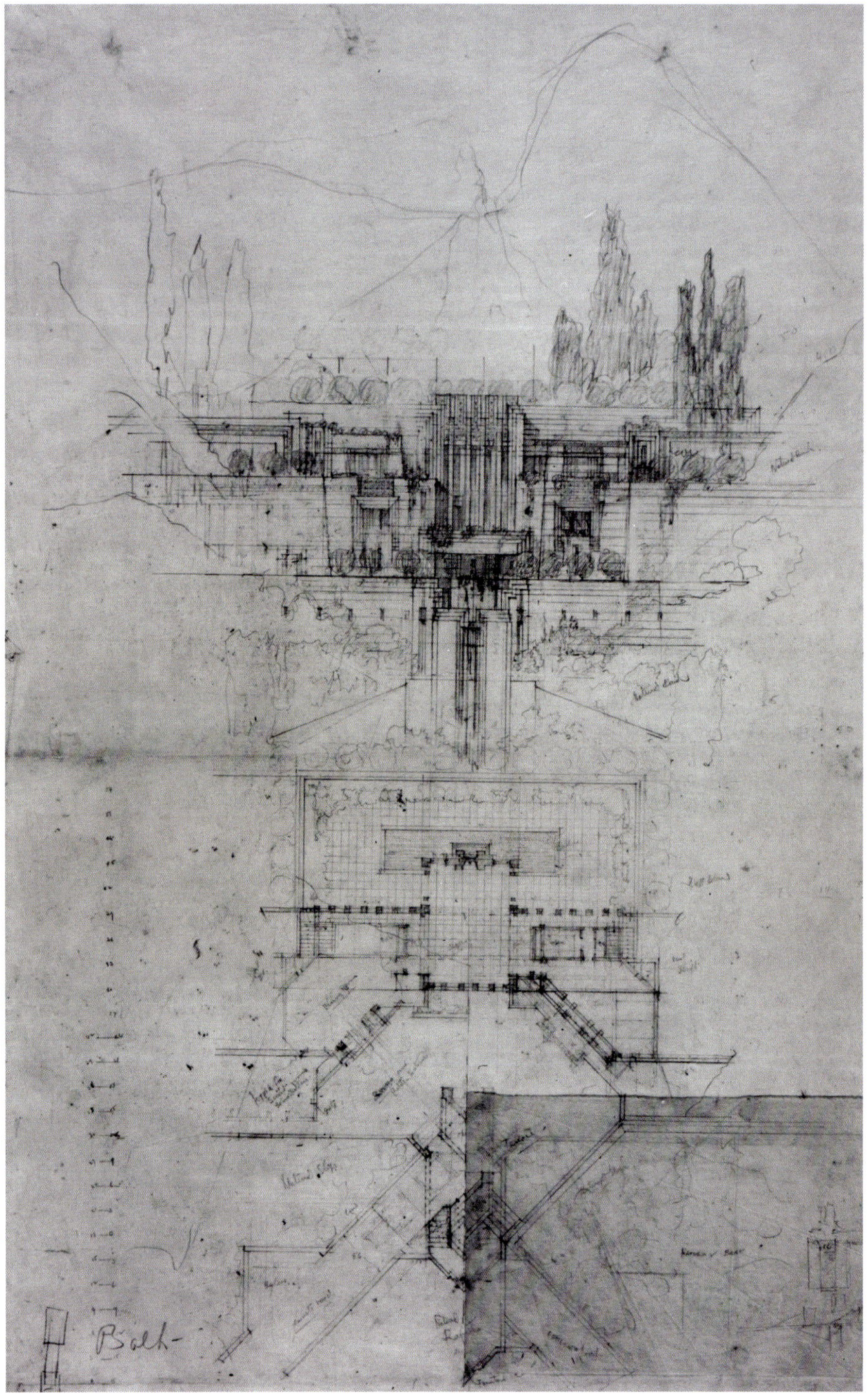

←←
Doheny Ranch tract map

←
View of typical development house, with landscaping and floor plan

→
Layered greenery and textile-block buildings

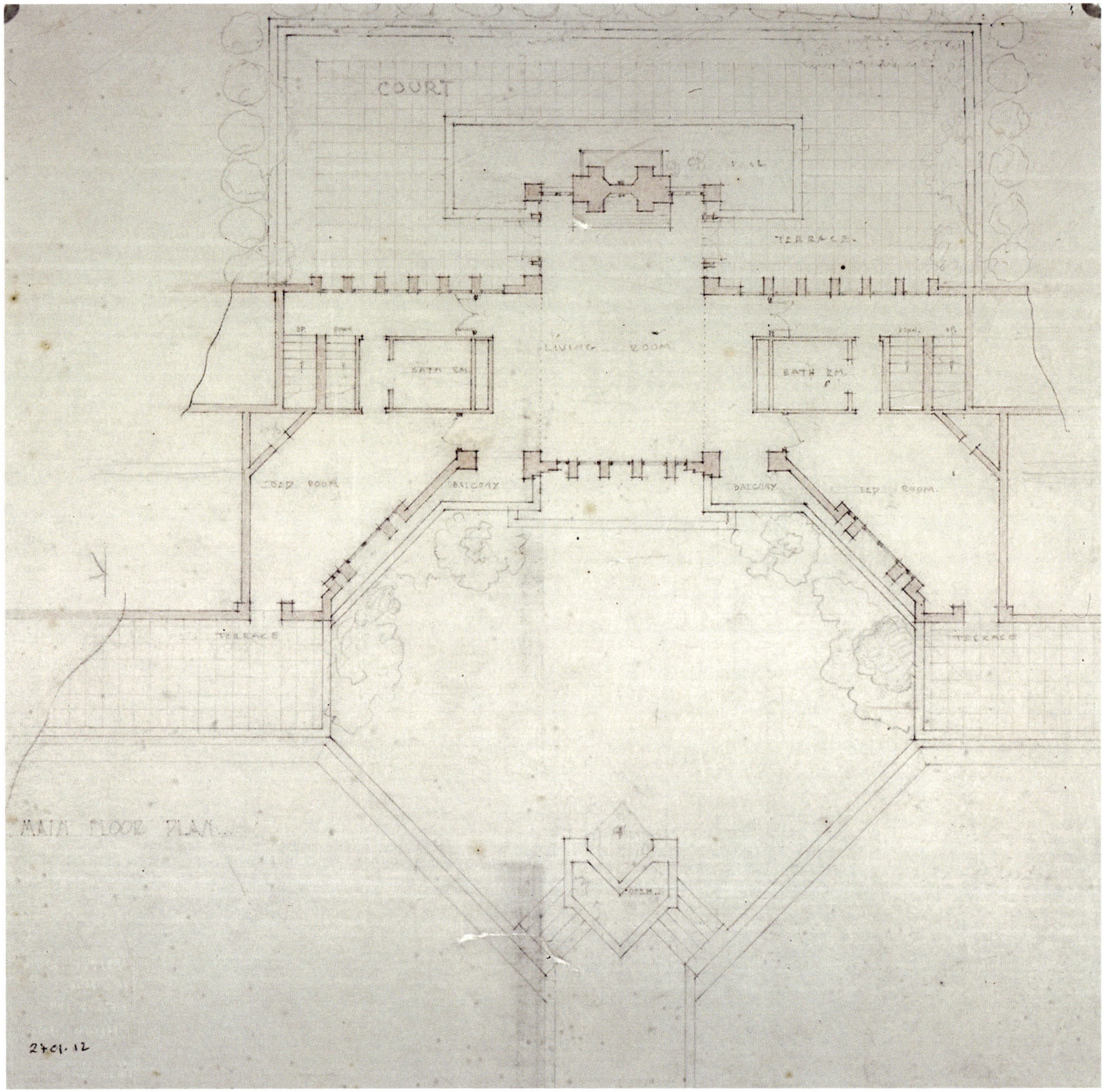

COURT
TERRACE
LIVING ROOM
BATH RM
BATH RM
BED ROOM
BALCONY
BALCONY
BED ROOM
TERRACE
TERRACE
MAIN FLOOR PLAN
2701.12

←←
View of bucolic hillside from raised patio

←
Main-floor plan of Doheny Ranch textile-block house

FRANK LLOYD WRIGHT
ALL-STEEL HOUSES

1937–40

Doheny Ranch wasn't the only Los Angeles hillside development that Frank Lloyd Wright envisioned. In the late 1930s, the architect and his apprentice John Lautner designed a cluster of 100 houses circling the slopes just west of La Cienega Boulevard in Baldwin Hills.

The multilevel homes, which stepped down steep ravines, consisted of vertical spines from which sizable balconies and sharp overhangs would radiate. They were built with steel foundations, framing, cladding, and even furniture, hence the name All-Steel. Vines and other plantings would soften the hard forms. While homes would be adapted to their specific sites, construction and detailing would be standardized, reducing costs and making building easier. The residences would be connected via a series of meandering walkways and bridges (made of steel, of course) with parking at the center of the tract.

Wright, the inspiration for the character Howard Roark in Ayn Rand's novel *The Fountainhead*, became friendly with the author and planned to use the All-Steel home design not just in Baldwin Hills but also as the basis for Rand's own cottage, which the two discussed for some time. "It is the particular kind of sculpture in space which I love and which nobody but you has ever been able to achieve," she gushed to Wright when she saw the design. But Wright could never find a taker on his All-Steel project—the New York banker he was counting on to fund it dropped out not once, but twice—and Rand never left the canyons of Manhattan, making both dreams figments of unfulfilled imagination.

MC

FRANK LLOYD WRIGHT
OLIVE HILL

1923

For I believe so firmly in your genius that I want to make it the keynote of my work.

Aline Barnsdall

Frank Lloyd Wright and Aline Barnsdall—the radical, free-spirited daughter of an East Coast oil baron—made extensive plans for Olive Hill, the Los Feliz spot on which Wright's Hollyhock House now sits. Her dream, wrote biographer Meryle Secrest, was to "build a community of her imagination on a tract of land that would conspicuously proclaim her freedom from petty constraints and flaunt her unconventionality before the world."

If Wright's original idea had been realized, the site would have included not only the house but also a children's playhouse and school, walking paths, actors' housing, artists' studios, a row of commercial spaces, a movie theater, a textile-block community playhouse called the Little Dipper, and, according to the *Los Angeles Examiner*, what was to be "one of the most exquisite theaters the world has ever seen." The Barnsdall Theater, which would have been the city's only avant-garde performance space, was indeed monumental, a circle in a square evoking a temple or an ancient ruin.

"You will put your freest dreams into it, won't you?" Barnsdall urged Wright. "For I believe so firmly in your genius that I want to make it the keynote of my work."

Barnsdall bought the 36-acre parcel, which had been planted with olive trees by its former owner, in 1919. While things started off well, Wright, distracted by other commissions—notably, the Imperial Hotel in Tokyo—was unable to focus. The mercurial Barnsdall, meanwhile, would float from one idea to the next, gradually spending her way through her inheritance. They fought over details large and small, with Wright, who later called Barnsdall his "worst-ever client," insisting that she bow to him on all design decisions. The project's cost soared beyond the original $75,000 budget, and contractors began dropping out. The dream soon fell apart.

Through the supervision of his son Lloyd and his protégés Richard Neutra and Rudolph M. Schindler, Wright was able to finish Hollyhock, another nod to Indo-American architecture. But Barnsdall hated its monumentality (and leaky roof) so much that she later commissioned Schindler and Neutra to design replacements. Neither Schindler's Transparent House nor Neutra's Greyhound House was built.

In 1926, Barnsdall bequeathed Olive Hill and Hollyhock, the home she had lived in for just one year, to a reluctant recipient: the city of Los Angeles.

→ View of Olive Hill, theater in foreground

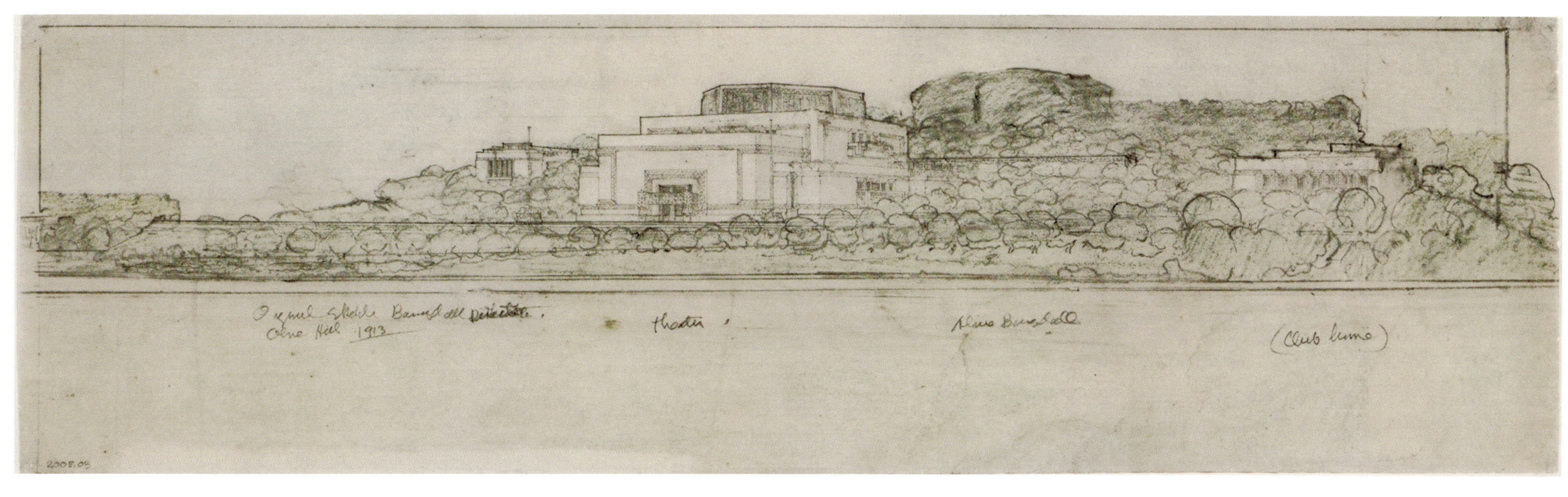

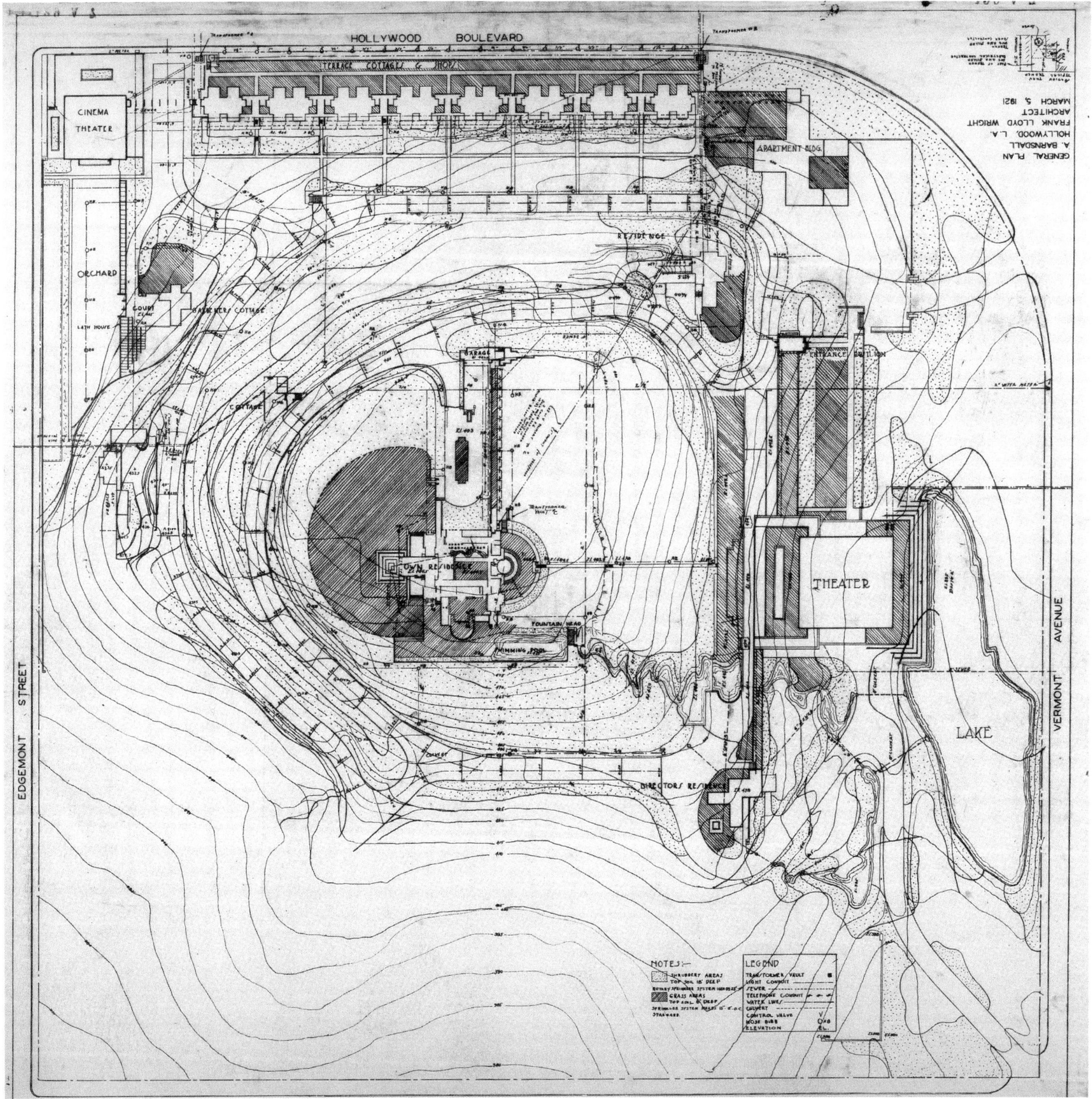

← Olive Hill site plan

→ Barnsdall Theater model, section, and elevation sketch

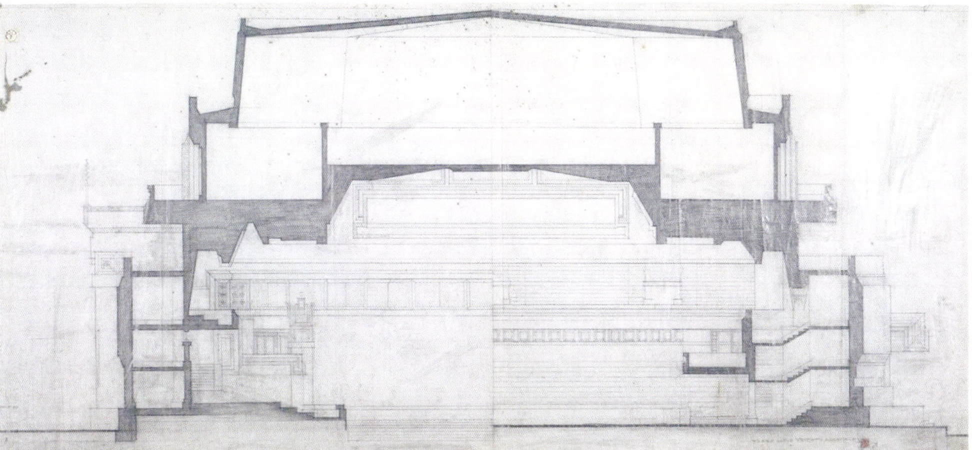

EATRE, OLIVE HILL 2005.01

↑
View of terrace cottages and shops (center) and cinema/theater (far right) from Hollywood Boulevard

DT

LLOYD WRIGHT
LOS ANGELES CIVIC CENTER

1925

We need not wait upon the costly and painful "force of circumstances" to erect a more or less tortured and deformed structure.

Lloyd Wright

Like the plans that preceded it and nearly every plan that followed, Lloyd Wright's 1925 competition entry—meant to guide "the present and future development of this to be the greatest of all cities"—emphasized the symbolism of public buildings sited atop Bunker Hill.

City leaders had invited Los Angeles's best architects to reconceive the metropolitan core. The winning scheme, by Wright's nemesis, the collection of firms known as Allied Architects, limited itself to the streets around L.A.'s current City Hall, which it designed. Wright's plan, however, was epic, stretching from the site of Bertram Goodhue's Central Library (then under construction) at Fifth and Grand and continuing north to Sunset Boulevard. Wright later called it an "acropolis for the city."

The design took the form of an elongated cross, following the existing north-south axis of Grand Avenue and the east-west line of what is today the 101 Freeway. Flanking a 500-foot-wide terraced walkway were twin pairs of connected buildings that grew in height as they progressed up Bunker Hill. When seen from afar, the megalith, which Wright called a "unified, organic structure," evoked an ancient Assyrian temple. Up close, the mitered edges and tight vertical lines of shops, offices, and government buildings revealed the ultimate expression of Wright's Art Deco bravura.

At the north end of the complex stood a duet of civic buildings, massive piles embracing City Hall, county offices, courthouses, a police station, a post office, and the chamber of commerce.

In his dreamlike transportation plan, Wright sketched layered and individual movement systems for vehicles (including aircraft) and pedestrians throughout the civic center site. Already, congestion was strangling downtown, and Wright's fantasy attacked the problem head-on. His excavated rapid-transit throughways presaged the freeway troughs that would be cut around downtown in the 1940s and 1950s, but Wright discreetly buried his "speedways" under broad terraces to give pedestrians the right-of-way. High-speed elevators whisked drivers from subterranean parking to sidewalks, offices, and rooftop helipads above.

Wright warned: "We need not wait upon the costly and painful 'force of circumstances' to erect a more or less tortured and deformed structure." While Allied Architects' City Hall (1928) has stood the test of time, the rest of the civic center, and Bunker Hill especially, has suffered exactly that fate.

Anais Nin, who visited Wright's studio sometime in the late 1940s, looked at his plans and wrote in her diary: "I saw [his] plans for Los Angeles. It could have been the most beautiful city in the world....But architecture had been taken over by businessmen, and Lloyd the artist was not allowed to carry out his incredibly rich, fecund concepts....If his plans had been carried out, the world would have been dazzled by them."

→ Civic Center, view from south along Grand Avenue

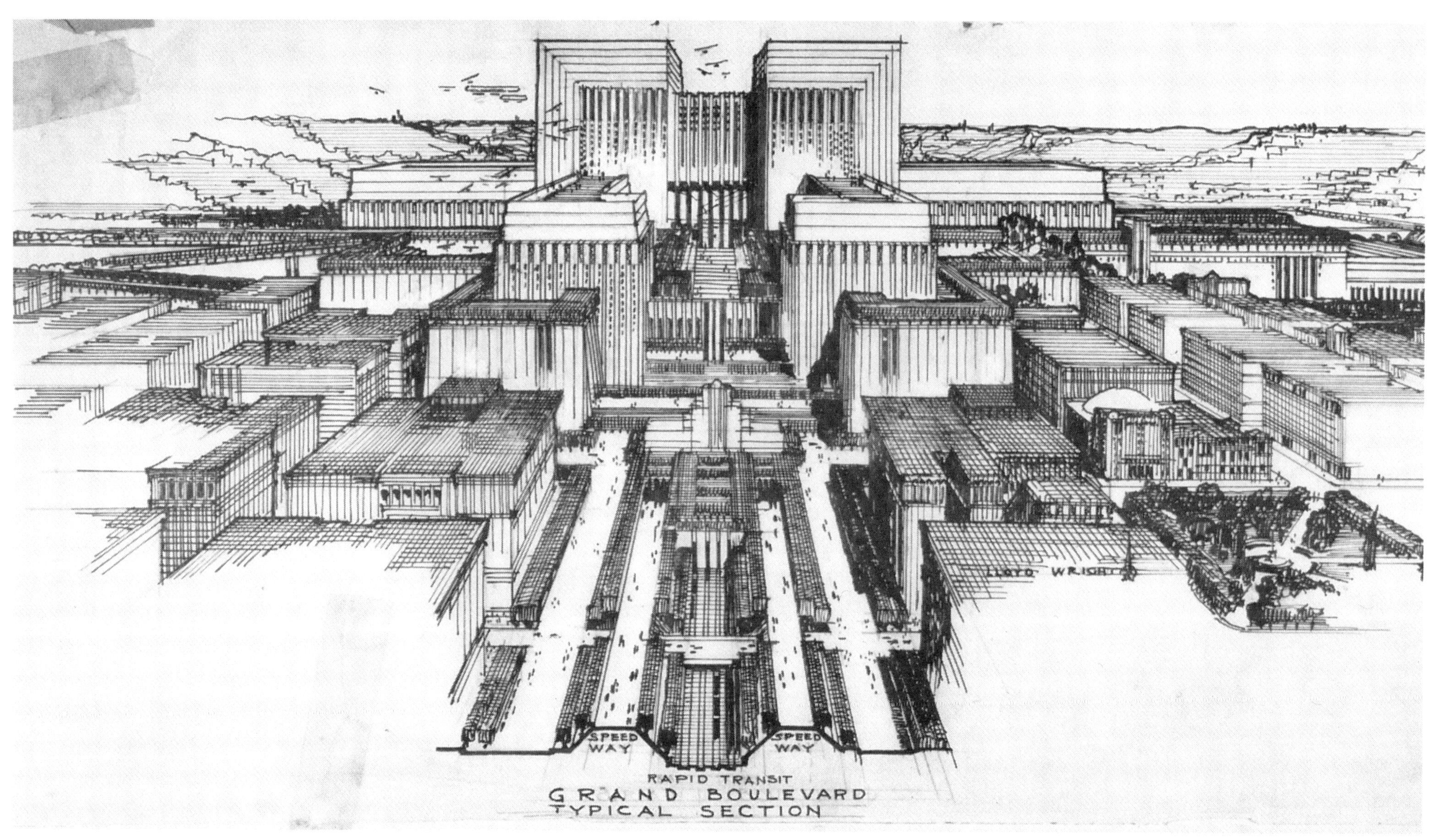
SPEED WAY
SPEED WAY
RAPID TRANSIT
GRAND BOULEVARD
TYPICAL SECTION
LLOYD WRIGHT

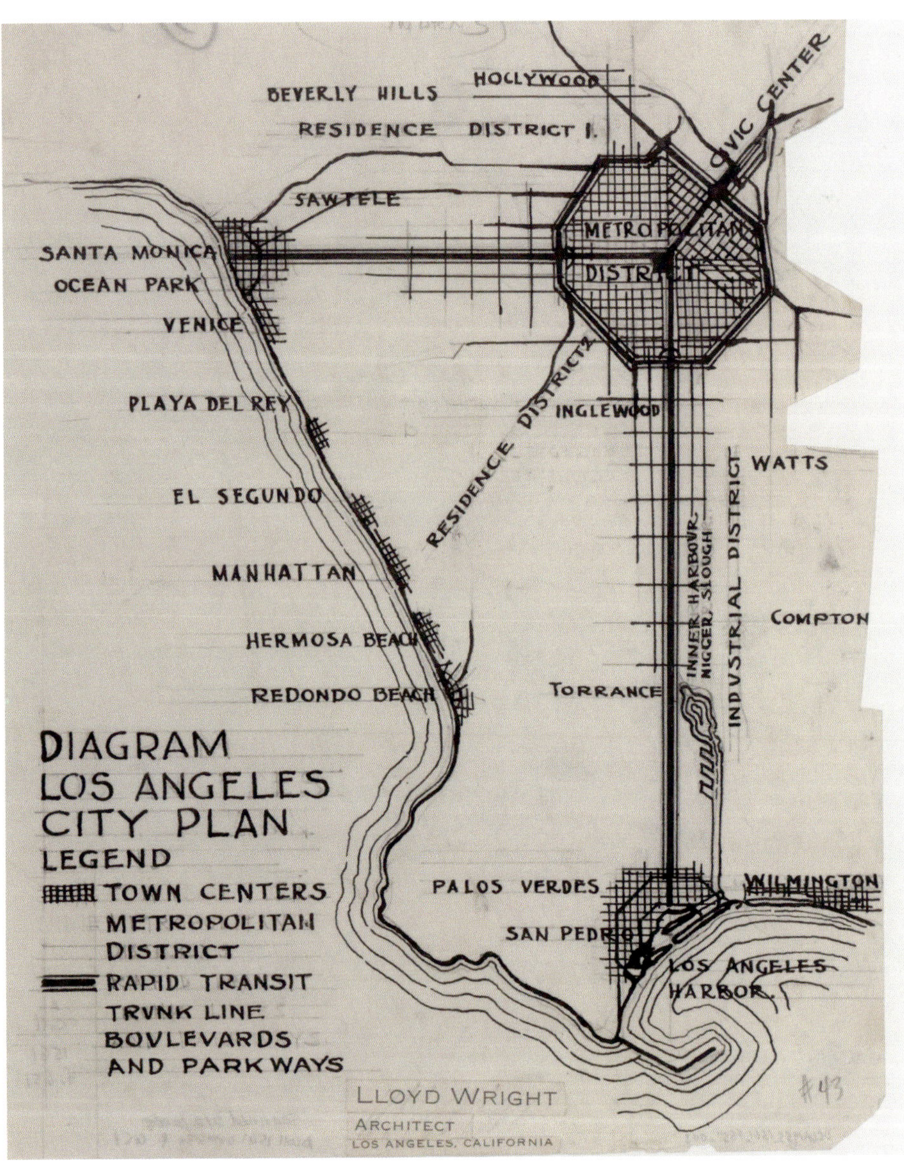

←←
Wright's vision of multiple town centers linked by rapid transit

↖
Early sketches

←
Early scheme with tall, cruciform buildings

→
Three conceptions of Wright's final plan

↘
Section view of infrastructure layers

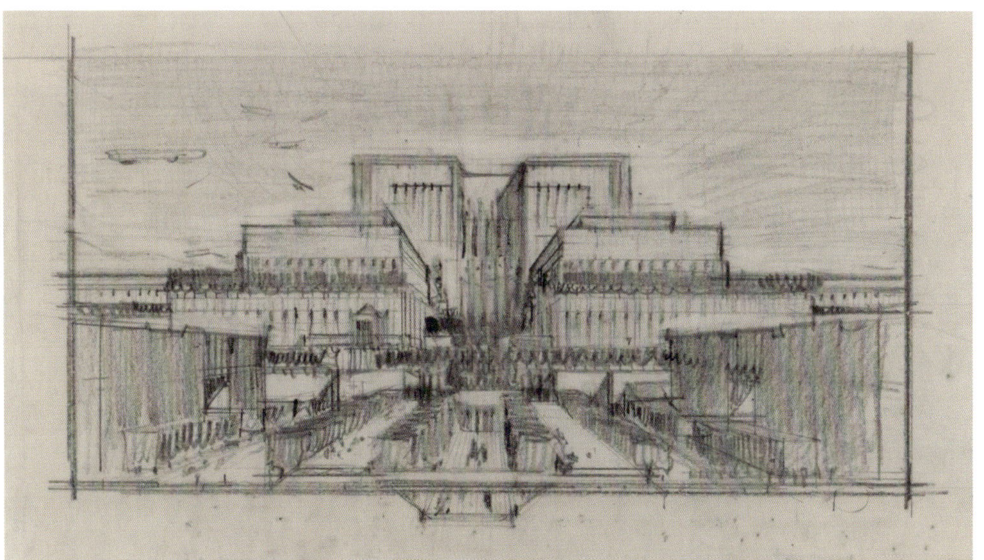

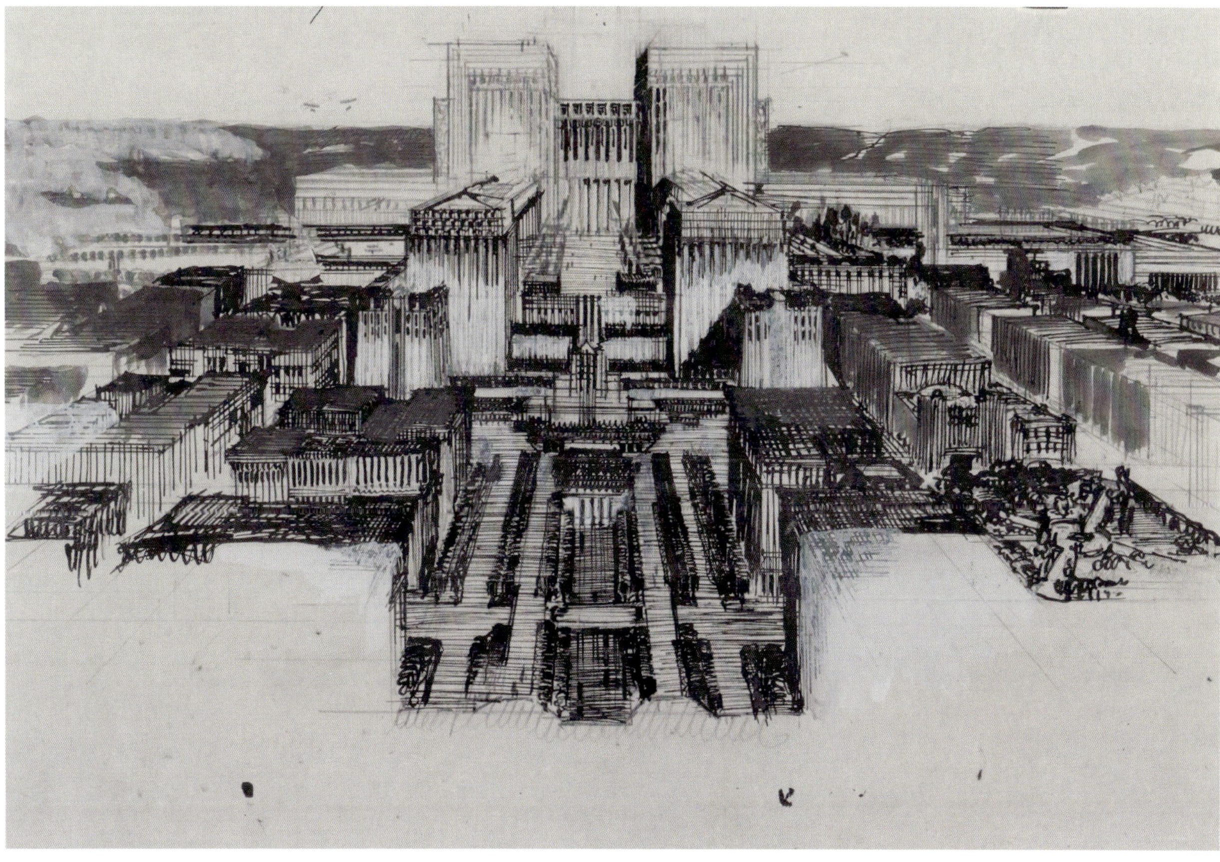

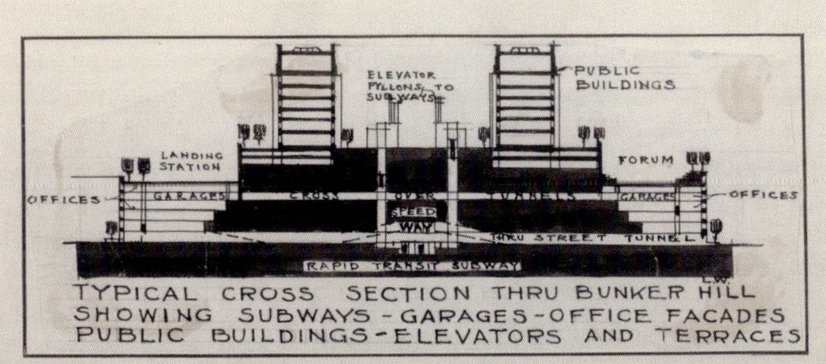
ELEVATOR PYLLONS TO SUBWAYS
PUBLIC BUILDINGS
LANDING STATION
FORUM
OFFICES
GARAGES
GARAGES
OFFICES
SPEED WAY
THRU STREET TUNNEL
RAPID TRANSIT SUBWAY
TYPICAL CROSS SECTION THRU BUNKER HILL
SHOWING SUBWAYS - GARAGES - OFFICE FACADES
PUBLIC BUILDINGS - ELEVATORS AND TERRACES

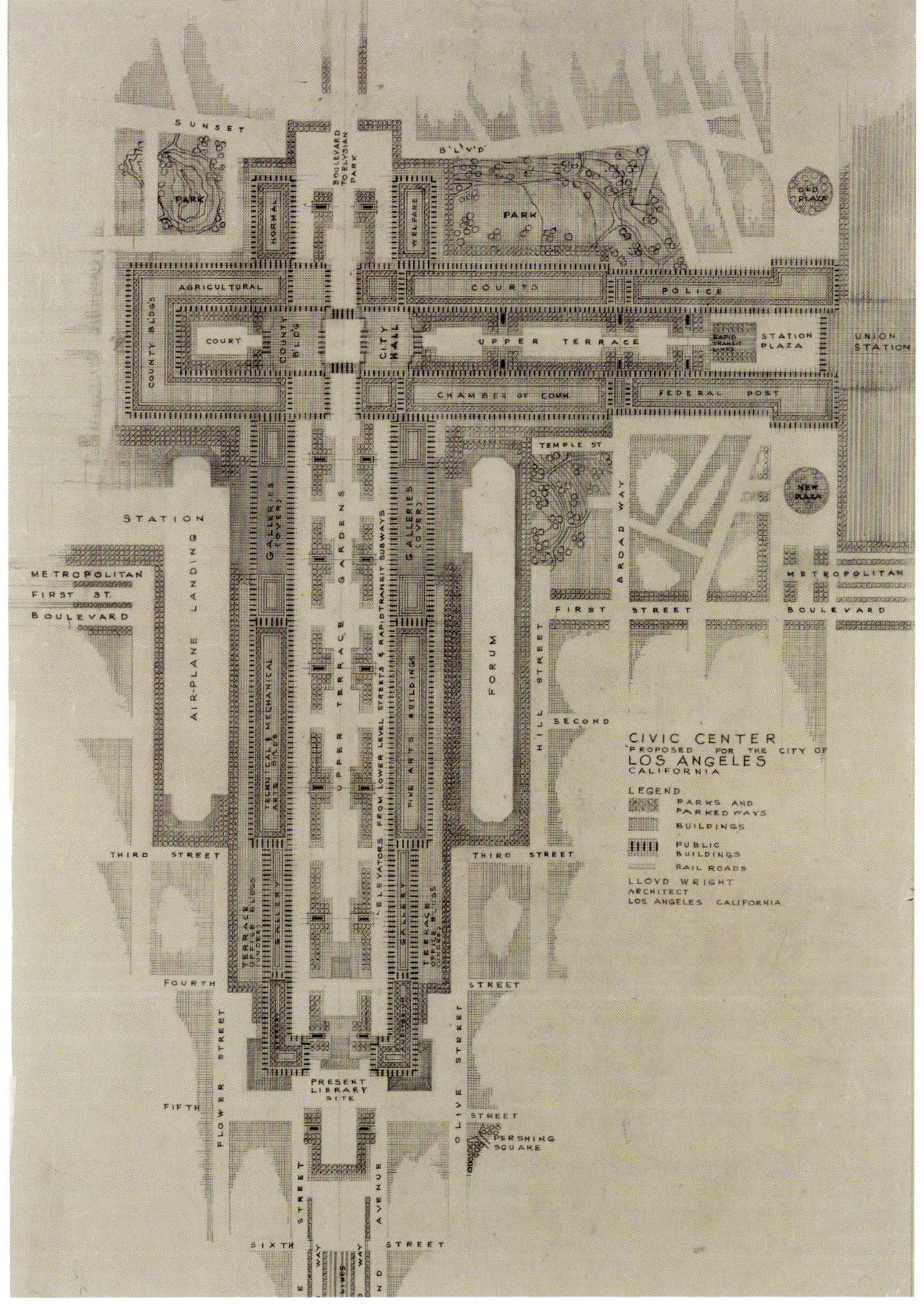

←
Cross-shaped site plan, stretching from Fifth Street to Sunset Boulevard and Figueroa to Broadway

→
Civic Center as seen from the east

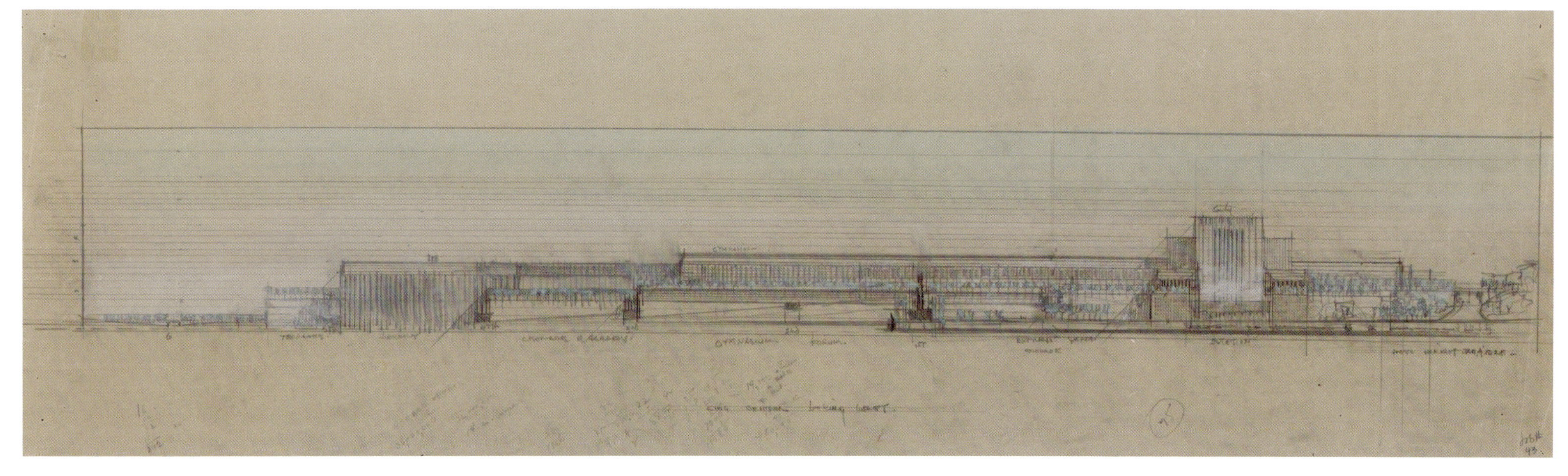
GYMNASIUM
FORUM.
CIVIC CENTER LOOKING WEST.

WS

GEORGE W. KELHAM AND ALLISON AND ALLISON
UCLA CAMPUS MASTER PLANS

1920s-45

Today, it is very difficult to discover anything positive to say about the UCLA campus.

David Gebhard and Robert Winter

The rolling hills of Westwood, cut by Stone Canyon Creek, brought to mind the undulating landscape of northern Italy, inspiring architects George W. Kelham and the firm of Allison and Allison to design in the style of Lombardy Romanesque. The aesthetic was an adaptation of UCLA's original buildings, on Vermont Avenue, and in many ways, of its sister university at Berkeley. The architects looked to the churches of Verona, Bologna, and Milan, sprinkling in a touch of Moorish and Byzantine. A sequence of Romanesques, faced in radiant red brick with elaborately detailed friezes, cupolas, semicircular archways, low-pitched tiled roofs, and stained-glass windows, would have progressed along a classical axis following the cardinal points on the compass.

While the plan called for 40 buildings, only the men's and women's gymnasiums, the Chemistry and Physics buildings, Powell Library, and Royce Hall were completed. Dodd Hall was added in 1948.

From the earliest stage, a campanile was proposed to rival Berkeley's 307-foot-tall 1914 Beaux-Arts tower (the third-tallest bell-and-clock tower in the world). "I wish someone would set the ball rolling by providing somewhere between $300,000 and $400,000 for a campanile, complete with clock and bells, at any appropriate place on this new campus," lamented university president William Wallace Campbell in early 1920. "Such a bell tower would be visible from afar and make a constant appeal."

A campanile remained an abiding symbol, on paper. As late as 1945, it was sketched in Allison and Allison's final master plan. It would have resided on the western edge of the school, to the far side of the ravine, approximately where Pauley Pavilion now stands. No doubt, the entire mood of the campus would have been different had the slender mast risen above the city's Westside.

In the end, the campanile, along with the original Romanesque idiom, was abandoned. It was too costly, plus the style created pockets of wasted space. By 1949, Welton Becket was summoned to fill in the campus with modernist boxes. From that time on, critics savaged the school's design. As architectural historians David Gebhard and Robert Winter put it: "Today, it is very difficult to discover anything positive to say about the UCLA campus." Architect and theorist Charles Moore commented that the landscaping "manages, thank heaven, at least partly to conceal most of the buildings."

→
Kelham's axial plan, with campanile

←
Drawing of main Allison and Allison plan, 1945

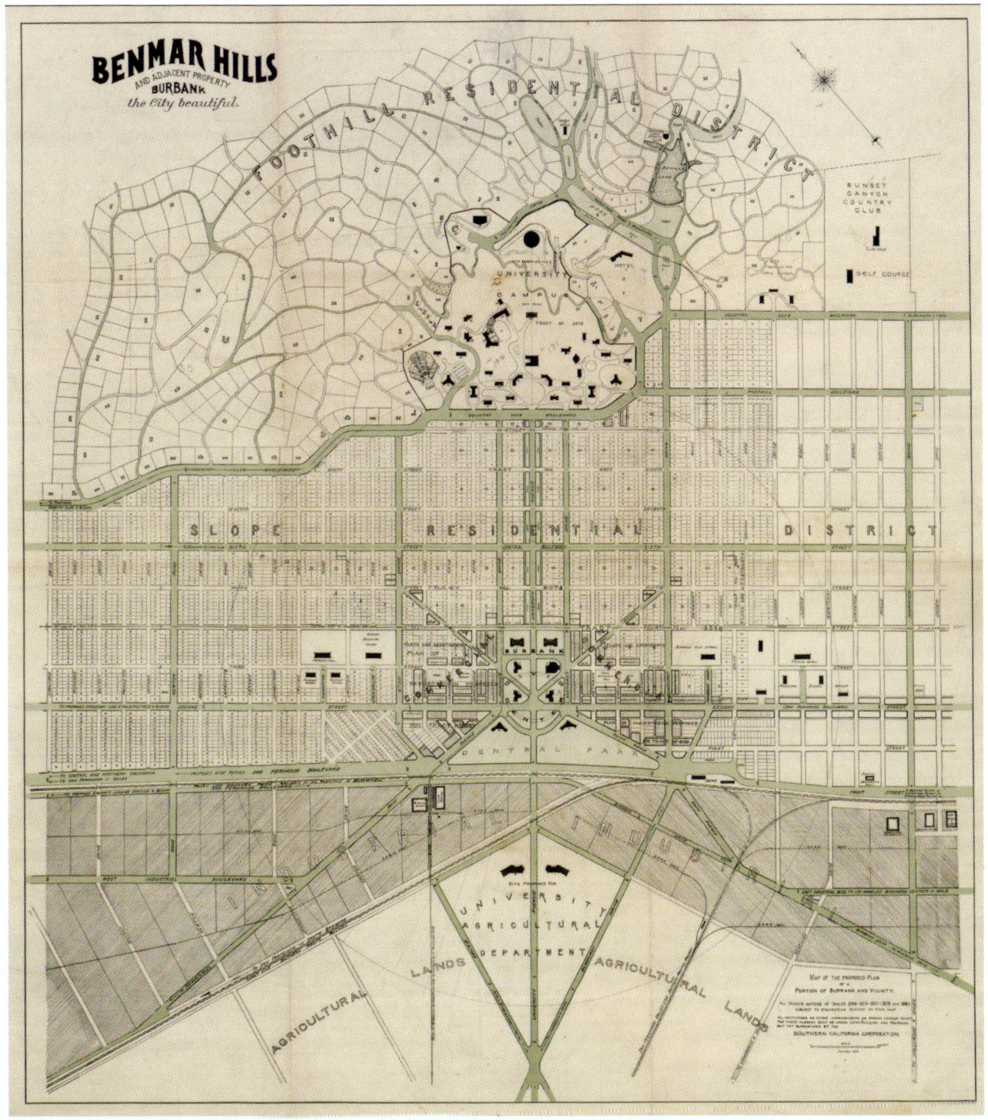

UNIVERSITY OF CALIFORNIA, BURBANK

1919–25

In 1919, Ben W. Marks, a real estate speculator, bought 5,100 acres of hillside in northern Burbank. Marks called the subdivision Benmar Hills—a name that has stuck—and tried to lure UCLA, then located on Vermont Avenue near downtown, to move to the barren slopes. A promotional brochure proclaimed, "The massive structures destined eventually to rise around about its spacious campus will include a wonderful College of Music, a perfectly appointed College of Arts and Drama, a two million dollar Museum, an Auditorium to seat 3,400 people, a complete Library, as well as a Stadium and Gridiron second to none in the United States. Each of these buildings will combine the high attainments of celebrated architects with the last word in the theory and practice of modern building construction." Just across the Southern Pacific railroad tracks, another huge swath was to be set aside for the university's Agriculture Department, reached by a number of intersecting boulevards laid out on an axis similar to the plan for Washington, D.C.

The Burbank site was rejected when the Janss Investment Company donated a chunk of acreage in West Los Angeles, enticing the newly minted university to what is now Westwood. The Burbank university idea did not fade, however. The Southern California Corporation, which succeeded Marks, continued to advance the scheme, and in 1925 the city of Burbank deeded 408 acres to UCLA's rival, the University of Southern California, to create a USC satellite called the Los Angeles University of International Relations. USC president Rufus B. von KleinSmid said he would need to raise $10 million for the new school, telling city trustees that he was about to embark on a trip to the East Coast to personally tap many "public spirited men of wealth...in an effort to obtain their financial support," the *Los Angeles Times* reported. USC was given two years to break ground, but fundraising failed. Benmar Hills became a housing development, whose streets, named for colleges around the nation, reflect the ambitions of Burbank's early city-builders.

MC

ROBERT ALEXANDER AND RICHARD NEUTRA
ELYSIAN PARK HEIGHTS

1950

Destined to become the most controversial unrealized project in the history of the city, the colossal plan for Elysian Park Heights, which came breathtakingly close to breaking ground, arose out of the dire postwar need for housing.

Los Angeles, flush with federal money, slated Chavez Ravine, an impoverished Mexican-American village nestled in the hillsides just northeast of downtown, to become its most ambitious housing development. Robert Alexander and Richard Neutra had misgivings about dismantling the tight-knit community, but the existing houses—many of them tin shacks with dirt floors—were deemed substandard, and the architects eventually came to believe that they could build a dense neighborhood while preserving the “human warmth and pleasantness” found in the existing “slum.”

To house more than 3,300 families—nearly triple the number there at the time—at least 24 13-story towers and 163 two-story garden apartments would have marched down the ravine in strictly ordered rows, like giant dominoes. The design borrowed heavily from monumentally scaled modernist utopian visions such as Le Corbusier’s Ville Radieuse and Neutra’s own Rush City Reformed. According to the $33-million plan, no major roads would bisect the area, interior streets would become culs-de-sac, and housing would face inward toward garden plots or “finger parks.”

The average rent for the one- to five-bedroom apartments was to be $35 a month, including utilities. Chavez Ravine required millions of cubic feet of hillside to be graded and moved to make way for the towers.

Hundreds of pages of blueprints—with specifications ranging from light fixtures to plant species—were ready to be handed over to builders. It was never to be. A red-baiting, anti-public-housing campaign launched by business, police, and political elites killed the plan three years after its conception. Elysian Park Heights would eventually be handed over, with a hefty public subsidy, to the Brooklyn Dodgers. On September 27, 1959, the team broke ground on a new stadium, ending the “battle of Chavez Ravine.”

→ Elysian Park Heights towers and garden apartments

ELYSIAN PARK HTS CAL 4
HOUSING AUTHORITY
CITY OF LOS ANGELES

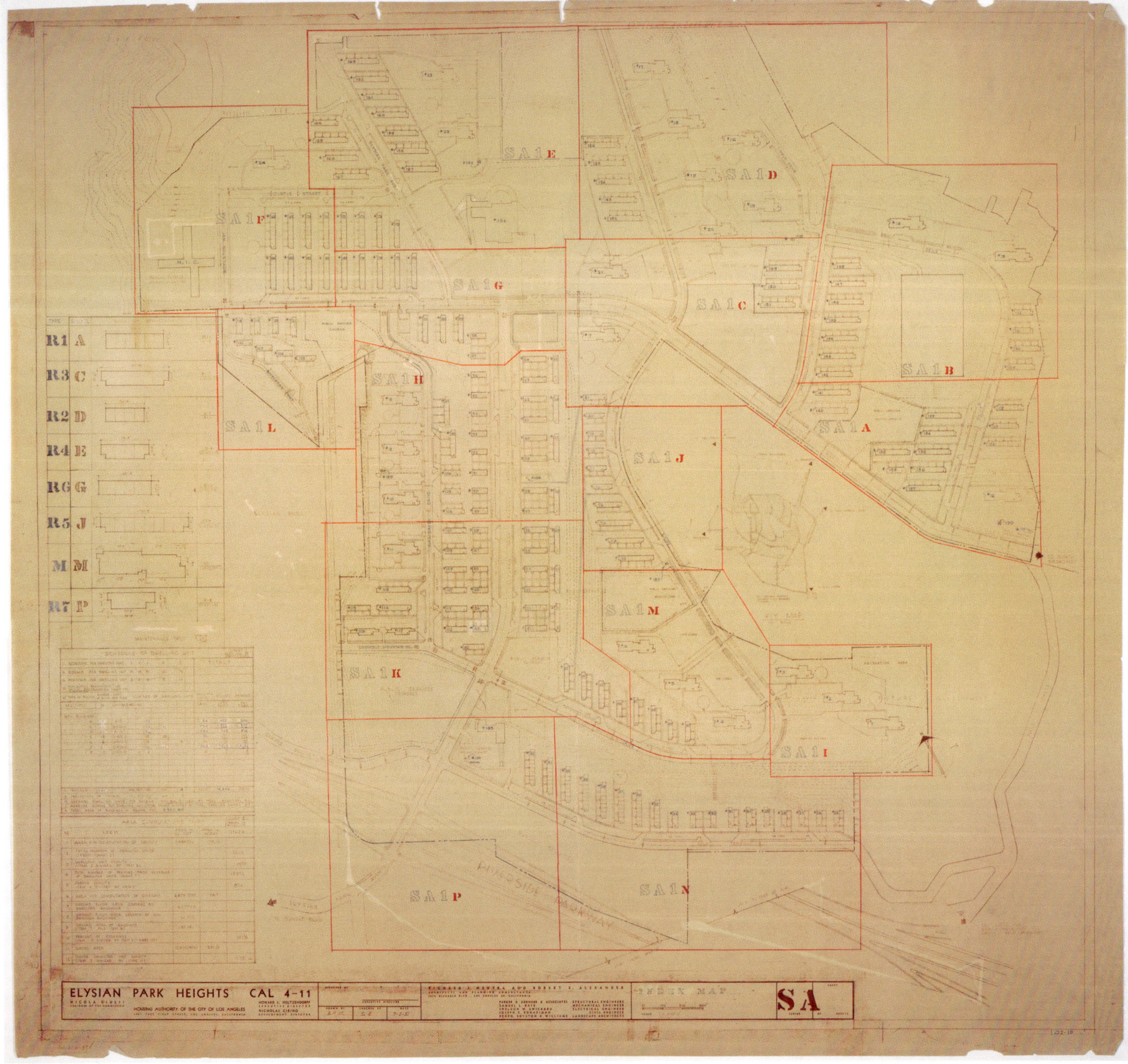

← Overall site plan

→ Landscape plan for one housing group

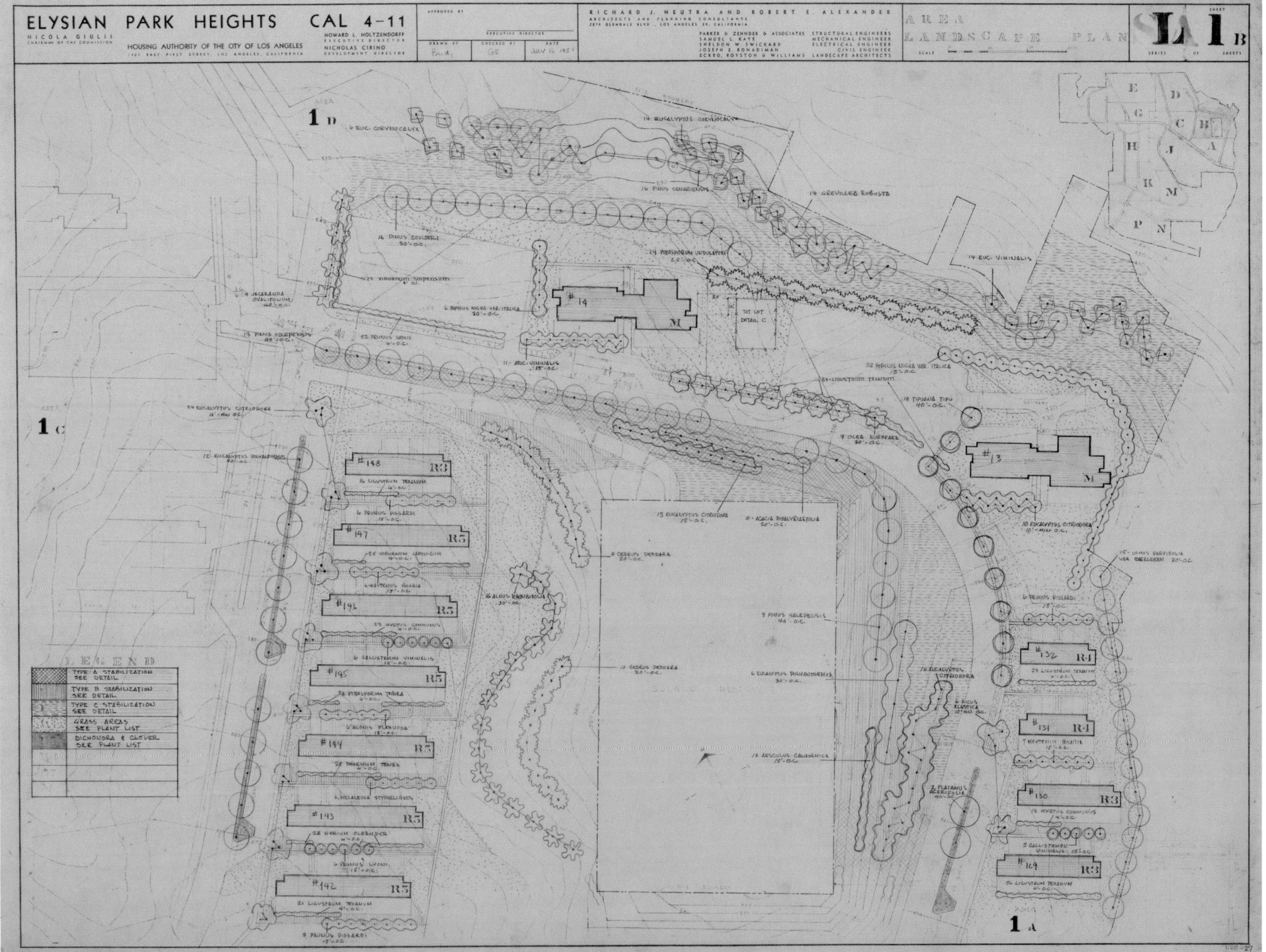
ELYSIAN PARK HEIGHTS CAL 4-11
NICOLA GIULII
HOUSING AUTHORITY OF THE CITY OF LOS ANGELES
HOWARD L. HOLTZENDORFF
NICHOLAS CIRINO
RICHARD J. NEUTRA AND ROBERT E. ALEXANDER
PARKER & ZEHNDER & ASSOCIATES STRUCTURAL ENGINEERS
SAMUEL L. KAYE MECHANICAL ENGINEER
SHELDON W. SWICKARD ELECTRICAL ENGINEER
JOSEPH E. BONADIMAN CIVIL ENGINEER
ECKBO, ROYSTON & WILLIAMS LANDSCAPE ARCHITECTS
AREA LANDSCAPE PLAN
L 1 B
LEGEND
TYPE A STABILIZATION SEE DETAIL
TYPE B STABILIZATION SEE DETAIL
TYPE C STABILIZATION SEE DETAIL
GRASS AREAS SEE PLANT LIST
DICHONDRA & CLOVER SEE PLANT LIST

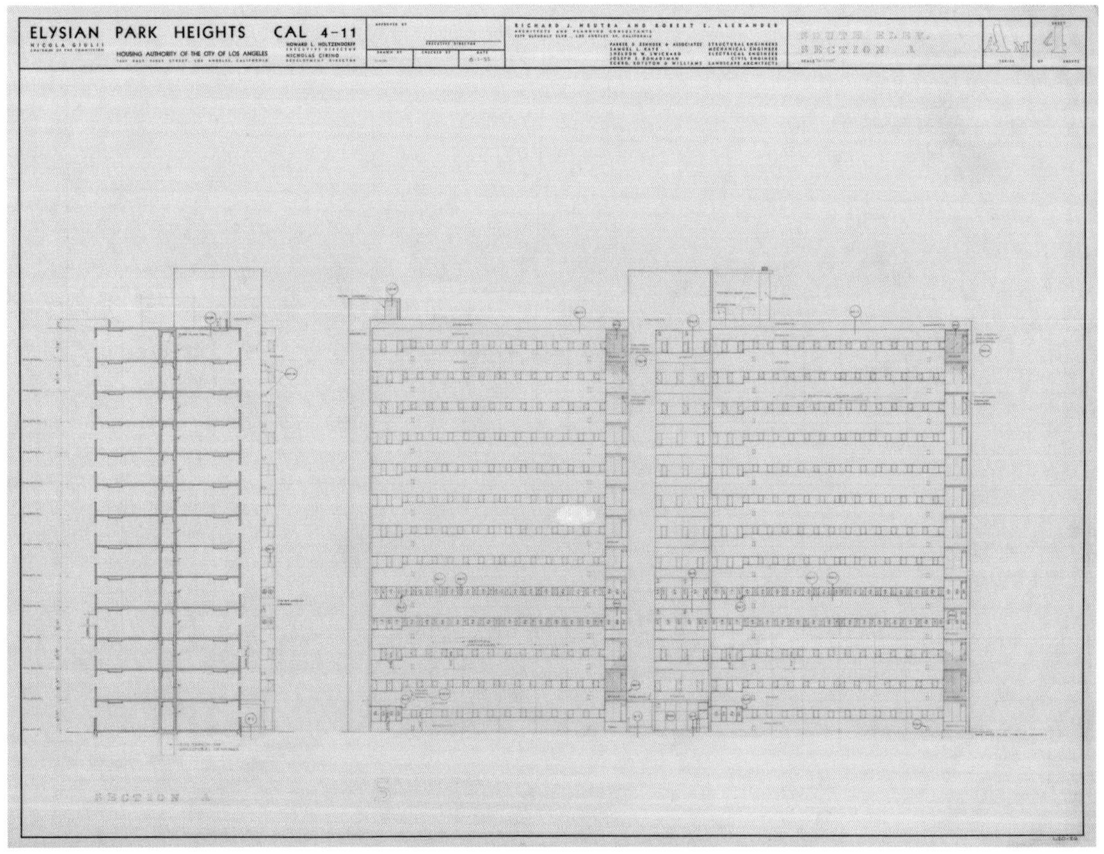
ELYSIAN PARK HEIGHTS CAL 4-11
NICOLA GIULII
HOUSING AUTHORITY OF THE CITY OF LOS ANGELES
HOWARD L. HOLTZENDORFF
NICHOLAS CIRINO
RICHARD J. NEUTRA AND ROBERT E. ALEXANDER
PARKER O. ZEHNDER & ASSOCIATES STRUCTURAL ENGINEERS
SAMUEL L. KAYE MECHANICAL ENGINEER
SHELDON W. SWICKARD ELECTRICAL ENGINEER
JOSEPH E. BONADIMAN CIVIL ENGINEERS
ECKBO, ROYSTON & WILLIAMS LANDSCAPE ARCHITECTS
SOUTH ELEV.
SECTION A
SECTION A

←←
Typical tower sections

←
Towers around landscaped courtyard

→
Interior of single-story apartment

↘
Community center

PEREIRA AND LUCKMAN
LOS ANGELES INTERNATIONAL AIRPORT (LAX)

1952

[LAX] was brand-new six years ago—and outmoded before the cement on its new runways was dry.

Time magazine

What began in 1951 as a design challenge for William Pereira's architecture students at the University of Southern California emerged as the centerpiece of his firm's original master plan for Los Angeles International Airport (LAX). Pereira and his students dreamed up the concept of a centralized, circular terminal building housed under an enormous glass dome. Six covered, elevated passageway "fingers" radiated from the periphery of the dome, like spindly spider legs, leading to outboard aircraft loading gates. The dome soared several stories above a grand concourse decked in palm and banana trees. Rising from the floor was a central column, in deep blue, with an etching depicting airline routes across North and South America. Far above, a circular platform housed a restaurant, an idea that would later morph into the LAX Theme Building.

This original plan died because the city's Building Department found it too radical, the cost of air-conditioning would have been exorbitant, and the airlines wanted their own individual terminals. These separate terminals became the basis for the firm's final master plan, developed later in the 1950s with Welton Becket and Paul R. Williams aboard. Every iteration of that plan, moving into the 1960s, added schemes that never made it, each more ambitious than the previous one.

"If we can land men on the moon before the end of this decade, the problems that face us as airport operators should be met with equally dynamic thinking," said one of the airport's annual reports from the mid-1960s.

In 1957, the dome vision was replaced by a hangarlike structure, reminiscent of Eero Saarinen's winged thin-shell-concrete roof for TWA at John F. Kennedy Airport. Extending from the corners of the architect's arched, tentlike design were the same concrete, spider-leg breezeways seen in the earlier version of the plan. As late as 1961, an "electronically controlled push-button horizontal elevator"—that is, an aerial tramway—was introduced as "the last word in modern vehicular systems." The overhead cars, glass-and-steel gondolas designed by Lockheed Aircraft Service, were propelled along a system of parallel tracks, carrying no more than a dozen passengers at a time. The tramway was intended to ferry people between the Theme Building and all ticketing buildings within four minutes, free to airline passengers but costing visitors 25 cents. The plan was abandoned in favor of a horseshoe-shaped, passenger-car roadway, known eventually as the world's largest cul-de-sac.

By 1967, *Time* magazine declared that the nation's most dramatic airport plans were those in Los Angeles, whose "airport was brand-new six years ago—and outmoded before the cement on its new runways was dry." Pereira alone was on the job, now proposing that five new terminals be constructed underground, each with its own subterranean garage and own giant dome-shaped skylight to allow in natural light from above. Jumbo jets, such as Boeing's 747 and SSTs, would be swiftly served, Pereira hoped, by huge, hydraulically operated underground "elevator-lounges" that would rise from the ground to unload their cargo of 250

→ Bird's-eye view of terminal and satellites

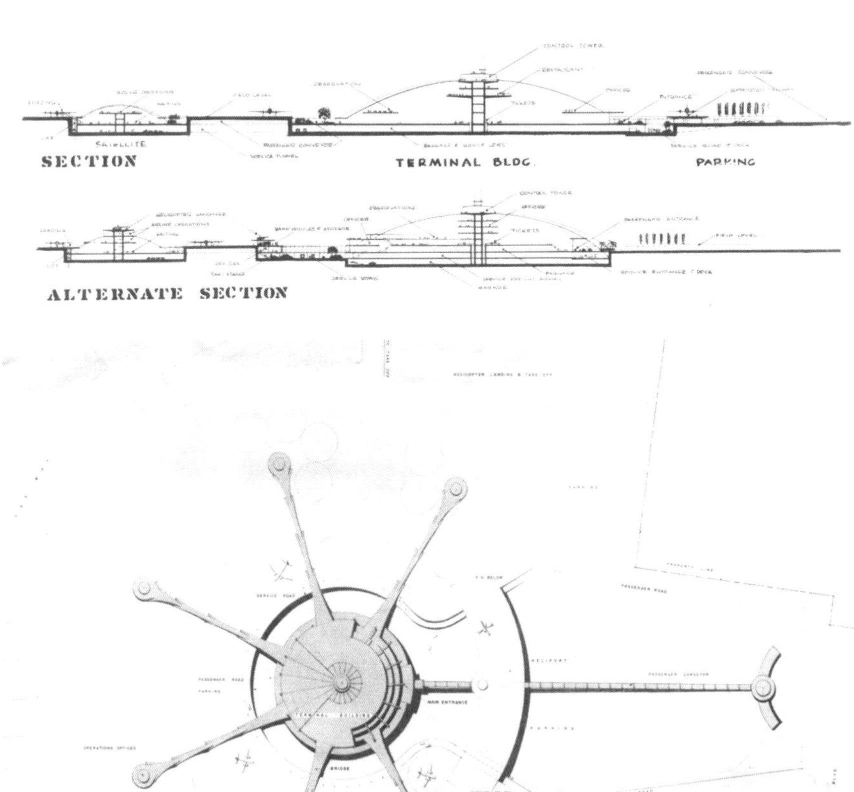

passengers via short, flexible telescoping bridges. Other lift mechanisms included "snorkel" escalator lounges rising out of the depths and "spiral ramps," or moving walkways that corkscrewed upward. Aboveground, five glass domes, imagined as giant skylights, would bring light to the caverns below.

That same year, airport authorities proposed another plan to deal with overcrowding: an offshore runway or Seadrome, located about 5 miles off the coast. The Board of Airport Commissioners approved a $15,000 contract with L.A.'s Transportation Systems Corp. for a three-phase preliminary study of the concept.

"I think it's something we need rather desperately to solve the crowding of the airways and the noise that is generated from the present-day airports and the noise problems as we see them in the future," said LAX general manager Francis T. Fox. He added: "Something like a super floating aircraft carrier might do it or something that is on pilings." For transport to and from the Seadrome, the initial plan called for hydrofoil vessels and helicopters. Another plan, involving a man-made island reached by a causeway extending from the 10 Freeway in Santa Monica or via subway tunnels extending from the mainland near Marina del Rey, would resemble a floating city. It would contain, among other elements, apartments, parks, beaches, a sports center, an art center, a convention center, and, of course, a new airport. Like the concoctions before them, the Seadrome and airport island were jet-age fantasies that eventually succumbed to reality, leaving an eyesore airport that to this day functions as if it were still the 1960s.

↖
Section through terminal building

←
Aerial plan of terminal building

→
Runways surrounding main terminal

← Glass-enclosed terminal interior, with world map etched on central column

↙↙ Open-air corridor encircling glass dome

↙ Pedestrian walkway to aircraft

→ Supersonic jet landing at offshore airport

↗ Interior of subterranean satellite terminal

→→ "Snorkel" escalator lounge

→→ Hydraulically operated elevator lounge

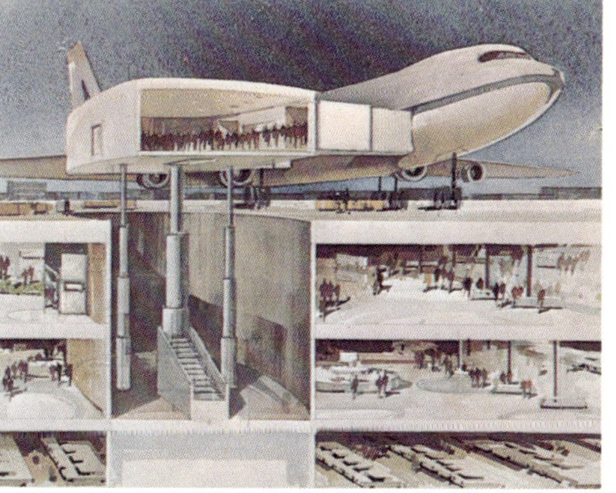

DT

PEREIRA AND LUCKMAN
BUNKER HILL URBAN RENEWAL

1958

We have a chance to create a dynamic city-within-a-city that would provide all the advantages of a major metropolis within a 500-acre site.

William Pereira

Other than the evisceration of Chavez Ravine, easily the most ambitious—and destructive—decision in Los Angeles history was the city's choice in 1951 to level Bunker Hill, a once-great but neglected Victorian neighborhood, to make way for its new cultural, residential, civic, and business hub. "It would be in the interest of the health, safety and general welfare of the people of Los Angeles to clear these blighted areas and redevelop them to their best social and economic use," California's 1954 Community Redevelopment Act pronounced.

The city and its new Community Redevelopment Agency hired the omnipresent firm Pereira and Luckman to draw the master plan for Bunker Hill's renewal in 1958. The initial scheme was even more far-reaching—or, more accurately, reckless—than what materialized a few years later. It remains one of the clearest examples of planning grandeur, which to this day has tempered the public's enthusiasm for "visionary work."

Mirroring conventional urban thinking—which promoted the separation of foot traffic from automobile traffic to "reduce accidents" and "facilitate movement of both pedestrians and vehicles"—the "New Heart of Los Angeles" was centered on massive interconnected superblocks raised above streets and parking structures, with freeways laced in below. In addition to segregating buildings and people from the grit of urban life with planted plazas and pedestrian bridges, the elevated plan, the firm said, would minimize land removal and provide 15,500 underground parking spots.

According to historian Eric Avila: "The corporatization of that neighborhood closely followed the discipline of modernist city planning, which embraced the principles of homogeneity, uniformity and monumentality over diversity, complexity and locality."

To convert the 150-acre hilltop from a "semi-slum," as the *Los Angeles Times* called it, or a "liability," as Pereira and Luckman termed it, the team proposed several "plazas" or "centers." These included a commercial plaza containing offices, hotels, and stores; a new trade center, offering a donut-shaped civic auditorium, a trade-fair area, and several hotels; a new Music Center, which included a wedge-shaped performance hall rising over a reflecting pool; and a residential plaza containing luxury apartments for white-collar elites. The cost for the plan: between $100 million and $150 million. And this was just the beginning. Further development, created along the same pattern, called for, among other things, a redesigned civic center, more trade, cultural, and residential buildings, and, vaguely, "future development."

→ Office plaza atop multistory parking structure

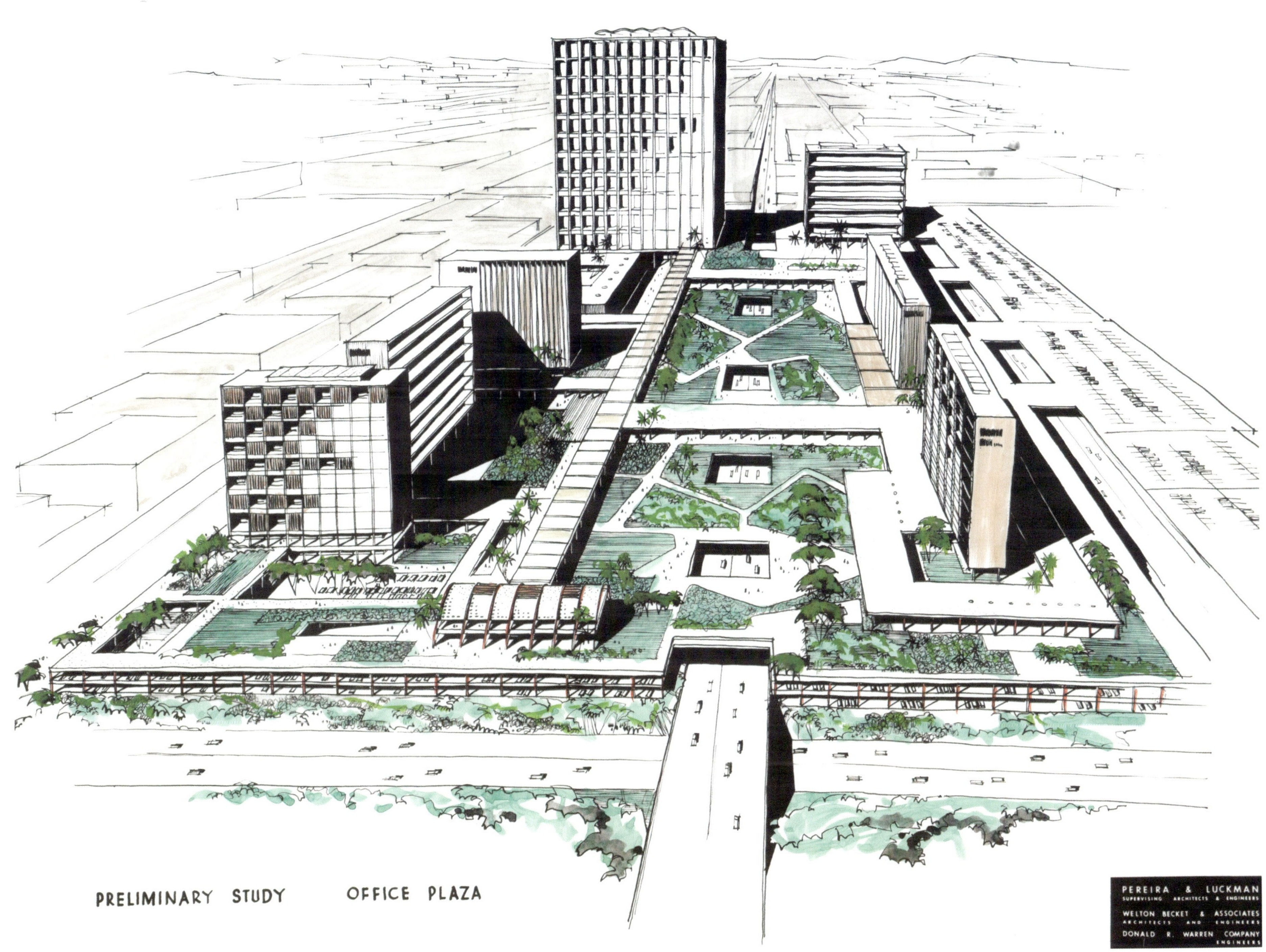
PRELIMINARY STUDY OFFICE PLAZA
PEREIRA & LUCKMAN
SUPERVISING ARCHITECTS & ENGINEERS
WELTON BECKET & ASSOCIATES
ARCHITECTS AND ENGINEERS
DONALD R. WARREN COMPANY
ENGINEERS

TRADE CENTER

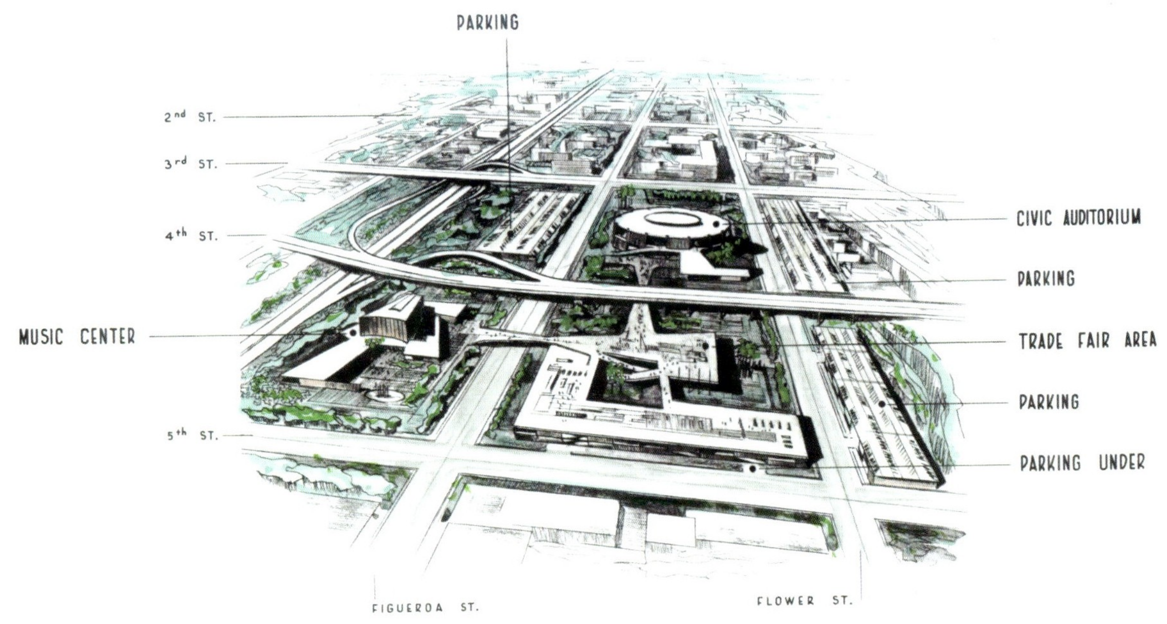

← Bunker Hill flattened and crisscrossed by elevated roadways

↙ Wedge-shaped Music Center, southwest of eventual location

→ Parking scheme for original superblock plan

→→ Urban redevelopment plan by Wurster, Bernardi and Emmons shows smaller, more plentiful parcels

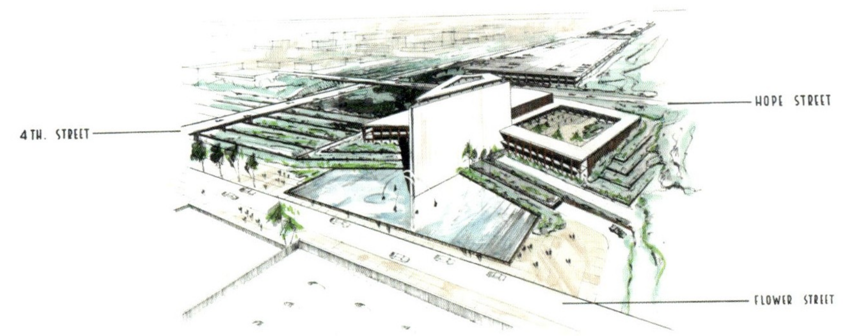

"We have a chance to create a dynamic city-within-a-city that would provide all the advantages of a major metropolis within a 500-acre site," said the ever-optimistic William Pereira.

While some superblocks, such as the Music Center, were completed (albeit in a different form), the majority of this plan never came to be. An update by Wurster, Bernardi and Emmons in 1971 decreased the number of parking spaces and increased density. Its outline, stretching from First through Fifth streets, integrated a staggering amount of parcels more tightly into the urban grid. Each building plot was given a letter, spanning the alphabet from A to Y.

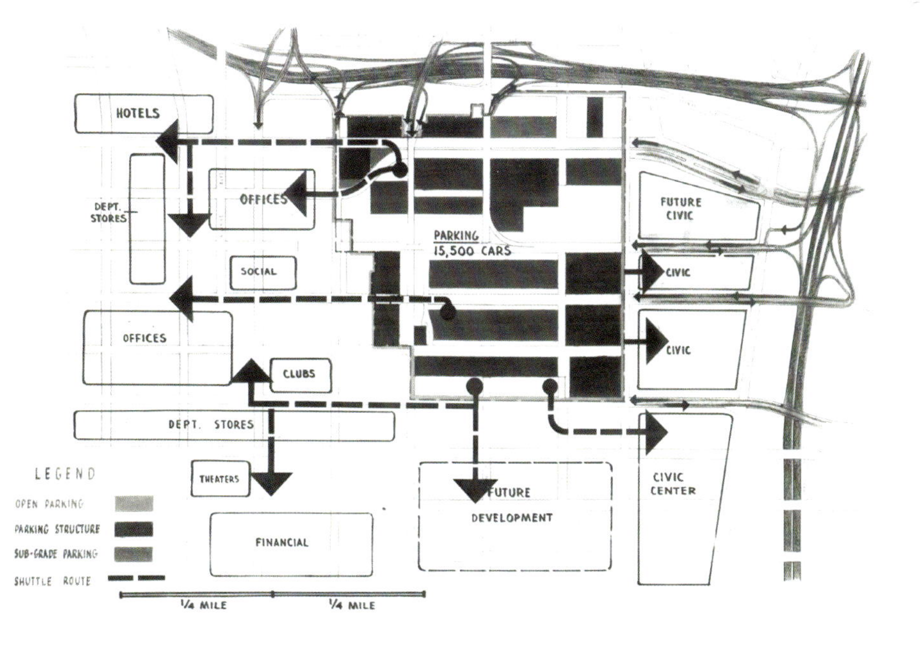

PARKING AND SHUTTLE

BUNKER HILL URBAN RENEWAL PROJECT
COMMUNITY REDEVELOPMENT AGENCY OF THE CITY OF LOS ANGELES, CALIFORNIA

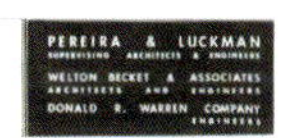

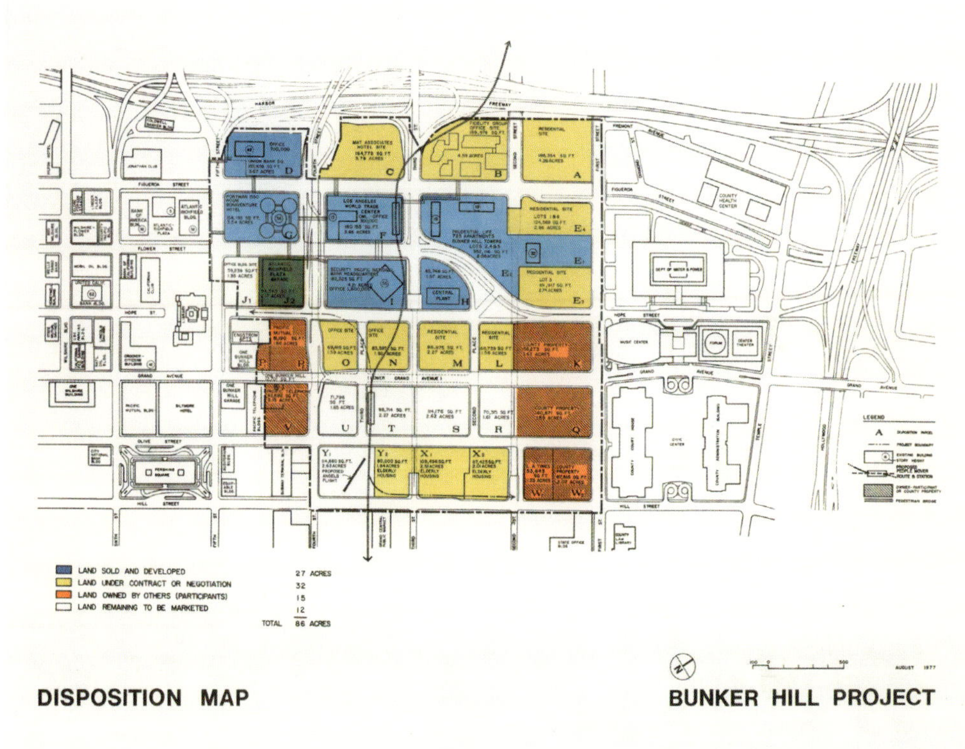

SB

JOHN LAUTNER
ALTO CAPISTRANO

1963–68

Alto Capistrano will one day be the very heart of the predicted Southern California super community bounded on the north and south by the downtowns of Los Angeles and San Diego.

Orange County Business Journal

Located in the mountains above San Juan Capistrano, a tony coastal town in southern Orange County, John Lautner's Alto Capistrano was planned as one of the largest, most profitable developments in Southern California. It was also going to be one of the most architecturally adventurous.

"Alto Capistrano will one day be the very heart of the predicted Southern California super community bounded on the north and south by the downtowns of Los Angeles and San Diego," wrote the *Orange County Business Journal*.

The self-contained community, the brainchild of developer Morris Nisbin, would include everything a 1960s family could ever need: a six-story shopping center; neighborhood-scale stores; restaurants, hotels, and theaters; medical offices; parks; schools; churches; a vacation spa and golf course; and, of course, plenty of housing, including high-rise apartments, condominiums, and single-family estates.

Lautner, who had studied developments on sloping terrain such as El Dorado Hills near Sacramento, called the complex "the greatest and most exciting challenge" of his career. It would no doubt have transformed his trajectory, and his bleak financial situation.

The community, providing homes with "no obstructions now or in the future," as Lautner put it, was to be created by carving into the mountains rising above the ocean, as if California had become the rice fields of Vietnam. The plan suspended multistory buildings above steep slopes in a dense pattern up the mountains, consciously reserving open space. Of the site's 11,000 acres, only a few hundred were to be disturbed.

There were three residential building types: clusters of capsule-shaped, two-story apartments with gardens and balconies; taller towers, stacked up the mountains like staircases; and clusters of single-family houses. The structures would fan out atop contoured mountainside terraces, overlooking the Pacific. The concrete apartments' rounded edges—containing outdoor balconies facing the ocean supported by conspicuous center columns—strongly evoked Lautner's eight-sided Chemosphere House. The project would have utilized inclined electric cars to transport residents to the shopping center and commercial complex below. Lautner had already reached out to Ehrsam, a company specializing in grain elevators and conveyor belts, to discuss the specifics of a "belt manlift" system.

Ultimately, Alto Capistrano was scrapped for several reasons: The county would not approve the project's compact density. Ehrsam and other companies could not figure out how to build and maintain inclined elevators in the area. And funding for the ambitious project was never finalized. The one built component was the visitors' center, an octagonal building also echoing the Chemosphere. For a time a museum of architecture, it now contains a health club.

→ Ocean-view housing contoured to hillside

JOHN LAUTNER
A.I.A. ARCHITECT
EL CERRITO PLACE
LOS ANGELES CALIF.

ALTO CAPISTRANO
SITE PLAN OF COMMERCIAL, APARTMENT
& RESIDENTIAL DEVELOPMENT FOR
IN THE CITY OF:
SAN JUAN CAPISTRANO CALIF.
SHT. S-P
John Lautner
A.I.A. ARCHITECT
EXISTING RESIDENTIAL TRACT

← Site plan of grading cuts, with football-shaped shopping center

→ Marina View Heights, part of Alto Capistrano development

↘ Rounded edge duplex echoes Lautner's Chemosphere House.

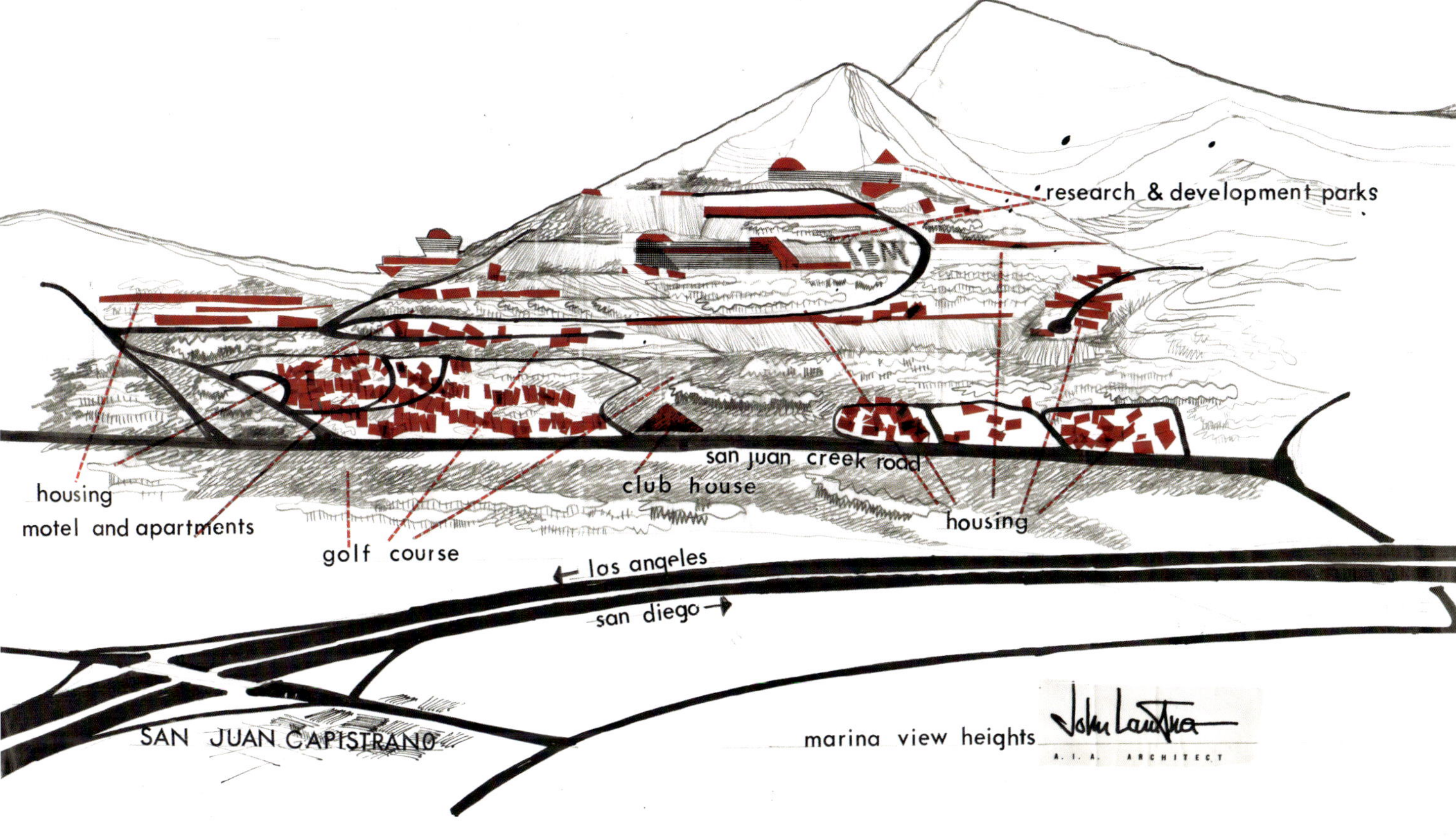

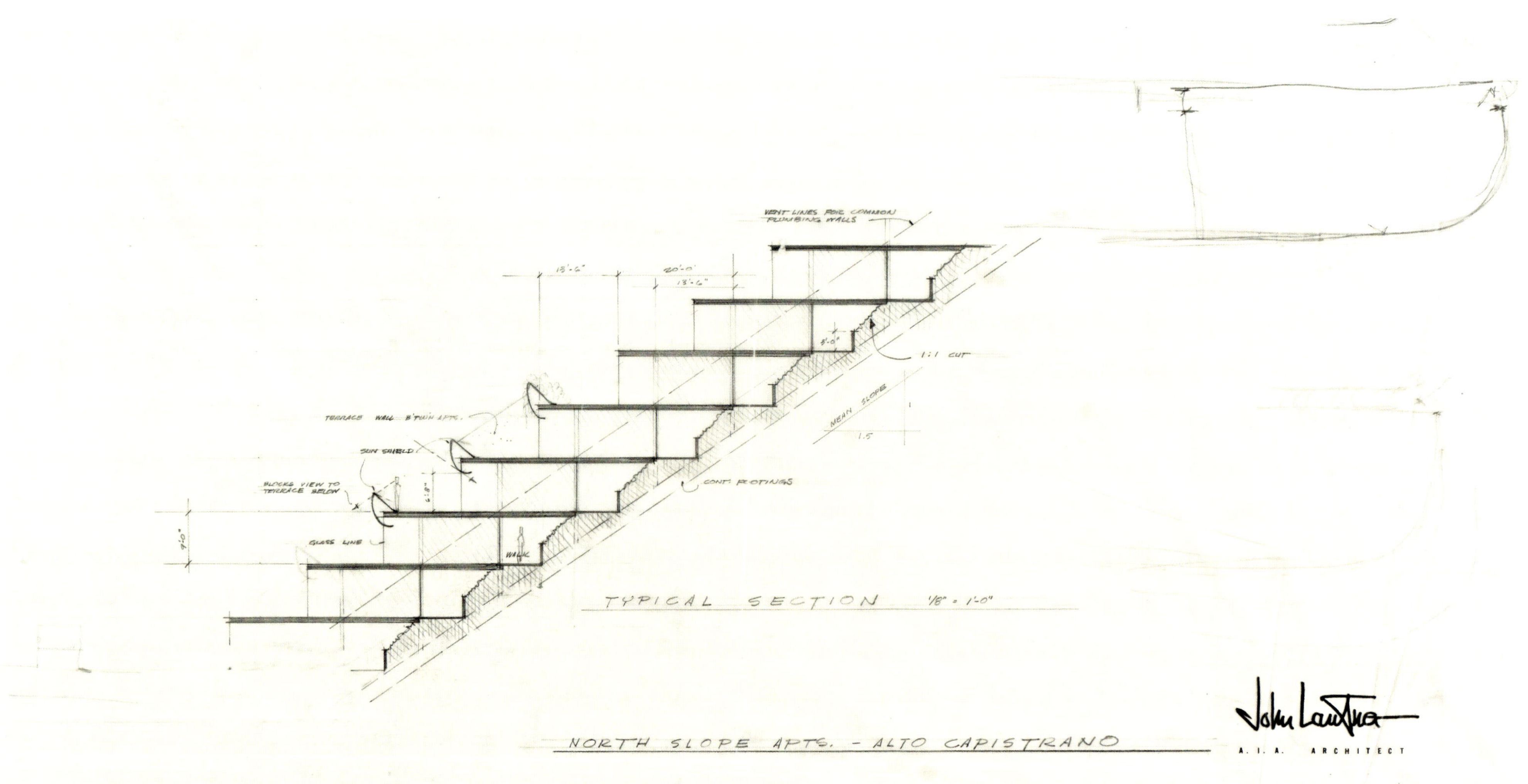

VENT LINES FOR COMMON PLUMBING WALLS
13'-6"
20'-0"
13'-6"
5'-0"
1:1 CUT
MEAN SLOPE
1
1.5
TERRACE WALL B'TWN APTS.
SUN SHIELD
BLOCKS VIEW TO TERRACE BELOW
6'-8"
CONT. FOOTINGS
9'-0"
GLASS LINE
WALK
TYPICAL SECTION 1/8" = 1'-0"
NORTH SLOPE APTS. - ALTO CAPISTRANO
John Lautner
A. I. A. ARCHITECT

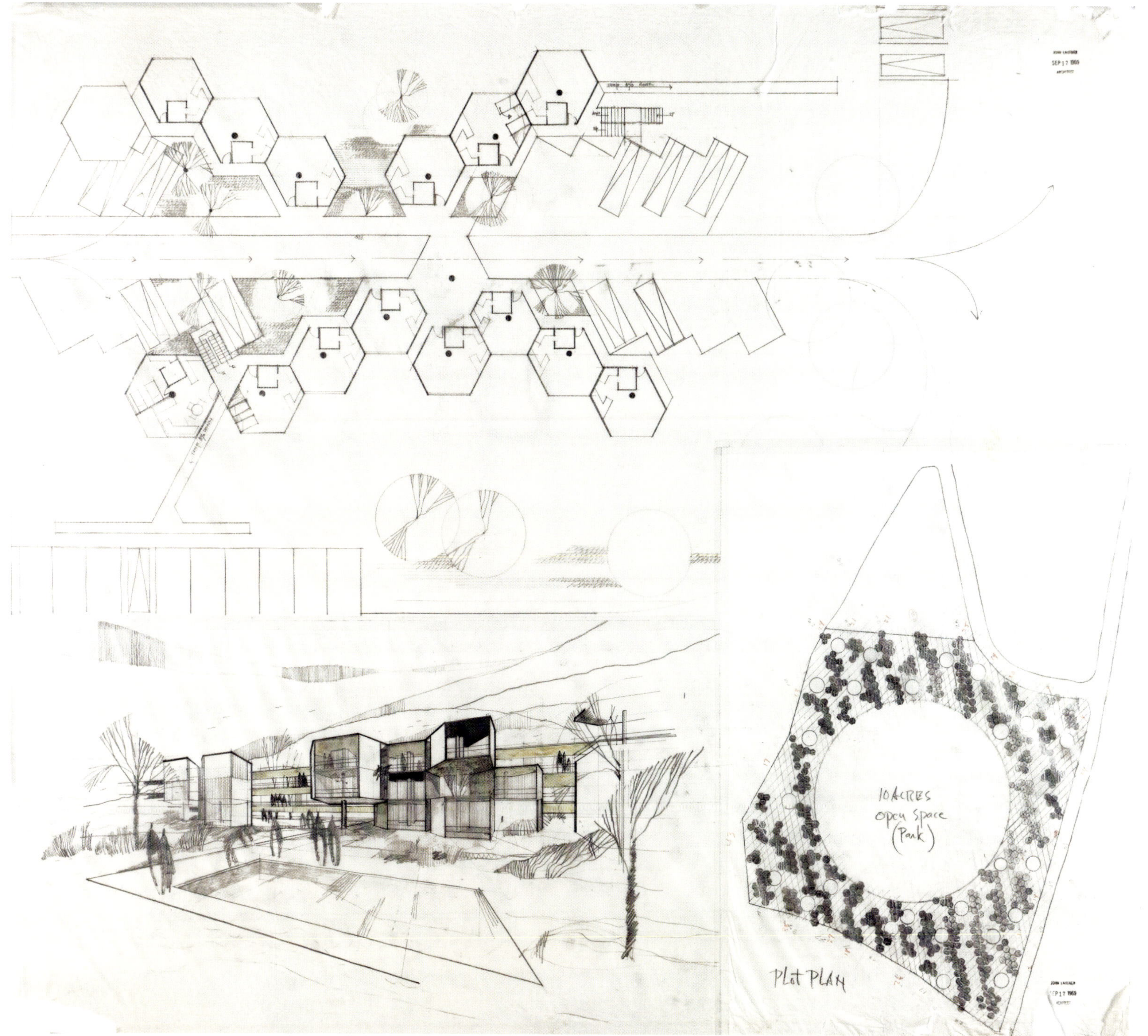

←

Multistory apartment steps down hillside.

→

Hexagonal townhouses surround circular park.

MC

CALARTS
CALARTS HOLLYWOOD

1964

Here is the CalArts of tomorrow.

Sebastian Cabot

At the 1964 premiere of *Mary Poppins*, Walt Disney made a rare appearance and played a short, titled *The CalArts Story*, ahead of his blockbuster. The 15-minute film, screened to the 1,500 tuxedo-clad, white-gloved stars in the audience at Grauman's Chinese Theatre, was propaganda. Disney was trying to raise money for his dream of building an arts college in the heart of Hollywood.

As celebrities including Julie Andrews and Dick Van Dyke sat captive, images of low-slung white buildings, in the idiom of the era's go-to architect William Pereira, flashed on the screen. Actor Sebastian Cabot's suave voice-over explained that Los Angeles was on the brink of getting a brand-new museum of art and a splashy new music center, and what it needed, to make a troika of cultural powerhouses, was a campus for the newly incorporated California Institute of the Arts.

"Here is the CalArts of tomorrow," Cabot intoned as the camera panned artists' renderings of the campus, perched between the Hollywood Freeway and Lake Hollywood and across from the Hollywood Bowl. A series of perfected geometric forms, complete with dormitories surrounding a swimming pool and a funicular connecting the roadside entrance to the campus high above, would occupy a shelf carved out of the hilltop. Cabot expanded: "An acropolis crowning the hills above Hollywood, if present plans materialize and the site can be made available. A hub of the art world chosen for its central location...within easy reach of the downtown Music Center, the art museum, and the galleries of the area."

Cabot was reading Disney's script, written to pressure the Los Angeles County Board of Supervisors to release land it owned directly across from the Bowl.

The first draft of the Hollywood Hills plan, drawn by Pasadena architect Thornton Ladd—whose firm, Ladd and Kelsey, would design the Norton Simon Museum—showed a typical college campus featuring individual buildings. But Disney, according to Ladd, said: "Nope, all under one roof. We want these arts to interact, not exist separately."

Why the Hollywood gambit failed is not known, although at the time Disney and other trustees were scrounging for money, which was slow in coming. By 1969, Cal Arts had broken ground on a 60-acre site in the rural town of Valencia, 32 miles northwest of downtown. The remote—and inexpensive—parcel was sold to the college by Newhall Land and Farming Company, which hoped that a residential subdivision would spring up around the new school. The failure to build in Hollywood turned out to be a boon for the boonies.

→ Illustration shows campus uphill from Hollywood Bowl and planned Hollywood Museum.

→→ Modernist academic buildings sandwiched between Hollywood Reservoir and Hollywood Freeway

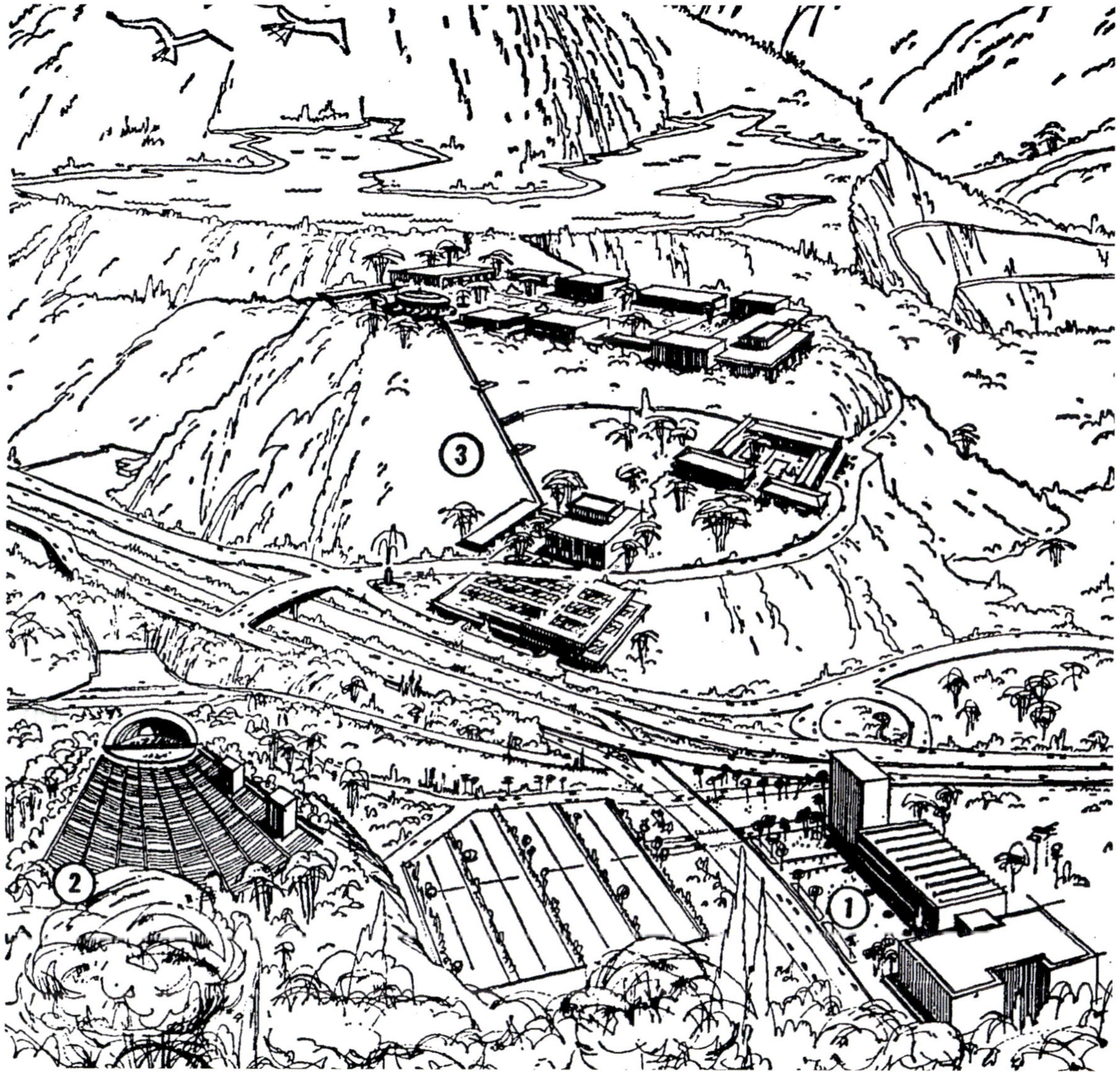

WS

HARLAN GEORGESCU
SKYLOTS

1965-67

Instead of going out, we went up.

Chris Georgesco

Harlan Georgescu remains one of Romania's most famous modernist architects. His work throughout that country ranged from high-rises to theaters to bridges to steel mills. Georgescu fled his Eastern European nation following the rise of Soviet-backed Communists in 1947. He never achieved prominence in his new home of Los Angeles, but he was able to establish a successful practice building mostly single-family residences. In his spare time, he developed visionary schemes designed to address urban ills. The most ambitious, Skylots, borrowed from his industrial-scale Romanian projects and was instigated by the creeping sprawl taking hold near his new house on the city's Westside.

Georgescu described Southern California as "bonanza land for the fast multiplying, self-appointed land developer." He predicted the coming of a single city stretching from San Francisco to San Diego, "paved, sliced and gift wrapped." Skylots was a reaction not only to this horizontal overdevelopment but also to rising land prices, pollution, and exhaustive commutes.

"Instead of going out, we went up," explained Chris Georgesco, a sculptor, who remembers his workaholic father complaining that his endless driving kept him from meaningful time at home. Georgescu enlisted Chris, then a teenager, to help build the project's gigantic models.

Stretching along both sides of the 405 Freeway from Brentwood to Laguna Beach, Skylots would consist of more than 100 "vertical villages," 300-by-300-foot plots of multistory housing supported on concrete slabs suspended from steel frames. Flying sidewalks, hung from cables, connected the buildings. The design was, in many ways, similar to that of a suspension bridge, a good choice in earthquake-prone Southern California. While the infrastructure was standardized, the houses could be individually tailored. The bases would contain centralized transport, shopping ("a modern Agora," Georgescu said), offices, schools, parks, and sports facilities. In total, the collection of villages would house about 5 million people.

Georgescu was shot and killed on the street in Venice, California, in 1977, a victim of random violence. He was 69. The remote chance of Skylots being built died along with him.

→ Towers joined by suspension bridges, with 405 Freeway and high-speed transit in foreground

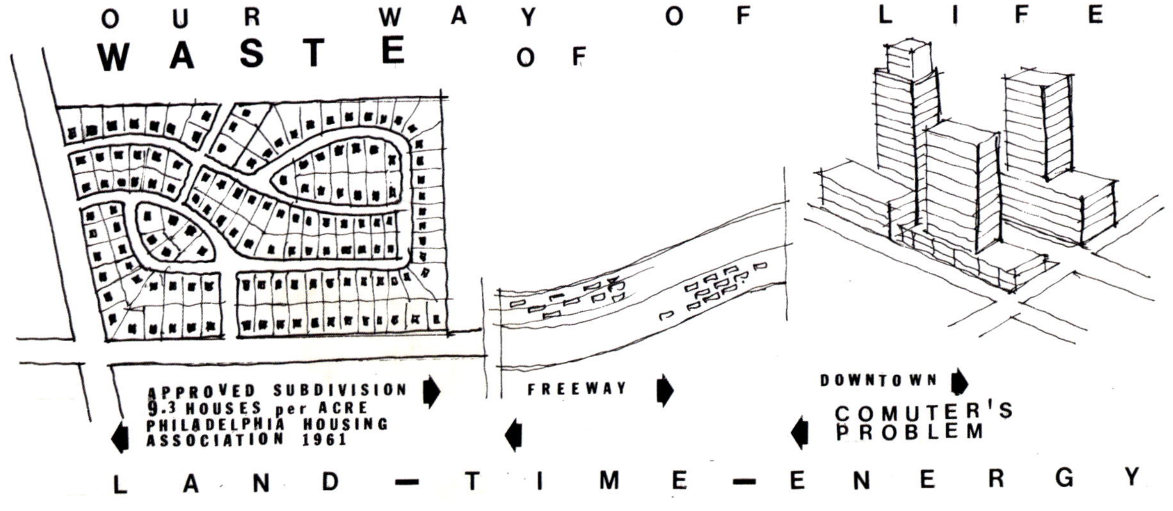

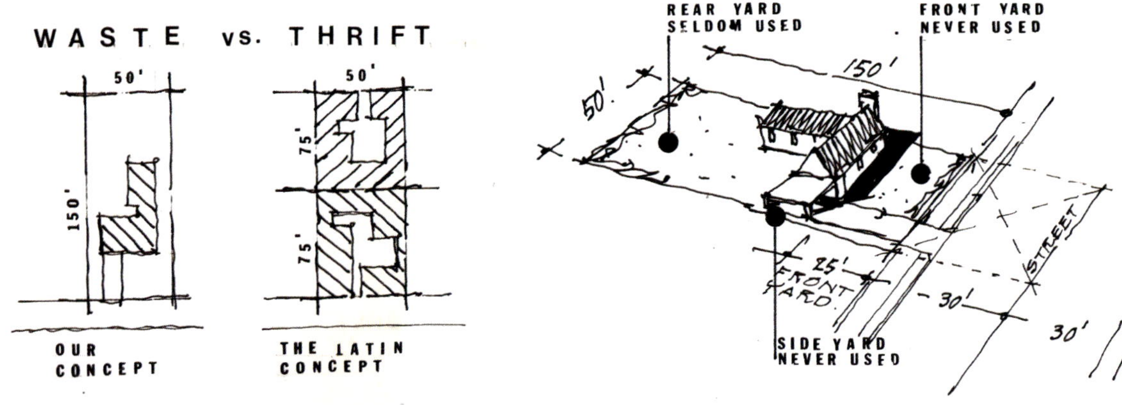

ANALYSIS FIND ~ HOUSES TAKE FIFTH OF LAND IN SOUTHERN CALIFORNIA
Los Angeles Times, July 23 1967
Sharply rising Southern California land prices are accelerated by the fact that only 20.4 % of the occupied land is being used for residences according to an analysis by the PRE-BUILDER LAND Co. of Beverly Hills. Another 32.7 % of available land is taken up by streets and highways, transport, commercial, military, industrial facilities to support this population. The result is that population increase exert an exaggerated leverage effect on the demand of land.
TO HOUSE - SUPPORT AND SERVICE SOUTHERN CALIFORNIA DAILY POPULATION RISE OF NEARLY 1000 PERSONS REQUIRES ABOUT 350 NEW ACRES A DAY.

WHERE DOES THE LAND COME FROM /?
The only remaining source is the 46.9 % still used for agriculture. As the supply diminishes, prices are certain to rise higher and higher.

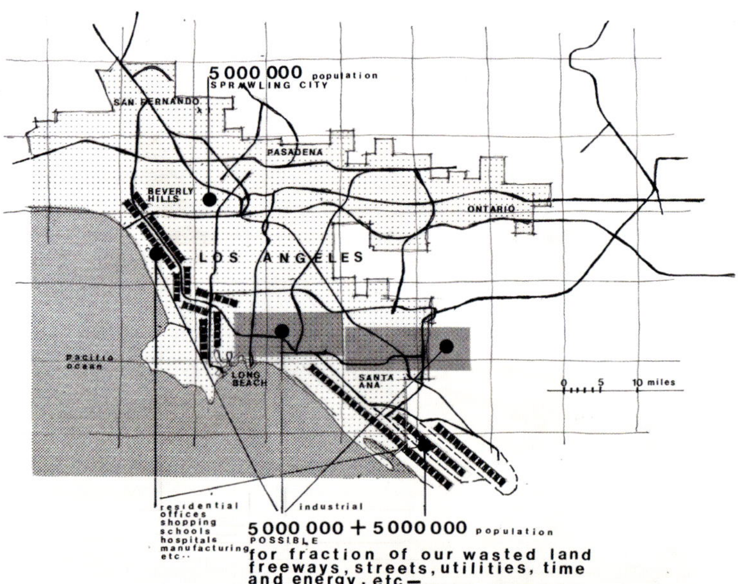

← Georgescu's analysis of sprawl versus density

↑ Map of vertical villages, extending from Brentwood to Laguna Beach

↗ Floor plates cantilevered off of central core via steel cables

↗↗ Tower elevation

→→ Residential interiors with indoor/outdoor rooms

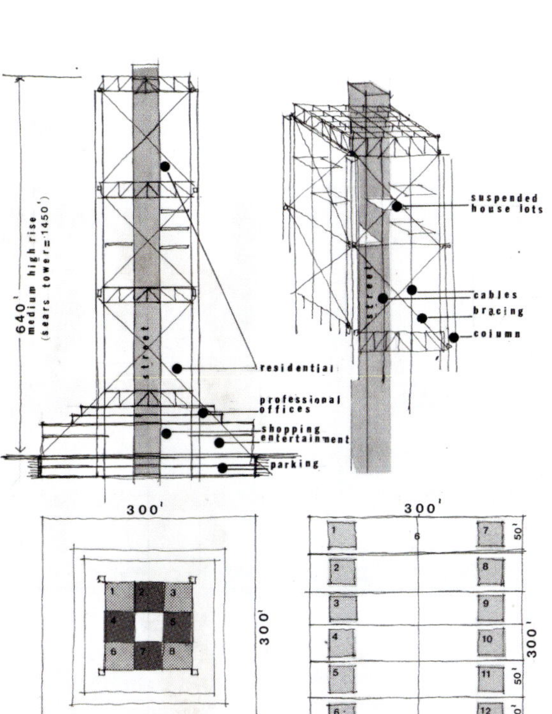
640'
medium high rise
(sears tower=1450')
street
residential
professional
offices
shopping
entertainment
parking
suspended
house lots
cables
bracing
column
300'
300'
300'
300'
150'
150'
50'
50'
30'

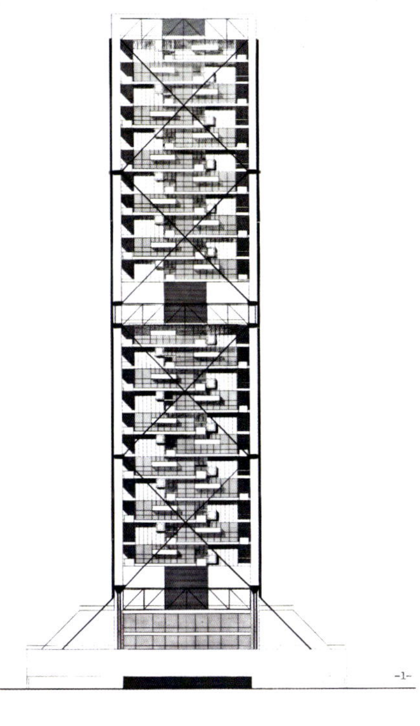

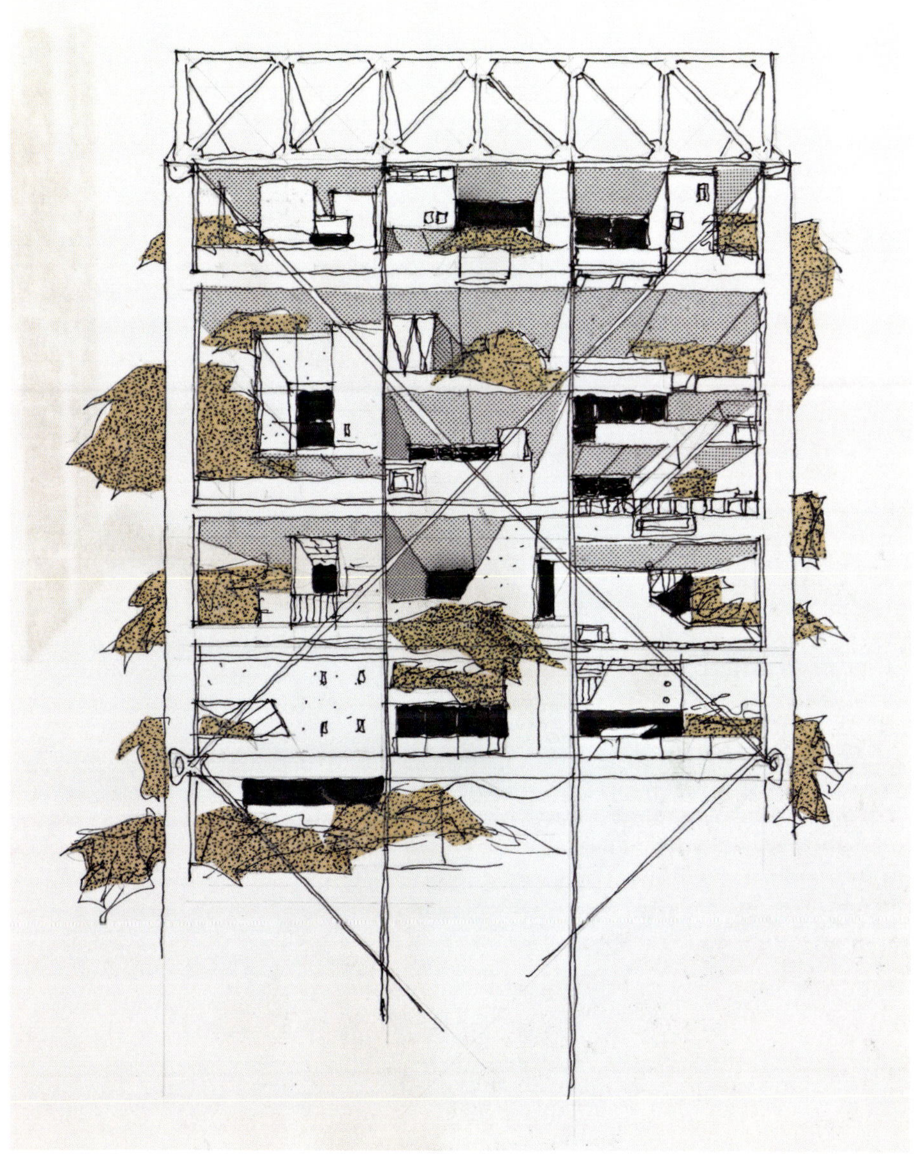

DANIEL, MANN, JOHNSON AND MENDENHALL (DMJM) AND SASAKI WALKER
SUNSET MOUNTAIN

1966

Reminiscent of Machu Picchu, the Spanish Steps, and a 1930s film setting of the City of the Future.

John Pastier

Imagine this scheme being proposed today: a mixed-use development on 2,100 uninhabited acres in the Santa Monica Mountains. That was the dream of the Sunset International Petroleum Corporation. Its $250-million Sunset Mountain would be a commercial and residential center consisting of shops, a school, restaurants, offices, and a hotel, located at the summit of a steep, craggy hillside. Clinging to the slopes were 4,771 terraced housing units, stepping downward as many as 60 stories and radiating from the commercial center in all directions. Accessible via inclined elevator, housing would be focused on neighborhood-like groupings of single-family homes and garden apartments.

When seen from above, the project, with its textured, barrel-like structural accumulations and fan shape, resembled a gigantic mothership about to meet its fleet. Architecture writer John Pastier described it as “reminiscent of Machu Picchu, the Spanish Steps, and a 1930s film setting of the City of the Future.”

In addition to Anthony Lumsden and Cesar Pelli of Daniel, Mann, Johnson and Mendenhall (DMJM), the project’s design team included landscape architect Peter Walker. In his presentation to the Los Angeles City Planning Commission, Walker stressed that the development, located in the hills west of the 405 Freeway, was an alternative to the mountain-leveling schemes so common across the region. Sunset Mountain, he stated, would “blend and contour with the natural topography.” Fifty percent was dedicated to undisturbed open space.

Sunset acquired the 3,500-acre site in 1964 for $14 million. But the project, made possible through changes to the Santa Monica General Plan, quickly drew fierce opposition, including busloads of protesters from the Pacific Palisades Property Owners Association. They loudly complained that the project would create traffic nightmares and eat up city services. They also feared the scheme would be located on “unstable, slide-prone land.” In the end, the protesters triumphed.

→
Mixed-use pinnacle, with 60 stories of terraced residences sloping downward

ROCK OUTCROP
BRUSH
OUTCROP
BRUSH
TREES

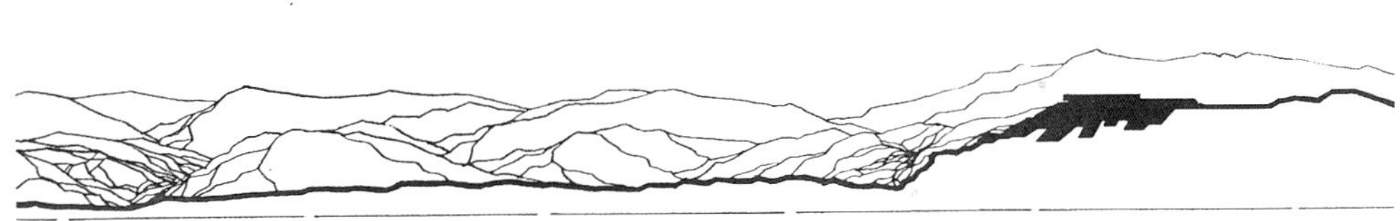

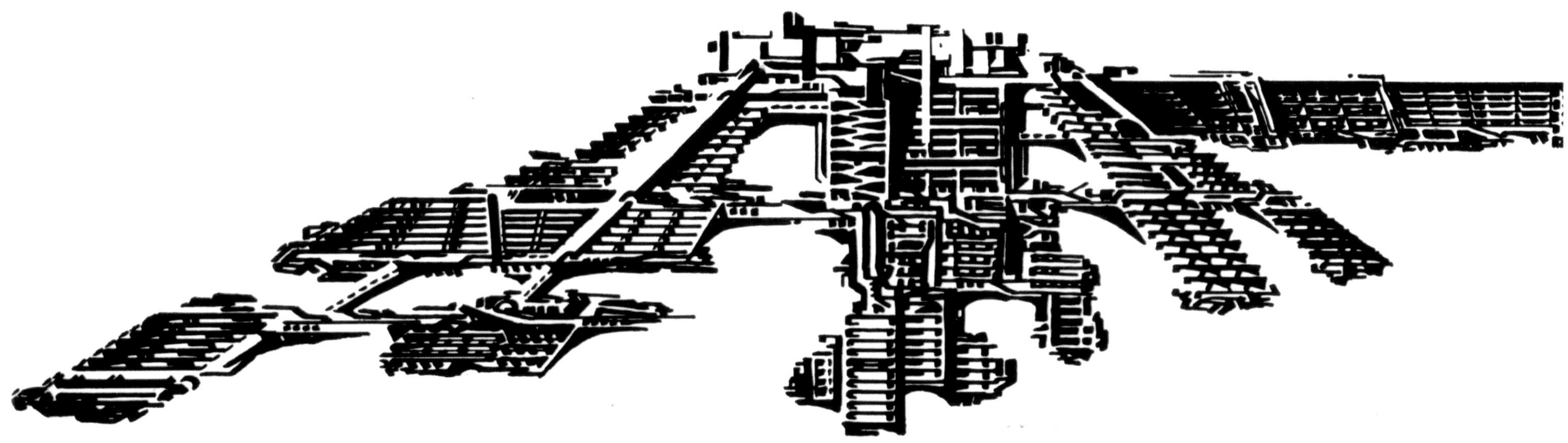

↖
Silhouette of project in Santa Monica Mountains

←
Fingers of development reach downslope.

→
Model resembles extrusion from the earth.

WS

DANIEL, MANN, JOHNSON AND MENDENHALL (DMJM)
PACIFIC OCEAN PARK REDEVELOPMENT

1969

[The hotel] is architecturally defined as a circle maximizing the 360-degree panorama of ocean, beach, mountains and city lights.

Anthony Lumsden

An unlikely developer named John "Jack" Morehart commissioned the most unlikely architectural wonder ever proposed for Santa Monica. Morehart, a savvy real estate speculator and rancher, owned the pier where the fabled but decaying amusement center, Pacific Ocean Park (POP), lay in wooden shambles. Or so he said. The city of Santa Monica had been eyeing Morehart's holding, hoping to fold it into a redevelopment slated for 20 acres in Ocean Park. A self-confessed "operator" who was "not ashamed of making a fast dollar," Morehart had purchased POP for $10 million, and he wasn't about to let the city turn his investment to dust. Boasting that he had something up his sleeve, he told Santa Monica officials in January 1969 that he was going to build a hotel that would be "unique to these United States."

One month later, he held a show-and-tell in the Los Angeles offices of DMJM. He revealed to the Santa Monica Redevelopment Agency the architects' alternative to its original plans for two prosaic 17-story residential buildings. Telling the commissioners that the POP pier would have to be demolished, he unveiled a rendering of a 30-story, 600-room hotel, seeming to float about 300 feet offshore. The round tower, entirely sheathed in glass, looked like a cylinder rising out of the waves, some kind of futuristic stele meant to absorb invisible inscriptions. The interior floors—stacked discs hung off a central core—looked like glass platters, just as transparent as the shell of the building. The whole thing pulsed with vascular energy, and it clearly came from the mind of DMJM's Anthony Lumsden, a master of undulating surfaces and curved-glass enclosures.

Lumsden told the agency that the hotel "is architecturally defined as a circle maximizing the 360-degree panorama of ocean, beach, mountains and city lights." A glass-enclosed bridge with a moving sidewalk would connect the hotel to a beach complex of apartments, shops, theaters, and restaurants.

It was never entirely clear if Morehart intended to move ahead with his plan, though he fought off a series of other projects that would have infringed on his parcel. The Redevelopment Agency had tried to push Morehart's land into the hands of Crescent Bay Properties, which proposed eight apartment buildings, 29 stories each, as well as a string of low-rise structures with 2,000 residential units—a small part of this development to be located on Morehart's parcel. That $60-million project was put in limbo when Morehart negotiated the right to develop as he saw fit.

Yet, two years later, in 1971, Morehart owed $281,000 in back taxes on the POP property, and, in an elaborate swap, the city of Los Angeles acquired the land. The wreckage of the old amusement park was finally carted away in 1975, and the land became an open beach, never to be subject again to development. Lumsden's sci-fi fantasy became just another piece of paper in the large pile that accumulated during a four-year real estate tug-of-war.

→ Drawing of cylindrical tower emerging from ocean by renowned renderer Carlos Diniz

WS

SAM WACHT AND RIBERA AND SUE
SANTA MONICA BAY VILLAGE

1968-73

It seems inappropriate to spend $1.5 million to create nothing but a pile of rock.

Perry Scott

No cluster of unrealized buildings in Los Angeles has ever had the impact of the 30-acre Santa Monica Bay Village development. The idea began on January 10, 1967, when Santa Monica city manager Perry Scott, a bulldog with unchained ambitions, informed the city council of plans to build a small island on top of the breakwater in the bay. For $5.5 million, Scott asserted, a man-made island could become the habitat of posh restaurants and shops. “It seems inappropriate to spend $1.5 million to create nothing but a pile of rock,” Scott said, when for a few million more the city could add a moneymaking attraction. The sausage-shaped, half-mile-long reef would be connected to shore by extending the Santa Monica Pier. (A more far-fetched version, envisioned by Scott’s staff, would cantilever a multi-level structure over the beach.)

Voters rejected a bond issue to fund the proposal, but Scott didn’t surrender. In late 1971, he was back with an even bolder concoction: a 30-acre island, a floating village 30 years ahead of Dubai, with five “quality” restaurants, a 60,000-square-foot convention center, theaters, a sports pavilion, a shopping mall, a network of pedestrian and bicycle pathways, a boating dock, and a heliport.

Most of the island would be covered by a lagoon, complete with a waterfall and its own jetty. Unbelievably, there would be underground parking for 5,000 cars. Entry to the island would be free.

The audacious plan—troubling in its own right to a nascent environmental movement—called for the demolition of the Santa Monica Pier. Opposition quickly coalesced around two groups: those who wanted to save the pier and those who didn’t want the waters of the bay turned into a contrived destination. Better to leave nature as it is, they argued.

The council, nevertheless, voted in 1972 to raze the pier and build the island. But city leaders had underestimated their opponents—and the tenor of the times. Californians would create the Coastal Commission that year, a bad harbinger for the island. Soon Robert Redford, whose hideaway in *The Sting* had been the carousel on the pier, arrived to defend the wooden planks and ramshackle arcades. The pier was beloved, and the proposed island sparked a civic uprising. In April 1973, incensed voters tossed out of office the three city council members who’d voted to replace the pier with the offshore resort. A new council majority promptly rescinded the island, and later that year, Santa Monica residents voted to permanently preserve the landmark pier while requiring voter approval for all future major projects along the waterfront.

The island plan had given birth to modern Santa Monica, committed to city planning scaled to public input and, above all, environmental consciousness. As for City Manager Scott, he was told his $40,000-a-year contract would not be renewed, a victim of his own stubborn mettle.

→ Model with hotel, convention center, sports complex, theater, lagoon, and causeway

MP

LA

LOS ANGELES CITY PLANNING DEPARTMENT, CALVIN HAMILTON
CONCEPT LOS ANGELES

1970

Created more than 40 years ago, L.A.'s long-range civic plan—known as Concept Los Angeles—continues to captivate urban thinkers despite its inability to move forward.

Conceived by Calvin Hamilton, the energetic and long-standing director of the City Planning Department, the scheme intended, among other things, to counter the forces of unchecked growth. It focused on the development of 48 "high intensity activity" centers zoned for housing, retail, business, government, and entertainment. These dense hubs would be connected via a comprehensive rapid transit and automobile roadway system, while low-density neighborhoods would be left as-is, preserving the city's sacrosanct single-family model.

The plan to organize the increasingly polycentric city stands as one of the first official acknowledgments that downtown would not remain the geographic or spiritual heart of Los Angeles. There were already too many other centers for that.

Activity within each designated hub would be focused on a core that contained rapid transit, high-rise office structures, department stores, hotels, apartment buildings, and theaters. Adhering to his strategy of "three-dimensional" design, Hamilton predicted: "Automobiles and delivery trucks will, for the most part, be restricted to the ground level. Interconnected pathways for pedestrian circulation will be provided at the second floor and higher levels. This nearly complete separation of vehicles, transit and pedestrians will enhance the convenience, safety and pleasantness of the core."

Each center would contain local concentrations, called nodes, with less intensely developed commercial, residential, and institutional blocks. Nodes would be connected via "secondary transit systems" like people movers and monorails. Along the periphery were more sparsely populated sections, called satellites and suburbs, connected via regional transit and, increasingly, the automobile.

In addition to promoting mass transit as a method of tying centers together, the concept called for an increase in "open spaces of various sizes," ranging from small public and private parks and plazas in centers to a network of trails and corridor parks.

Although the idea was incorporated into the city's 1974 general plan, neither officials, developers, nor the public got on board. Political pressure and economic downturns were the last nails in the coffin. The city continued along its path of untamed growth, and Concept Los Angeles was never realized.

→
Sketch of various nodes scattered around the city

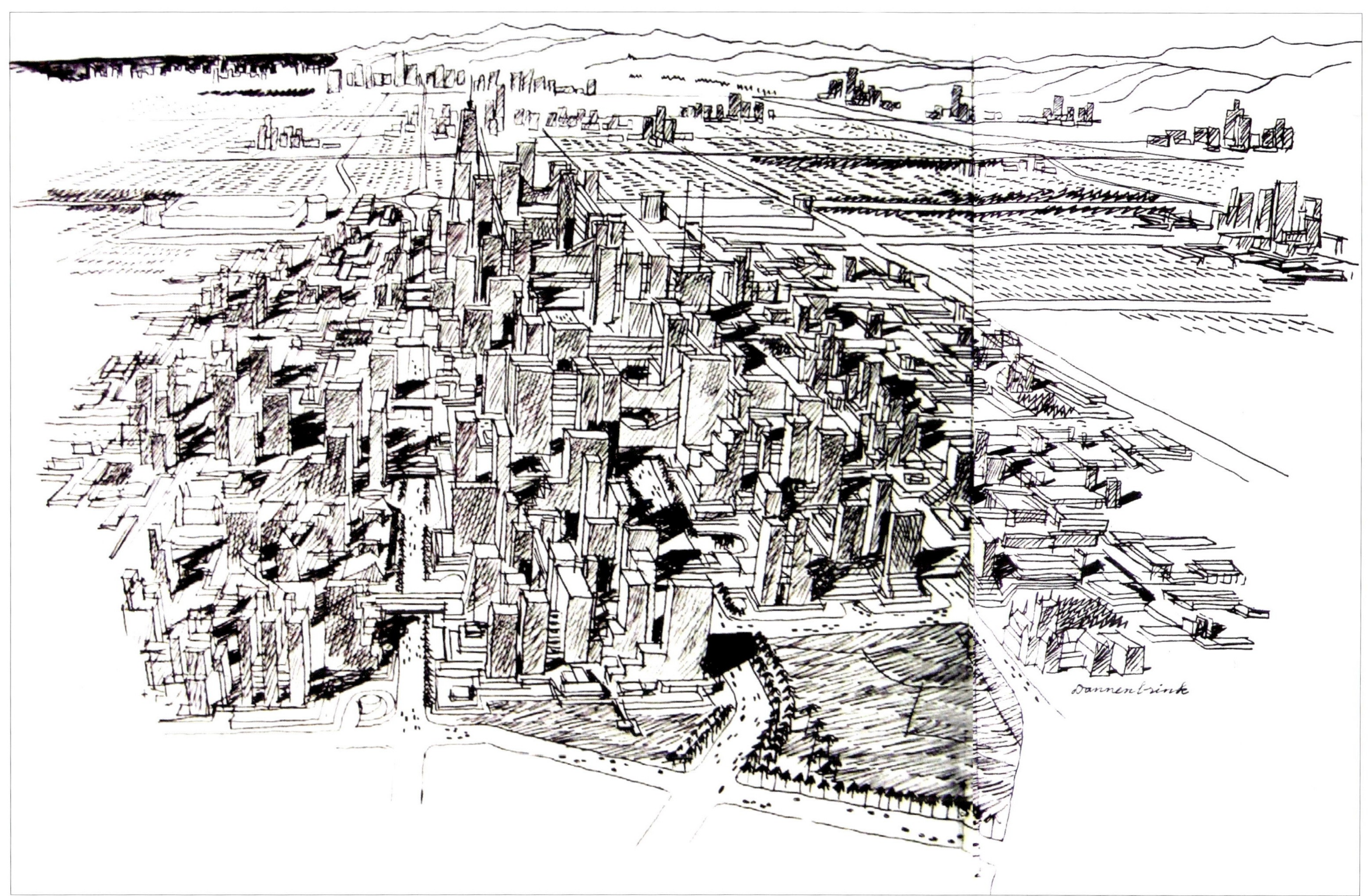
Dannenbrink

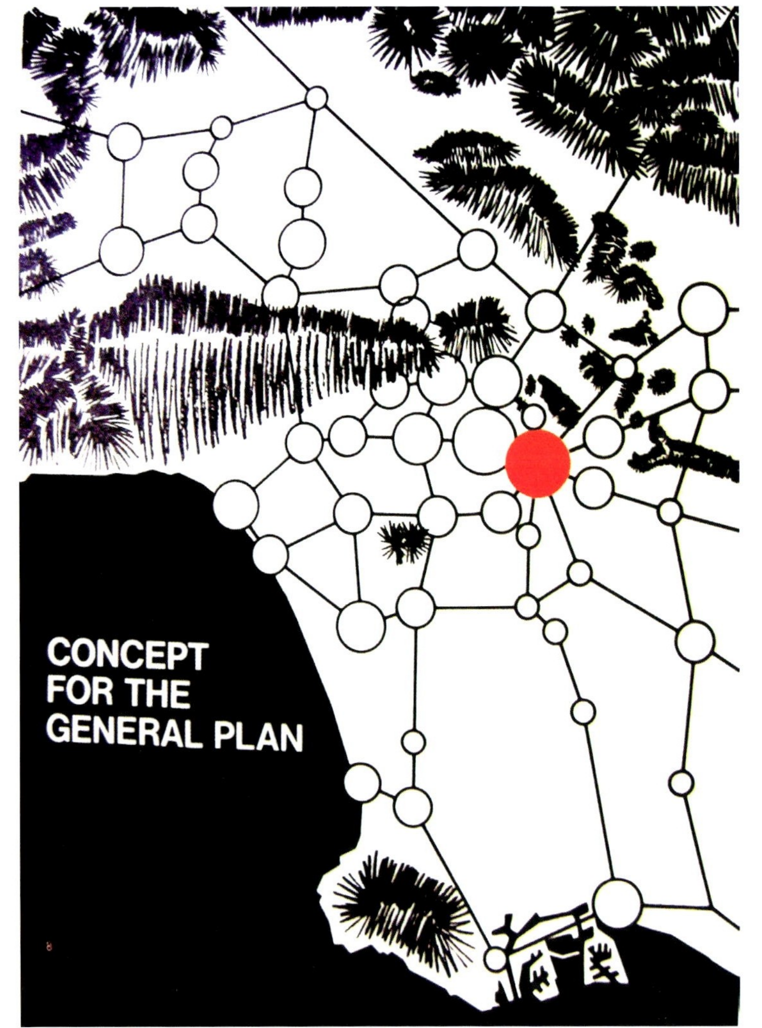
CONCEPT
FOR THE
GENERAL PLAN

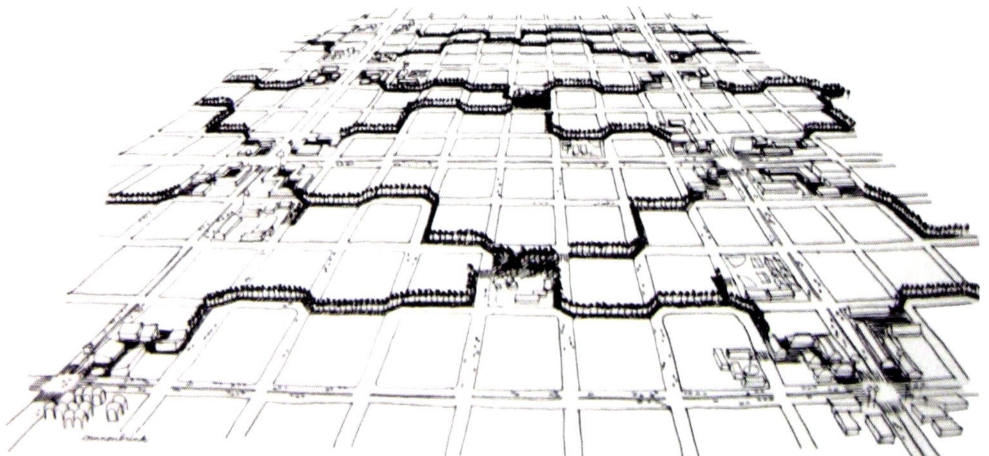

Cinema

←←
Concept Los Angeles booklet illustration showing connected nodes of development

↖
Sketch of transit connections

←
"High-intensity activity" center

↗
Rapid-transit station

→
Dense housing clusters

→→
Automobile-oriented commercial facility

DT

WALLACE, MCHARG, ROBERTS AND TODD
SILVER BOOK

1972

Downtown 1990 is a diversified urban center which has fully accepted its role as the region's most important focus.

Wallace, McHarg, Roberts and Todd

Aptly nicknamed for the reflective cover of this project's 113-page report, the Central City Los Angeles 1972/1990 Silver Book plan envisioned downtown through the lens of 1990. The study, which took 18 months to complete, was funded by the Committee for Central City Planning, the precursor to today's Central City Association. The city's heaviest hitters chipped in, including Times Mirror, Prudential Insurance, Bank of America, Union Bank, Title Insurance and Trust, and the Southern California Gas Company. The book, the size of an LP-record album, delivered a powerful graphic and intellectual wallop. It tackled the entire problem of downtown, from employment to traffic to the arrangement of physical space.

Consulting planners Wallace, McHarg, Roberts and Todd offered this view from their time machine: "Downtown 1990 is a diversified urban center which has fully accepted its role as the region's most important focus. Office and commercial space and employees have nearly doubled since 1972, and there are six times the number of high-rise residential units. Projects underway in 1972 are now complete; Bunker Hill is a mature, commercial/residential center and Little Tokyo is a rich, Japanese/American trade, cultural, and residential community." Mass transit, they predicted, had relieved traffic congestion. Skid Row's downtrodden residents were uplifted through detoxification and rehabilitation. A people mover provided round-trip jaunts from Olvera Street on downtown's northern edge, to the Convention Center, on its southern. A subway hurried riders about 10 miles from Bunker Hill to Beverly Hills for lunch and back in time for their predinner siestas.

The focus of downtown construction in 1990, their crystal ball told them, would be an area they named "South Park Urban Village." Bounded by Eighth Street, Pico Boulevard, the Harbor Freeway, and Broadway, the new residential village would be built around a lake and a park, a setting the planners compared to Copenhagen's Tivoli Gardens. In the shadow of the office towers and hotels that rimmed the park, families would play, grandparents would snooze on park benches, and couples would embrace. A museum and art gallery, a school, restaurants, tennis courts, a bicycle path, and peaceful, shaded dells would make the neighborhood a pedestrian enclave. Residents would "WALK to work, only a few blocks away. Along the Lake, you stop for breakfast and to read the paper at a small outdoor restaurant in the Park. Three times a week, you get up a half-hour early and jog the mile-long bicycle path around the Lake."

In all, 7,000 dwellings would be constructed, along with 7.3 million square feet of office space, 3 million square feet of retail, and hotels with a total of 4,100 rooms. A combination of low- and high-rise buildings would emerge, and a whole new district would burgeon. The Silver Book was submitted as a preliminary general-development plan, but the city never officially adopted it. The park, its lake plied by a regatta of toy boats, never materialized, yet the name stuck, perhaps the only legacy of the last truly complete plan for downtown.

→
Downtown Los Angeles, circa 1990, with lake in southern half

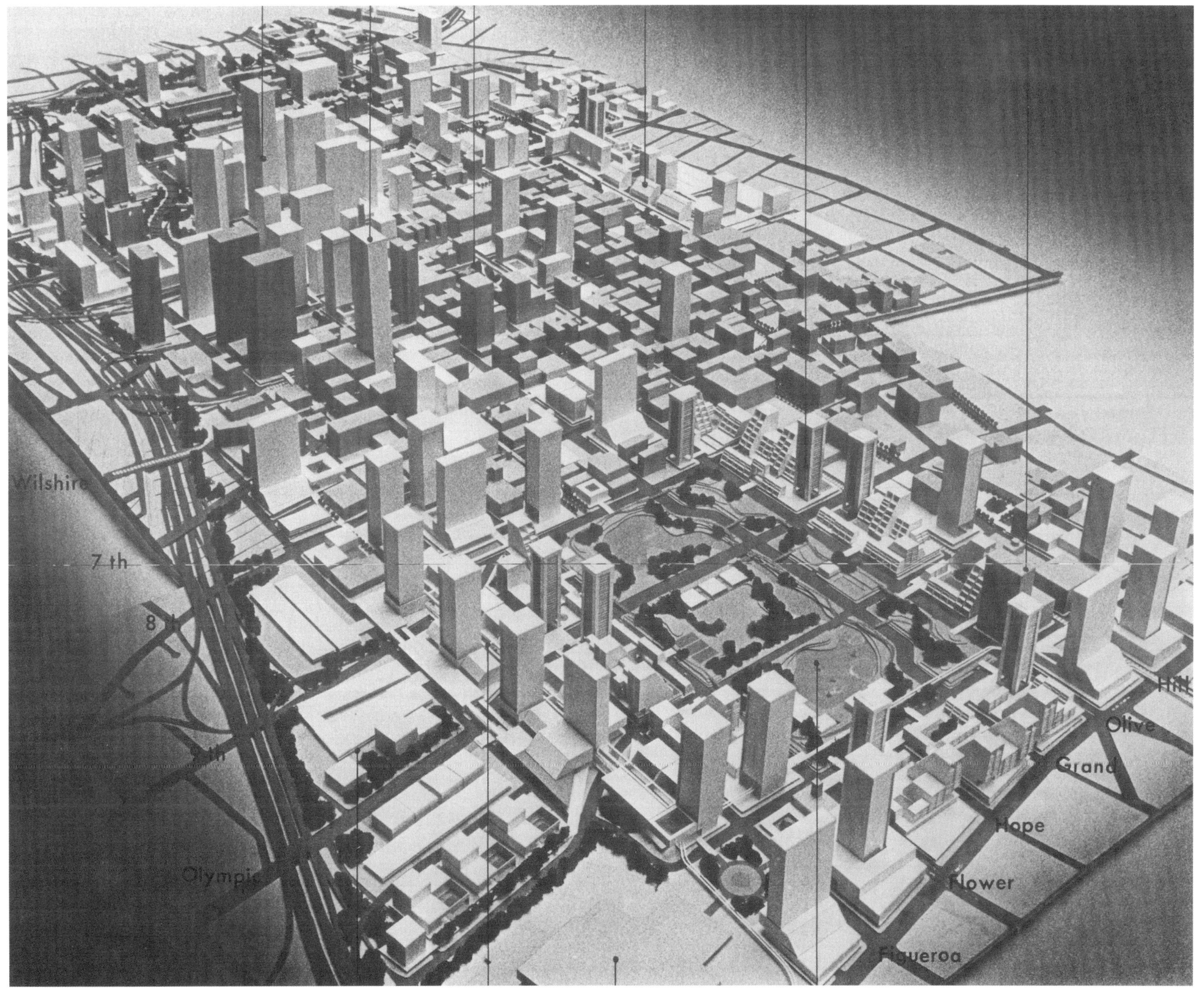
Wilshire
7 th
8 th
9 th
Olympic
Hill
Olive
Grand
Hope
Flower
Figueroa

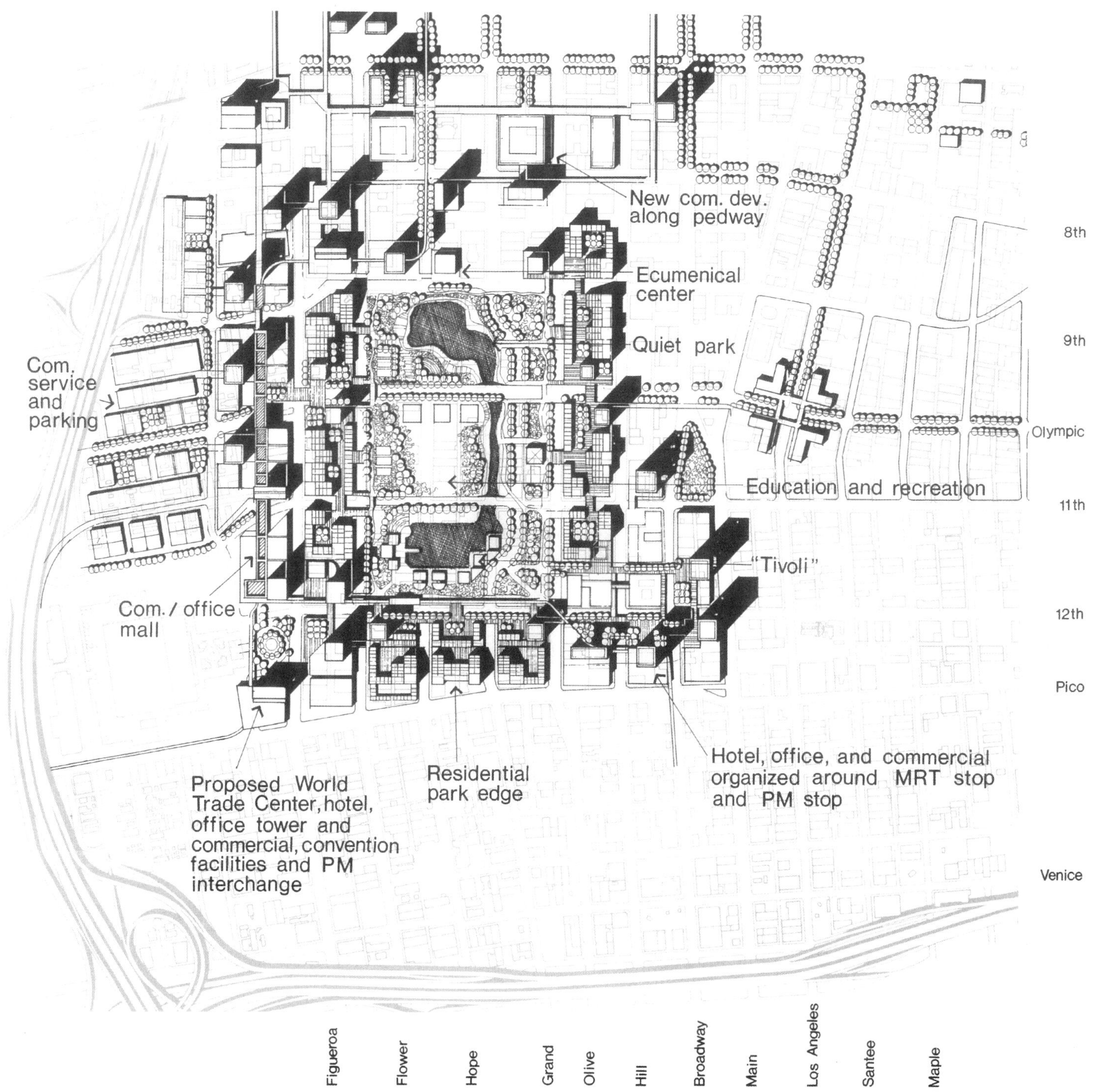

← South Park becomes a self-contained neighborhood of residential, commercial, and entertainment buildings around a central green space.

→ Landscaped promenade

→→ Along the water's edge

THOMAS A. TODD
1972

MP

DT

BARTON MYERS, CESAR PELLI, FRANK GEHRY, AND OTHERS
A GRAND AVENUE

1979–80

What we've got here are some unified towers, a somewhat unified base and pockets of madness.

Hugh Hardy

The Maguire Partners' storied effort to reinterpret Grand Avenue—today a forbidding fortress of concrete, granite, and glass—as an animated pedestrian-and-cultural precinct in the heart of downtown lost in competition to a team led by Canadian architect Arthur Erickson. The losing lineup consisted of Edgardo Contini, Frank Gehry, Lawrence Halprin, Hardy Holzman Pfeiffer, Robert Kennard, Ricardo Legorreta, Charles Moore, Barton Myers, Cesar Pelli, Harry Perloff, and Sussman Prejza. As Robert Maguire said, you can't "build a city with just one architect."

Answering the Community Redevelopment Agency's call to rebuild the 11-acre site on the east side of Grand Avenue from Fourth to Second streets, Maguire's architects carved a mix of high- and low-rise towers; a museum of modern art; and office, residential, and entertainment spaces. Instead of a unified master plan, the "All Stars," as the group became known, presented a $700-million architectural exquisite corpse—nine projects connected along a linear plaza modeled by Moore and Halprin after the Piazza Navona in Rome. Titled "A Grand Avenue," the plan would have connected upper Grand Avenue to the city's historic core through a series of intersecting parks, plazas, fountains, and promenades, an outdoor theater, and a variety of pavilions for restaurants and cafes.

Scaled from the sidewalk up, A Grand Avenue was meant to be dotted with spaces where people could meet face-to-face, wandering, lingering, chatting, or lounging, without the large office towers overwhelming them. The notion was to reimpose the tightly spaced nineteenth-century street grid of Bunker Hill. On the Olive Street side, the mothballed funicular Angel's Flight, re-envisioned by Gehry, would have been restored and smaller apartment buildings and artists' studios built along a meandering promenade filled with colorful, jumbled architectural pieces.

The apex of the skyline, meanwhile, was the North Office Tower. Pelli's granite-and-glass building would soar 62 stories, making it the tallest structure on Grand Avenue. A tower within a tower, the skyscraper looked etched by acid, exposing a slender building within the arms of a larger one. The pinkish-brown granite and bronzed-glass building had an evolutionary quality, as if a 1930s stepped skyscraper had eroded to reveal a 1980s modernist shaft.

The other visual focus of the avenue was Hugh Hardy's museum of modern art. Described by the architect as a "crystal cube," it seemed to defy gravity as it jutted out over Grand Avenue. Formed like upturned plates of glass, the building was set 45 degrees akimbo to the street, adding to its troubling, vertiginous quality.

In the end, the genius of the proposition was not its architecture but its infusion of life into a topography suspended in the doldrums. Maguire invested $400,000 in the proposal, which some attacked as architectural anarchy. Hardy perhaps summed it up best: "What we've got here are some unified towers, a somewhat unified base and pockets of madness."

→ Architectural icons march down Grand Avenue.

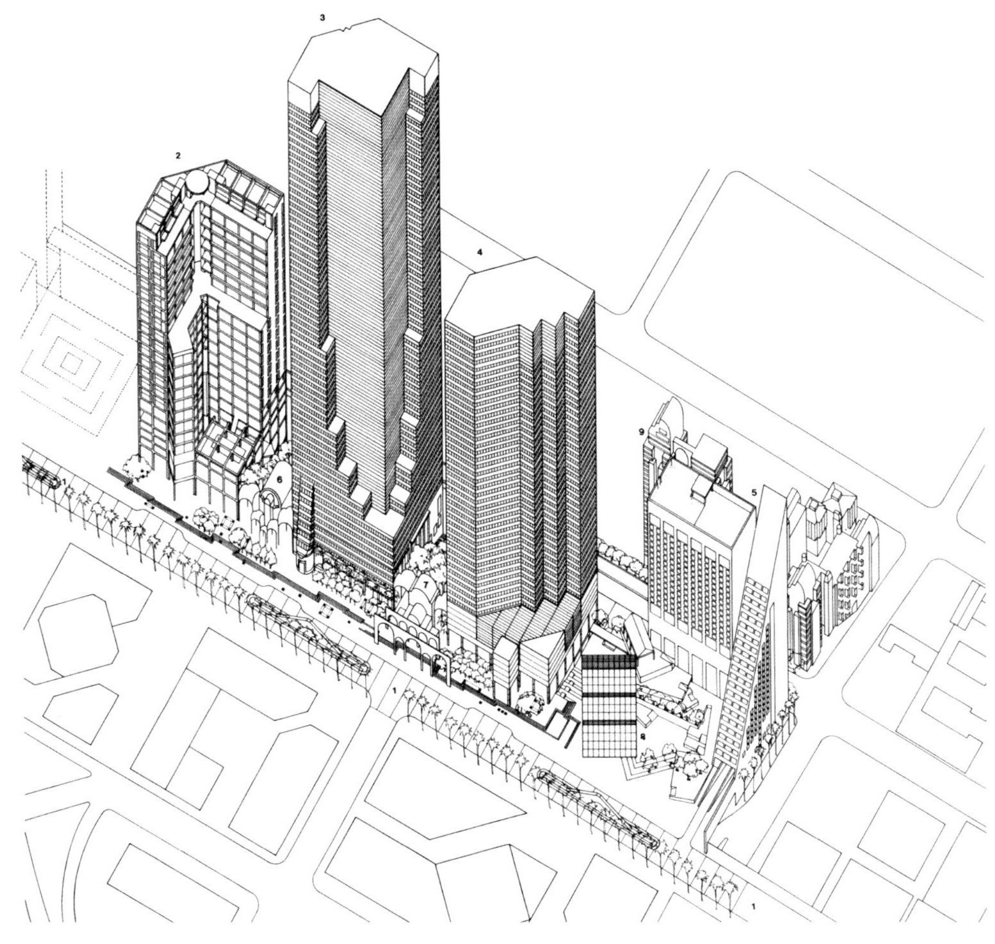

The playfulness of the design, wrote the critic John Pastier, "was a mighty affront to the sensibilities of the bureaucrats, citizen commissioners, and unevolved modernists. The intimacy and intricacy of those elements seemed inappropriate to an audience that expected, and indeed demanded, monumentality and polite blandness." Ultimately, the naysayers got what they wanted: a dull boulevard haunted by the legend of A Grand Avenue.

←←
Aerial view of boulevard

←
Cesar Pelli's cutaway tower

→
A row of buildings by star architects

→→
Residences stepped down to street level.

↘
Bunker Hill with new buildings superimposed

← Interior alleys connect Bunker Hill to historic district

→ Hugh Hardy's geometric modern-art museum

↘ Frank Gehry's version of Angel's Flight funicular railroad

SKIDMORE, OWINGS & MERRILL (SOM) AND OLYMPIA & YORK/TRIZEC
GRAND PARK/BUNKER HILL

1979

One of Robert Maguire's formidable opponents as part of the Community Redevelopment Agency's competition for the dense, mixed-use portion of upper Grand Avenue was Olympia & York/Trizec with SOM. Their Grand Park development was not only intended as a major destination, but also zeroed in on one of downtown's biggest flaws: its emptiness on evenings and weekends, a conundrum that still plagues Bunker Hill.

A grassy park was to be surrounded by shops, restaurants, cafes, an art museum, apartments, offices, and an entertainment complex. Its "front door" was to be a large archway on Grand Avenue leading visitors to an indoor display area via a glazed canopy. Angel's Flight, the historic funicular, was to be rerouted to run diagonally from Fourth and Hill to an upper station and a complex containing cinemas, restaurants, a theater, and other attractions. Grand Avenue itself was to be lined with shops and cafes, complemented by a covered arcade. The Grand Avenue Plaza, flanked by two office towers, was to become the entryway to the project's commercial areas.

DT

BARTON MYERS, HANS HOLLEIN, GOTTFRIED BÖHM, AND JAMES STIRLING
MUSIC CENTER EXPANSION/WALT DISNEY CONCERT HALL

1982–87

A lush garden oasis nestled among towers.

Frank Gehry

Long before Frank Gehry's consultants began polishing titanium for the Walt Disney Concert Hall, another plan took shape just down the street, when Los Angeles County hired Barton Myers Associates to prepare a master plan for three city blocks near the Music Center. The design laid out 9.3 acres of office space, hotels, and retail. But most important, it contemplated expanding the Music Center east, not to the south across First Street, where Disney Hall now stands. Myers and several officials insisted that bridging Grand Avenue would be the best link to the existing Music Center theaters.

Myers's 2,700-seat concert hall would directly face the Music Center's raised plaza, spanning the wide avenue with two flanking pedestrian bridges. On its backside, thanks to a large glass curtain wall, the building would gaze on City Hall, made visible, and accessible by foot, through the reconfiguration of the mall. The principal shoebox theater would be circled by lobbies and have glass stair towers at its corners. A smaller theater would slip underneath.

Myers strongly opposed building the hall on "Lot K," the county-owned land where Disney eventually rose, claiming, correctly, that the site would be cut off from the Music Center. But the Music Center's leadership, headed by its chairman, F. Daniel Frost, endorsed Lot K. Frost argued that the parking lot would be cheaper to build on. Many in the county, including chief administrative officer James C. Hankla, opposed Lot K, but they were checkmated once Frost secured a major donation from Roy and Edna Disney, earmarked for his preferred site.

Once Lot K won, the next step was picking an architect, a task headed by Richard Koshalek, then director of the Museum of Contemporary Art (MOCA) and chairman of the new hall's building subcommittee. The finalists for what was billed as a 2,500-seat, $50-million chamber were Gehry, German architect Gottfried Böhm, Austrian Hans Hollein, and Englishman James Stirling.

Differing wildly from his final wavy-steel masterpiece, Gehry's original proposal revealed his fascination with postmodernism. It was an angular, stacked, and glazed white "conservatory," surrounded by the architect's trademark steel screens, several small pavilions, and thick groupings of trees and landscaping. Gehry described it as "a lush garden oasis nestled among towers." Böhm sketched a glazed sphere reminiscent of a birdcage, which the *Los Angeles Times* described as both "a vast, open-web cupola of concrete ribs and tinted glass" and "a huge Brünnhilde bra cup in an Olympian-scale performance of the Twilight of the Gods." Hollein's scheme, vaguely reminiscent of a 1980s office

→
View of Myers's new concert hall from Music Center plaza

Andre Previn
Civic Light Opera
Joffrey Ballet

←
Myers's building reaches across Grand Avenue to Music Center via pedestrian bridges.

↗
Hollein's postmodern smorgasbord

→
Böhm's birdcage

↘
Stirling's turntable

park, was a postmodern mash-up of upthrusting green glass shafts, metallic cylinders, and red sandstone. Finally, the legendary Stirling seemed to be slightly out of his element in the searing sunshine: His plan called for a circular theater fronted by a large, square box office topped with a rotating electronic billboard. Gehry won, but his plan changed radically in the painful—and exorbitantly expensive—decade and a half it took to get his building done.

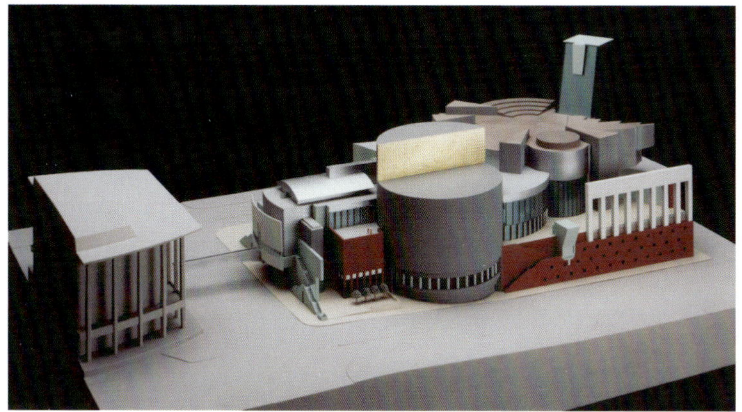

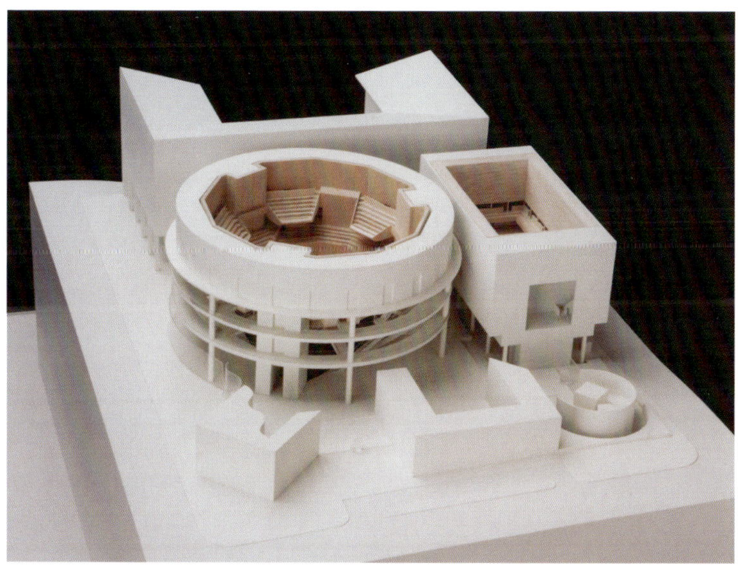

MUSIC CENTER, SIXTH AND HOOVER STREETS

1945

The push to create a new music facility dates to the late 1930s, when plans were drawn up for a complex containing both a music auditorium and a trade and exhibition hall. Proponents believed that the best approach was to marry culture to money. Seven firms each pledged $50,000 toward the exhibition hall/music center, but World War II intervened. Efforts were revived in 1945 with the formation of the group Greater Los Angeles Plans. The following year, it acquired two pieces of property for the proposed building: one a 26-acre parcel between Third, Fifth, Figueroa, and Fremont streets, and the other on Sixth Street opposite Lafayette Park. Voters rejected the bond issue for the two projects. The Lafayette Park property was sold and attention was focused on the downtown site.

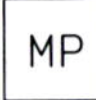

DT

BARTON MYERS
STATE MALL, EXPOSITION PARK

1984

Since 1914, Exposition Park has been one of L.A.'s cultural centers, home to its Natural History Museum, Science Center, the Beaux-Arts Rose Garden and, of course, the Memorial Coliseum. But if you ask most tourists, and plenty of residents, they don't know what or where Exposition Park is. The park is a set of detached, disorienting parking lots and through streets, and buildings that seem to have nothing to do with one another.

In the buildup to the 1984 Olympics, local and state officials hired Barton Myers Associates as part of their effort to correct the mess and breathe life into the park. The resulting plan was a cluster of new cultural facilities organized around an $11-million promenade known as State Mall.

The scheme would replace a small and mostly irrelevant street in the middle of the complex, State Drive, with a 2,000-foot-long boardwalk, defined by a series of large steel-framed archways connected by overhead cables, lights, and banners. Myers called them “wickets.” A bulky tower, evocative of the Coliseum's classically inspired front portal, would mark the entrance.

Officials planned a number of new buildings along the mall's length, interspersed with a series of outdoor courtyards known as “rooms.” Among these, Frank Gehry's Aerospace Museum and Jack Haywood and Vincent Proby's Museum of Afro-American History and Culture went forward. But Myers's Multicultural Center—a series of seven geometric steel pavilions and an outdoor theater united by a 70-foot-tall triangular entrance marquee and viewing pavilion—never materialized. Nor did the State Mall itself. The “self-financing” Olympic Games didn't have the budget. “Call it part of the Ueberroth dividend,” joked John Wyka, a former associate at Myers's office, referring to Peter Ueberroth, the games' tightfisted director.

→ Boardwalk connects Exposition Park's scattered museums.

LOS ANGELES
USA
TACO

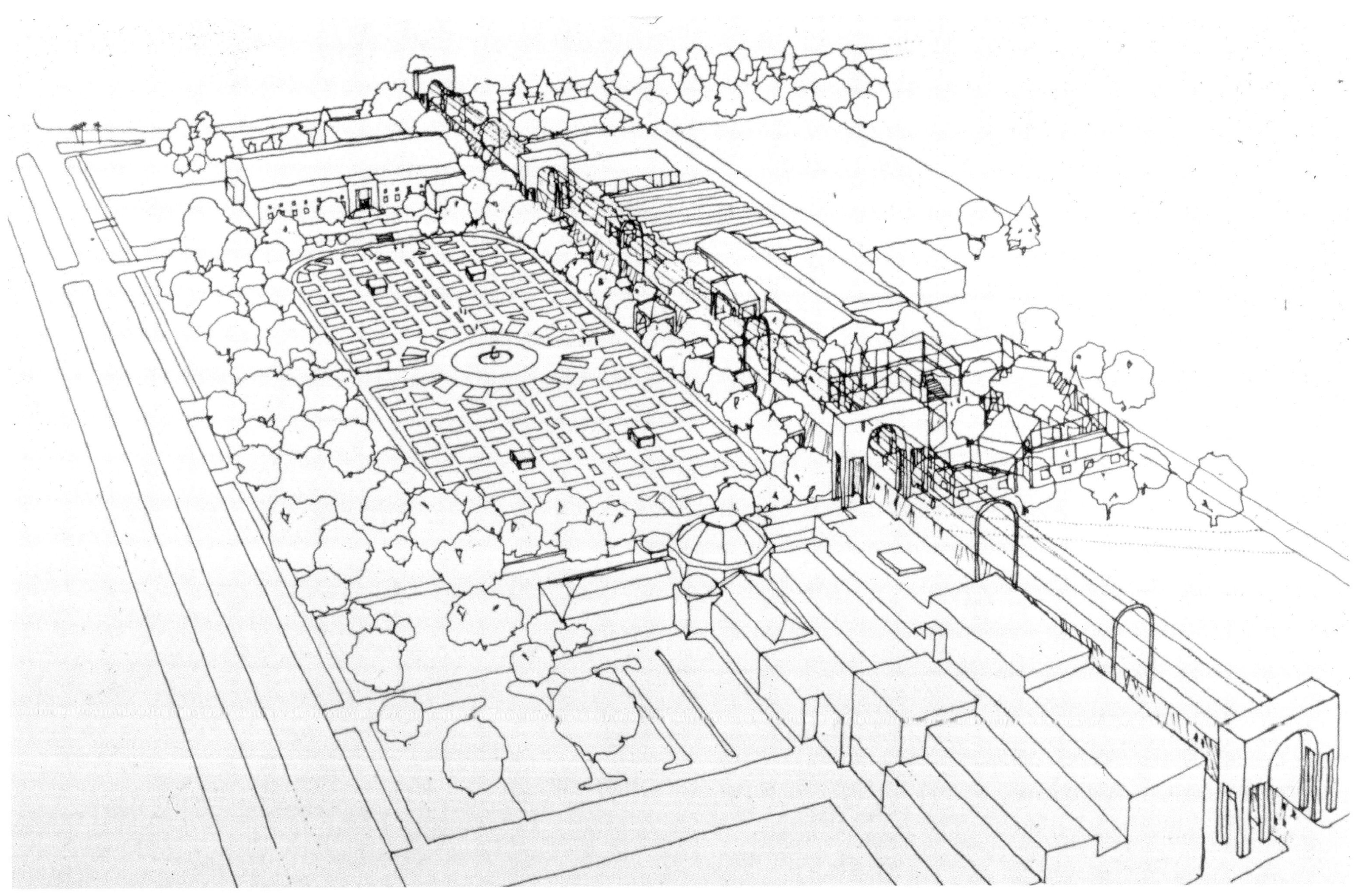

←
Arches define pathway next to historic rose garden.

→
Multicultural Center

MP

DT

DOUGLAS SUISMAN
TEN MINUTE DIAMOND PLAN

1997

Using the rotunda of City Hall as the locus of civic activity, Douglas Suisman, one of the city's most influential planners, drew a boundary line 10 minutes' walking distance, or a half-mile, in every direction. Within this "diamond" would be a pedestrian-oriented district, made friendly by the introduction of a network of what Suisman called *paseos* heading east to the Geffen Contemporary and Little Tokyo, and a retail arcade running north to Olvera Street and the plaza—the main square of the Spanish Colonial pueblo where the city's first families settled, in 1781. The plan called for a pedestrian bridge along Main Street to span the fissure created by the 101 Freeway. Suisman wanted to levitate the Los Angeles Mall, a subterranean hole on Main Street, to sidewalk level. He also proposed tearing open the sides of the third-floor "pedway" connecting City Hall to the City Hall East tower, while adding exterior staircases to put a bit of life back in the street.

The most important intervention, however, was to be a Civic Plaza covering the entire block due south of City Hall. This was not intended as another tree-filled park but as a genuine arena of civic affairs, an open space dedicated to citizen action—from political rallies to New Year's Eve celebrations. As such, the plaza would serve as the symbolic heart of Los Angeles. Like Hyde Park Corner or Union Square, it would have been the one spot, situated at the very hub of a gilded government ghetto, where spontaneous public encounters might occur. It would have been the most democratic institution in the city—Zuccotti Park under public ownership.

The $13.5-million proposal, which fell under city, county, state, and federal authority, became the last official master plan adopted by the Los Angeles City Council, with the Civic Plaza inked in a city ordinance. Then, this core idea for the civic core was betrayed. An expedient land grab, engineered by Ron Deaton, the city's chief bureaucrat, and Jan Perry, a key city councilwoman, slipped police headquarters onto the parcel set aside for the plaza.

On October 25, 2009, the land bounded by First, Second, Spring, and Main streets emerged, in the words of urban critic Sam Hall Kaplan, as "the site of a security encrusted fortress."

→ All roads lead to City Hall rotunda.

→→ Civic center is an easy walk from all directions.

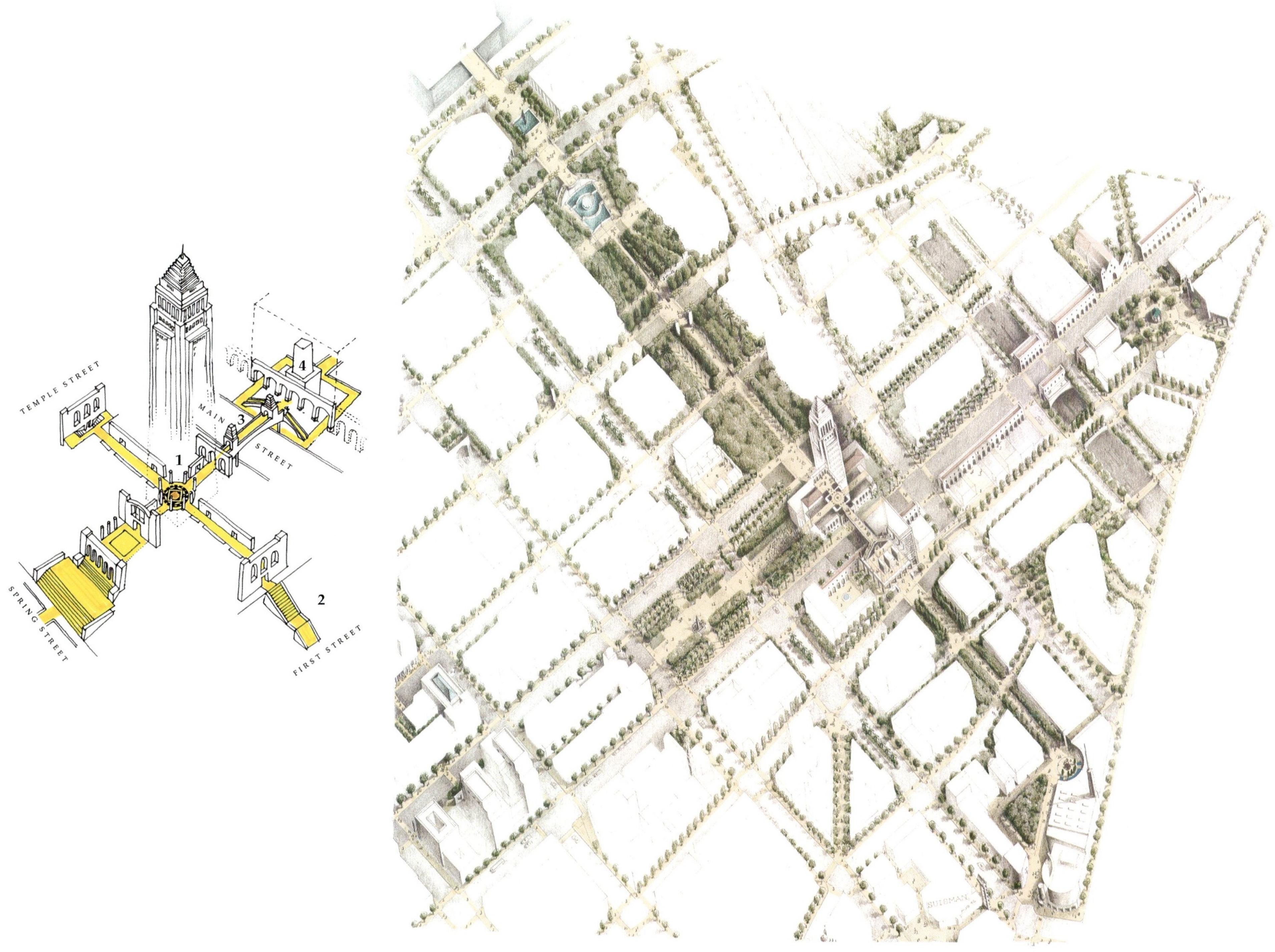

TEMPLE STREET
MAIN STREET
SPRING STREET
FIRST STREET
1
2
3
4

DUANY/PLATER-ZYBERK, HANNA/OLIN, LEGORRETA ARQUITECTOS, MOORE RUBLE YUDELL, AND MOULE AND POLIZOIDES PLAYA VISTA

1993-2001

It is the biggest business win that any city has ever had....Our economy is vibrant, our future is great.

Richard J. Riordan

Confronted with an environmentally sensitive site, which was also the last remaining open space on the city's Westside, architect Buzz Yudell asked rhetorically, "How do you create a sense of community in this complex context?" The answer was Playa Vista, a "city within a city," a Los Angeles version of Seaside, Florida, built on the wetlands south of Marina del Rey. Robert Maguire, the powerhouse who a decade earlier launched the ill-fated plan for A Grand Avenue, had acquired development rights to the 1,087-acre plot and once again assembled a "dream team." This time it was Duany/Plater-Zyberk, Ricardo Legorreta, Moore Ruble Yudell, Moule and Polizoides, and landscape designers Hanna/Olin.

They composed a settlement with 13,000 townhouses and courtyard homes clustered around hotels, restaurants, shops, and a marina, with 5 million square feet of office space, freeing nearly 500 acres of wetlands and parks. The idea was to create mixed-use zones subdivided into six neighborhoods and three districts: the marina, the office campus, and the town center. They proposed a system of blocks and streets, dotted with open spaces, greenbelts, and pedestrian walkways, woven into a medium-density city of corner retail and office complexes. Every home would be within walking distance of transportation, stores, schools, parks, and workplaces. There would be a riparian corridor to recycle gray water, and magnetic cables buried in the streets would power electric transit. Here was the New Urbanists' answer to the Los Angeles that, they said, was "chaos by design."

The renderings show a bucolic landscape ordered in Renaissance fashion. Red-tiled roofs capped buildings of smoothly troweled white-plaster stucco. Towers, archways, and deep-set windows nodded to 1920s Spanish Colonial Revival, but instead of being laid out along a grid of streets, the homes and shops faced lush expanses of lawns shaded by pepper and palm trees. This was suburbia with an urban zest.

To make all this happen, Maguire inked a deal with DreamWorks, the film company controlled by billionaires David Geffen, Jeffrey Katzenberg, and Steven Spielberg. The Hollywood magnates, promising to spend upward of $250 million, turned to Johnson Fain to design a production lot, which would have been the first major studio to open in the city since Warner Bros. opened in Burbank in 1937. Within a walled compound, two- to four-story buildings were to be clustered around an eight-acre lake, just the sort of fantasy a movie director would conjure. IBM and Silicon Graphics were to move in. Mayor Richard J. Riordan gushed, "It is the biggest business win that any city has ever had...Our economy is vibrant, our future is great."

↗ Map of development and restored wetlands

→ Views of Dreamworks studio surrounding man-made lake

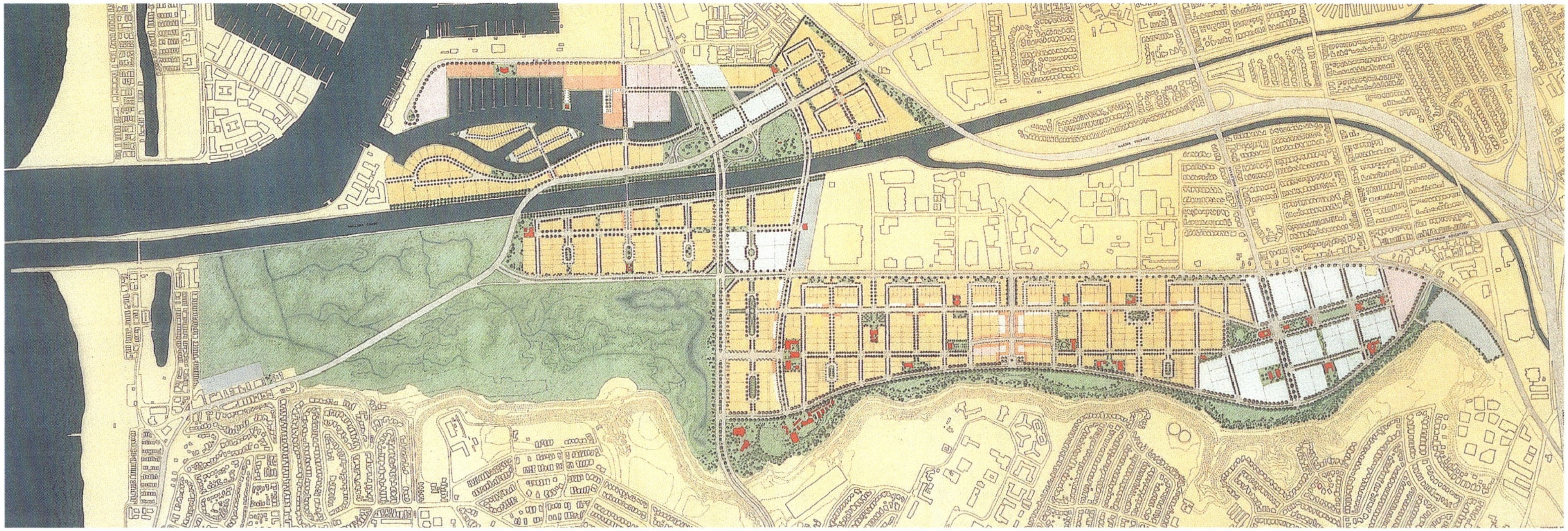

But court battles with environmentalists, and a bitter feud between Maguire and DreamWorks, cost the project time and money. The economy tanked in the early '90s, and Maguire, unable to pay his backers, lost control of all but a small stake. DreamWorks never did ante up, erasing the lake and the New Urbanists' town from the blueprints. The site was eventually developed, not as a well-tuned urban village but as a stucco cavalcade of generic homes crammed shoulder to shoulder in a placeless place.

↖
Busy commercial corner disguises urban setting within.

↑
New Urbanist interior courtyard

cc Los Angeles Times

Gehry's Putting Stamp on Playa Vista

Real estate: The famed architect is hired to help plan and design key elements of the massive coastal development.

By MORRIS NEWMAN
SPECIAL TO THE TIMES

FRANK GEHRY
PLAYA VISTA

2001

In July 2001, Robert Maguire made another of his signature moves. He hired Frank Gehry to conceive a master plan for the remaining 60 acres of his original holdings. Gehry was supposed to design four new buildings, near Centinela Avenue and Jefferson Boulevard, and then move his offices from Santa Monica to a 45,000-square-foot former helicopter factory "I've been wanting to work with [Maguire] for years because he's the best," Gehry proclaimed. "No other developer has that history out here."

The *Los Angeles Times* reported, "In contrast to the billowing, twisting shapes of his museums in Bilbao and Seattle, Gehry's designs for Playa Vista are hard-edged buildings that were inspired, in part, by the simple, industrial form of the hangar where Howard Hughes built the giant Spruce Goose seaplane....The largest building is a multistory office building covered in a glass curtain wall—a material not often associated with Gehry—that features floors 12 feet in height."

Landscape architect Laurie Olin, brought in to shape the open space around Gehry's buildings, proposed a meadow and a jogging trail along a tree-lined canal down the middle of the project.

A year after he signed on, Gehry announced he wasn't going to relocate to Maguire's property and withdrew his design services.

(FER) STUDIO
PLAYA VISTA ARTS COLONY

2006

A decade after Maguire's New Urbanist plan came to naught, Inglewood architects (fer) Studio issued a conceptual master plan for The Art Colony at Playa Vista. Laddie John Dill, the Venice-based artist known for his colored-cement-and-glass work, persuaded a number of his contemporaries to support the idea to convert an old Hughes Aircraft facility. The plan called for artists' studios and live-work lofts. Some of the studios would have 32-foot ceilings and private courtyards, to allow artists freedom to work outside. There would be gallery spaces, great natural light, and views of the bordering wetlands. Peter Alexander, Charles Arword, Trone Barnett, Robert Graham, Dennis Hopper, Anjelica Huston, Callie Khouri, Kristin Klosterman, Peter Lodato, Ed Moses, Ed Ruscha, Alan Shaffer, and Francisco X. Siqueiros all signed on.

In a letter to Steve Soboroff, Playa Vista's newest developer, Dill said, "I believe that this portion of your Playa Vista property might be the last place on the Westside where a divorce group of artists with an eye to the future can create a self-sustaining center for the arts for the next 100 years, and in the process, make excellent use of a group of wonderful and historic buildings with personalities unto themselves."

101
134
101
188
158
5
178
164
146
144
148
172
182
234
110
405
SANTA MONICA BLVD
101
238
192
184
214
222
WILSHIRE BLVD
10
206
170
210
248
202
140
224
208
194
10
232
228
218
N
174
186
E
168
242
S
200
212
226
198
1
LA
142
150
110
156
160
244

BD

SB

7

BUILDINGS

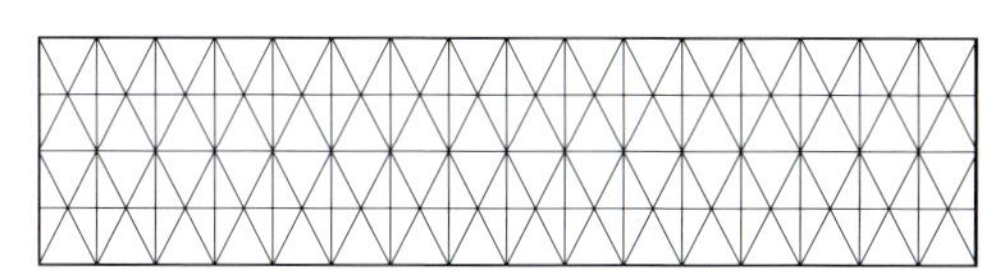

DT

C. E. NOERENBERG NOERENBERG PASSENGER RAILROAD TERMINAL FOR LOS ANGELES

1926

A pair of ventilators upon the carapace of iron and concrete.

William Alexander McClung

C. E. Noerenberg was a prominent architect of the 1920s and 1930s. He designed libraries, movie theaters, hotels, office buildings, and the Streamline Moderne Dorsey High School, and was an early member of the city's Building and Safety Commission.

In 1926, as civic and business elites were choosing sides in the battle over creating a unified railway terminal—there were three small ones at the time—the architect weighed in with his "Noerenberg Plan for a Passenger Railroad Terminal for Los Angeles." The idea was to cap the Los Angeles River, putting a 1,000-foot-long-by-2,000-foot-wide lid on the space between what subsequently would become the Fourth Street and Sixth Street bridges. For the previous half-decade, Noerenberg had been arguing to make Sixth Street into the city's "most important connecting link," spanning the river, rail yards, and trucking lanes, and connecting the bluff along Boyle Avenue to the flats of Mateo Street, in downtown.

The towers of Noerenberg's bridges, supporting an enormous railway plinth, had the forbidding appearance of an ancient Judaic fortress. Suspended between these viaducts were two terminal buildings: symmetrical, light-filled sheds surmounted by four vaults trimmed in glass. The structures faced each other across a courtyard, penetrated by an oblong slot located directly over the riverbed. Critic William Alexander McClung described the station in his book *Landscapes of Desire* as "a pair of ventilators upon the carapace of iron and concrete." Beneath, hugging either side of the river, were double rows of sculpted trees shading a man-made riparian walkway that seemed to continue for miles in either direction. It would be the Jardin des Tuileries transplanted to a flood plane whose banks were lined in railroad tracks.

The idea of transforming the Los Angeles River into a channel, more than a dozen years before the U.S. Army Corps of Engineers would make that a reality, and subordinating it to a mechanized juggernaut, was prescient. Although Noerenberg's vision of a terminal suspended above the river never caught on, the subjugation of the natural setting would soon be completed.

→ Los Angeles River bridged by twin pavilions and land-scaped as civic park

FOURTH STREET
SIXTH STREET
LOS ANGELES RIVER
SEVENTH STREET
THE NOERENBERG PLAN FOR A PASSENGER RAILROAD TERMINAL FOR LOS ANGELES

BD

LA

RUDOLPH M. SCHINDLER

SCHINDLER SHELTERS PROTOTYPE HOUSING

1930s

All units interlock and require a minimum of fastening by nails, screws and bolts, and the appearance of each house may be individualized.

Rudolph M. Schindler

Schindler's prefabricated "Schindler Shelters" were low-cost, flexible, mass-produced units intended for Los Angeles and beyond. Built with a series of interchangeable and "rhythmically spaced" plastic and wood panels and posts (hence the architect's term "panel-post construction"), they were designed as an alternative to mass-produced housing that was usually repetitive and bland.

Similar in their modularity to Schindler's famous Kings Road residence—and exhibiting his typical clerestory windows and intersecting and projecting planes—the one- and two-bedroom houses could take on several configurations, opposed to the usual "erection and re-erection of the same building," Schindler wrote. "All units interlock and require a minimum of fastening by nails, screws and bolts," and "the appearance of each house may be individualized." The system also allowed for diversity in ceiling height and could be further customized with awnings, plantings, and different-size glass walls.

Steeping himself in the minutiae of government bureaucracy, Schindler persistently proposed the shelters to local and federal agencies (producing huge hand-drawn flow charts of their inner workings), including the Department of Defense (for military housing) and the Department of Housing (for public housing).

However, the modern styling, the innovative and unfamiliar configurations, and the roughly $2,000 price tag made them unappealing to cost-conscious and obdurate government bureaucrats. And since prefabrication was rarely used in the private markets of the 1930s and '40s, Schindler couldn't persuade a builder to take them on either.

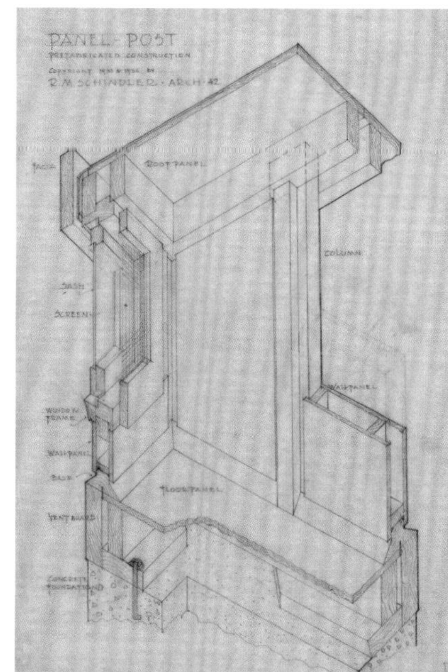

← 3-D diagram of plywood components

→ Basic building blocks yield a complex form with clerestories, intersecting planes, and deep eaves.

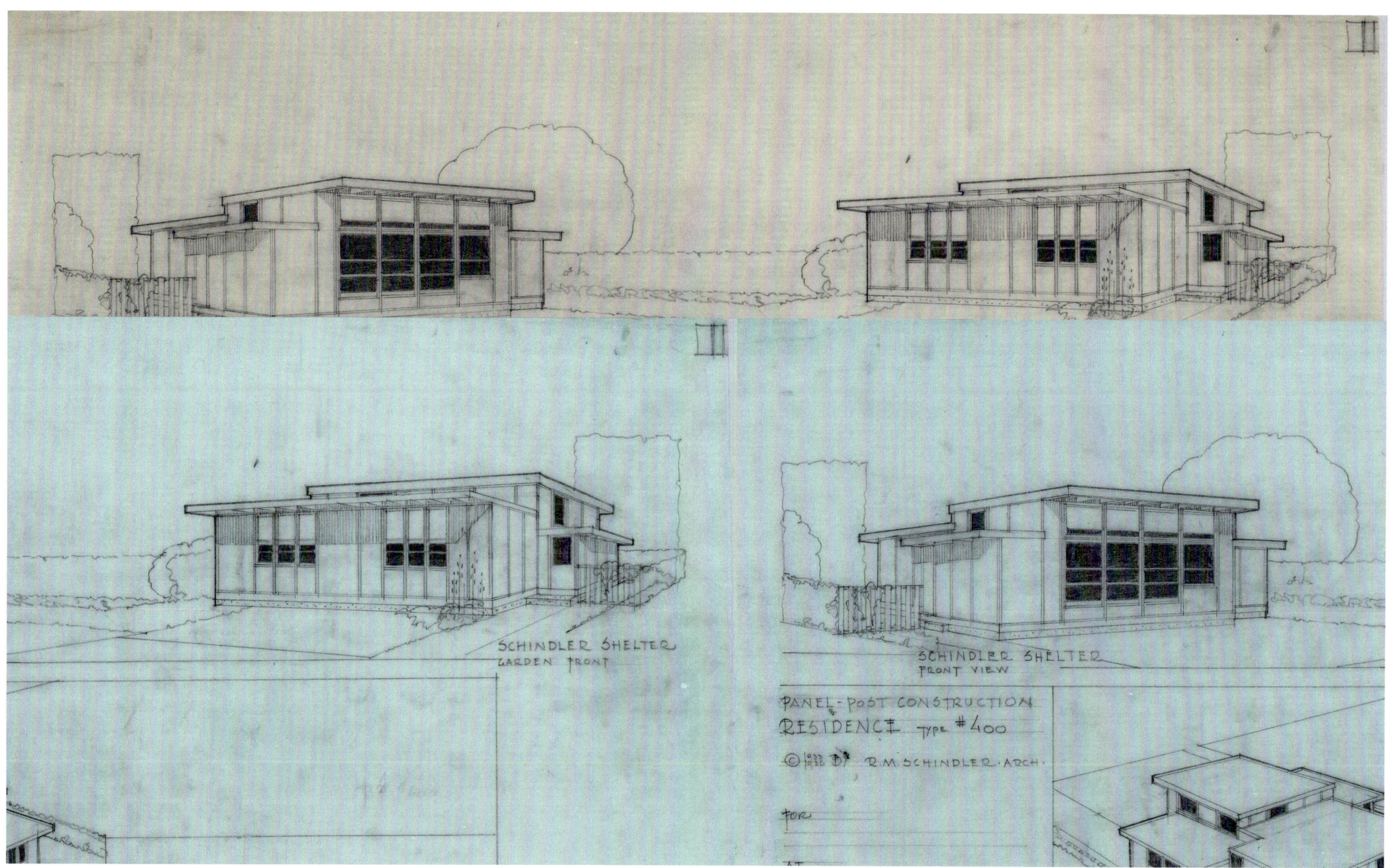
SCHINDLER SHELTER
GARDEN FRONT
SCHINDLER SHELTER
FRONT VIEW
PANEL-POST CONSTRUCTION
RESIDENCE TYPE #400
R.M. SCHINDLER · ARCH.
FOR

BD

MC

GORDON B. KAUFMANN HOLLYWOOD RITZ-CARLTON HOTEL

1930

On the night of February 7, 1930, a large party of the city's rich and swanky gathered beneath a circus tent on the vacant hilltop site of what was supposed to become "the most sumptuous banquet hall in one of the premier hotels in the world." The 200 diners—including *Los Angeles Times* sovereign Harry Chandler and theater magnate Sid Grauman—mingled under the rays of 20 huge searchlights casting multicolored beams skyward. The Goodyear blimp *Volunteer* hovered above, dodging in and out of the shafts of light, a scene described in a local radio broadcast as a man-made aurora borealis.

Thus was launched the Hollywood Ritz-Carlton Hotel, to be built on the slopes at the head of Argyle Avenue. Advertised as the crown jewel of the globe-spanning chain, the proposed $5-million hotel would have presided over Hollywood like Mont Saint-Michel over the coast of Normandy. The 15-story behemoth was designed by Gordon B. Kaufmann, whose Boulder (now Hoover) Dam and Los Angeles Times Building were examples of high modernism at its most heroic. The hotel, by contrast, was a Mediterranean mishmash, combining Moorish domes, Romanesque arches, Spanish roofs, and a Renaissance observation tower into a fortress that would have consumed the skyline. After meeting with Ritz-Carlton executives in New York, Kaufmann revised his drawings, giving the pile a more uniformly Italianate feel.

Kaufmann lavished the hotel with Turkish baths, beauty parlors, stock-trading suites (with direct private Western Union wires), private screening rooms, and a ballroom for 500. The main lobby opened onto a large patio, which, Kaufmann declared, "faces down over the city, offering the entire panorama reaching from Los Angeles to the ocean."

Downslope, among 22 acres of roses and bougainvillea, the architect designed lush villas. According to contemporaneous accounts, wealthy buyers gobbled these up before even a speck of dirt was turned.

The man behind all this activity was Gilbert H. Beesemyer, a banker who'd recruited Cecil B. DeMille, Edward L. Doheny, Kodak inventor George Eastman, Henry O'Melveny, and Mack Sennett to invest. He'd sold them on the superscaled, posh hotel in no small part because it was scheduled to open by November 1931 in anticipation of the 1932 Summer Olympics. Beesemyer, it turned out, was a crook. He'd been busy stealing from his Guarantee Building and Loan Association by toting gold bullion out of the bank. His $8-million theft was discovered in December 1930. The equivalent of more than $100 million in today's money, it remains the largest embezzlement in the nation's history.

Ritz-Carlton withdrew its endorsement, and the hotel plan collapsed. Soon, native sagebrush sprouted around rusting equipment abandoned by the contractors. In 1937, 15 acres of the former site were subdivided into individual lots, a development promoted as Ritz-Carlton Manor.

→ Massive hotel dwarfs Hollywood Hills.

J. R. DAVIDSON
DRIV-IN-CURB MARKET

1931

German émigré J. R. Davidson, who later would be the architect of Case Study House No. 1, was interested in commercial design. He'd been a set designer for Cecil B. DeMille, and he redid the interior of the Cocoanut Grove Restaurant in Hollywood. His work on the Satyr Bookshop, a literary hangout in Hollywood, and the High Hat Restaurant gained some acclaim. But his uncommissioned, speculative 1931 scheme for a corner market was a clear departure from the prevailing notion that a grocery be a traditional bow-truss box with produce piled in front. As the architectural historian Richard Longstreth notes, Davidson "emphasized transparency." His supermarket, strategically placed on a busy boulevard corner, was a backlit billboard floating above a storefront completely open to the intersection. It was as if the street, sidewalk, and shop floor were one continuous space.

He may have escaped the upheaval of the Weimar Republic, but Davidson tried to fold some of that period's dynamic, glittering energy into the car culture of Los Angeles. Had it been built, the aptly named Driv-in-Curb Market would have been an animated lobby, blurring the line between those motoring past and those lingering inside. This was visionary civic architecture that, in the right location, would still be valued today had Davidson's drawings been more than conjecture.

← Ink drawing of market with interior aglow

→ Colored-pencil tracing shows cars dashing to the curb.

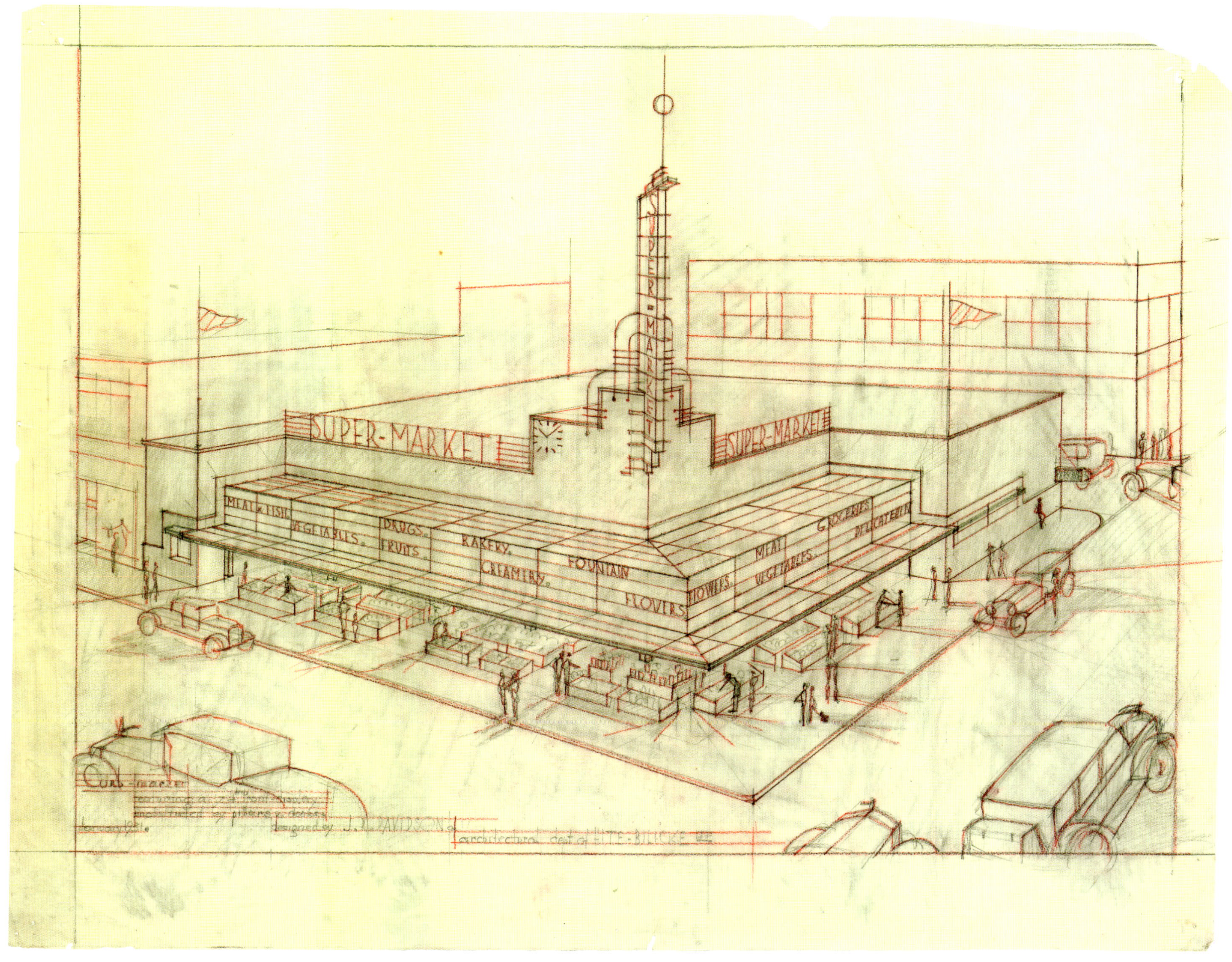
SUPER-MARKET
SUPER-MARKET
SUPER-MARKET
MEAT & FISH
VEGETABLES
DRUGS
FRUITS
BAKERY
CREAMERY
FOUNTAIN
FLOWERS
FLOWERS
MEAT
VEGETABLES
GROCERIES
designed by J. R. DAVIDSON of
architectural dept of

MC

ROBERT STACY-JUDD
NATIONAL HALL

1931

Perhaps the most ardent practitioner of the Mayan Revival style—and well-known for his explorations throughout Latin America—Robert Stacy-Judd proselytized that "indigenous" design should become the template for a distinctive American vernacular, far removed from the influence of Europe.

Stacy-Judd's projects in California, often merging Art Deco lines with ancient Aztec and Mayan motifs, were plentiful, highlighted by his legendary pre-Columbian showpiece, the Aztec Hotel in Monrovia. Most of Stacy-Judd's ornamental, cast-concrete schemes were never built, including "the world's largest airplane" for Hughes Aircraft; the Laguna Beach Hotel; a restaurant, church, and university building in North Hollywood; and an "Indian Center" for Beverly Hills.

But perhaps no project would have been as remarkable or influential as his Mayan-themed National Hall. Covering two city blocks along the southwest corner of Sunset Boulevard and Vine Street, in Hollywood, the complex would have included an enormous domed auditorium capable of seating 23,000, a 13-story Art Deco department store, a stepped-and-chamfered office block, and a hotel. Its most ornate feature was a tower topped by a Mayan arch, a motif that carried through the office block and the entrance to the department store. The exposed facade of that store consisted of V-shaped plate-glass windows in continuous bays, 11 stories high.

After World War II, Stacy-Judd's work fell quickly out of favor. As author Marjorie Ingle, a devotee of the Mayan Revival, put it, "Kookiness and flamboyance seemed desperately inappropriate after a sobering world war." She added: "Of course it was a style that eventually would have died a natural death without a world war to see it off. Everyone tires of fancy dress after a while."

→ Meso-American palette for walls, pediments, corbels, and friezes

Robt Stacy-Judd. A.I.A
Architect
Hollywood. Cal.
1931
National Hall Project. S.W. Corner (Two City Blocks) Vine & Sunset Blvd. Hollywood, Calif. Hotel, Office Bldg., Department Store, Convention Hall (Seat 25000) and Theater, N.E. Corner.
Maya Art Motifs throughout.

LA

LLOYD WRIGHT
TWENTIETH-CENTURY METROPOLITAN CATHOLIC CATHEDRAL

1931

A monumental shaft of glowing light, articulate with color and variety of expression, yet all correlated and totally integrated with the purpose and concept of the building and its symbol.

Lloyd Wright

At the beginning of the 1930s, Lloyd Wright was approached by Marguerite Brunswig, the heir to a large pharmaceutical fortune, to design a cathedral. Brunswig was not only a devout Catholic but also a sculptor, which led to a close collaboration between herself and Wright. What emerged was an enormous tower, with a cruciform theme throughout. Indeed, the cathedral took the form of a cross when viewed along its height, from above and below, and even in the outlines of the 16-by-16-foot precast-concrete blocks from which the entire structure was to be made. This followed an inspiration Brunswig had in New York, gazing at the newly completed Empire State Building. "When viewed from a certain angle," she later wrote, "a cross seemed to impose itself through the very core of the structure. What an idea for a church!"

Made of reinforced-concrete modular units (similar to those Wright and his father were using in their textile-block homes), the 50-story tower would contain 2,800 small rooms, each measuring 256 square feet. The 950-foot-tall monolith of concrete lace was to be inset with colored glass or plastic panels and lit from within at night, producing, Wright said, "a monumental shaft of glowing light, articulate with color and variety of expression, yet all correlated and totally integrated with the purpose and concept of the building and its symbol." Certainly, no one could miss the symbol. The glowing, illuminated cross—800 feet high and 160 feet wide—would assert its dynamic presence even by day, in silhouette against the setting sun.

The center of the church would have had a deep atrium soaring uninterrupted from ground level to the top of the massive tower. A large metal pendulum, suspended from a cable above the altar, would swing freely, "symbolizing the path of the Earth and other planets in the universe." Along the perimeter, the stations of the cross, which Wright spelled out in his drawings, would be portrayed by a 20-foot-high frieze "with the life of St. Vibian continuing on either side of the sanctuary with the four evangelists Matthew, Mark, Luke, and John and meeting over the altar of lady Guadalupe with a great mural of the blessed Virgin Mary."

Wright arranged a rigidly symmetrical pattern, with the central tower standing in the middle of four cloistered courtyards protected from the street by an overgrowth of trees and vines. A rectory, chancery, synod hall and offices, library, Episcopal residence, and school were laid along the axis of the cross. These took shape as identical three-story buildings, deferential supplicants bowing at the foot of the triumphal tower.

Could this bold, somber undertaking have become the city's Sagrada Familia? Archbishop John J. Cantwell, whose diocese this was proposed for, was "much impressed" but "had no intention of building a cathedral at the moment," according to Brunswig's unpublished memoir. Having failed to interest the local church, Brunswig, in 1937, moved on to Budapest, hoping to erect a similar cathedral in the hills overlooking the Danube. World War II put an end to her effort.

→ Model of Wright's textile-block bravado

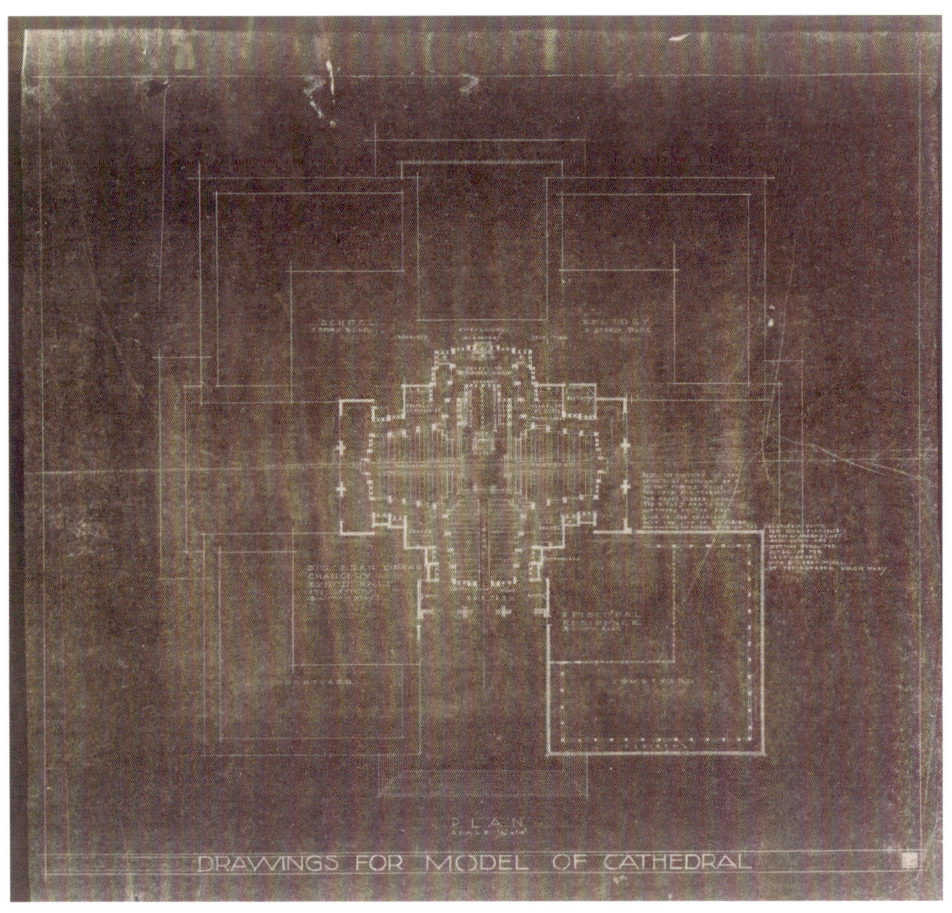

DRAWING FOR MODEL OF CATHEDRAL

←←
Site plan of sanctuary surrounded by cloisters and courtyards

←
Cathedral appears as a cross from all directions.

→
Drawing of mural suspended above the altar

←←
Early pencil sketches

←
Preliminary detail

→
Exterior elements textured with biblical references

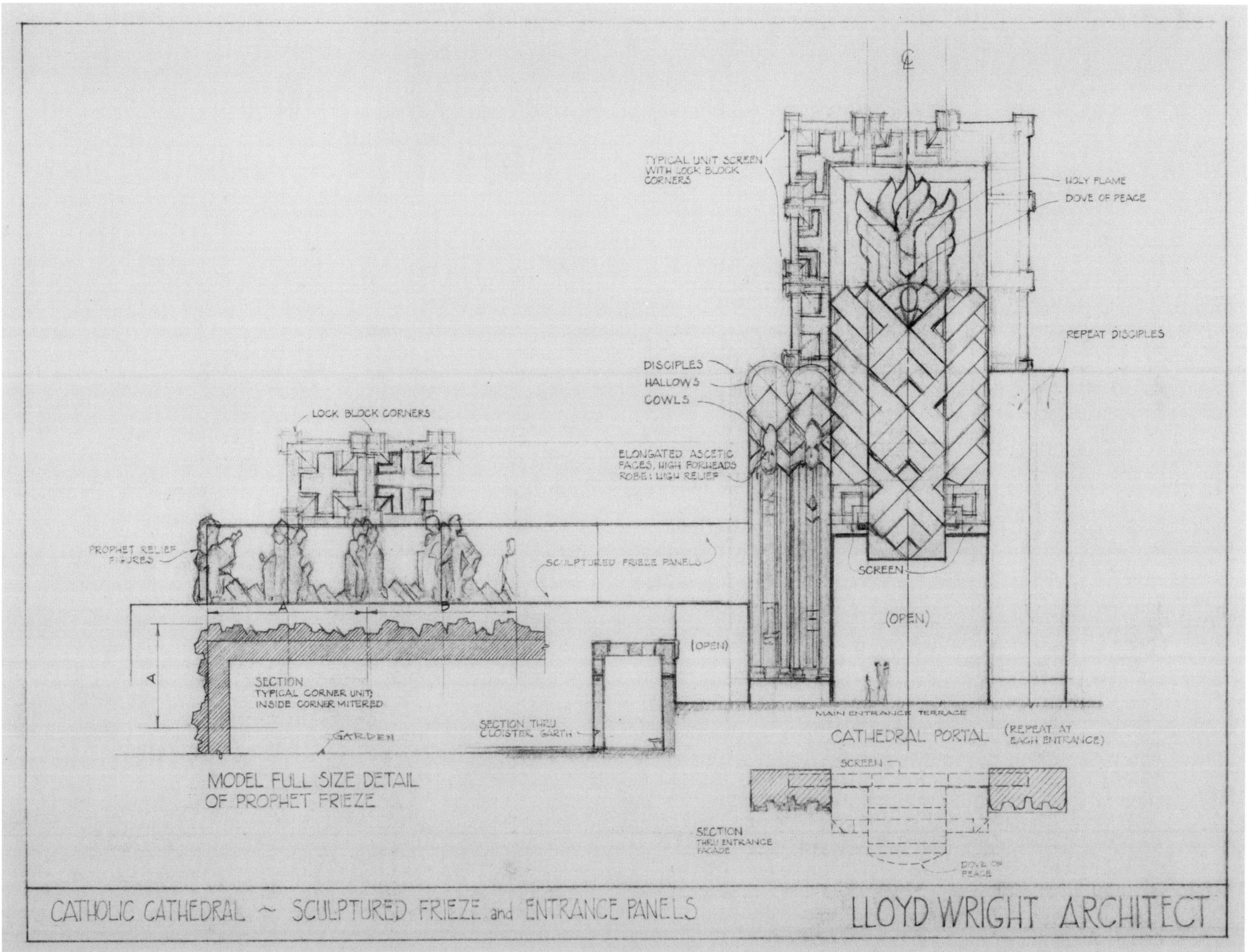
TYPICAL UNIT SCREEN WITH LOCK BLOCK CORNERS
HOLY FLAME
DOVE OF PEACE
REPEAT DISCIPLES
DISCIPLES
HALLOWS
COWLS
LOCK BLOCK CORNERS
ELONGATED ASCETIC FACES, HIGH FORHEADS ROBE: HIGH RELIEF
PROPHET RELIEF FIGURES
SCULPTURED FRIEZE PANELS
SCREEN
(OPEN)
(OPEN)
SECTION TYPICAL CORNER UNIT; INSIDE CORNER MITERED
GARDEN
SECTION THRU CLOISTER GARTH
MAIN ENTRANCE TERRACE
CATHEDRAL PORTAL (REPEAT AT EACH ENTRANCE)
MODEL FULL SIZE DETAIL OF PROPHET FRIEZE
SCREEN
SECTION THRU ENTRANCE FACADE
DOVE OF PEACE
CATHOLIC CATHEDRAL ~ SCULPTURED FRIEZE and ENTRANCE PANELS
LLOYD WRIGHT ARCHITECT

LA

RUDOLPH M. SCHINDLER
GAS STATIONS

1933

The design is not futuristic in any way but modern or contemporary in the sense of an up-to-date piece of machinery.

Rudolph M. Schindler

In 1933, Rudolph M. Schindler designed a prototype gas station for Union Oil. As always, the transplanted Austrian architect was concerned with simplifying construction and creating a kit that, he said, "may become standard parts for all future gas stations." He was looking to keep the price down while putting amperage into a design composed of varying planes of concrete, glass, and thin metal panels. The intersecting beams and surfaces, said historian David Gebhard, became "a piece of De Stijl sculpture." This was roadway architecture, intended to turn the entire building into a sign—just at the moment when motoring was beginning to grip the city.

Set back from the street, an illuminated tower enclosed in orange glass bisected a small building made of interlocking offset rectangles. Ornamental shrubbery spilled out from an overhang, guarding the attendant's booth, while a pendant flapped on a tall flagpole overhead. Two flying canopies were split by a single supporting beam, which doubled as a lit billboard for the station. At the ends of the beam, facing the street, Schindler proposed a three-color neon light to beckon drivers. "The beam and the canopies may be manufactured as standardized units," Schindler wrote, "to be used on stations otherwise varied to fit particular lots."

Slender round pumps and skinny columns would give the station an inviting, open appearance. The station was to be essentially transparent, giving drivers an unobstructed sense of the road ahead. "The design is not futuristic in any way but modern or contemporary in the sense of an up-to-date piece of machinery, and will fit into all surroundings in the same way as a modern automobile does," the architect concluded.

Schindler created a similar model, decked in vivid red, white, and blue, for Standard Oil. A last version, more reminiscent of Piet Mondrian's color schemes than Gerrit Rietveld's angular constructions, was proposed for "Mrs. Nerenbaum," a client, like the stations, lost to history.

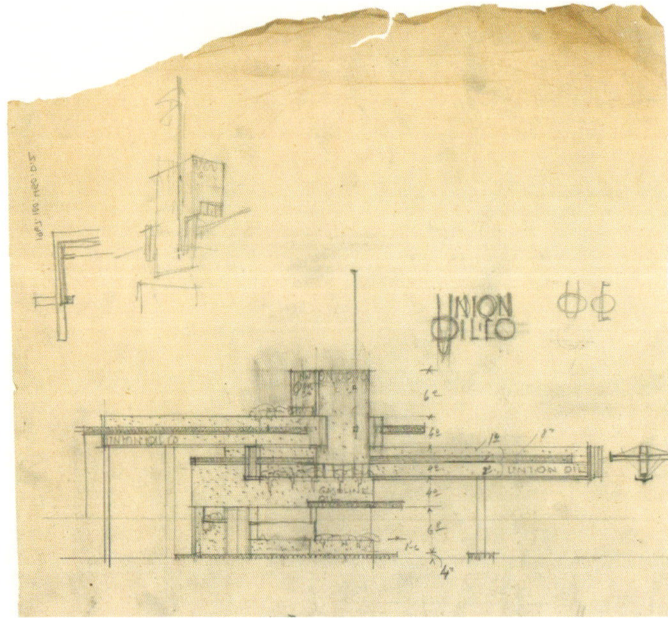

← Pencil drawing of thin canopies hovering over gas pumps

→ The ultimate roadside stop woven into the urban fabric

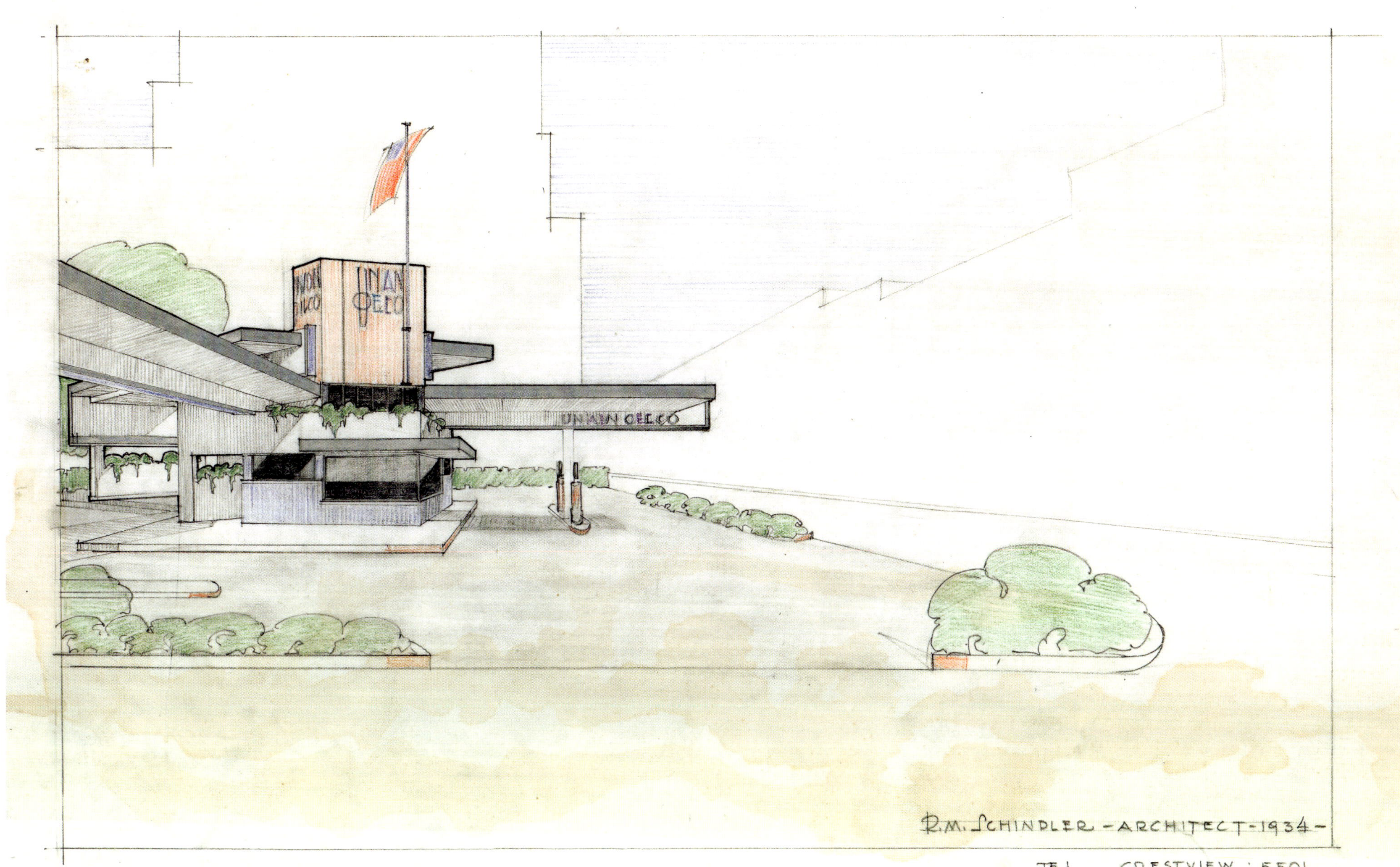
R.M. SCHINDLER -ARCHITECT-1934-
TEL . . . CRESTVIEW : 5501

MC

PARKINSON AND PARKINSON
LORADO TAFT'S DREAM MUSEUM

1934

It would be one of the art marvels of the world—it would be a shrine for the lovers of beauty.

Lorado Taft

Beginning in 1930, Lorado Zadoc Taft, described in news accounts as "the dean of living American sculptors," started talking up his Dream Museum, an institution dedicated to the masterworks of architecture and sculpture from around the world. He envisioned it as a pageant of civilization that would use replicas to re-create the great periods of human history, from fifth-century-BC Greece to Michelangelo's Medici tombs in Florence to the buddhas of China and the Hindu deities of India.

He found a receptive audience in Los Angeles, where his lectures were crammed with spectators hungry for his grandiloquent pronouncements. "If Los Angeles builds my 'dream museum' her citizens will come closer to the meaning of life," he preached. "Southern California is destined to be the new Hellas."

For the location, he chose 10 relatively level acres in Griffith Park at the end of Commonwealth Avenue. Parkinson and Parkinson, who had designed the Los Angeles Memorial Coliseum and were then drawing Union Station, penciled an enormous temple to sit on the summit, commanding a panoramic city view. The concrete structure would have no windows and be lit entirely by skylights. The road leading to the museum would pass directly beneath the building and spill onto a landscaped parking lot.

This million-dollar Acropolis would be 750 feet long by 250 feet wide. There would be no pillars or interior walls. At its peak, its ceiling would reach 80 feet, tapering to 50 feet at the sides, much like a railway concourse. The huge exhibition hall would have been the largest single room in the West. It was so large, in fact, that a planned full-size model of the Parthenon could have been comfortably housed within, still leaving ample room for a reproduction Trajan's Arch. The hall would be arranged with seven aisles tracing the development of Greek, Egyptian, Oriental, Assyrian, and other art from inception to demise. Rows bisecting the aisles would allow patrons to interrupt the flow of one culture to march across time and place to encounter others. (These subversive shifts would become the guiding idea, 77 years later, of Rem Koolhaas's bid to rebuild the Los Angeles County Museum of Art [LACMA] from scratch.)

On February 9, 1934, with his brother-in-law, novelist Hamlin Garland, and Los Angeles Art Museum director Clarence B. Mitchell at his side, the white-haired and -bearded sculptor hammered a surveyor's stake into the hard soil, inaugurating the Griffith Park plateau. Completing the museum, he said, "will give to this city a cultural supremacy almost unsurpassed in the entire world. Surely no more beautiful place could be found than this site. It would be one of the art marvels of the world—it would be a shrine for the lovers of beauty and of tremendous value as an educational project."

→ Museum large enough to contain the Parthenon and Trajan's Arch

Taft was sincere in his lofty ambitions—and backed by the city's power elite. But the 74-year-old sculptor didn't have long to live. Suffering a series of strokes, he died on October 30, 1936, his Dream Museum still but a dream.

OJ · JOHNSON · ARCH'T ·

S. CHARLES LEE THEATERS

Early 1940s

Bold replaced sleek. The entire building, not just the marquee, was now readable from the car.

Maggie Valentine

S. Charles Lee, one of Los Angeles's most prolific and talented theater architects, was best known for his palatial Los Angeles Theater (1931), downtown on Broadway, and his Streamline Moderne Academy Theater (1939), in Inglewood. But later in his career, his designs began to drastically change, adapting to a parade of advancing technologies and circumstances.

While both materials and construction had been severely limited during World War II, the period following produced a short-lived movie theater resurgence, thanks to plentiful labor and supplies of new, lightweight materials developed for the war effort. Plastics, fiberglass, Plexiglas, and aluminum provided a creative palette. Growing automobile traffic spurred theaters to become more visible and dramatic from the street. The scale and proportions of exteriors began to grow, while drive-through marquees literally drew people into buildings.

"Bold replaced sleek....The entire building, not just the marquee, was now readable from the car," wrote theater historian Maggie Valentine.

Lee was Los Angeles's leader in dreaming up designs for these car-culture movie palaces. His sculptural visions merged architecture and signage with a flamboyance and audacity that few had ever accomplished.

The facade of the Diana Theater would be built entirely of plastic, allowing a clear modernist box to rise from a streamlined, wing-motif base and giving the building the ability to light up or disappear at will. The Sign Theater would have an all-glass front, allowing drivers to see into the lobby from the street. The Town's centerpiece was a giant spinning globe hovering over the entrance canopy. Perhaps the most expressive theater of all was the Rio, which featured giant three-dimensional letters spelling out its name in copper and metal. The sides of its vertical marquee were angled, making the sign more legible for motorists and pedestrians.

The theater interiors were equally inspired. Rows of seating in the La Vona would have multihued lighting arrangements, creating what Lee called "a blaze of color with the new fluorescent lighting units." Auditoriums had huge prosceniums framed with giant graphics. The architect also began to experiment with black light, giving theatergoers a whole new thrill when the house went dark.

Unfortunately, few of Lee's late-career theater designs were realized. In the early 1950s, the major movie studios lost a series of antitrust cases, forcing them to relinquish their theater holdings. Smaller, independent operators couldn't finance Lee's schemes. Television bit even deeper into movie theater revenues, cutting attendance in half. Lee anticipated the end of the movie palace era and retired from architecture at the age of 50, leaving most of his last designs taped to the drawing board.

→ Rio Theater is its own marquee.

FOUR
LINES
OF

SIGN
A B C D E F
G H I J K
L M N O
LA VONA
PARKI

CORREA
NEWS
COMEDY
STREET
MAIN STREET
DESIGN AND RENDERING BY
S. Charles Lee
architect
DESIGN NO 1.
THEATRE.
THE DESIGN IS ADAPTABLE TO ANY CORNER LOT 40X140 + OR - LETTERS IN SIGN TOWER TO BE 36 HIGH CHANGEABLE FROM INSIDE THEATRE PORTION CAN BE ONE FLOOR AS SHOW OR BALCONY TYPE IF DESIRED.
A - CIRCLE LIFT BOOTH TO CEILING. FOR POSTER CASES IN ITS PLACE.
B - LOBBY WITH GLASS CEILING
C - FOYER.
CIRCULAR CEILING OVER TICKET BOOTH WITH HIGH REFLECTING SURFACE.
SINGLE & 2 WAY POSTER CASES. ENTIRE FRONT OF GLASS INCG DOORS. & CEILING

SIGN
LETTERS

←→
Supersize lettering and detailing are clearly legible to passing cars.

MC

FRANK LLOYD WRIGHT HUNTINGTON HARTFORD SPORTS CLUB AND COTTAGE GROUP CENTER

1947

Hovering above Runyon Canyon in the Hollywood Hills, the Huntington Hartford Sports Club—part of a planned 130-acre hotel development—would have been the most futuristic of Wright's Los Angeles designs.

Huntington Hartford II, heir to the A&P grocery chain and known equally as a playboy and a cultural patron, commissioned the project. Hartford had built the Beaux-Arts Huntington Hartford Theater on Vine, while spearheading various failed ventures around the world. Wright, a man of equal bluster and vision, was the ideal designer for the complex.

A multibuilding hotel, called the Cottage Group Center, would be located a few blocks off Hollywood Boulevard, insulated from the hubbub by the secluded canyon. Guests and members would check in at a glass-walled welcome hall and then proceed to timber cottages nestled in the steep surrounding hillsides. Perched on a promontory high above the hotel was what Hartford called the Play Resort. Supported by a seven-story masonry core containing a lobby, kitchen, changing rooms, and an apartment for the bon-vivant owner, the club was composed of three concentric concrete-and-glass saucers projecting over the ravine. Wright used the saucer in several of his later projects to convey weightlessness and a futuristic feel.

The three saucers, supported by reinforced concrete and inset with glass tubes like those Wright used in the Johnson Wax Building, included a lounge, a dining and dancing area, and a space for cinema and cabaret. Each had a balcony. Above the saucers was a dome-covered bowl that served as a sunbathing terrace; below were two uncovered disks, one for a swimming pool (its contents dramatically spilling over the edge like a waterfall, years before the infinity pool became an L.A. status symbol), the other for tennis courts with their own stands, as well as spaces for croquet and badminton.

Local residents, worried that Hartford's free living would corrupt their children, fought zoning changes that would have allowed commercial buildings in the residential area. Wright's grandson Eric Lloyd Wright, who was in high school at the time, remembers one neighbor calling the idea "the ugliest thing I've ever seen." Wright, usually above the fray, told his grandson there was "no use casting pearls among swine." The battle lasted two years before Hartford and Wright surrendered. Hartford eventually built a pool and a pool house for himself on the ridge. In 1972, the pool house was consumed by fire. All that remains is the stone foundation.

→ Sketch of infinity pool among saucers perched on promontory

PLAY RESORT IN HOLLYWOOD HILLS FOR HUNTINGTON HARTFO
FRANK LLOYD WRIGHT LLOYD WRIGHT ASSOCIATE

COUNTRY CLUB FOR HUNTINGTON HARTFORD HOLLYWOOD
FRANK LLOYD WRIGHT ARCHITECT

PLAY RESORT HOLLYWOOD HILLS
FOR HUNTINGTON HARTFORD
FRANK LLOYD WRIGHT LLOYD WRIGHT ASSOCIATE

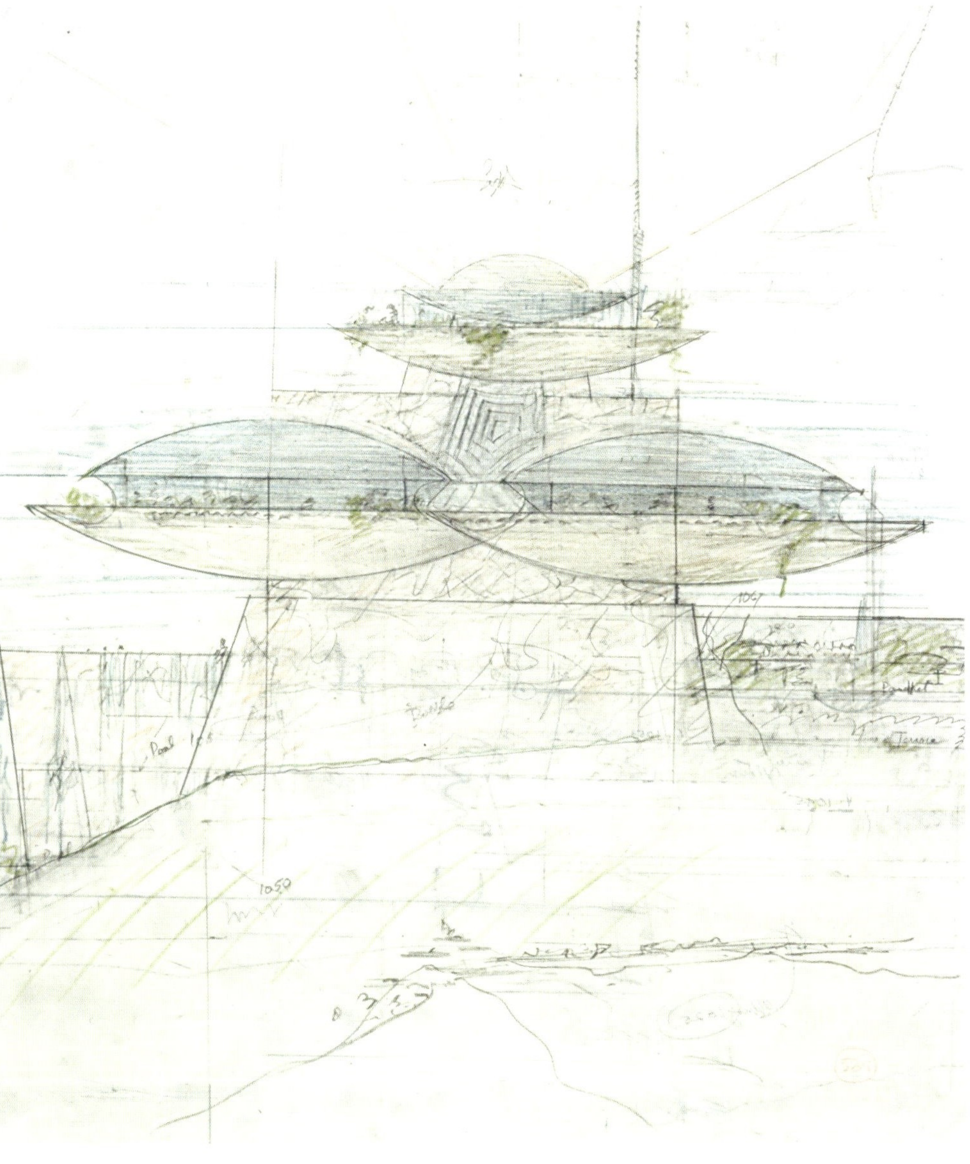

↖↖
Concrete walkway leads visitors to club merged with hillside.

←
Lids suspended above glass enclosures cap sculpted floors.

↙↙
Site plan of saucers cantilevered from triangular base

↗
Hotel and cottages in foreground; sports club in background, left

→
Graphite and colored pencil depiction of hotel reception hall

SB

GRUEN AND KRUMMECK
OLYMPIC SHOPPING CIRCLE

1950

Austrian-born architect Victor Gruen, father of the modern shopping mall, presided over the suburbanization of the United States, devising master plans, housing projects, and, of course, malls. With the Olympic Shopping Circle, he rejiggered the essential form he had created and reconsidered the typical demographic it served. The Circle was slated for East Los Angeles, a blue-collar neighborhood halfway between downtown and Whittier.

The $20-million, 70-acre project, spearheaded by New York developer Leonard S. Gans, would be one of the largest regional malls in the nation, equal to 12 downtown business blocks.

Gruen, who was brought in on the heels of a prior attempt to develop the same spot, dismissed earlier mall ideas—his own and others: The "strip plan," which put storefronts behind street-side parking lots, invited "pirating and commercial slums" and made the parking lot the most important feature of the development. The "block development," built on its own grid, discouraged pedestrian traffic and isolated certain stores. Finally, the "mall development" was put aside because the walking distances were too far and shoppers couldn't see the entire center from most points.

So Gruen introduced his "circle solution," declaring: "This scheme provides all the advantages of the strip, the block and the mall plans." Gruen's innovation was how he conceived of the interaction between cars and pedestrians and the shops themselves. Cars would shoot through four underpasses to reach an enclosed parking lot, in the center of which was the drive-in restaurant. Here was the new civic square, dedicated as much to the car as to shoppers.

The breezeway encircling the parking lot crossed above the traffic lanes, creating a broad, comfortable loggia reminiscent of the edging around a European town marketplace. The anchor store would be housed in a circular building around whose perimeter ran a ramp whisking cars to the rooftop parking lot.

Gruen's huge circle, which evokes the Tevatron particle accelerator, was ahead of its time. There would be 710,000 square feet of shopping space, rooftop terraces for 300 cars, a 1,500-seat theater, a nursery and playground ("a place for harried mothers to check their children while shopping"), a gas station, and a drive-in restaurant with a roof garden terrace.

Gans withdrew, made skittish by the onset of the Korean War, and the kind of strip mall Gruen denounced eventually came to occupy the spot. Kmart, Target, and Pacific Theaters now reside under big-box roofs, with a deep parking lot filling the Whittier Boulevard frontage where Gruen had envisioned his Olympic Shopping Circle.

↗ Cars pass beneath circular shopping center to park around central restaurant.

→ Shoppers in loggia

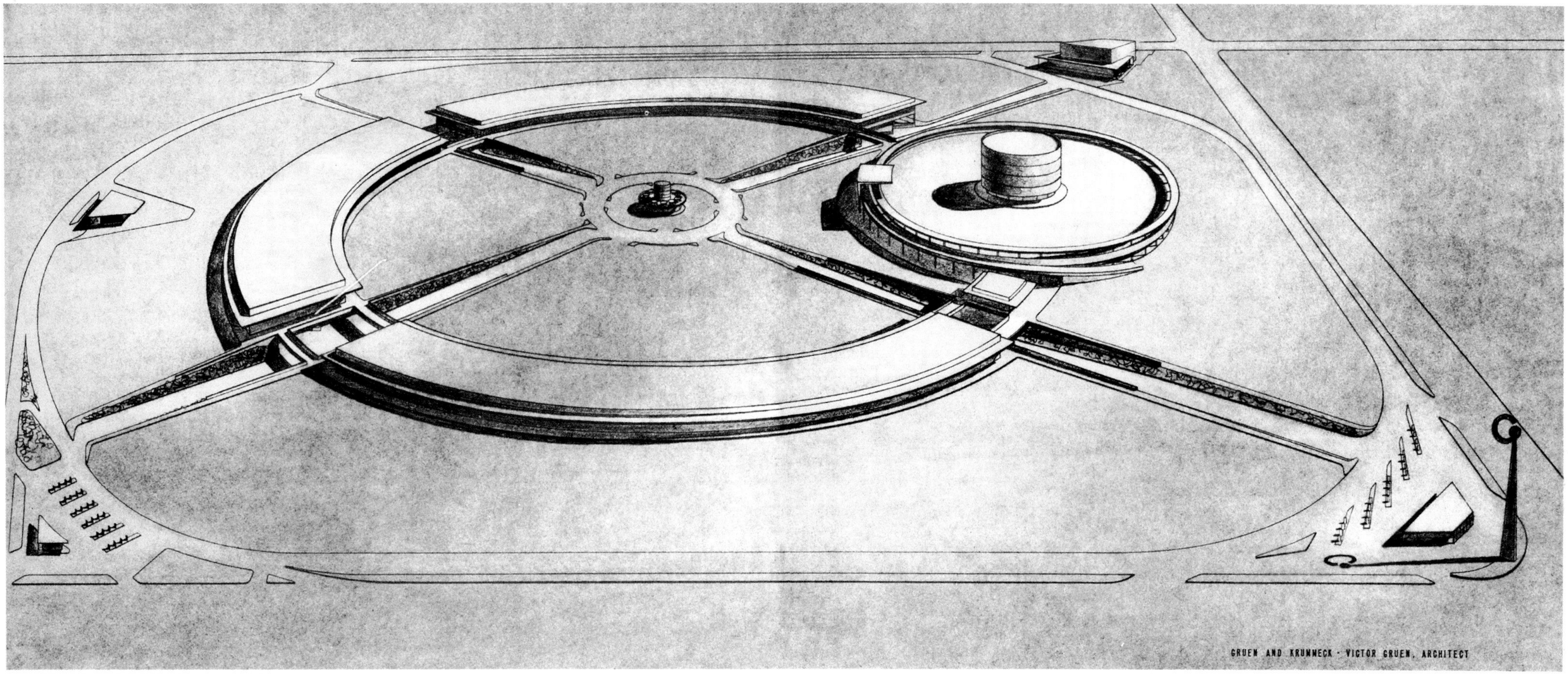

GRUEN AND KRUMMECK · VICTOR GRUEN, ARCHITECT

A. C. MARTIN UNION STATION TRANSPORTATION CENTER

1954

We were all going to be using helicopters for public transportation. It was just a matter of time.

Chris Martin

One of countless doomed attempts to unify the city's disjointed transportation matrix, A. C. Martin's six-story, $20-million hub, situated behind historic Union Station, was to be a giant bus terminal that also accommodated rail, auto, and helicopter travel. The project had the enthusiastic backing of powerful county supervisor Kenneth Hahn, among others.

The round bus terminal, with its protruding pilasters, clerestory windows, and monolithic form, looked a lot like the L.A. Forum, in Inglewood. Its shape also mirrored the giant gas tanks dotting the surrounding industrial landscape. Fanning out from this core were administrative buildings, a long-span rectangular train shed, and several parking structures. Indeed, the project wore the city's automotive bias on its sleeve. Parking for 10,000 cars was spread across 60 acres. But the terminal's most ambitious goal was to make helicopters a more vital part of regional transit. "Helicabs," said A. C. Martin partner J. Edward Martin, would become "the aerial version of a street taxi"—lifting off from the roof and providing quick jaunts around town.

"It was a certainty," A. C. Martin principal Chris Martin remembers. "We were all going to be using helicopters for public transportation. It was just a matter of time." (Subways were not part of the plan.)

In fact, the futuristic Helicabs sank the entire scheme. While the idea was in vogue—it's hard to find a 1950s architectural rendering without a copter somewhere in the picture—helicopter travel proved impractical for public use. Maintenance and fuel were too expensive, and the risks of flying were too high. A. C. Martin, however, remained partial to the project, proposing the helicopter-based Metroport for the same location a decade later. In 1991, Ehrenkrantz Eckstut and Kuhn's Union Station East Portal was built, sans copters, partially fulfilling the original transit-center concept.

→ Corrugated train shed next to circular bus station topped with helipad

BD

MC

PAUL WILLIAMS
THE HOLLYWOOD

1960

Paul Williams's mixed-use complex, planned for the corner of Sunset and Vine, was perhaps too much of a leap ahead. Facing away from the street into an interior courtyard, the three 31-story towers—potentially the tallest and largest such development of its time on the West Coast—would have created a controlled envelope at odds with Hollywood's single-use, sidewalk-friendly commercial grid.

The office-and-residential project also included outdoor mezzanines and sunken plazas, a heliport (another example of that technology's popularity) with four flights leaving per hour, a 5,000-car garage, an air terminal with luggage service that would let travelers check their bags before heading to the airport, a hotel, theaters, restaurants, and a shopping center.

Williams's prototype of a multiuse city center anticipated today's live-in malls. In fact, the W Hollywood, a 2010 mixed-use residential complex that bears a striking resemblance to The Hollywood, sits just a few blocks from where Williams's towers would have been built.

THE HOLLYWOOD
SUNSET AND VINE, CALIFORNIA
VIEW OF THE ESPLANADE

← High-rise towers increase density in Hollywood.

↑ Thin-shell-concrete canopy shades courtyard.

PAUL WILLIAMS
SATELLITE CITY

Williams was constantly dreaming up ambitious schemes, most of which never progressed beyond his drawing board. His Satellite City, which he designed for the Cornfields site north of downtown (the same site that Thom Mayne and Michael Maltzan envisioned transforming decades later), comprised a cluster of tall office and residential buildings mixed with shopping centers and restaurants, all situated on top of a parking podium for autos. He also made plans for a Wilshire Boulevard monorail, an Art Deco stadium, and a seashell-shaped convention center for Anaheim.

A. QUINCY JONES AND FREDERICK E. EMMONS

EICHLER HOMES/ CASE STUDY HOUSE NO. 24

1961

The project was designed as an earth sculpture.

Cory Buckner

In 1961, *Arts & Architecture* editor John Entenza asked A. Quincy Jones and Frederick E. Emmons if they had a plan that might fit into his Case Study program, the influential examination of the American home that ran from 1945 to 1966. Indeed, they did, and with Case Study House No. 24, Jones and Emmons announced their intention to radically rework suburbia and suburban living, and to prove that innovative architecture did not have to be a one-off proposition. They proposed to Entenza a project that they had designed for Joseph Eichler, the unorthodox developer whose houses are coveted today as supremely livable, and which Eichler intended to build. On 148 acres in the rolling hills of Chatsworth, where orange and oaks trees were being pulled up as fast as freeways could be extended into the north San Fernando Valley, Eichler Homes was preparing to construct a tract of 260 dwellings designed by Jones and Emmons, which were fully adapted to searing summer temperatures and integrated into the undulating landscape.

At the Chatsworth site, the architects proposed to partially sink the houses two feet below grade, huddled behind and beneath seven-foot-high earthen banks heaped from soil excavated on site. The berms would not only mimic and maintain the contours of the rolling hills but also act as thermal insulation and block the chatter and prying eyes of neighbors. In their aim to produce as comfortable a living space as possible, Jones and Emmons employed a rooftop water-circulation system. In hot weather, a fine-spray fog—not unlike the misters used today in Palm Springs and Las Vegas—would keep the roof temperature below 70 degrees. As they noted to Entenza, “Because water and earth are among the best insulators, the Case Study House will be considerably easier to heat and cool than a conventional above-grade house.”

The architects conceived five models, each 1,700 square feet with four bedrooms and three bathrooms. A post-and-beam frame permitted sliding glass doors on three sides, extending the living area out to the line of the retaining walls. Two fire pits flanking the living room, an open kitchen, and a flexible floor plan combined to suggest an easy lifestyle, indoors and out. Trellised overhangs blended the house into the landscape, where ancient stands of oaks were to be preserved. As architect and author Cory Buckner put it: “The project was designed as an earth sculpture.”

By reducing lot sizes from 20,000 to 11,000 square feet, Eichler and his architects carved room for a wide commons, bridle paths, and a community center, connected to one another by green walkways. The Los Angeles City Planning Commission approved the master plan, but the city council’s Committee on Zoning refused to shrink the lots, citing concerns that the greenbelts might not be properly maintained. With that, the concept died. Eichler never commissioned a prototype so, like many Case Study Houses, No. 24 remained a study on paper.

→ Tract home buried in the rolling landscape

442
A. QUINCY JONES · FREDERICK E. EMMONS & ASSOCIATES
EMIEL BECSKY
HARRY SAUNDERS
KAZ NOMURA
LOUIS LIETS
WILLIAM LAFFIN
JOHN THOMAN
ASSOCIATES
ARCHITECTS & SITE PLANNERS
MEMBERS OF THE AMERICAN INSTITUTE OF ARCHITECTS
12248 SANTA MONICA BLVD.
LOS ANGELES 25, CALIFORNIA
PHONE: BRADSHAW 2-8208
ALL IDEAS, DESIGN ARRANGEMENTS AND PLANS INDICATED OR REPRESENTED BY THIS DRAWING ARE OWNED BY AND THE PROPERTY OF A. QUINCY JONES, FREDERICK E. EMMONS & ASSOCIATES, ARCHITECTS, AND WERE CREATED, EVOLVED AND DEVELOPED FOR USE ON, AND IN CONNECTION WITH, THE SPECIFIED PROJECT. NONE OF SUCH IDEAS, DESIGNS, ARRANGEMENTS OR PLANS SHALL BE USED BY OR DISCLOSED TO ANY PERSON FIRM OR CORPORATION FOR ANY PURPOSE WHATSOEVER WITHOUT THE WRITTEN PERMISSION OF A. QUINCY JONES-FREDERICK E. EMMONS & ASSOCIATES, ARCHITECTS.
DRAWN
CHECKED
DATE
JOB NO.
NO.
DATE
REVISION

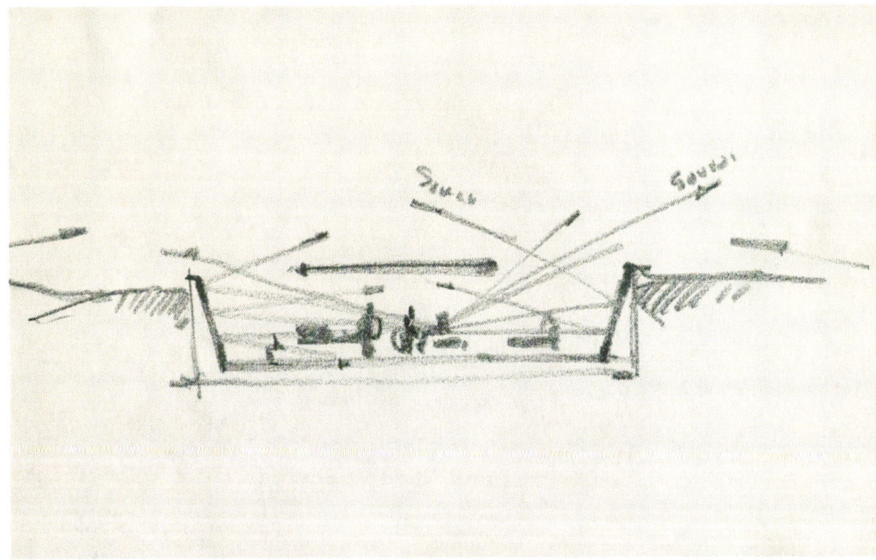

Entrance Walk

←←
Open space and pathways preserve natural setting.

↙↙
Berms act as sound barriers and privacy screens.

←
Low roof frames house entryway.

→
Sunken living room, two kitchens, and multiple patios

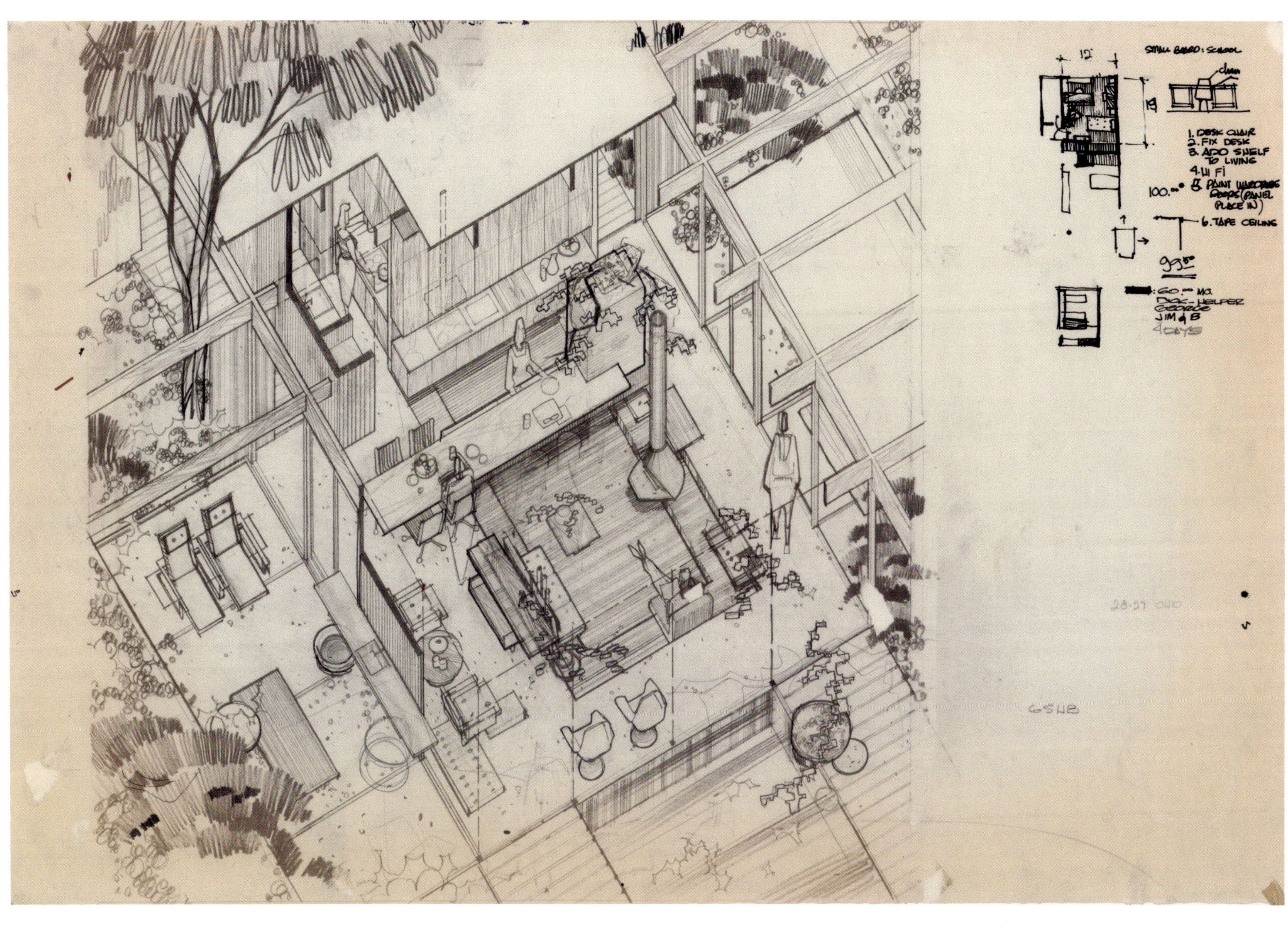

WILLIAM PEREIRA AND ASSOCIATES
HOLLYWOOD MOTION PICTURE AND TELEVISION MUSEUM

1962–63

The goal was to dramatize the dramatists, to star them in their own epic.

William Pereira

As if William Pereira hadn't already designed enough in Los Angeles, a committee headed by the Board of Supervisors and Hollywood film veteran Sol Lesser (who produced the original *Tarzan* franchise as well as several classic Westerns) chose the architect to create what the city considered the final piece in its cultural puzzle after the Music Center and LACMA. The concept: a $6.5-million showcase of film and television treasures from the world capital of entertainment. Numerous efforts to build such a museum had failed, but that didn't deter the team.

Upon signing a $76,000 contract, Pereira's firm drew a cluster of modernist boxes for Highland Avenue, just across from the Hollywood Bowl and down the hill from the proposed home for Cal Arts. First, inside what Pereira called "a solid structural mass" would be a motion-picture sound stage. Next to that, within what *Progressive Architecture* magazine described as "a series of large platforms suspended in a structural 'cage' of pre-stressed concrete," would be the principal exhibition and theater space. Last, a vertically oriented, solid cube, similar to the firm's office projects sprouting up all over town, would contain a library, offices, and an education center.

The project broke ground on October 20, 1963, before an audience of 5,000. Luminaries studded the guest list: Gene Autry, governor Edmund G. "Pat" Brown, Walt Disney, Lesser, Mary Pickford, Ronald Reagan, Rosalind Russell, Jack Warner, and the stars of *The Beverly Hillbillies*.

Inside the complex, Pereira said, the goal was "to dramatize the dramatists, to star them in their own epic." Using miniatures, process photography, and other special effects, numerous re-created film and television sets—such as a simulacrum of imperial Rome—would resemble Hollywood originals. Besides the working sound stage and television studio, the museum would sport a hall of fame, a wax museum, a 600-seat movie theater, electronic study rooms, and private screening rooms.

According to Pereira, the facility would be an "electronic wonderland," truly a house of curiosities. Animatronic celebrities would dispense tickets; there would be "television forests" containing row after row of working sets, a massive winding staircase tracing the history of film and television, and a blank, egg-shaped room made to show off sound technologies.

The story was typical Hollywood. The *Los Angeles Times* reported that over 90 people were hired and fired during the five-year history of the project. The budget ballooned from $6.5 million to $21 million, prompting several to nickname it a "Taj Mahal." County supervisor Kenneth Hahn weighed in, calling it a "white elephant" and a "shocking example of waste." The county eventually insisted on a new design to cut costs, which Pereira and the museum directors were reluctant to provide. Lesser resigned in 1965, dogged by questions about his leadership. Meanwhile, local opponents piled on. Said one resident, "To me, these people sound like the Pharaohs, eager to build a monument to themselves with the sweat of others." Such a

→ Museum with 101 Freeway and Capitol Records Building in background

sentiment, which deepened when the county seized homes on the site, was the final blow.

Or was it? Like a B-movie monster, the Hollywood Museum kept creeping back, only to stumble again into the grave—a plot played out against a backdrop of studio infighting, civic timidity, bureaucratic blockades, and financial woes. The list of dead museums could fill Hollywood Forever Cemetery: a Hollywood Hall of Fame above Griffith Park; an archive at Universal Studios; an installation within a renovated Pan Pacific Auditorium; a space within the Hollywood Masonic Temple; and a museum off Vine Street designed by Christian de Portzamparc. Debbie Reynolds—who exclaimed that “Hollywood without a museum is like a person without a heart”—pitched a project that had two death scenes, one in Tinseltown, the other in Pigeon Forge, Tennessee. Today, despite a new plan to put a museum inside the former May Company building on Wilshire Boulevard (will it happen?), the closest Hollywood has to an institution devoted to its legacy is the Hollywood Heritage Museum, a small, ramshackle operation located in a 1901 barn that was moved in 1983 to a site across the street from the Hollywood Bowl—the same parcel that Pereira’s museum was to have occupied.

←
"Cage" construction, with floor slabs supported by exterior pillars

↙
Movie set of classical city

→
Museumgoers admiring exhibits

→→
Cover of invitation to ground-breaking ceremony

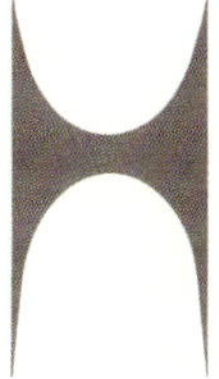

The Los Angeles County

HOLLYWOOD MUSEUM

Ground Breaking / October 20, 1963

BD

MC

PIERRE KOENIG
HOLLYWOOD MOSQUE

1963

It might have seemed an unlikely match, but Pierre Koenig, famous for his spare, flat-roof residences in Southern California, was the perfect architect to design a mosque for the center of Hollywood: After all, to paraphrase Mohammed, one must live a simple life, and adornment is a sin.

The Moslem Association of America commissioned Koenig to draft the mosque from funds promised by the Kuwaiti government. The precast-concrete structure, set with brick-infill walls, would be punctuated by a square, pencil-thin three-story minaret containing a passenger elevator. The mosque would have a perimeter colonnade shading a courtyard, where fountains would burble serenely in reflecting pools. Sliding solid and glass walls would provide flexibility, accommodating larger crowds and formal occasions. But the Kuwaiti funds never materialized, and the project never gained political support. It quickly died.

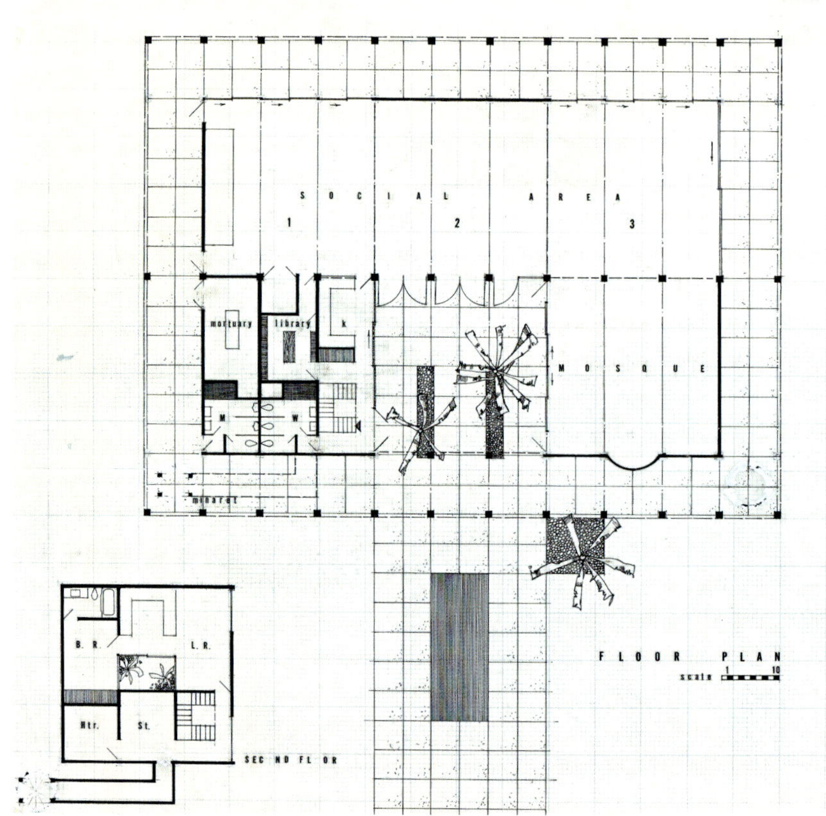

← Floor plan showing flexible indoor and outdoor spaces

→ Thin columns front entryway and support minaret.

KOENIG

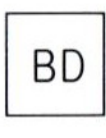

WS

WELTON BECKET CENTURY CITY THEME BUILDING

1963

A complex big enough to awe the Pharaohs.

Alcoa

When the Aluminum Company of America (Alcoa) purchased 260 acres of back lot from 20th Century Fox Studios, in 1961, it hired Welton Becket to create the master plan for Century City. Becket emerged with an ultramodern city within a city, described by its promoters as "a complex big enough to awe the Pharaohs." In all, 88 buildings were to have been scattered around Becket's never-to-be-built Theme Building—the centerpiece that would, Alcoa claimed, "make this a showcase for 20th Century American architecture."

The rolling hills were bulldozed and remolded, with tree-lined boulevards as wide as airport runways, most of them eventually punctuated by rows of office towers. The lineage, and transformation, was pure Le Corbusier towers-in-the-park.

To complete the picture, Becket, who had built his own headquarters adjacent to Century City before construction began, had wanted the Theme Building, a 50-story tower intended to be both a cultural center and a landmark, for the patch of land directly across the street from what would become the Century Plaza Hotel. In architectural renderer Carlos Diniz's images, it appeared as a shining beacon of light. Yet with its dorsal-like armor, it looked vaguely like something harnessed to the launch pad at Cape Canaveral. A tunnel beneath the Avenue of the Stars, which was eventually built, would connect the Theme Building and its cultural complex to the hotel, creating what the developer said would be "one of the liveliest spots in the world."

The project was put on hold, but Becket and Alcoa still entertained a desire to build the Theme Building until the architect's death, in 1969. Afterward, Century City, Inc., bought out Alcoa and abandoned Becket's original design. Charles Luckman updated Becket's master plan, but the Theme Building vanished forever from the renderings.

→ With protruding fins, Theme Building towers over Century City.

SB

KONRAD WACHSMANN
CALIFORNIA CITY CIVIC CENTER

1966–71

Nathan K. Mendelsohn, a Czech-born sociologist who taught at Columbia University before becoming a land speculator, incorporated California City in 1965. He'd seen the boom in the San Fernando Valley and thought he could amalgamate his grand theories about community development with his prospector's keen sense for turning a quick buck. He bought 82,000 acres near Edwards Air Force Base, in the Mojave Desert, and founded what would become the state's third-largest city in terms of area. Streets were laid out across its 186.5 square miles, while Mendelsohn dreamed of a metropolis to rival Los Angeles, with a population of 3 million, stocked with great industries, universities, shopping centers, banks, doctors, skyscrapers, and, of course, a civic center.

Enter Konrad Wachsmann. The adventurous Mendelsohn, to his credit, sought out the little-known architect, who'd made a lifelong career of exploring ways to put lightness and poetry into the mechanics of building. Wachsmann worked mostly in steel, figuring out how to build long-span structures whose roofs required little if any support.

Wachsmann's technically elaborate design for the civic center would have used high-tension cables strung between massive abutments to form a 192-foot-long floating roof. The 1.5-inch cables, each tensioned at 105,000 pounds, were secured by steel anchorages, able to resist a thrust of 1 million pounds. According to Wachsmann's calculations, the cables could resist winds of 100 miles per hour.

Ten roof panels, made of fiberglass and filled with urethane foam, would be stitched together using a neoprene expansion joint, forming a roof skin that was incredibly light yet strong. Wachsmann wrote that "the insertion of essentially unlimited variations of enclosed spaces" was possible under the open, plastic roof. Public and private spaces could be built, expanded, and rearranged as the city saw fit.

Did Mendelsohn hire Wachsmann as some kind of publicity stunt? The real estate speculator cut out in 1969, selling to Great Western United Corp., a Denver-based sugar and mining company, which in turn was swallowed by the Hunt Brothers of Texas. The city never took off, stranding Wachsmann's plan. California City today is a schematic, population 10,000, with badly paved roads slowly eroding into sand, leaving behind the traces of a roadmap to nowhere.

→ Model shows tensioned cables supporting floating roof.

→→ Clear-span roof frames view of mountains.

MC

JOHN LAUTNER
GRIFFITH PARK NATURE CENTER

1972–74

In September 1972, the Los Angeles Department of Recreation and Parks selected Lautner to design what would have been his highest-profile commission within the city limits. The Griffith Park Nature Center, located near the zoo, was surrounded by a sprawling, wooded camping retreat and the 22-acre Pecan Grove picnic area. The center, a welcome and exhibition outpost, measured 14,000 square feet and was set for completion in 1974, its $790,000 price tag covered by state bonds.

Lautner first envisioned the center being dug into a huge earthen mound, accessible by zigzagging underground ramps. But that was just early doodling. His final plan, projecting off the top of a hill, was a three-pronged building whose thin, steel-reinforced, concrete shell “wings” would cantilever 40 feet from its central core. Sloped glazing along the flanks allowed natural light to pour inside.

Perched on the hillside, the building looked like a bird spreading its arched concrete-and-glass wings. “That was his great inspiration: nature. And the way nature designs,” pointed out Helena Arahuete, an associate at Lautner’s office from 1971 until the architect’s death in 1994.

Inside, park offices and an auditorium would be clad in a Bouquet Canyon Stone veneer, an appropriate motif for the idyllic site. Exhibition rooms would contain a scale model of the park and other nature-inspired presentations. Graphic artist John Follis, who designed the Disney logo, signed on to assist with the displays.

While initially funded, the project unraveled during the 1973 oil crisis, which sent construction costs sky-high and kept the county from supporting the inventive scheme. County representatives insisted that Lautner abandon his thin concrete roof structure to cut costs, but the architect refused. The county eventually decided on a prosaic building, which opened in 1981.

→
Nature center nestled into idyllic setting

GRIFFITH PARK NATURE CENTER
DEPARTMENT OF RECREATION & PARKS – CITY OF LOS ANGELES, CALIFORNIA
JOHN LAUTNER ARCHITECT F.A.I.A.

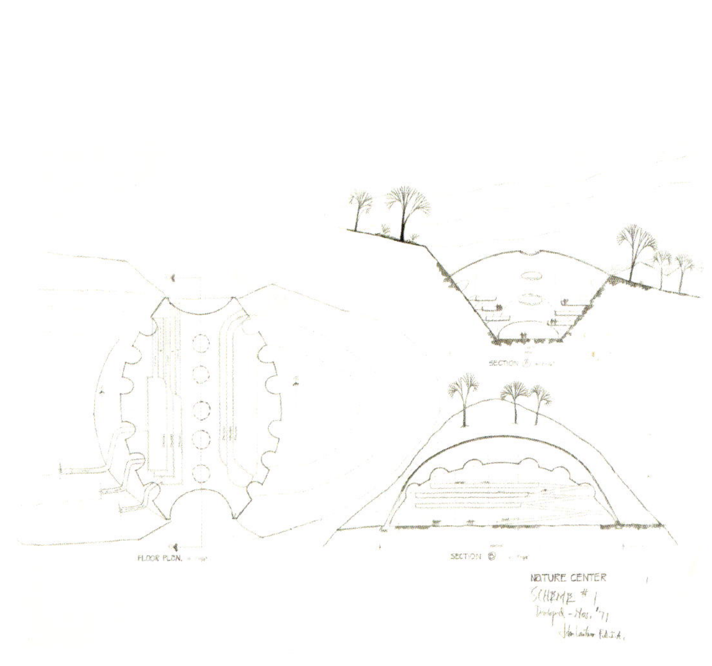

SECTION
FLOOR PLAN
SECTION
NATURE CENTER
SCHEME # 1

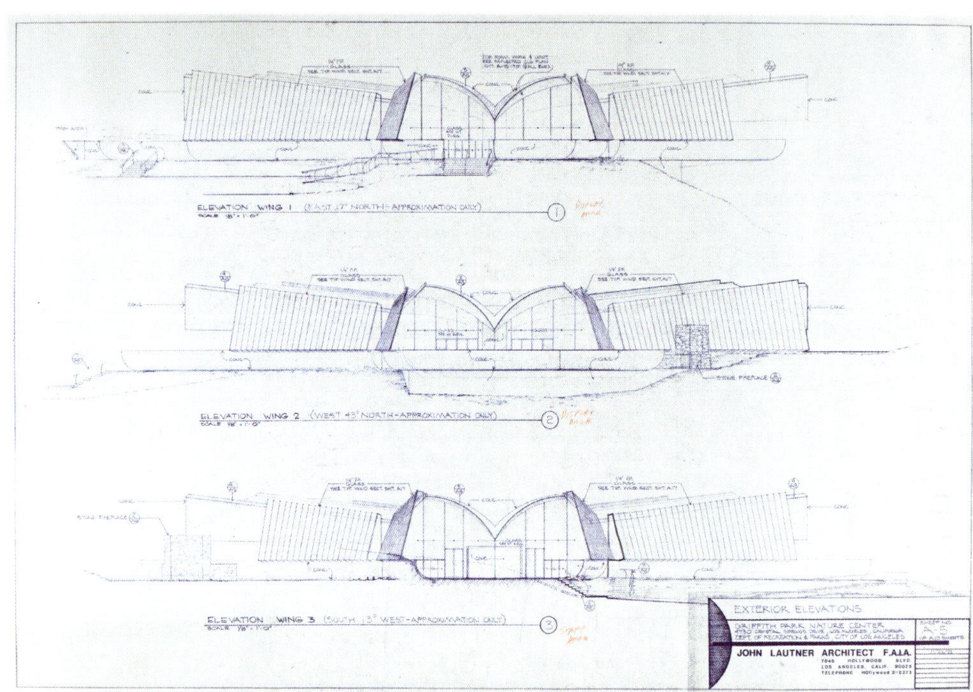

ELEVATION WING 1 (EAST 17° NORTH - APPROXIMATION ONLY)
ELEVATION WING 2 (WEST 43° NORTH - APPROXIMATION ONLY)
ELEVATION WING 3 (SOUTH 13° WEST - APPROXIMATION ONLY)
EXTERIOR ELEVATIONS
GRIFFITH PARK NATURE CENTER
DEPT. OF RECREATION & PARKS, CITY OF LOS ANGELES
A-5
JOHN LAUTNER ARCHITECT F.A.I.A.
7046 HOLLYWOOD BLVD.
LOS ANGELES, CALIF. 90028

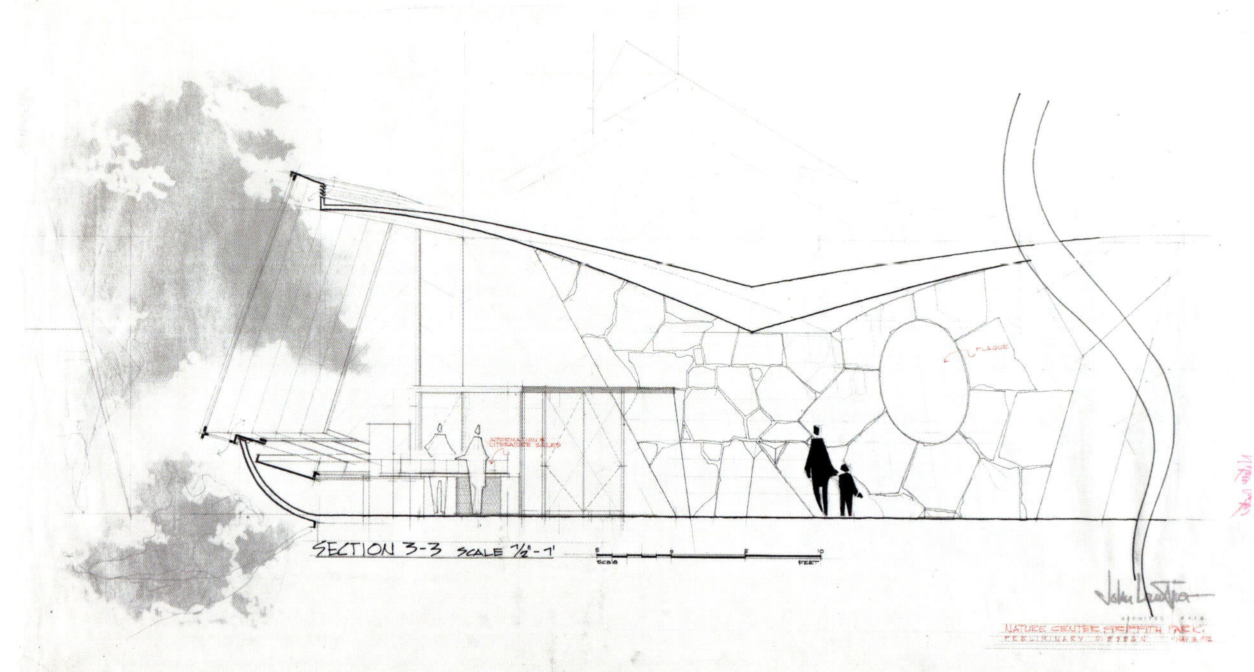

PLAQUE
SECTION 3-3 SCALE ½"-1'

↖↖
Early version, dug into hillside

↖
Blueprint of winged concrete roof and angled glass walls

←
Exhibition space

→
Painting reveals how building is inspired by land and sky.

BD

WS

ANTHONY LUMSDEN
BEVERLY HILLS HOTEL

1973

Anthony Lumsden, a master at sculpting curving glass walls and evoking shifting tectonics, devised an eight-story, 450-room hotel for the corner of Wilshire and Santa Monica boulevards. The cube-shaped building, with its sleek, silver mirrored-glass skin, shifted dramatically in complexity below its raised lobby. At that point, the structure terraced down in long, extruded horizontal cylinders, revealing different functions beneath—meeting rooms, restaurants, a lobby, and a cocktail lounge. The building's varied, fragmented base was highly reminiscent of another perhaps overambitious unbuilt Lumsden project: his rippling Lugano Convention Center in the Swiss Alps. The plan for the hotel was abandoned, and the site became home to I. M. Pei's CAA Building—itself abandoned in 2007 when the talent agency moved into larger headquarters in Century City.

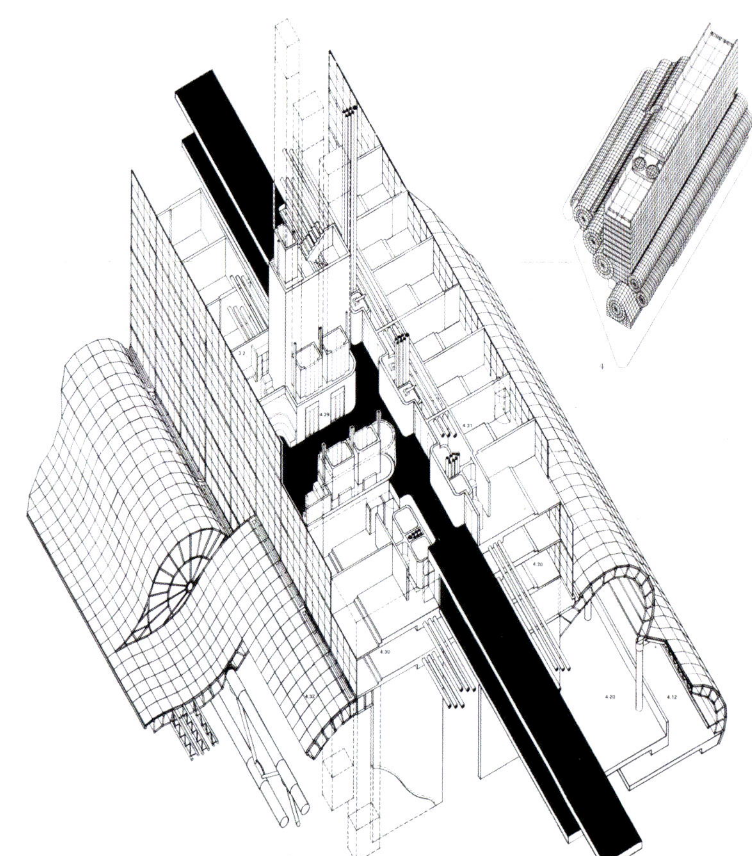

← Cutaways reveal where square tower meets rounded base.

→ Horizontal cylinders seem to roll off building's edge.

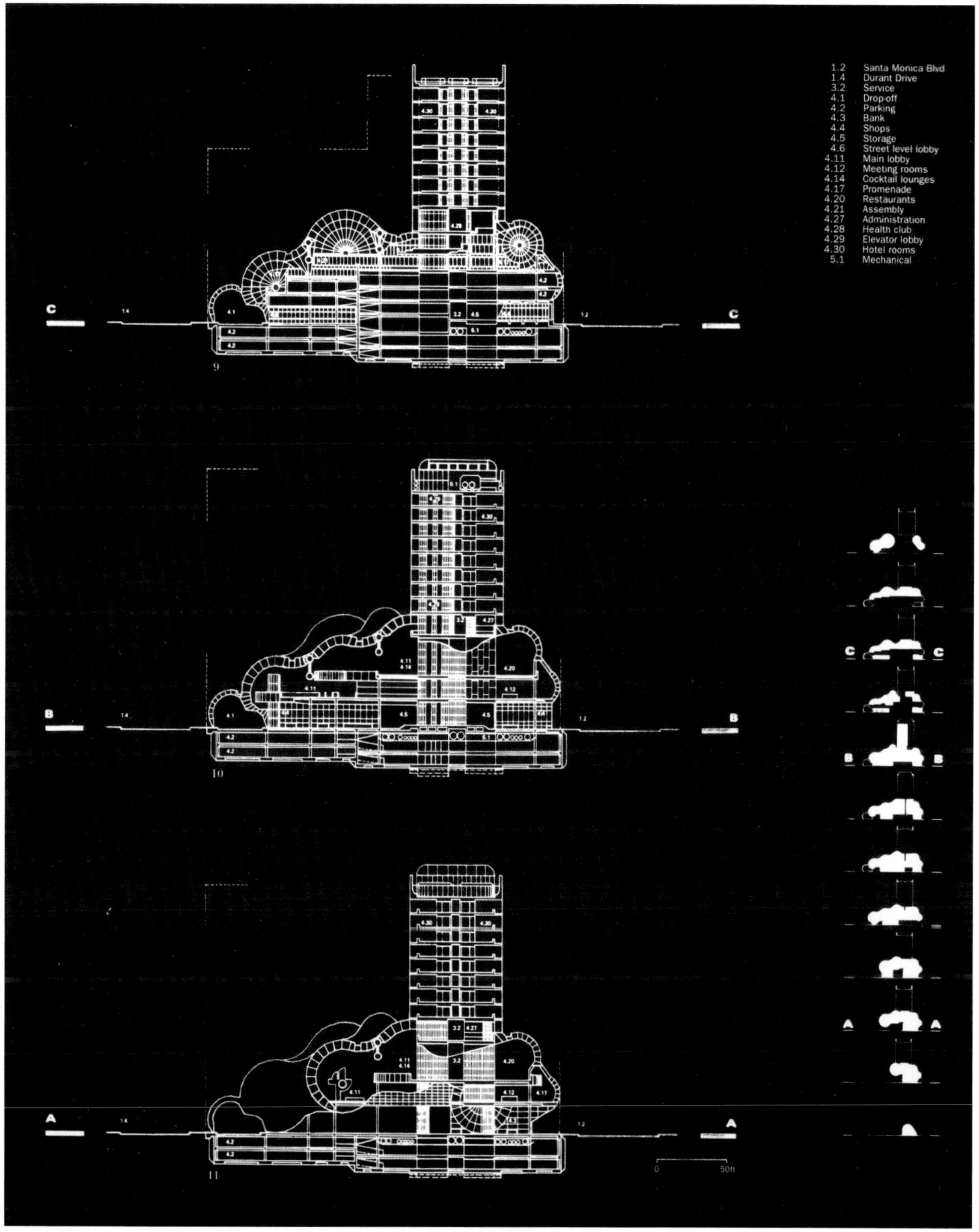

1.2 Santa Monica Blvd
1.4 Durant Drive
3.2 Service
4.1 Drop-off
4.2 Parking
4.3 Bank
4.4 Shops
4.5 Storage
4.6 Street level lobby
4.11 Main lobby
4.12 Meeting rooms
4.14 Cocktail lounges
4.17 Promenade
4.20 Restaurants
4.21 Assembly
4.27 Administration
4.28 Health club
4.29 Elevator lobby
4.30 Hotel rooms
5.1 Mechanical

9

10

11

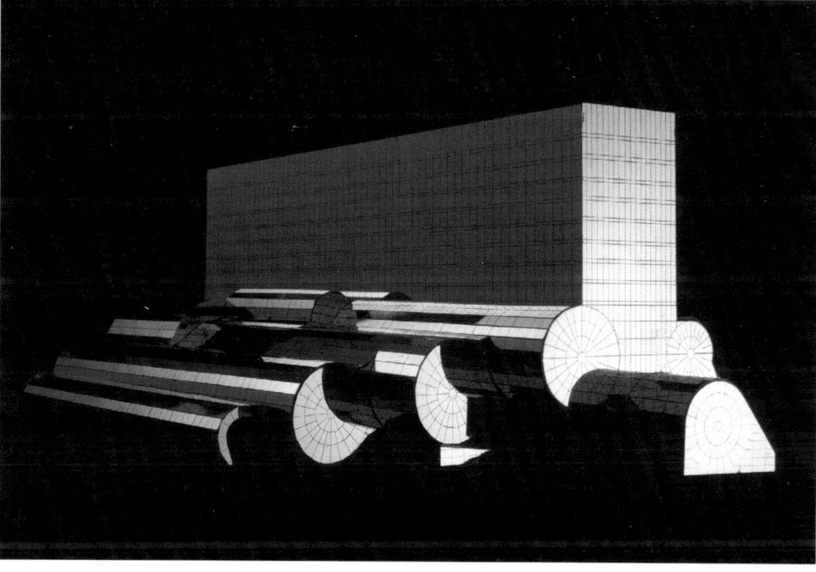

CHARLES LUCKMAN, BARTON MYERS, AND I. M. PEI
LOS ANGELES CENTRAL LIBRARY EXPANSION PLANS

1974–82

The historic central library building may instead be altered so dramatically that its value as a cultural and architectural landmark is diminished.

John Pastier

Timing is everything. Charles Luckman had recently endured nationwide revulsion for replacing New York's exquisite Beaux-Arts Penn Station with the oppressive Madison Square Garden. Now, he was hired to develop a blueprint for revamping another sensitive site: Bertram Goodhue's beloved Art Deco–style Los Angeles Central Library (1926).

Luckman was a pragmatist, not a preservationist. As he once told the *New Yorker*: "I am firm in my belief that architecture is a business and not an art."

Aware that the '20s building had become inefficient and cramped, library officials considered replacing their home altogether. A feasibility study examined 23 possible sites, including Pershing Square, Bunker Hill, and the library's existing location at Fifth and Flower streets, downtown. Luckman estimated the cost of building anew at over $83 million. He was hired, instead, to develop a much cheaper $38-million restoration of the original building, increasing shelf space by 86 percent (from 1.3 million volumes to 2.4 million), and almost doubling the usable area.

Luckman proposed appending wide, single-story modernist boxes to the library's east and west sides, and digging a level of reading and shelving space belowground with two levels of parking below that. Inside, the architect would renovate everything from floors, walls, and ceilings to heating and electrical systems. An open bank of escalators, descending from the library's fresco-covered rotunda, would unite the expanded project, while light wells would illuminate the belowground stacks.

Even though he had recently called the structure "a lousy library," Luckman said the new architecture would defer to the original building. "The low-level additions will incorporate materials and colors to make the total complex look as if it had been constructed at the same time," the architect said. In a memo to the city council, he predicted that his planned improvements would serve the library "to about the year 2000."

Landscaping would surround more than 60 percent of the site, "creating a garden oasis," according to a press release from the firm. The plan also called for open plazas, with fountains reminiscent of New York's Lincoln Center. The improvements, noted Luckman, would create a "ripple effect," spurring other development in what was a fairly depressed area.

The city council approved the expansion on June 21, 1977, opting to finance the project with Community Redevelopment Agency funds. But public opinion soon began to sour, inflamed by the furor over Penn Station. In favor of Luckman's plan, predictably, were editorial boards and public officials. Arrayed against, perhaps just as predictably, were citizens, historians, journalists, and the American Institute of Architects (AIA), which wanted all additions to be underground. "The historic central library building may instead be altered so dramatically that its value as a cultural and architectural landmark is diminished," noted critic John Pastier in *New West* magazine. Luckman, who

→ Luckman's west wing fronted by large plaza with fountain

filed a libel suit against the magazine, eventually said he was "tired of being a scapegoat."

This controversy—and a persistent parade of complaints that included a fight over Luckman's right to design the building—stalled the project. By 1979, rising costs, the city's dwindling budget, and officials' recurring ambivalence caused the city council to reverse course. Out of the battle arose a vital preservationist movement: the Los Angeles Conservancy.

In 1981, Maguire Partners and architect Barton Myers proposed an underground expansion of the library to the east. Topped with a staggered plaza resembling a shallow Aztec mound, the project would be naturally lit by a large pyramid inside a glass cube, which Myers claims inspired I. M. Pei's Louvre Pyramid a year later. To the west, Pei himself and developer Arco proposed a Museum of the Southwest, another underground structure, this one topped by a circular plaza bisected by a multilevel park. In 1993, the library was finally renovated by Hardy Holtzman Pfeiffer. As per the AIA's earlier wishes, the expansion proceeded underground and the library facade was left unobstructed. Once completed, Hardy Holtzman's bombastic, derivative addition was derided across the city.

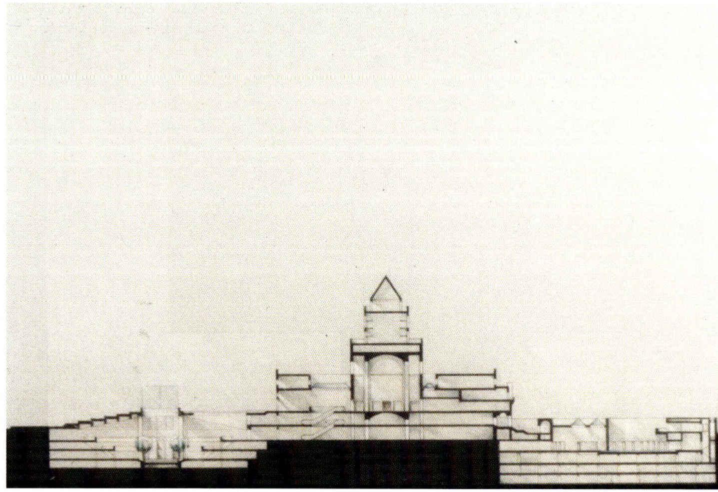

←
In Luckman's scheme, open escalator unites rotunda with newly added floors below.

↙
Section showing depth of the two new wings underground: Myers's library expansion on left, Pei's museum on right

→
Pei's Museum of the Southwest (top); Myers's library (bottom)

↗↗
Inside Myers's subterranean addition

→→
Myers's stepped plaza with central glass pyramid

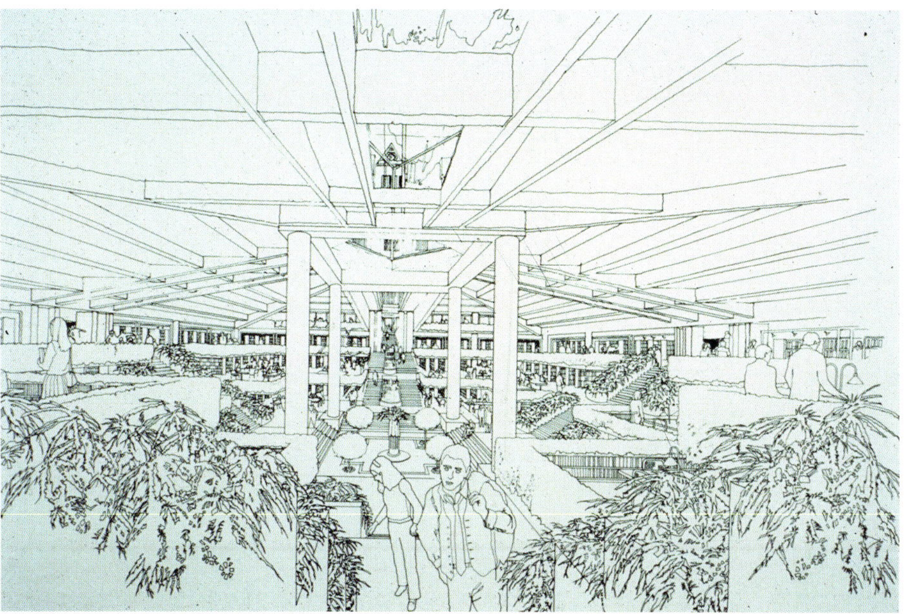

STUDIO WORKS
VENICE INTERARTS

1982

In 1979, the city of Los Angeles announced plans to tear down the old Venice City Hall and jail to make way for a new library. The buildings were home to a cluster of upstart arts groups: the literary center Beyond Baroque; Los Angeles Theater Works; and the artists and muralists of the Social and Public Art Resource Center (SPARC). Threatened with eviction, the groups turned to Studio Works, the team of Robert Mangurian and Craig Hodgetts, who devised an alternative. The architects proposed renovating the buildings into offices and artists' workshops, while constructing two theaters, one with 99 seats, the other with 500, and a 250-foot-long mural space. They positioned the library prominently along Venice Boulevard's median strip—a former right-of-way for the abandoned Red Car light-rail system that served Southern California until the 1950s—and connected it to the arts cluster by a bridge. A courtyard, formed by the new buildings and the old jail, would become an outdoor gathering and reception area.

The idea, which won a *Progressive Architecture* design citation in 1983, used the library to define the fourth side of the plaza, evoking an Italian city square. Because Venice Boulevard was—and is—a speedway, having the buildings face each other would have carved out a welcome public arena.

This touch of Renaissance city planning was carried through in the library design. Mangurian and Hodgetts—opponents of the then-prevailing taste for postmodernist pastiche—conceived a building that reinterpreted the Italian Renaissance commitment to proportion, symmetry, and geometry. They sketched a long, narrow structure divided in two by a low tower. One wing housed the library beneath a continuous, clear-span skylight, topped by a low-slung metal roof that was a tribute to the tiled roofs of Italy. The other wing was a tube whose cutout radius formed a vault that echoed the Laurentian Library in Florence.

The exterior, meanwhile, was composed of evenly spaced columns that defined bays filled with well-proportioned windows, lintels, and corbels. The overall effect would have been a concise reprise of classical architecture seen through modern eyes.

Despite lobbying hard, the nonprofit arts groups failed in their library bid, although they managed to save the old City Hall and jail from demolition. The city council member representing Venice wanted to hire a marquee architect and so gave the assignment to Michael Graves. The result was a postmodern library situated a half-mile west along the median and standing alone, an advertisement for itself and the memory of its civic-minded, unbuilt rival.

→ Bridge over Venice Boulevard connects library to plaza and arts center.

→→ View across new plaza

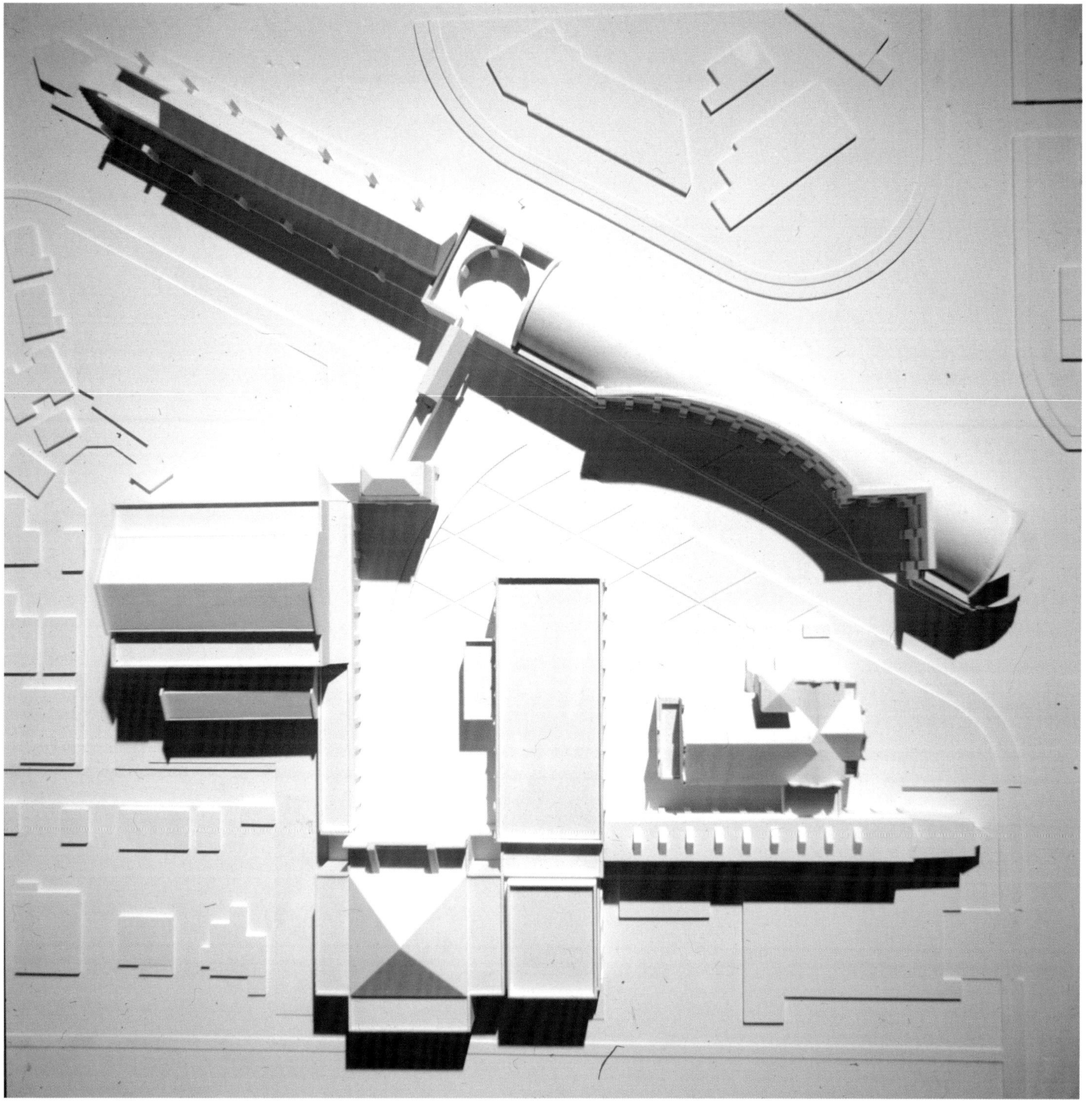

BD

SB

PETER EISENMAN UNIVERSITY ART MUSEUM, CALIFORNIA STATE UNIVERSITY AT LONG BEACH

1986

A specialist in creating theoretical and theatrical storylines for his projects, Eisenman considered the University Art Museum, set on a grassy, undulating 23-acre arboretum site next to Cal State Long Beach, more of an "archaeological artifact" than a building.

His idea was to base the T-shaped building and its landscape on the superimposition of several maps, modeling the site's geography, history, and topography. Inspirations included the ranch that once occupied the site; local oil derricks; the massive Rainbow Pier that once arced beyond the Long Beach shoreline; overlapping fault lines that helped form the local coast; the canalization of the Los Angeles River near the site; and the gridded division of property in the area.

The collision of these inspirations resulted in a building filled with overlapping planes and irregularly shaped geometries, sometimes dug into the land, which itself was terraced, sculpted, and curved to merge with the building's cacophony.

The 67,500-square-foot building would contain four exhibition galleries, a black-box theater, an auditorium, a cafe, conference rooms, a library, offices, and storage and preparation spaces. It would even include a life-size re-creation of an oil derrick and a curved walkway evoking the Rainbow Pier. Outside were sculpture courtyards, botanical gardens, and a two-acre pond. An elevated passageway would slice through and above the museum, linking it to the arboretum. In 1987, Stephen Horn, president of the Long Beach campus, abruptly resigned, and construction was immediately abandoned.

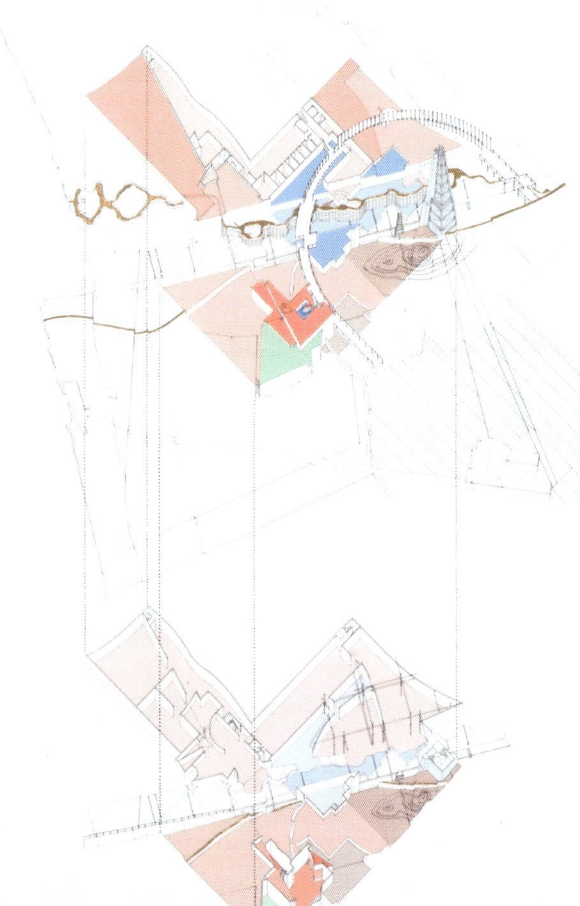

← "Archaeological artifacts" falling into place

→ Oil derrick and pier dominate sculpted museum grounds.

DT

MURPHY/JAHN
CIVIC CENTER PLAZA

1987

I wanted to see something like you would see in Los Angeles in the year 2000.

Raffi Cohen

Helmut Jahn's 21-story, $125-million Civic Center Plaza office complex was to be located on the site of the earthquake-damaged Los Angeles State Building, smack in the heart of the city.

Jahn's design, set back from First Street to leave room for a large plaza, would be clad with a grid of diagonal steel cross-bracing. The H-shaped building resembled two towers linked by a bridge or one broad edifice pierced by a 12-story opening. The project formed an impressive entryway to the plaza, connecting Broadway to Spring Street on axis with City Hall. Topping the building was a four-story steel-frame pyramid, echoing the ziggurat-like pinnacle of that Art Deco landmark. The shape was again employed in the glass-and-steel food kiosks dotting the project's retail arcade.

"I wanted to see something like you would see in Los Angeles in the year 2000," said developer Raffi Cohen, whose vision for the 4.5 acre site included a futuristic complex containing offices and ground-level retail.

Cohen, a wealthy Israeli-American who enjoyed recounting how he immigrated to the United States as a pauper, made his fortune as a developer in the San Fernando Valley. But with this project and his nearby Figueroa Plaza, designed by Ellerbe Becket, he made a firm commitment to downtown. When the commercial office market tanked, the Civic Center Plaza died. Ironically, Cohen's current company, Galaxy Holding, today develops properties primarily outside of the city center.

→
Pyramid atop 12-story atrium echoes City Hall crown (background, right)

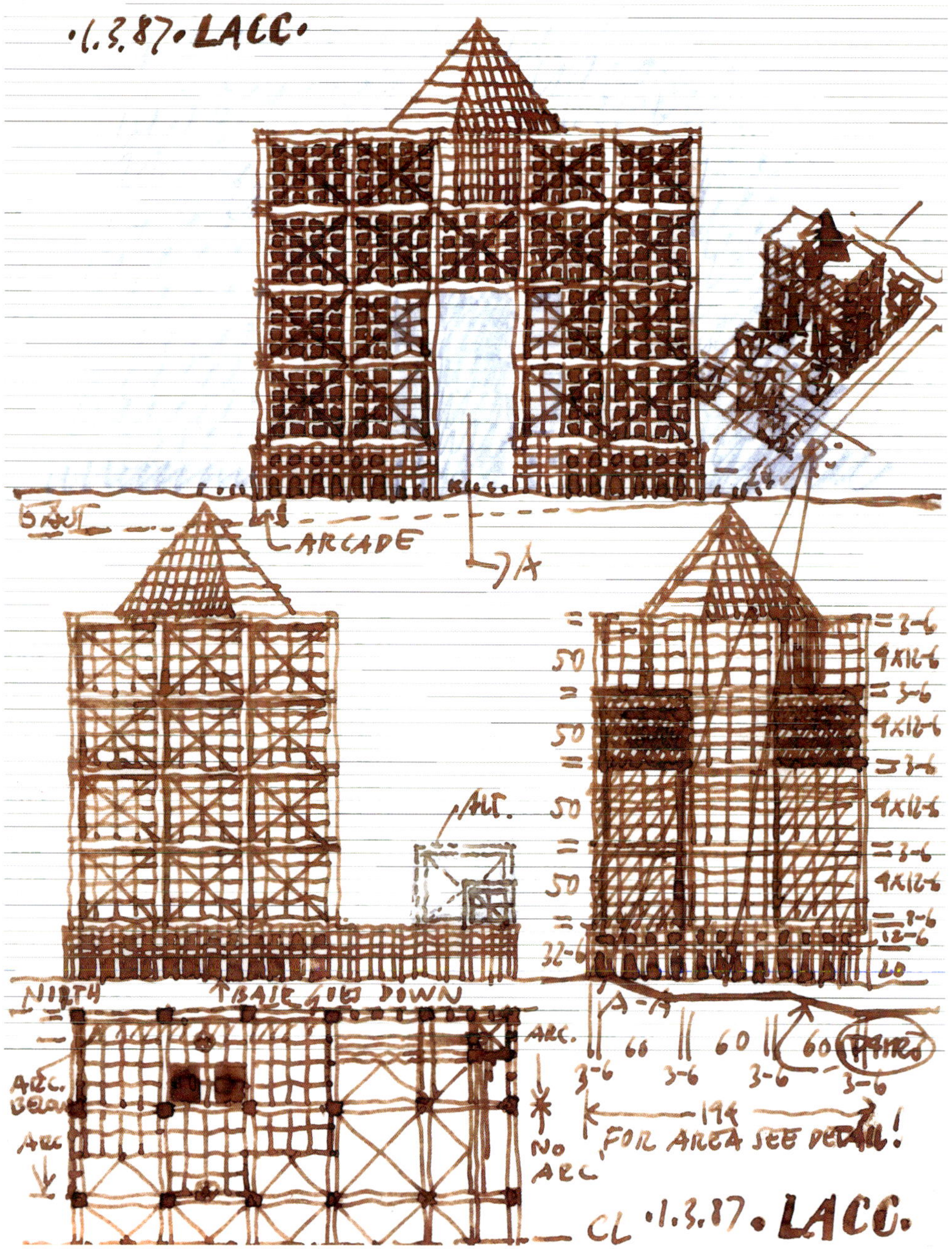

←← Ink sketch hashing out scale and proportion

← Drawing of building elevations and view through arcade

→ New Civic Center Plaza building sits between City Hall and Law Library.

→→ Close-up of model reveals bridge linking two buildings.

↘↘ Grid expressed in steel and glass

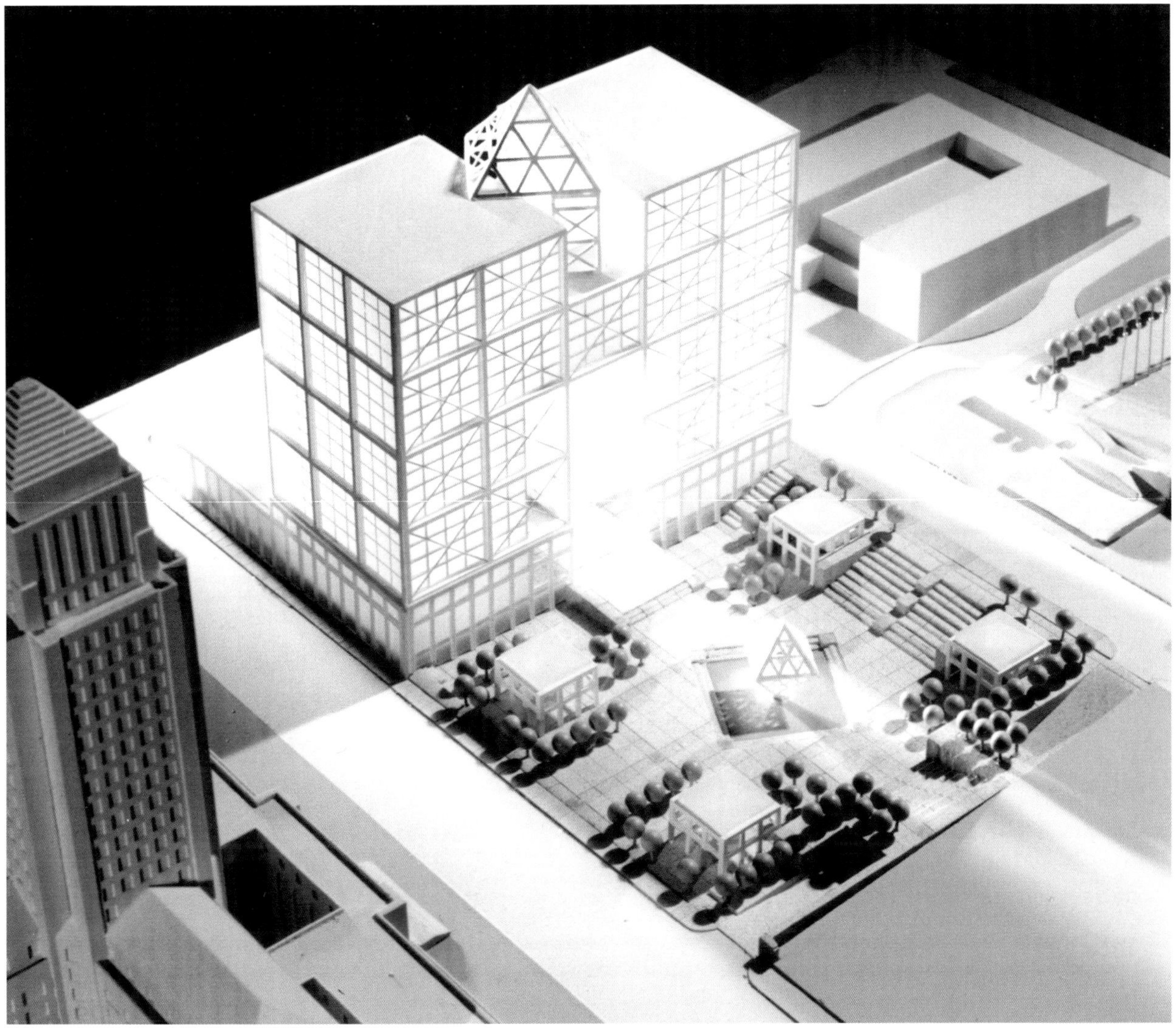

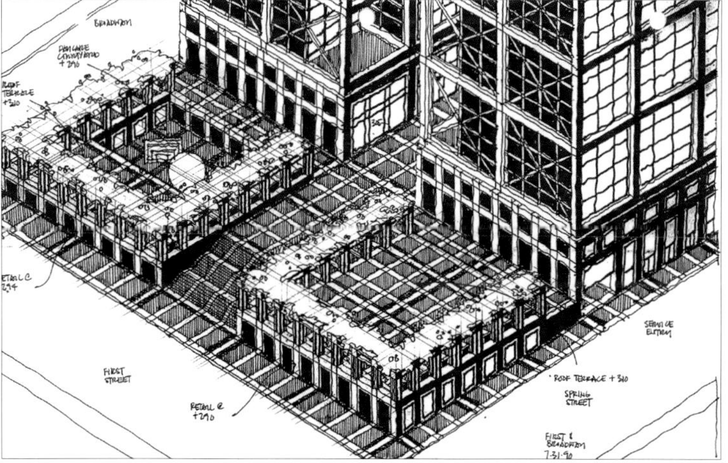
FIRST STREET
RETAIL B
+290
ROOF TERRACE + 310
SPRING STREET
FIRST & BROADWAY
7-31-90

JOHNSON FAIN
TRUMP TOWER

1989

In 1989, when he acquired the 24-acre site of the landmark Ambassador Hotel, Donald Trump boasted that he was going to spend a billion dollars putting up the world's tallest building. Besting competition designs by A. C. Martin and Skidmore, Owings & Merrill (SOM), Johnson Fain developed a tapering 148-story office tower with a braced-steel exoskeleton and gold-colored glazing. The project also included a large mixed-use component at street level with retail, a large hotel, and public open space.

SOM had presented a soaring, 125-story white obelisk crowned with a porkpie hat, a tower that would have loomed over its surroundings like a sequoia in a pygmy forest. A. C. Martin had proposed a hotel-condo-and-office complex set around a circular plaza, topped with two diamond shapes: "When I told Ivana that the basis of the idea was to put two diamonds together, she lit up," remembers A. C. Martin's David Martin. "I think they were divorced a week later."

In 2001, after a 12-year courtroom battle over the property, the Los Angeles Unified School District wrested control from Trump and other developers, who had managed to collect $76.5 million in public money. The hotel and its glamorous Cocoanut Grove nightclub were demolished by the school district in 2005. Five years later, the district opened the Robert F. Kennedy Community Schools to commemorate the site where the presidential hopeful was assassinated shortly after midnight on June 5, 1968.

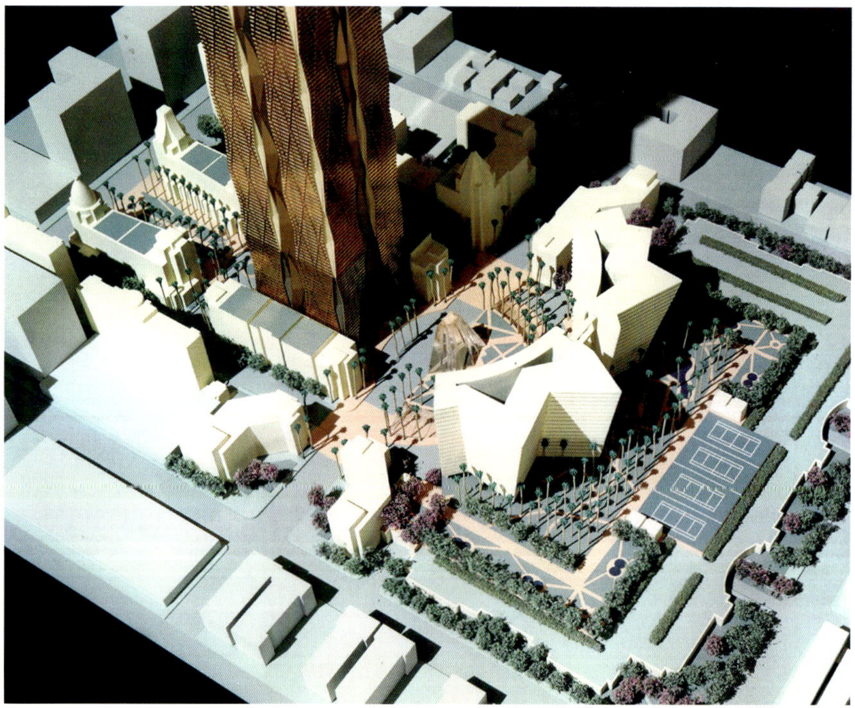

← Golden cladding and diamond reliefs emphasize towering height.

→ Gardens and buildings around world's tallest skyscraper

DANIEL, MANN, JOHNSON AND MENDENHALL (DMJM)
AMBASSADOR INTERNATIONAL

1957

DMJM had been hired to reconfigure and replace the venerated Ambassador Hotel, with its world-famous Cocoanut Grove nightclub (designed by Paul Williams). The firm proposed to engulf the 1920s hotel in a streamlined 32-story tower surrounded by a cluster of sleek, modern steel-and-glass high-rises. The hotel would have disappeared beneath a rambling deck covering the lobby and a convention hall/ballroom (capacity 2,500). Cars would have crossed a wide plaza to reach a porte-cochere deep inside the grounds. A lake would have separated the new structures from the hotel, which slowly declined for another 30 years, until it closed in 1989.

DT

MICHAEL GRAVES
METROPOLIS

1990

It's going to strangle the city.

Marvin Braude

Michael Graves's Metropolis was one of the earliest efforts to bring megascale development to a downtown slowly making its way back after decades of decline. Postmodern master Graves beat out Chicago firm Murphy/Jahn and Australian architect John Andrews for the $650-million project, which consisted of 4.4 million square feet of hotel, office, and residential towers looming above parking, retail, and a cultural center in the shadow of the Harbor Freeway. The eclectic site, which was anchored by a long, thin public plaza, would showcase Graves's colorful masonry, splashy geometries, and simplified historical references.

Metropolis would be built in several phases over about 10 years. Its two southernmost office towers, identical in design and both rising 28 stories, would create a visual entryway to downtown for motorists on the freeway. The central plaza, which contained a tree-lined garden court, an amphitheater, and a cultural center, would form a public corridor between what would later become the Staples Center to the south and the heart of the downtown business district to the north.

Several city council members strongly opposed the gargantuan, freeway-adjacent project, fretting most of all about traffic. "It's going to strangle the city," councilman Marvin Braude said. While it garnered enough votes in the council, Metropolis could not survive the crippled early '90s economy. Beaten by the recession, the owner, City Center Development, decided to sell the property. The project briefly resurfaced in the mid-aughts, only to succumb to yet another recession.

→ Postmodern exterior resembles, among other things, Legos and a player-piano scroll.

→→ Five buildings surround a courtyard.

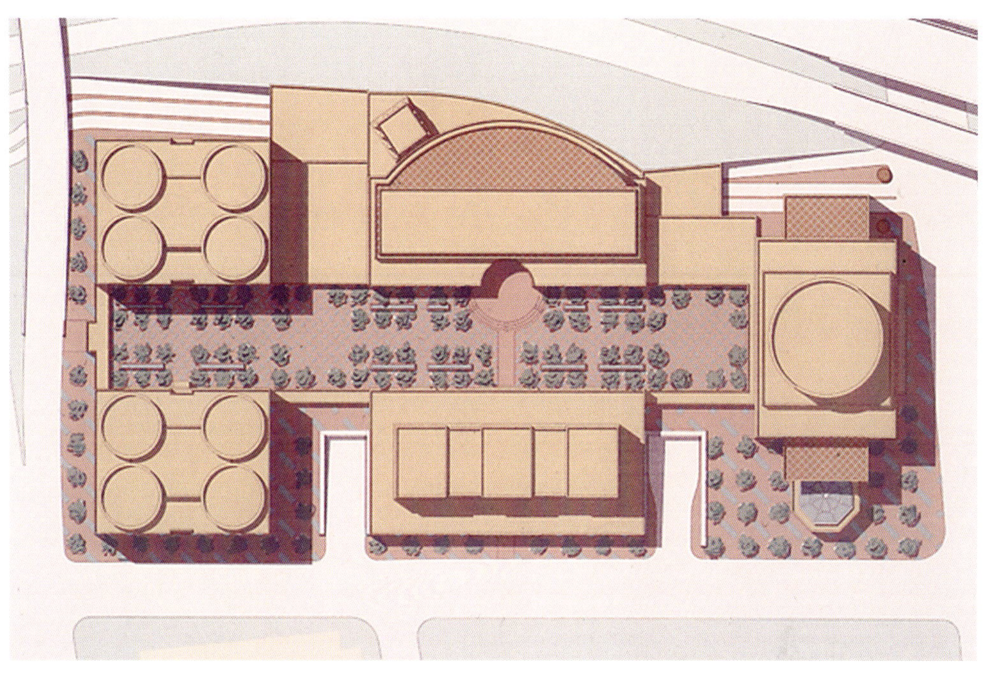

DT

FRANK GEHRY
LOS ANGELES RAPID TRANSIT DISTRICT (RTD) HEADQUARTERS

1991

→
Years before Bilbao, an undulating metal exterior wraps a bulky tower.

→→
Site model shows half a dozen new buildings behind Union Station.

The front page of the August 1991 issue of *Headway*, the newsletter of the Southern California Rapid Transit District (RTD), featured a photo of Samuel Morales, winner of the district's annual Bus Roadeo driving-skills competition, sticking out of the sunroof of a minibus. Meanwhile, buried on page 18 came the important news: The Orange County firm McLarend Vasquez and Partners had been chosen by the Catellus Development Corporation, owners of L.A.'s Union Station and the land around it, to design the 26-story, 595,000-square-foot RTD headquarters.

The announcement did not hide the fact that the building would become the focal point of downtown construction north of the Harbor Freeway. But what the district omitted from its newsletter was that McLarend Vasquez had beaten out none other than Frank Gehry and Cesar Pelli for the job. The winner, said Catellus, had demonstrated the "strongest overall response to the project's needs and requirements...having worked on major projects comparable in size and scope to the RTD headquarters." As has been the case with much of the city's public-realm architecture, caution trounced risk. The result: one of the least notable high-rises in Los Angeles.

Gehry's proposal, by contrast, would have been an unfolding skyscraper wrapped in a metallic skin. Its base would have had flanks flapping like trousers in the wind, while its pinnacle would have looked like a jester's cap tousled into three riotous towers. Conceived more than 10 years before Walt Disney Concert Hall, it would have been the most adventurous building in a skyline that sorely lacked brio.

SB

MOORE RUBLE YUDELL
SUNLAW POWER PLANT

1997

They weren't tastemakers. They were energy guys used to getting their hands dirty. But they wanted to do something unique.

James Mary O'Connor

Hoping to capitalize on a newly deregulated electricity market and showcase its clean-energy technologies, the relatively unknown Sunlaw Energy Corporation proposed an 810-megawatt, natural-gas-fired power plant in Vernon, a largely Hispanic city southeast of downtown Los Angeles.

To help sell the unlikely prospect—and to celebrate the $450-million scheme instead of camouflaging it—the company hired local architects Moore Ruble Yudell. Blending history and myth, the firm sought inspiration from, among other sources, Vladimir Tatlin's Constructivist *Monument to the Third International* (also never built). The architects also looked at Watts Towers, Simon Rodia's iconic assemblage of found materials.

In the final design, two leaning elliptical cylinders encasing the cooling towers were juxtaposed against a sweeping steel-mesh canopy that covered the plant itself. This composition not only united the plant's smokestacks, power generators, and scrubbers in one building but also created a kinetic view from the 710 Freeway. The leaning towers would be clad with LED-embedded glass, programmed to display messages about the plant to freeway drivers speeding by. Designed as a kit, the project could be reproduced and assembled anywhere in the country.

Moore Ruble Yudell principal James Mary O'Connor was amazed that Sunlaw was willing to pursue the ambitious design. "They weren't tastemakers," he recounted. "They were energy guys used to getting their hands dirty. But they wanted to do something unique."

Local environmentalists, citizens, and officials denounced the project because of its potentially harmful emissions. The firm dropped the plan in 2001. As O'Connor remembered: "They received so much negativity that they just went away and started building plants the way they normally build them."

→ Power plant faces freeway.

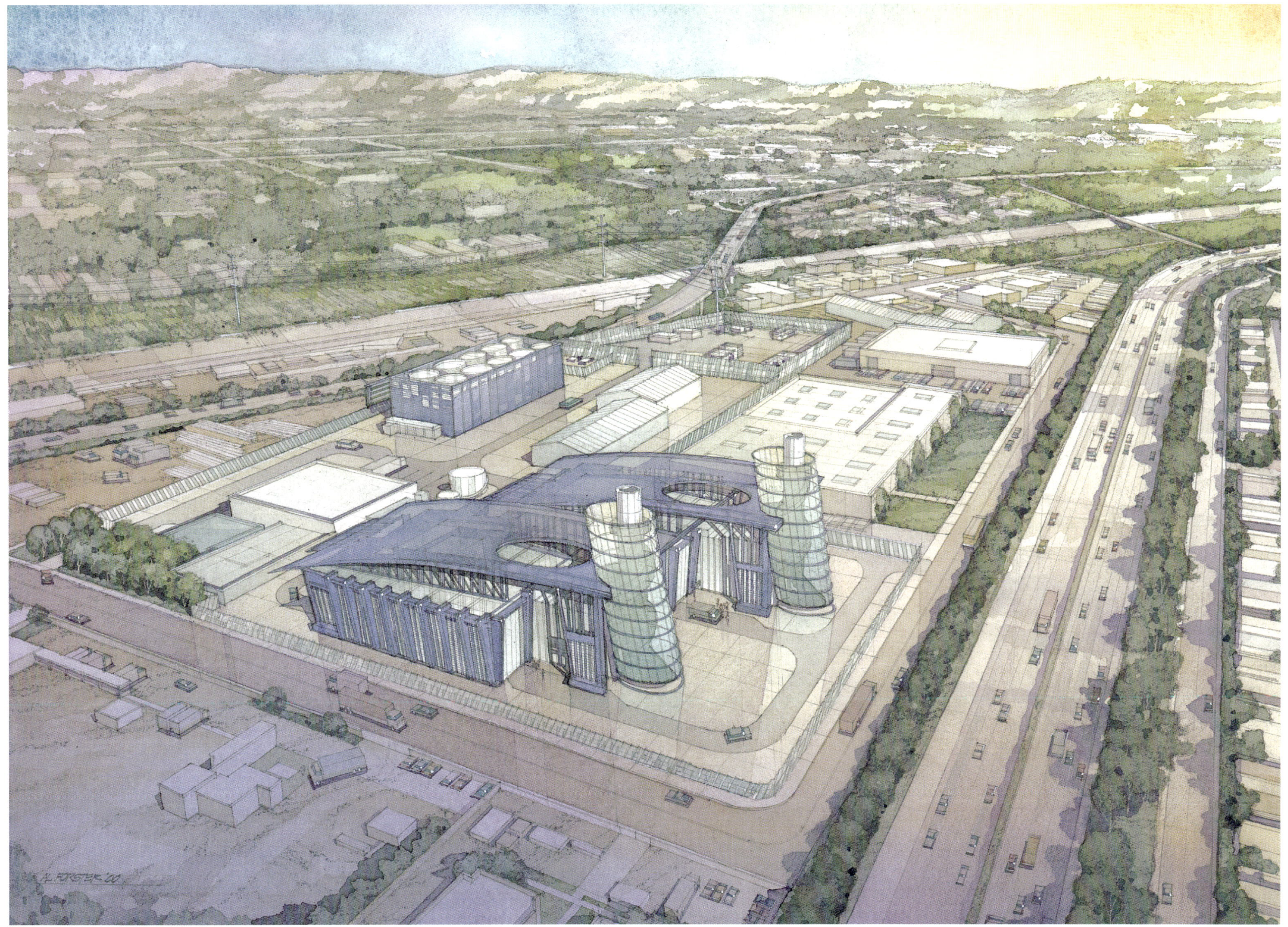

BD

MC

OFFICE FOR METROPOLITAN ARCHITECTURE (OMA) LACMA

2001

We discovered that a consolidated LACMA could...create a sense of coherence... that this museum has lacked for decades. Any other approach would exacerbate its problems.

Rem Koolhaas

Over a span of four decades, LACMA had emerged, in its own words, as "a disconnected and disorienting experience for the public." William Pereira's original 1965 design—the result of a compromise that passed over architectural heavyweights Ludwig Mies van der Rohe, Eero Saarinen, and Edward Durell Stone—had become a stylistic hodgepodge of unwieldy additions.

The Office for Metropolitan Architecture (OMA), famous for its radical solutions to some of architecture's most difficult problems, proposed to undo what it called LACMA's "continental" separation of jumbled and disconnected buildings.

The firm's solution: tear down the museum's Ahmanson, Anderson, Bing, and Hammer buildings, leaving only the Bruce Goff-designed Pavilion for Japanese Art and the landmarked former May Company building. Next, out of this tabula rasa, create a unified system of horizontal layers, with exhibition spaces stacked above a large plaza. OMA founder Rem Koolhaas, with a wink, called this his "Miesean plaza."

The architect, rejecting the notion that art should be displayed chronologically or geographically, created a more fluid floor plan. Epochs, regions, and movements could be accessed via diagonals slicing through the layers and across floor planes. Visitors—and curators—would be forced to confront art in a completely different, more dynamic manner.

Focusing on "transparency and uplift," the firm designed a translucent, pillowed roof made of the plasticlike polymers ETFE and PTFE for the new building, supported by a grid of cables on steel stilts spanning the entire museum floor.

"We discovered that a consolidated LACMA could perform more efficiently, expend less money on renovation, open up more of the park to the city, and create a sense of coherence and the much-needed presence that this museum has lacked for decades. Any other approach would only exacerbate its problems," said Koolhaas.

"I'm exhilarated that [the architects] took the leap to energize and transform the museum so dramatically and profoundly," commented former MOCA curator Elizabeth A. T. Smith, echoing a common art-world sentiment that the plan, while painful, would have benefited the museum. But OMA's brash makeover elicited a severe backlash, for both its $200-million price tag and scorched-earth approach.

The museum, facing budget shortages and nervous donors, abandoned the design. The ghosts of Mies, Saarinen, and Stone continued to haunt the museum as, once again, LACMA was unable to hire a world-class architect.

→ OMA's translucent roof puts all of LACMA under a single lid.

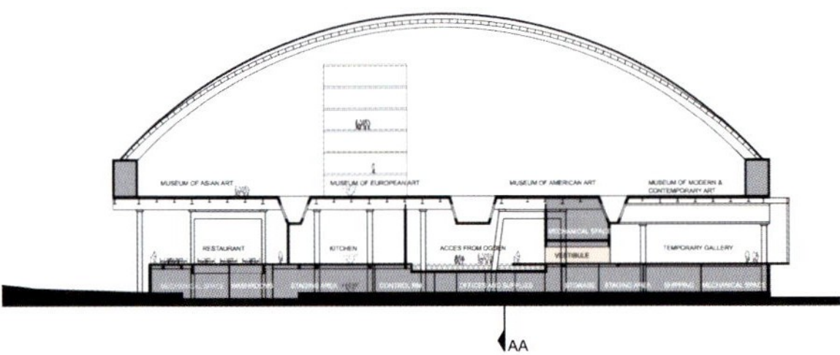

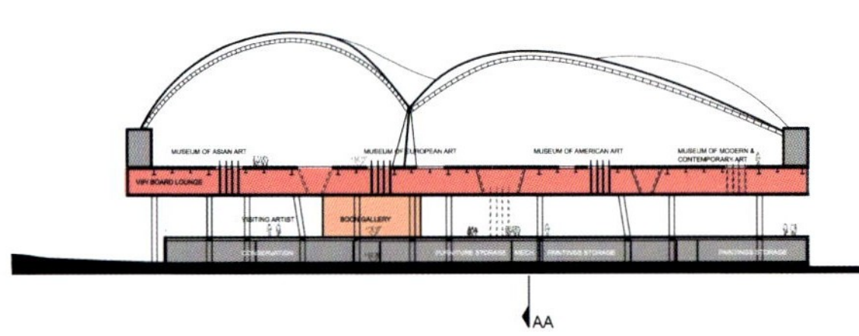

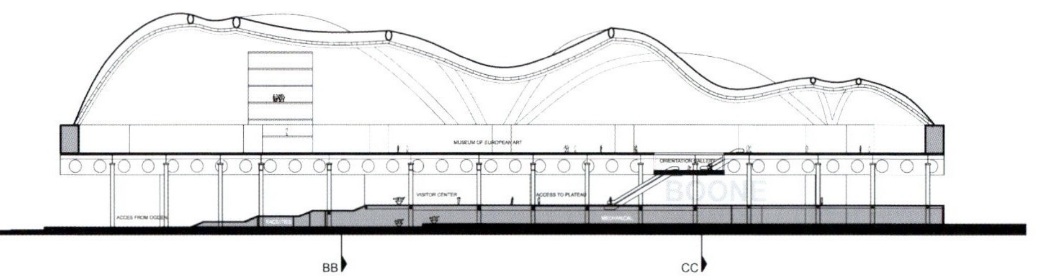

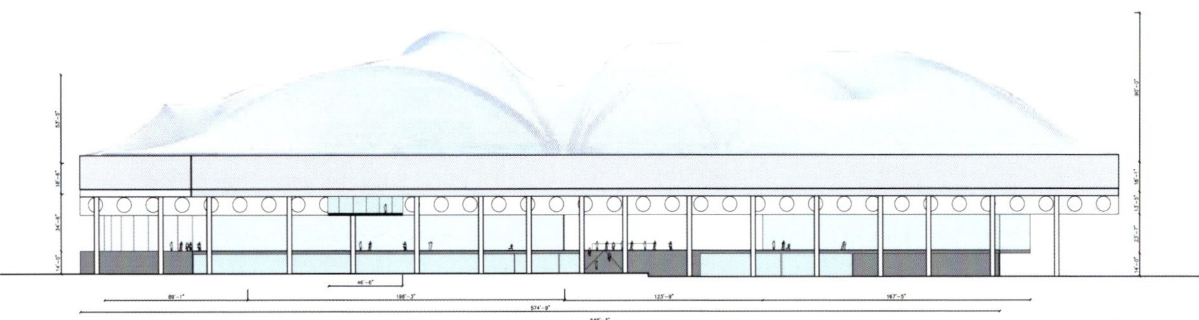

←
Slices through museum show roof puckering and dimpling.

↗
Crosshatched cables support lightweight roof.

→
Art displayed in a fluid fashion

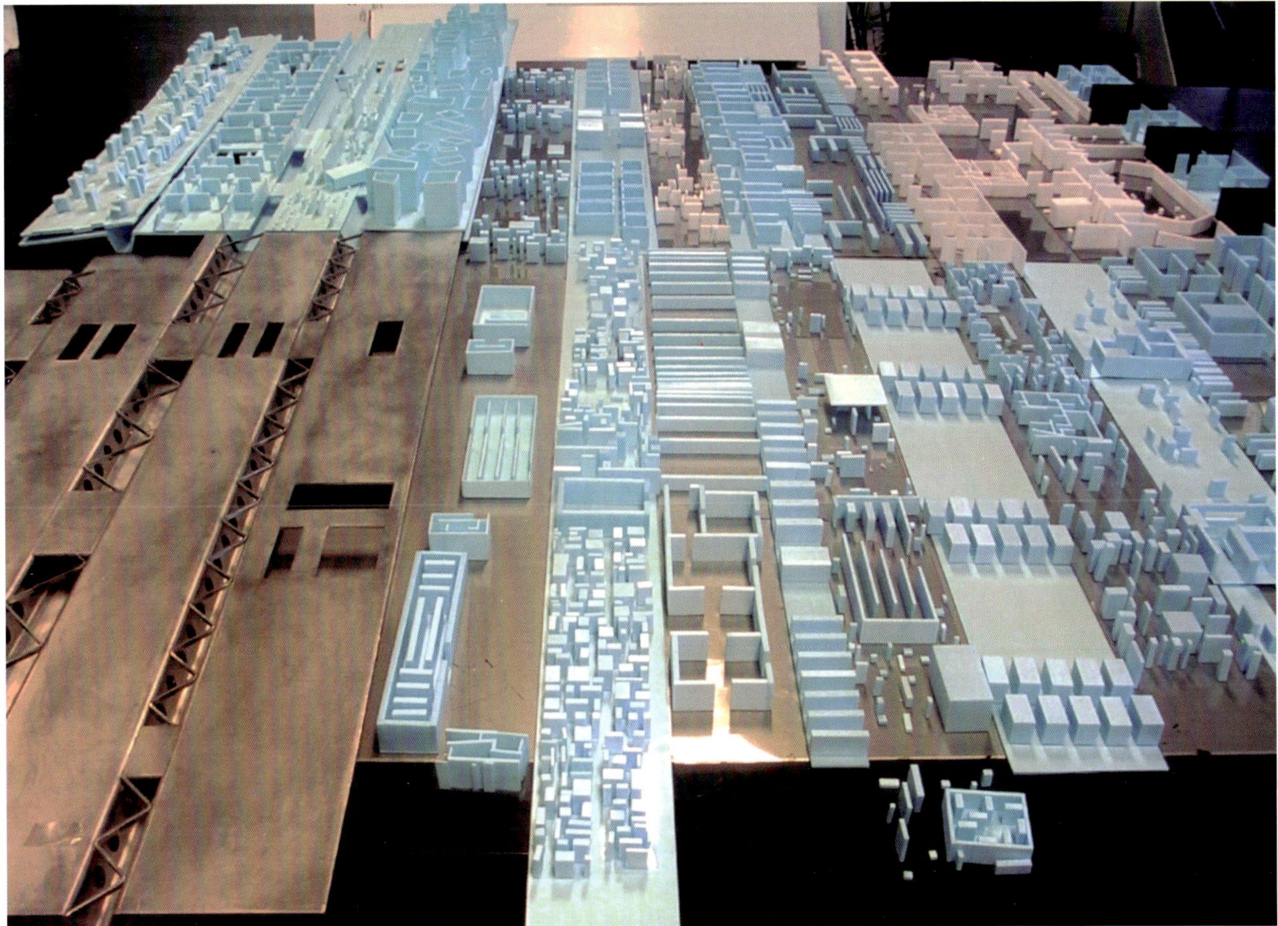

SPF:A
6006 WILSHIRE BOULEVARD

2006

Commissioned by LACMA, 6006 Wilshire was designed primarily to contain overflow art storage for the Broad Contemporary Art Museum (BCAM), the Renzo Piano-designed building inaugurated by billionaire philanthropist Eli Broad. There would be gallery space as well as a residential mini-tower facing Wilshire Boulevard. This was when property values were still red hot and LACMA and Broad were still friends. Shortly thereafter, in late 2006, real estate plummeted, Broad and LACMA started feuding, and the project died an acrimonious death.

DT

STEVEN HOLL NATURAL HISTORY MUSEUM TRANSFORMATION

2002

Despite its beautiful 1913 Beaux-Arts core, the Natural History Museum of Los Angeles—with its mismatched additions, brutalist facade, and less-than-ideal siting at the edge of Exposition Park—has long suffered from a lack of connection to its neighborhood and a lack of interest among city dwellers.

In 2002, to remedy the situation, an invited international competition was held. New York architect Steven Holl won with a proposal that combined landscape, urbanism, and architecture in a single, $200- to $300-million package.

To help unify the museum, Holl would strip away the unfinished exterior of its 1927 addition. An L-shaped building, the *Los Angeles Times* reported, "would slip over the halls like a sleeve," extending to the west and flanking the museum's existing south lawn. The new structure would feature a glassy Mobius-strip tower (containing a restaurant that Holl nicknamed the Observatory of Life on Earth), a glazed main lobby with its own plaza, a planted roof, a sizable reflecting pool, and a large "science garden" showcasing outdoor exhibits. The building would open to the surrounding park and neighborhood with multiple entries and clear pathways.

When the museum failed to secure the land for the science garden and plaza, the architects updated their plan, making the building itself the botanical and public spaces. The roof garden would now slope down in tilted segments from top floor to ground level, creating a new arena for outdoor learning and strolling. The main entry would be clad with a faceted wall of angled structural glass pieces and fronted with a patinated copper canopy projecting toward the park. Many of the museum's exterior walls would be covered in vines.

Inside, the museum would be completely rethought. An open-ended, nonlinear format would guide visitors past large digital projections merged with displays of original specimens in an "open and flexible architecture." Large, amorphous courtyards, known as "spiracles" (a scientific term for animals' respiratory openings), would become focal points, organizing both the collection and the building. On the roof, visitors could gaze at the city from a cafe wrapped in floor-to-ceiling glass.

There would be no forgetting this museum—until it perished from a lack of fundraising and a surfeit of internal strife. While the board of trustees promised to raise the seed money to keep the project on track, it never did. "The museum fizzled," as Steven Holl principal Chris McVoy put it. "We kept trying to check in. We eventually stopped trying because nothing was happening."

→ New entry with dramatic cantilever and green wall facing reconfigured park grounds

NATURAL
HISTORY
MUSEUM
OF
LOS
ANGELES
COUNTY

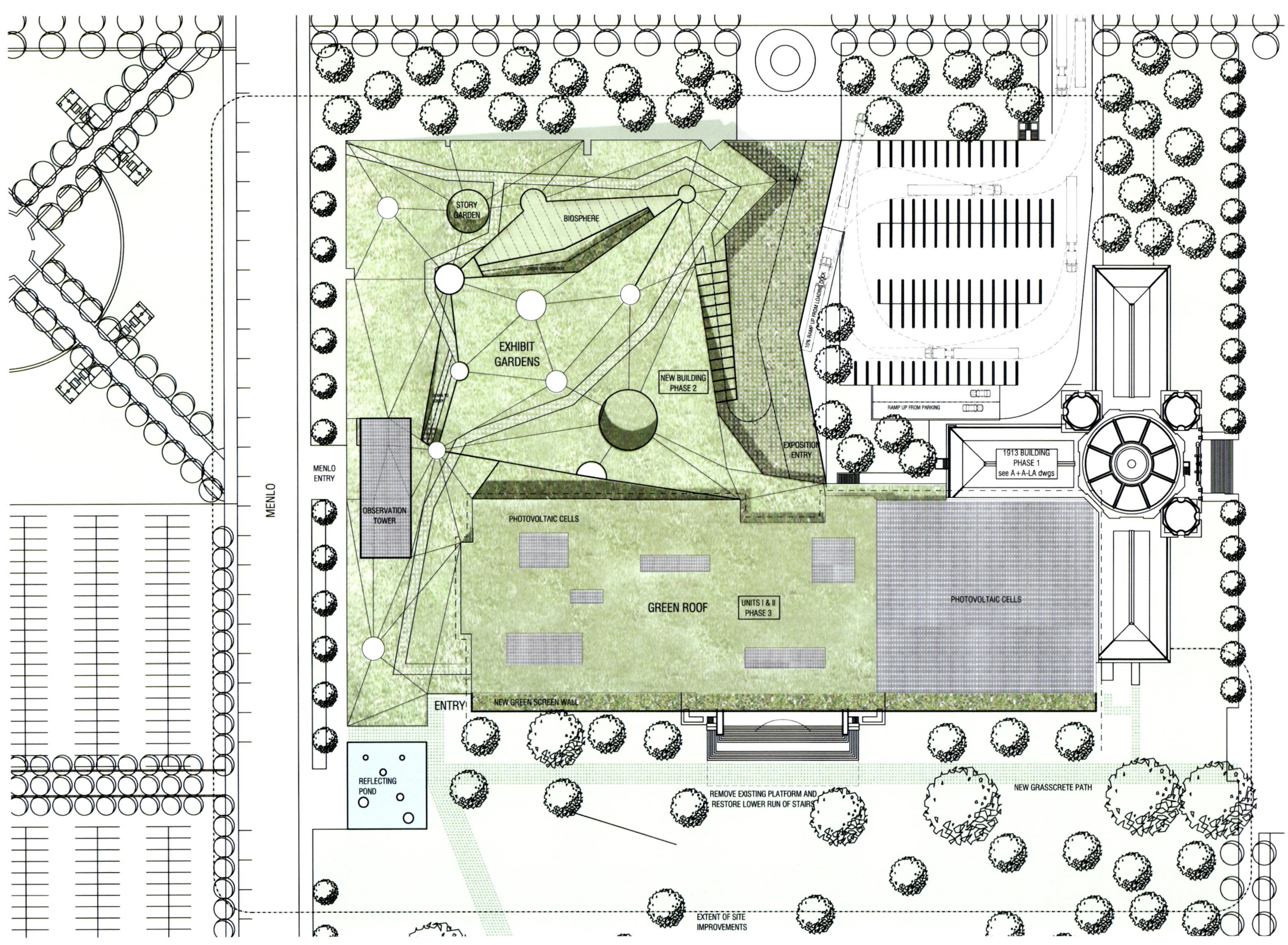
STORY GARDEN
BIOSPHERE
EXHIBIT GARDENS
NEW BUILDING PHASE 2
10% RAMP UP FROM LOADING DOCK
RAMP UP FROM PARKING
EXPOSITION ENTRY
1913 BUILDING PHASE 1 see A+A-LA dwgs
MENLO ENTRY
MENLO
OBSERVATION TOWER
PHOTOVOLTAIC CELLS
GREEN ROOF
UNITS I & II PHASE 3
PHOTOVOLTAIC CELLS
ENTRY
NEW GREEN SCREEN WALL
REFLECTING POND
REMOVE EXISTING PLATFORM AND RESTORE LOWER RUN OF STAIRS
NEW GRASSCRETE PATH
EXTENT OF SITE IMPROVEMENTS

←
New gardens and courtyards, on roof and at ground level

↗
Green roof ramps to ground level

→
Watercolor of Mobius tower

→→
Clerestory windows bring natural light to interior

KEATING/KHANG
PETERSEN MUSEUM

2002

The Petersen Automotive Museum resides at a critical intersection. Wilshire and Fairfax is more than a spot where the city's vertical downtown meets an important north-south axis. The corner is a cultural and architectural convergence. The landmark May Company building, by A. C. Martin and Samuel Marx, anchors the corner with its gold Art Deco pylon. LACMA is just up the block. Wilshire Boulevard, lined with art galleries, also features the La Brea Tar Pits.

The original structure was designed by Welton Becket in 1962 as the Japanese department store Seibu, which had glass elevators, a Japanese garden, and a glass-pavilion rooftop restaurant. Over the decades, the building had faded and suffered a botched renovation, which blacked out the Wilshire facade and turned its back to the street. So it seemed fitting that the automotive museum might want a makeover.

Richard Keating's approach was to open the building back up. He moved the escalators to the small triangular piece of land at the corner of Wilshire and Fairfax and added a looping, continuous pedestrian ramp set in a glass-wrapped atrium at the structure's northern edge—an homage to the curved face of the May building. The new walkway would have allowed visitors to move through the cars on display and then up or down ramps to other levels while peering over Wilshire Boulevard.

The entire Wilshire side of the building would be a wall of glass protected by a scrim of gridded metal. A new ballroom and exhibition space on the fourth floor would have a sinuous balcony, curving around the corner to offer spectacular city views. Extended escalators would reach all floors, and a glassed-in automobile lift would rise through the middle of the newly configured interior.

Keating's design would have transformed not only the building but also the corner and, conceivably, the boulevard. Light and open, it would have animated what, sadly, remains a somber zone dominated by an impenetrable wall camouflaging a major cultural institution.

→
Solid box becomes glassy white lantern.

Petersen
AUTOMOTIVE MUSEUM
MILLION DOLLAR CARS AT PETERSEN AUTOMOTIVE MUSEUM
TERSEN AUTOMOTIVE MUSEUM

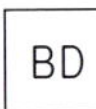

DT

COOP HIMMELB(L)AU
SKY-ARC

2005

A horizontal force field—a loose field of public spaces catering to culture, arts and entertainment.

Wolf Prix

The high-flying real estate firm Meruelo Maddux Properties owned a large, open piece of land next to the Southern California Institute of Architecture (SCI-Arc) at the former Santa Fe Freight Yard, in the Arts District east of Los Angeles City Hall. Then the largest landlord in downtown, the firm wanted to take advantage of its neighbor's edgy reputation by commissioning a piece of edgy architecture. It got more than it bargained for by hiring a provocateur like Coop Himmelb(l)au founder Wolf Prix.

Ignoring the client's admonition against building towers, Prix offered two pairs of them. One pair was made up of single helixes. The other, more dramatic, was linked by what the architect called "the drop," a bridge extending beyond the buildings' walls via a deck that appeared to float in thin air. Slung from the bridge between the skyscrapers was a sagging, elliptical paraboloid dangling 700 feet above the ground. The drop would contain restaurants, a pool, a terrace, and a bar. "This area offers views to downtown Los Angeles and across the entire city," the Himmelb(l)au team said. "As a reformulation of the shape of an 'ARC' the drop and the two towers give the new development its name and identity—SKY-ARC—while offering the city a highly visible symbol of the importance of culture and the arts."

The 36-story towers were flexible spaces that could become hotel rooms, offices, or housing for 1,000 people. At the base was an eight-story village of terraced lofts—some with 20-foot ceilings—which resembled aisles of stacked shipping containers that had inadvertently shifted. To ensure that SCI-Arc, located next door in a two-story, quarter-mile-long building, did not disappear behind the newly created skyline, a large public space was cut into the center of the project. Called the SCI-Arc Plaza, it was to be the school's front door and a backyard for students. The centerpiece was a peanut-shaped sculpture, similar to Anish Kapoor's *Cloud Gate* in Chicago's Millennium Park, meant to ooze over the edge of a 40-foot-high plinth, like an overstuffed Slinky descending stairs. This spot alone would cover some 300,000 square feet.

Prix called the graduated buildings "a horizontal force field—a loose field of public spaces catering to culture, arts and entertainment." But the developer balked. With smirks and shudders, the dangling bridge was compared to a jockstrap. The project, undertaken as a way to abort a bitter lawsuit pitting Meruelo against the architecture school, came to be viewed by the developer as no more than agitprop. The bottom line: Meruelo Maddux never took the design seriously, and the $50,000 cost of the outlandish drawings was a write-off. The site remains barren.

→
Shiny towers and stacked boxes preside over new plaza.

SB

JOHN FRIEDMAN ALICE KIMM ARCHITECTS
MIRA

2006

The brainchild of Chinese businessman Jason Kim—and a sign of escalating Chinese ambition on U.S. shores—MIRA (named after the giant, pulsating red star) was the perfect roadside development. A 2-million-square-foot international trade center in Santa Ana, the building would stretch along the 55 Freeway, its seven-story, 2,000-foot-long south facade serving as a giant billboard advertising new products through bright graphics.

Typical of Chinese developments, which lean heavily on architectural symbolism, the project's shape and texture were inspired by the koi fish. The "head" was to accommodate the main entrance, an auditorium, a conference center, and a narrow, glass-and-steel, twisting corridor to transport visitors via escalator from the ground to rooftop gardens and restaurants. (The green roof would also support photovoltaic panels and several windmills.) The "spine" was made up of 600 back-to-back showrooms punctuated by freestanding conference pods and gathering spaces; a perforated metal skin and gigantic skylights would provide natural light and views. Finally, the "tail" would feature a three-level exhibition space.

Like so many other daring projects of its time, MIRA could not survive the economic downturn of the late aughts. Kim's company, First California Equity Group, put the project on hold and eventually the real estate transaction collapsed.

← Long balconies shape interior courtyard, where curving glass corridor transports visitors to upper floors.

→ Fishlike form topped with wind turbines

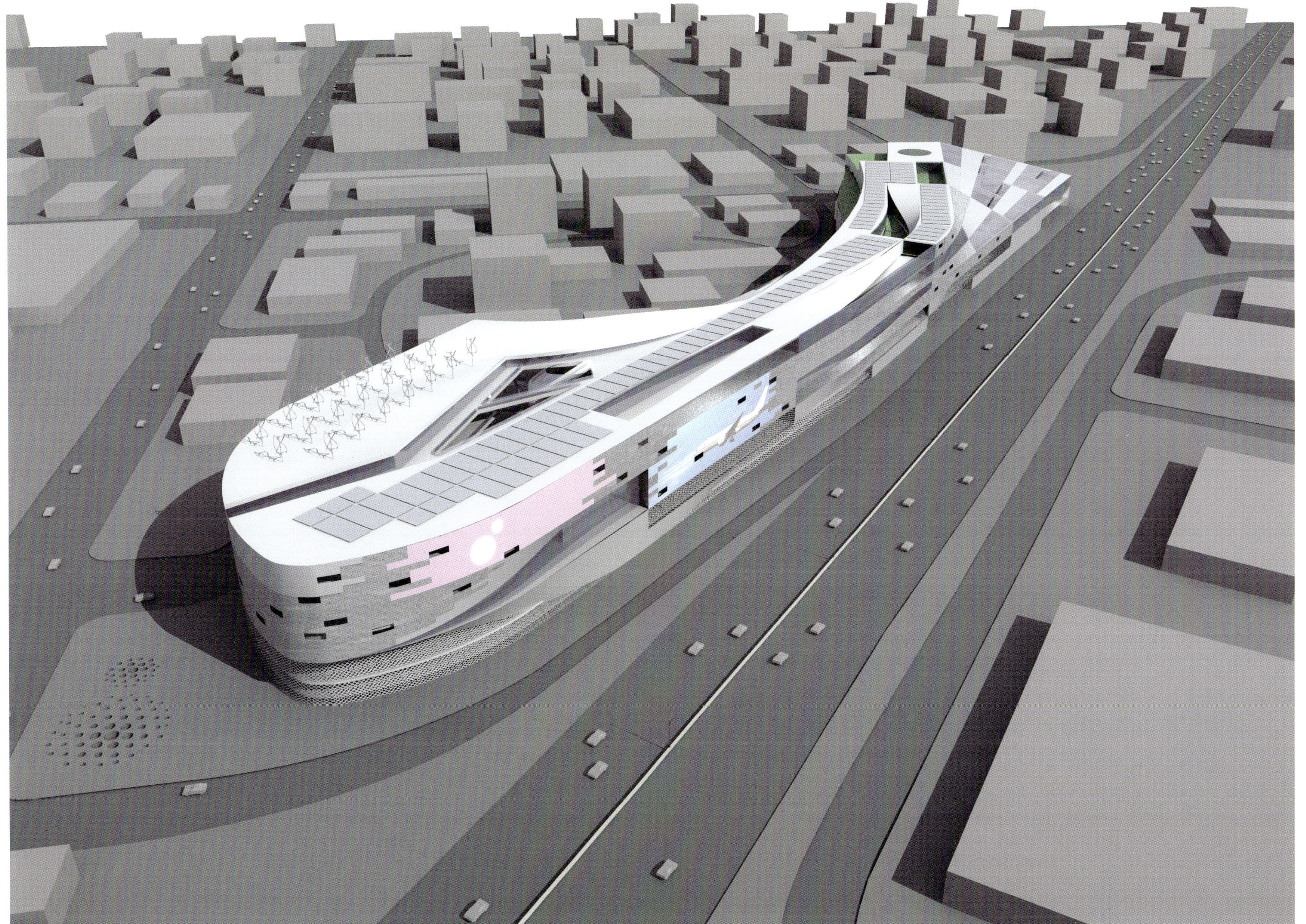

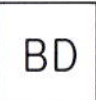

BD

WS

ERIC OWEN MOSS ARCHITECTS
CONJUNCTIVE POINTS THEATER COMPLEX

2006

Few architects have had clients as loyal as Frederick and Laurie Smith, who for more than 20 years have sponsored Eric Owen Moss's myriad experimental buildings inside Culver City's industrial plot turned high-tech office park, Hayden Tract. The architectural laboratory includes projects that resemble their names, such as Beehive, Stealth, and the Umbrella. But the most ambitious would have been the mixed-use Conjunctive Points Theater Complex, a performing arts center with three theaters, retail, offices, and an outdoor plaza.

Although it's tempting to think so, Conjunctive Points' twisting, elastic form wasn't just a grand formal experiment. Moss designed it to embrace a diverse program, with a vision of creating a new, major cultural center for Los Angeles. To the east, the structure was curved to render a 750-seat theater-in-the-round; highlight city views; and shape a large plaza with outdoor seating, gardens, and an amphitheater. To the west, the configuration would twist 90 degrees to accommodate a two-level thrust theater with raked seating for 1,650. A third, multiuse theater was positioned directly above that space at the westernmost tip of the project.

Although detailed plans were drawn up, Conjunctive Points never went beyond the drawing board. Neighbors and officials worried about the project's scale and possible impact on congestion, despite the fact that a light-rail line—the Expo, now in operation—was already planned for the district. The Smiths, battered by the opposition and unable to buy a portion of the site from UCLA, withdrew.

→ Theater complex rises above revamped industrial tract.

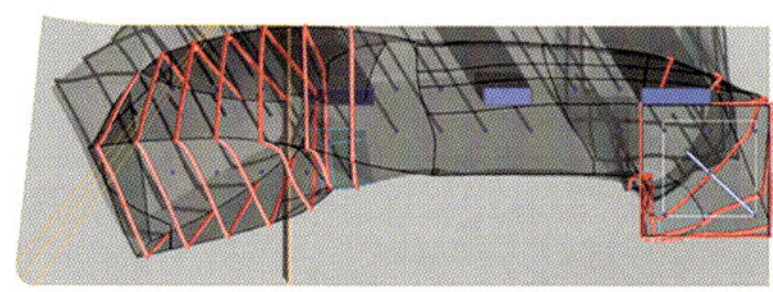

Red Structure synonymous with foam contours

Gold Structure synonymous with orthogonal grid

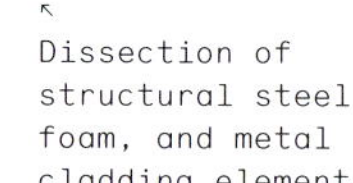

↖
Dissection of structural steel, foam, and metal cladding elements

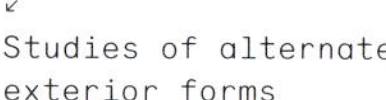

↙
Studies of alternate exterior forms

→
Multiple theaters under undulating roof, with plaza and amphitheater outside

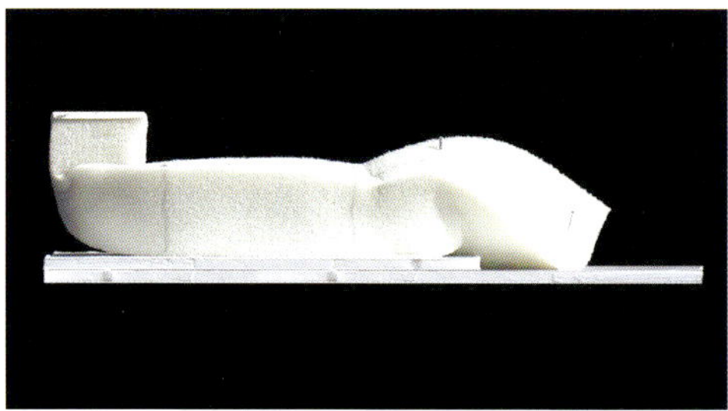

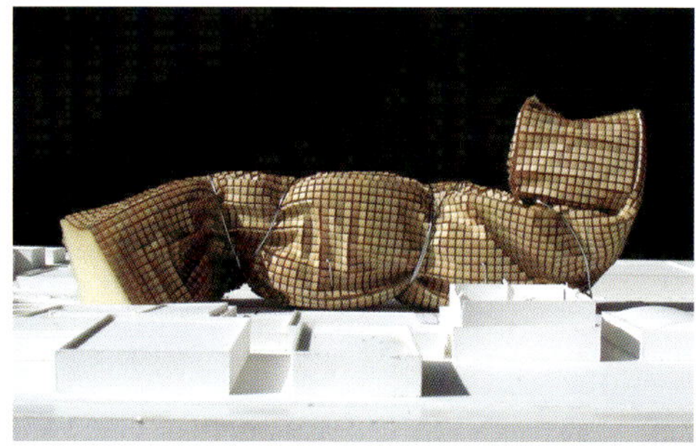

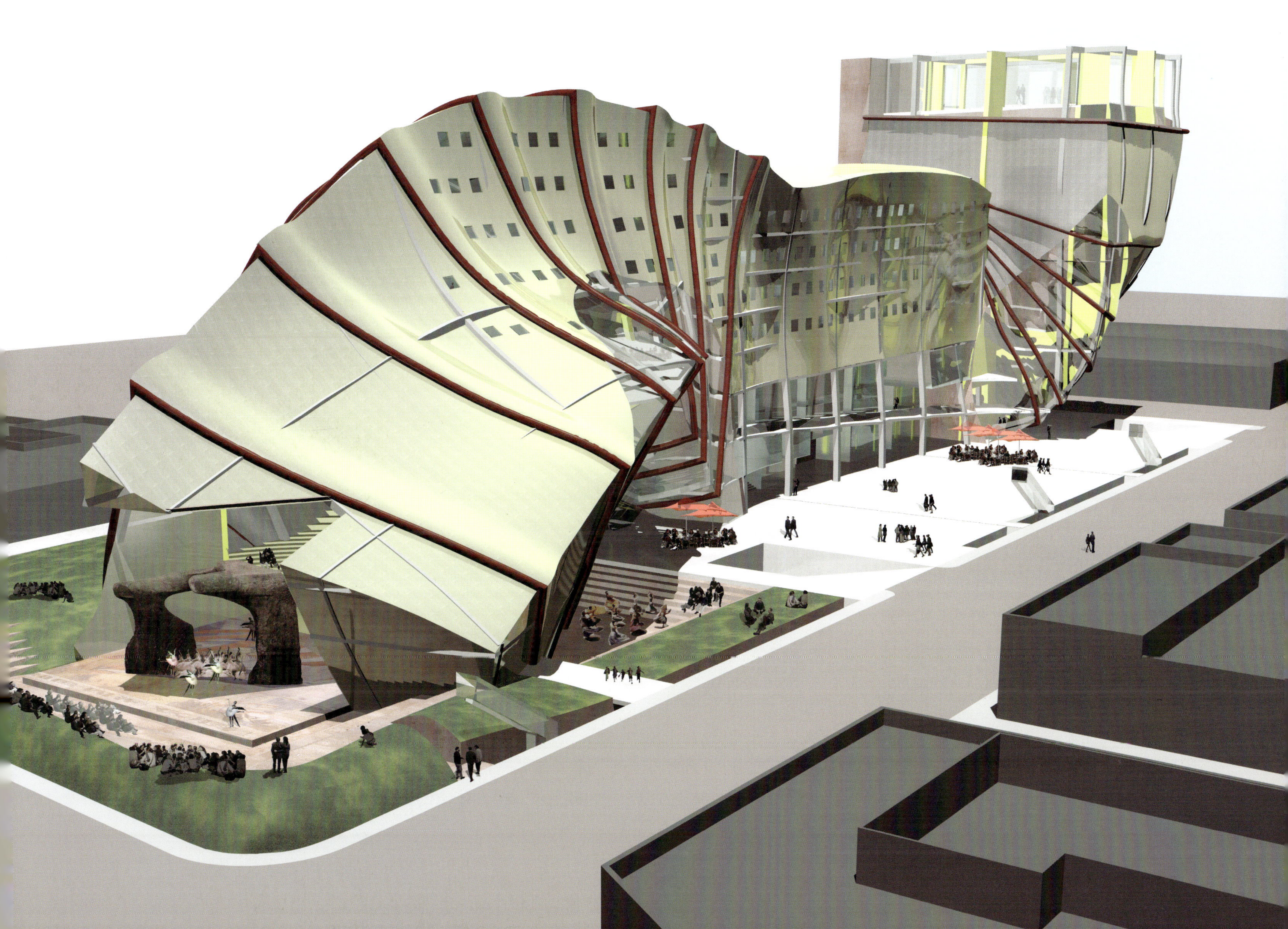

BD

DT

MORPHOSIS
HERALD EXAMINER TOWER

2007

Riding the final wave of the new century's real estate boom, Morphosis's Herald Examiner project was meant to provide a center of energy in the seedy Garment District of Los Angeles. The first step was to rehabilitate Julia Morgan's masterful, and shamefully discarded, Mission Revival building on Broadway as office and retail space. Next up, a 256-unit condo, followed by another 319 luxury dwellings designed to maximize space and, of course, attract maximum attention.

Developed by Hearst and Urban Partners, the project's precast-concrete walls would have been clad with a deconstructed latticework of terra cotta, red cement fiberboard, and prefinished sheet metal, a loose interpretation of the Morgan building's red tile roof. Multistory loft spaces were to sit at the upper levels, vaguely resembling the head of the robot Wall-E.

The project fell victim to the real estate collapse that began not long after construction was set to begin. Morgan's block-long Moorish and Mission structure still sits empty, its colonnades filled in and its yellow-and-blue mosaic cupolas gathering soot from truck traffic rumbling down Broadway.

→ Julia Morgan's newspaper building stares up at fractured condo tower.

↗↗ Head-on elevation displays complex facade.

CHRISTIAN DE PORTZAMPARC
ACADEMY OF MOTION PICTURE ARTS AND SCIENCES MUSEUM

2007

To call L.A.'s long-dreamed-of Hollywood Museum cursed would be an epic understatement. Since the advent of the motion picture, elected officials, producers, actors, and movie buffs have tried to build the definitive repository for industry treasures. Each time, they've failed miserably.

The most recent attempt took place in 2007, when the Academy of Motion Picture Arts and Sciences selected Pritzker Prize-winning French architect Christian de Portzamparc from a field of 154 to design a 200,000-square-foot museum, described by the Academy as "a place for watching and learning about film and filmmaking." Located just off the corner of Vine Street and Homewood Avenue in the gritty heart of Hollywood, it would become a permanent home for the Academy's collection of films and film memorabilia, now scattered across the city in largely inaccessible locations. It also would contain several theaters and exhibition galleries.

Portzamparc's proposal called for a series of floating concrete boxes, stacked and staggered, and thin concrete shards, all projecting toward the street in front and wafting serenely over a ramped berm in back. The minimal interior would essentially become a canvas on which to place memorabilia, posters, graphics, and projections, many of them stretching the entire length and height of the space. Lofty bridges and large ramps would offer unique viewpoints, and an auditorium would host regular screenings.

Plans for the museum halted as the economic downturn took its toll. In 2011, the Academy abandoned a $400-million capital campaign, instead electing to install a more modest museum inside the May Company building at Wilshire and Fairfax. On the site of the planned Portzamparc museum, the Academy recently completed a 17,000-square-foot event space, including a large amphitheater and public patio.

→ Portzamparc's kinetic museum waltzes with its neighbor, the Academy's Pickford Center.

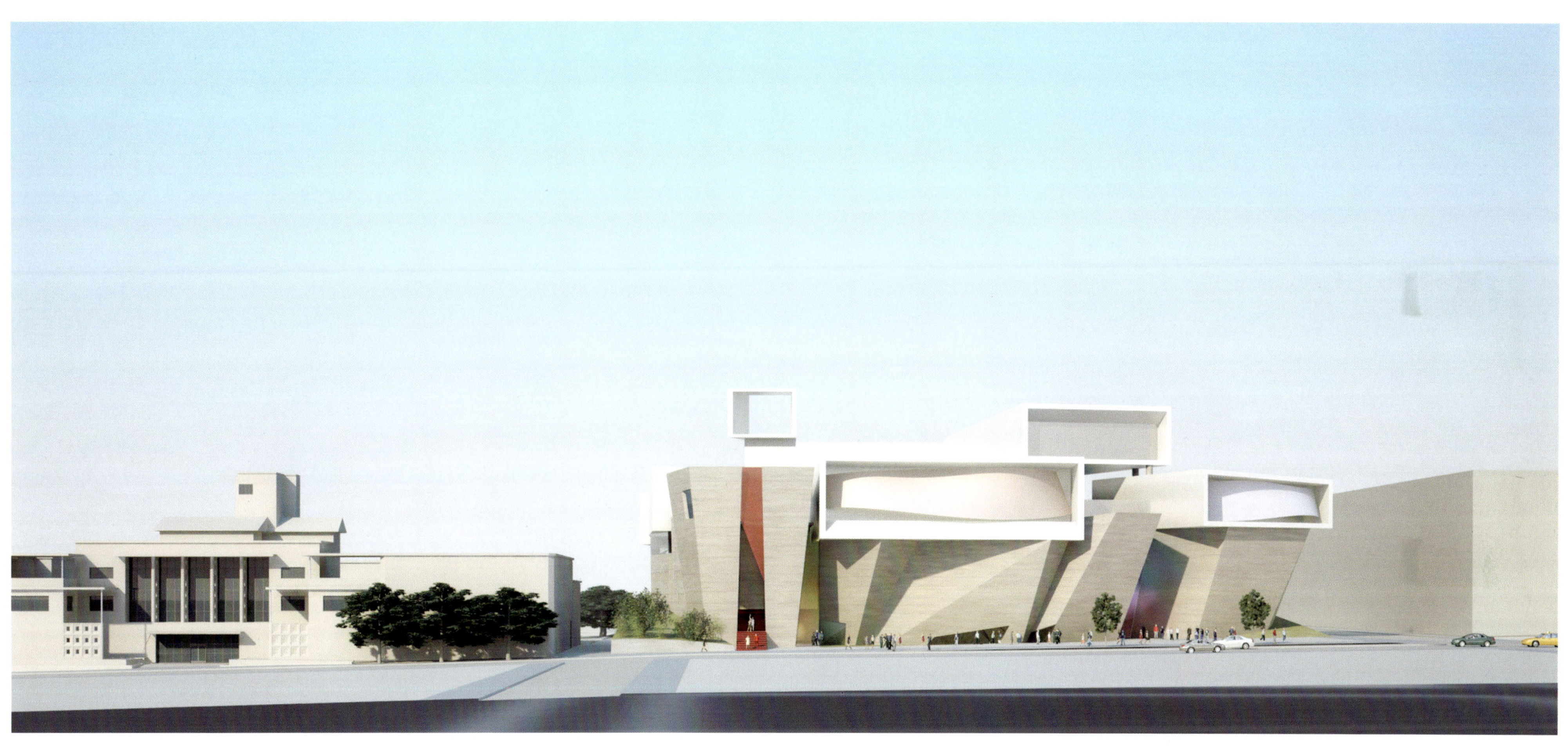

←
Site model shows thin, stacked building boxes projecting toward street, with park at rear.

→
Sloped park doubles as amphitheater and screening room.

→→
Giant movie screens and large gallery windows overlook Vine Street.

↘
Interior gallery

WS

ATELIERS JEAN NOUVEL
GREEN BLADE

2008

There was much fanfare when Pritzker Prize-winner Jean Nouvel unveiled his design for this 45-story, $400-million condominium tower. The building—intended to rise above the intersection of Century Park East and Santa Monica Boulevard—would have been the French architect's first on U.S. soil west of the Mississippi. A slender high-rise 50 feet wide and 350 feet long, the structure was a hydroponic version of the ancient Hanging Gardens of Babylon. Nouvel proposed to graft two ecosystems—desert flora facing south, Mediterranean plants facing north—onto 4-foot brims extending from each floor of the long, narrow tower.

The Orange County developer SunCal sprang for an elaborate luncheon at which Nouvel narrated a scroll of PowerPoint images. "In the perspective of Santa Monica Boulevard, the building is a blade...a green blade," he said, giving the building its moniker. "The green blade is thin, 11 times higher than it is wide. It tries to prove that it is possible to tame height by simple pleasures like reflections, shadows, and vegetation vibrating against the depth of faraway horizons."

Every condo was a throughway apartment, taking up the full width of the building. The landscaped exterior building skin would become a scrim through which residents could experience the city. Nouvel explained: "The interior space of each unit extends out beyond the glass line onto a planted balcony landscape. Long views are had through a foreground of plants. Foreground, background: That is the secret of the atmosphere specific to each apartment." Interior gardens, furnished for each residence, tied interior to exterior.

Unlike the usual presentation, however, in this one the architect furnished no model. His assistant, when asked about the omission, said slyly, "There will be a full-scale model. We're installing it on Santa Monica Boulevard."

Nouvel wasn't so sanguine. Upon being introduced with lavish praise for his design, he said in rugged English: "Too many compliments. Usually so many compliments means you are dead."

He was right. SunCal had been trapped in a bidding war with Donald Trump for the land and wound up paying $110 million. Within a month of Nouvel's presentation, SunCal filed for bankruptcy, another victim of the real estate plunge.

→ Tower rises above north end of Century City.

Westfield
1000

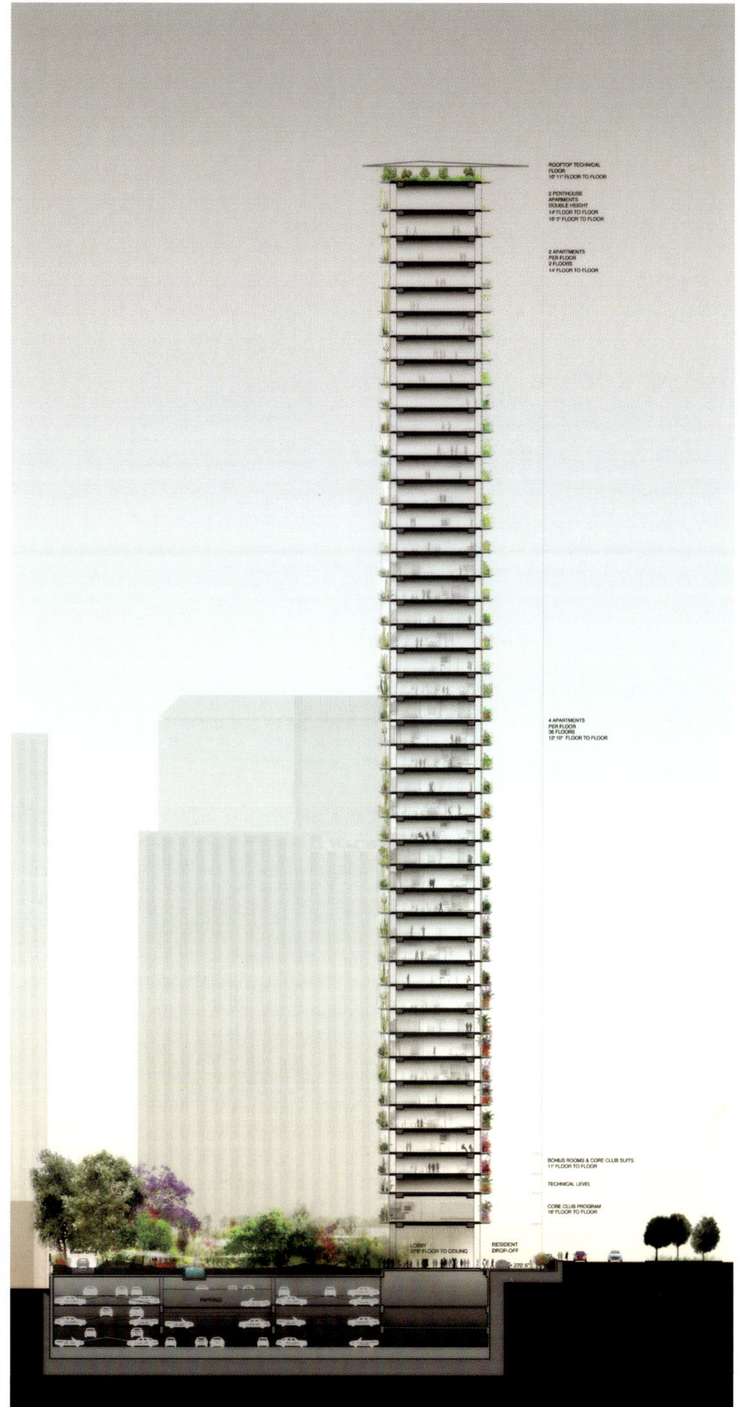

←
Soft green foliage seems to reflect golf course below.

→
Impossibly thin, with two apartments per floor

→→
Semitropical and desert plants screen interior rooms.

BD

SB

B+U
FIRESTONE MIXED-USE OFFICE BUILDING

2009

World-class landmarks don't often sprout up in Downey, an industrial city located southeast of downtown Los Angeles. But that didn't stop L.A. firm B+U from proposing a striking mixed-use building for local financier Jesse Flores.

Located on Downey's swarming main thoroughfare, Firestone Boulevard, the three-level structure would include a cafe, retail spaces, and a ground-floor plaza with two levels of office space above, all configured around a central atrium opening to the street.

Wrapping the building—and providing its wow factor—would be a swooping enclosure system made up of ornately braided layers of fabric with varying levels of transparency. The insulated fiberglass fabric would provide consistent shading and daylight levels inside. On the ground floor, a glass facade would open up retail spaces to the street. The firm also designed undulating landscaping to link an outdoor seating area to the boulevard.

While the project looked quite complex, firm partner Herwig Baumgartner pointed out that the fabric system that made the building pop was relatively affordable and easily installed. The city was receptive to the project, seeing it as a way to revitalize the southeast L.A. community. But Downey never experienced the Bilbao effect, as yet another project was sucked into the vortex of a sinking economy.

← Fabric roof and large opening illuminate sweeping bridges.

→ Swirling landmark for one of the nation's busiest intersections

LA

LOS ANGELES FOOTBALL STADIUM

John and Donald Parkinson's Los Angeles Memorial Coliseum in Exposition Park and Myron Hunt's Rose Bowl in Pasadena each opened to great acclaim in 1923. Since then, not a single professional football stadium has been built in Los Angeles. In a sports world that worships the next big thing, this is hardly a recipe for attracting franchises. In the 1980s and '90s, the Rams and the Raiders both threatened to leave town and then actually followed through. A raft of proposals across the region—more than 15 in all, from Carson to Irwindale to Inglewood to the Dodgers' home at Chavez Ravine—were floated by developers and municipalities in an effort to first keep the teams and then to attract new ones. One of the most frequently targeted sites was none other than the venerable but neglected Coliseum itself. Here are a few notable proposals.

BARTON MYERS
L.A. COLISEUM TRANSFORMATION

1996

Part of the city's push to make the Coliseum attractive to NFL teams, architect Barton Myers's proposal would have created a contemporary seating bowl within the stadium's existing shell. The facility would have provided improved sightlines, closer seating, private boxes, and large open-air concourses for concessions, located between the new bowl and the building's original structure. In a setting vaguely recalling the tournament grounds for a medieval joust, the plan included large fabric shades supported by massive steel struts, intended to minimize the stadium's legendary glare. Like many other Coliseum plans, this one never found political will or civic financing.

NBBJ
L.A. COLISEUM TRANSFORMATION

1998–2003

Architecture firm NBBJ's design for the Coliseum was commissioned in 1998 by a group called New Coliseum Venture, led by developer Ed Roski and developer-turned-philanthropist Eli Broad. Also backed by powerful Los Angeles County supervisor Mark Ridley-Thomas, the plan featured a modernized stadium with a new, smaller bowl and a sharply angled glass-steel-and-fabric canopy that not only drew attention to the building but also served as a shading device. In addition, it called for a splashy mixed-use entertainment zone surrounding the stadium—a place to eat, drink, and even play sports—filled with wavy signage, loud logos, and a large formal park along its perimeter.

ROCKWELL GROUP
HACIENDA
COLISEUM AT EXPOSITION PARK
HOLLYWOOD PARK STADIUM

1999

Going head-to-head with Houston for an NFL expansion team, former über-agent and Disney chief Michael Ovitz (and an investment group that included supermarket king Ron Burkle and movie star Tom Cruise) pumped up the Hollywood glitz with several stadium proposals in 1999.

Ovitz's group, led by New York designer David Rockwell, first came up with a Mission-style stadium and entertainment complex for the oil-rich city of Carson called the Hacienda, which featured, among other things, several bell towers, Spanish Colonial arches, a clutch of jumbotrons, and a giant mall and concourse. The team next proposed a Roman-themed renovation of the Coliseum (which also went up against the Eli Broad-Ed Roski scheme). Dubbed the Coliseum at Exposition Park, it was somehow more classical looking than the original. The 68,000-seat stadium, built into the existing shell, would have glass end-zone towers, reflecting pools, a picnic area, gurgling fountains, and a band of lights along its upper brim. Just as important, the overhaul envisioned several parking structures covered with grass and trees, and called for razing the adjacent Los Angeles Memorial Sports Arena to create a huge, unified green space at Exposition Park. After this plan failed, Ovitz made one final push: His investors offered to put up $400 million to build a new stadium on a 97-acre site at Hollywood Park, in Inglewood. None of the schemes managed to lure an NFL team.

NBBJ
ANGELES FIELD

2007

In 2007, Irvine-based developer DDM Group hired NBBJ to create a 70,000-seat stadium as the centerpiece of a large master plan for Lynwood, a poor, primarily Latino neighborhood south of downtown. The focus of the stadium design was its "protective armor," evocative of football players' shoulder pads. The stadium was oriented inward, concentrating attention on the game, although pieces cut in the envelope would allow glimpses of the city beyond.

A concrete plaza, softened with large pools of water, would lead spectators inside and guide them to the development's three districts: the Marketplace, a large retail center; Las Ramblas Center, a residential and performing arts zone; and Sportstown, a mixed-use district anchored by the stadium. Neither the public nor bankers jumped in to support the master plan.

RICHARD KEATING
DOWNTOWN STADIUM

2010

While much recent attention has been focused on AEG's still-pending plans to install a Gensler-designed stadium downtown, there was at one point another idea for the same site. Architect Richard Keating, working with an anonymous "American Music Entertainer with ambitions of NFL ownership," as Keating put it, in 2010 proposed a stadium adjacent to the city's convention center with a weblike roof structure that would "cast its shadowy presence during the day" and be "illuminated at night." With a playing field set 40 feet below the sidewalk, the design minimized bulk and carved out a plaza leading to nearby transit as well as the mammoth LA Live entertainment complex. The anonymous client pulled out, not only for financial reasons but also because of a reluctance to work with AEG, which owns LA Live, the Staples Center, and most of the South Park neighborhood.

DOWNTOWN TOWERS OF THE 2000s

Thanks to questionable planning and harsh demographic shifts, downtown Los Angeles has long been the object of ridicule. People have dismissed the city's center as a sterile corporate workplace or a hostile urban jungle. But during the economic expansion of the early 2000s, the area morphed into a viable 24-hour neighborhood, with residents filing into converted historic office blocks, restaurants and shops transforming barren storefronts, and condo towers sprouting like glassy bamboo shoots. At the height of the expansion, more than 30 new buildings, each more than 11 stories tall, were planned for downtown, according to the *Los Angeles Times*. But rampant speculation overinflated demand, and when the real estate bubble popped, many of those grand skyscraper plans imploded just as quickly. Here are a few examples.

KANNER ARCHITECTS
PARK TOWER

2006

Kanner Architects' Park Tower, located at Hope and Ninth streets, was to hover above the emerging South Park district, adjacent to the Staples Center and LA Live. At its base, the 43-story condominium complex contained double-height retail spaces, a parking garage, and a pool and gardens. Above that, the building's shell would be composed of thin, diagonal concrete patterning and glass curtain walls.

KEATING/KHANG ARCHITECTS
755 SOUTH FIGUEROA

2006

Richard Keating's 50-story 755 South Figueroa—a.k.a 7+Fig—was hailed by developer Robert Maguire as the first new office tower in the city in the last 15 years. It hugged the western edge of downtown, making it the first structure commuters would see when approaching on the 110 Freeway. Keating said the project, containing a million square feet of office space, would help establish "a new image for downtown L.A." The gentle slope of the east wall was intended to "provide a graceful line toward the sky," the architect noted, while the relatively narrow form contrasted with downtown's mostly bulky buildings. The aperture, or "sky window," some 40 stories up may have looked like a gimmick, but it was actually meant to reduce wind load at higher elevation, and would have provided a canvas for nighttime illumination.

A. C. MARTIN
BILTMORE HOTEL TOWER

2006

As part of a planned overhaul of Schultze and Weaver's 1923 landmark, Millenium Hotels—hoping to leverage the residential building boom—hired A. C. Martin to design a 60-story condominium tower above the Renaissance Revival structure's northwest corner. The glassy tower's form would be generated through a twist of its envelope and a sharp cut at its property line. The controversial tower, already under intense scrutiny from preservation officials, couldn't survive the financial crisis.

KOHN PEDERSEN FOX (KPF)
PARK FIFTH

2007

In May 2007, New York firm KPF unveiled Park Fifth, a 71-story, 850-foot-high tower on Pershing Square that would have been the tallest residential skyscraper west of Chicago.

The glass-clad building, whose floor plates changed configuration from floor to floor, was covered with staggered horizontal louvers, creating a variegated exterior. It was designed, said the firm, to incorporate attributes of single-family housing into a high-rise. Each of the tower's dwellings would contain its own "backyard," or large covered terrace, carved out of the building's envelope. Residents could enjoy a semiprivate roof park atop a glass bridge connected to an adjacent 41-story tower. And at the tower's base, a monumental "urban window" was to frame views into an elevated plaza.

At the time the project was proposed, Peter Slatin of the real estate Web site TheSlatinReport.com, predicted Park Fifth's demise. "It's risky to start building into a market that's starting to decline without knowing how long the decline will last," he wrote.

DANIEL LIBESKIND
1340 SOUTH FIGUEROA

2009

In true Libeskind fashion, this 43-story residential tower across from the Convention Center consisted of a square concrete shell clad with an angular glass-and-steel facade. It included 273 market-rate units—each with its own balcony—two stories of retail, a spa, and seven stories of parking. The building's developer, a consortium of Korean companies with a sci-fi-sounding name—CA Human Technologies—claimed to have in-house financing, but that fell apart in the wake of the downturn.

JOHNSON FAIN
426 SOUTH SPRING STREET

2007

Johnson Fain and developer Gilmore Associates submitted plans for what would be the first skyscraper in downtown's quickly growing historic core: a 23-story, 200,000-square-foot condo tower and boutique hotel. The building's unusual massing featured a rectangular podium containing retail, a lobby, and parking that would dramatically step back at hotel level and angle inward as the building transformed into condos farther up. The skin would be a highly reflective combination of metal panels and glass. A small pocket park next door would open up to Spring Street, creating a badly needed public retreat in the neighborhood.

101
264
134
101
284
5
110
405
SANTA MONICA BLVD
101
282
WILSHIRE BLVD
256
10
278
10
N
E
270
S
254
266
274
1
LA
110
260

FOLLIES & AMUSEMENTS

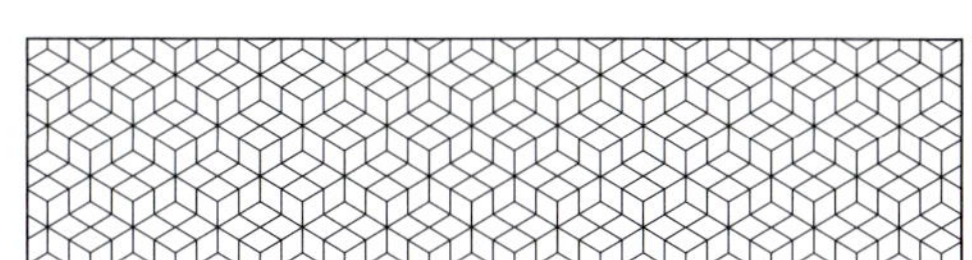

FA

WS

VENICE AMUSEMENT PIERS

1912
1924

Today, the Los Angeles coastline has only one remaining amusement pier, in Santa Monica, but the city's beachfronts were once brimming with such attractions. During the 1930s, it was like a Coney Island West, with roller coasters, novelty shows, and dance halls stretching down the length of the Pacific shore. The Santa Monica Pier, the Crystal Pier, the Ocean Park Pier, the Venice Pier, and the Sunset Pier jutted into the ocean like five concrete-and-wood fingers. Over the years, these and other piers burned down, succumbed to storms, collapsed in fiscal ruins, or were removed by their future landlord, the city of Los Angeles.

Still, in this heyday, dozens more pleasure centers were never built. The most ambitious were in Venice, which at the beginning of the twentieth century made a name for itself as a center of ingenuity, hedonism, and chutzpah.

Local brewer Eddie Maier announced plans in August 1912 to build a new $2-million amusement pier at Center Street, five blocks south of the Abbot Kinney Pier. The reinforced-concrete structure, built by contractor Augustus Stutzer, would measure 1,300 feet long and 550 feet wide. Supported by 800 solid reinforced-concrete piles, the pier would contain an ornate Beaux-Arts dance palace designed by Large and La Casse Architects and guaranteed as fireproof. Also in the works were a giant swimming pool, a cafe in the shape of a passenger liner, various rides, and a children's Pavilion of Fun.

That plan was scuttled when workers, protesting the contractor's management, destroyed much of the almost-complete project. But Maier was undaunted. He commissioned architect C. H. Russell to design a smaller pier, this time 300 feet long by 100 feet wide. Its highlight: a large-scale dance pavilion and, down the pier toward the ocean, a sizable bandstand. "Many engineering difficulties have been encountered, but these, it is declared by the architect, will all be overcome," said Maier. It never happened.

A competing project by architect O. L. Clark would have extended 1,200 feet into the ocean from Electric Street, just south of the Venice Pier. Proposed in 1924 by the Electric Pier and Amusement Company, the $1.5-million project, said the *Los Angeles Times*, was poised to become "the most complete amusement zone in the country." It would contain the world's largest outdoor swimming pool, measuring 600 feet by 300 feet, equipped with what would have been, by all accounts, the world's first wave machine (or, in the parlance of the day, "wave making device"). An electric fountain would adorn the center of the pier; at its end, an open-air theater would have seating for 20,000. Such an ambitious project required the skills of Walter Clark, the engineer who later consulted on Boulder (now Hoover) Dam.

"The men behind the project state that when completed the pier will be operated as a miniature world's fair throughout all seasons of the year with constant new features," wrote the *Times*. Construction began on the Electric Pier in 1924, but after that, all mention of the project disappeared.

↗ Architect C. H. Russell's 1,000-foot "Pleasure Wharf" for Maier

→ Maier's Beaux-Arts dance hall

pg. VII

GREATEST OF CRESCENT BAY AMUSEMENT PIERS NOW BUILDING.

Yet another extravaganza, also extending 1,200 feet into the Pacific, the Washington Pier was touted as the largest jetty on the West Coast. Ride designer “Fred A. Church, amusement man,” as newspapers called him, planned to open the new attraction in 1926. Washington Pier would begin at Leona Boulevard, an extension of Washington Boulevard. A huge plaza on the sand would merge into the pier some 500 feet out on the water. Beyond would stand a “mammoth dance hall,” a bathhouse, an auto park accommodating 1,500 vehicles, and “every possible amusement device” known, boasted Church. He promised not one but two roller coasters. But before the pier could get under way, Los Angeles annexed Venice in 1925. City officials, wary of the amusement piers' carny atmosphere—and planning to turn their beaches over to the sober administrators at the parks department—nixed the scheme.

DT

PACIFIC EXPOSITION CORPORATION
PACIFIC MERCADO

1936–40

Exploiting the city's ambition, pride, and mythologized past, the nonprofit Pacific Exposition Corporation proposed a permanent exposition grounds modeled after similar fairs in Europe. Pacific Mercado, or the marketplace of the Pacific Area, had a simple, if far-reaching, goal: "to make of Los Angeles the commercial, industrial and cultural center of the Pacific Basin."

The $2.7-million Mercado would house commercial booths for U.S. companies and products as well as a fine-arts and cultural center. Unlike other world expositions, the attractions would remain in place after the inaugural fair in 1940 and a subsequent celebration of the four-hundredth anniversary of Portuguese explorer Juan Rodriguez Cabrillo's landing in California in 1542. The organizers hoped the parklike grounds would become home to a much-needed art museum, opera house, theater, libraries, and several art colleges.

The corporation initially secured a promise of $1.5 million from the state. The city's Department of Water and Power, hoping to boost its public identity and capitalize on the amount of electricity the Mercado would consume, chipped in $1.24 million.

In researching an appropriate location, the corporation, led by its "committee of 15"—including City Hall architect John C. Austin and ubiquitous power broker Henry O'Melveny—solicited proposals centered around more than 20 neighborhoods, from downtown to Palos Verdes. A proposal for Griffith Park included a completely revamped Los Angeles River, plied by boats and lined with amusements.

In 1938, the committee finally chose Elysian Park and Chavez Ravine. The area seemed ideal: It was close to downtown and shielded from the elements by surrounding hills and tree-filled dales.

A glossy promotional book depicted a wonderland of Spanish Colonial structures, dotted with colonnades and campaniles, organized along a grand axis and around a lake crossed by elegantly arched bridges. More buildings, some evocative of Asian temples, would rise in the hills above. The concentration of commercial pavilions would help the city "become trade capital and market place for 21 countries bordering the Pacific Ocean," said prominent businessman Marion R. Gray.

The rhetoric outpaced the reality. Bitter arguments over the location—many citizens wanted a public vote rather than a closed-door committee selection—added delay and stymied state and federal funding. In 1939, the promised appropriation of $1.5 million from the state legislature evaporated, a result largely of the project's sluggish pace. It's unclear what dealt the knockout blow, but the onset of World War II certainly eclipsed the idea, forevermore.

→ Elysian Park resembles a lost civilization.

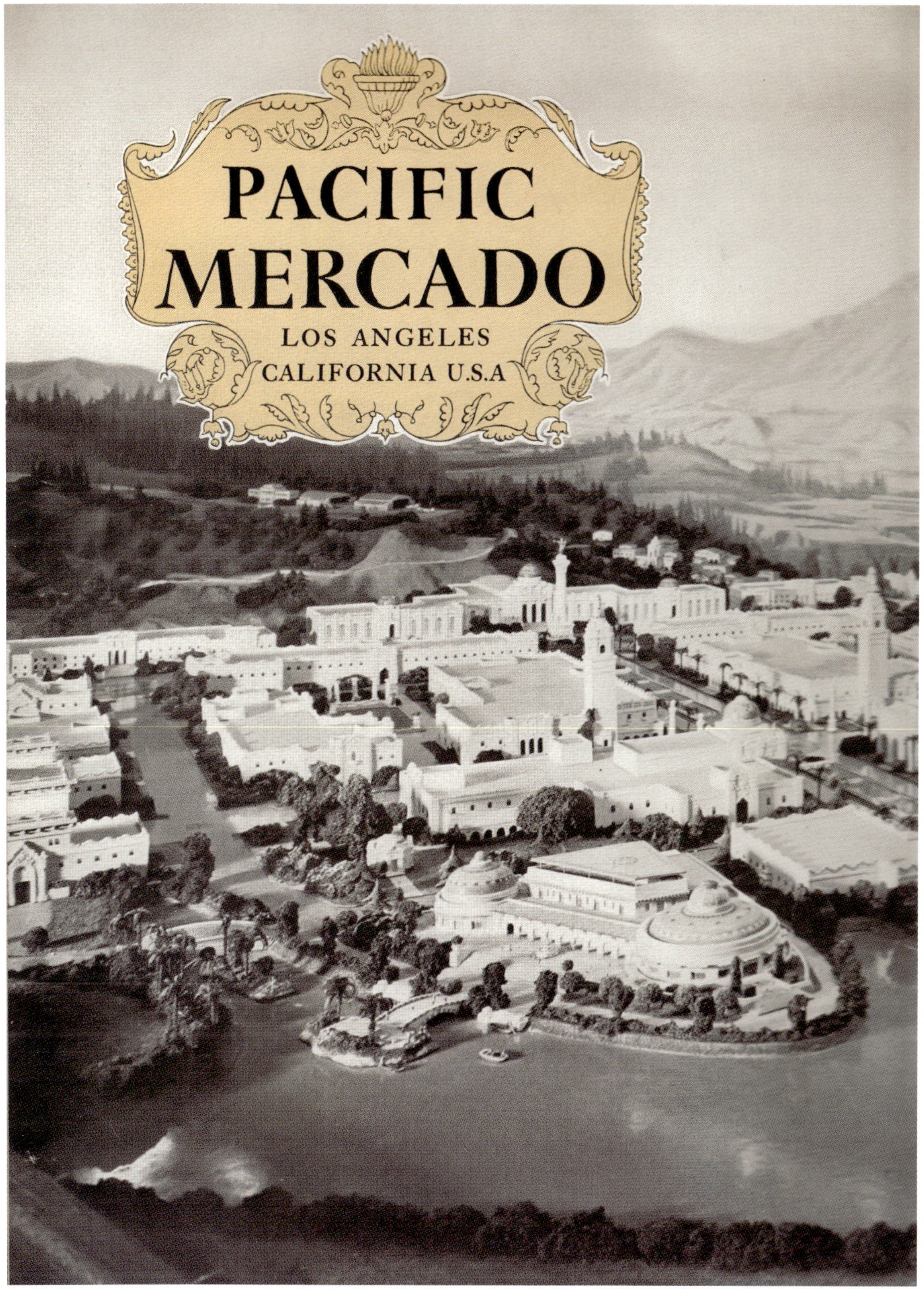

PACIFIC
MERCADO
LOS ANGELES
CALIFORNIA U.S.A

COMMERCE AND TRADE

Los Angeles Times

HOMES AND BUILDERS

SUNDAY MORNING, FEBRUARY 6, 1938.

Beautification Plan Urged

Prompt Start of Local Stream Project Declared Essential

BY CHARLES C. COHAN

In 1940 Los Angeles expects to make notable contribution to world progress and amity by inaugurating a permanent Pacific Mercado or trade exposition. In 1942, this will take the form of a world's fair to commemorate the four hundredth anniversary of Cabrillo's discovery of California.

There is public-spirited desire that the city should then be ready to offer an exposition created with unique architectural artistry in a setting of rare beauty within a community whose charm has kept even pace with its economic stride.

Selection of a site suitable for the permanent exposition and lending itself to expansion for the purposes of the Cabrillo celebration is therefore seen of paramount importance.

Held likewise important is elimination of unsightly physical flaws in the city.

In this latter respect Los Angeles has accomplished much. It is especially emphasized that demanding immediate attention is improvement of the Los Angeles River channel.

CONSPICUOUS

Obviously, this stream course is in a most conspicuous place in the city's topography. For many years the importance and possibility of its conversion from its present condition of raw cleft and receptacle for tin cans and other debris into a feature of thorough attractiveness have been studied and urged.

Now presented is the desirability of having the transformation completed by the time the exposition's gates swing open.

When recently Fred H. Howard, prominent Southern California horticulturist and landscape expert, pointed out in an interview that Los Angeles has in the

CONCEPT OF HOW LOS ANGELES RIVER CHANNEL CAN BE IMPROVED

Above drawing by Charles H. Owens visualizes the possibilities of beautifying the Los Angeles River channel. Also shown is how the improvement would be a notable feature of the Pacific Mercado, or trade exposition, for which the vast natural amphitheater in the northeast section of Griffith Park has been suggested as a site. The exposition is scheduled to be ready to open its gates in 1940.

FACT AND COMMENT

With its enactment, the revamped housing act has ceased to be a theory and has become a fact.

And having been created, what's going to be done with it?

It's the topic of the day.

Predictions about its effect are flying thick and fast throughout the nation.

Following on the heels of the enactment have come reports from some other regions so enthusiastic that they would seem based on new building booms already launched.

Obviously, there's some hysteria in that.

Statements from lending sources and the attitude of the F.H.A. itself encourage the belief, at least the hope, that opportunities under the revised housing law are not going to be allowed to run hog

SOUTHLAND RECORDS LARGE JANUARY CONSTRUCTION GAIN

Factory's Space Increase Great

REPORTS FOR MONTH SHOW BUILDING ACTIVITY'S INCREASE

←
A proposal to locate the Pacific Mercado in and around Griffith Park included a revitalization of the Los Angeles River. Elysian Park was chosen as the site instead.

→
1937 congressional resolution calling for U.S. participation in an "international exposition to be known as the Pacific Mercado"

→→
Cover of Pacific Mercado promotional book

75TH CONGRESS
1ST SESSION

H. J. RES. 484

IN THE HOUSE OF REPRESENTATIVES

AUGUST 9, 1937

Mr. FORD of California introduced the following joint resolution; which was referred to the Committee on Foreign Affairs and ordered to be printed

JOINT RESOLUTION

Providing for the participation of the United States in the continuing international exposition to be known as Pacific Mercado, to be held in the city of Los Angeles, California, commencing in the year 1940, and in the year 1942 commemorating the landing of Cabrillo, and for other reasons.

Whereas there is to be held in the city of Los Angeles, State of California, commencing in the year 1940, a continuing international exposition to be known as the Pacific Mercado, designed to promote closer relations and better understandings among the countries and nations of the world, through the furtherance of trade, industry, and cultural arts, by gathering, arranging, and exhibiting the varied cultures of such countries and nations and the origins, progress, and accomplishments in science, the arts, education, industry, business, and transportation of such countries and nations; and by other appropriate means; and

WILLIAM H. EVANS
LOS ANGELES WORLD'S FAIR

1939–50

It is doubtful that [fairs] have a useful economic purpose. They are carnival in their spirit and their actuality and they do little to assist in the permanent building of a community.

Los Angeles Chamber of Commerce

A Los Angeles World's Fair was the dream of William H. Evans, a real estate developer who'd built hundreds of homes in Long Beach and, during the Great Depression, helped author the National Housing Act. Evans started pushing his idea in 1939 and by the middle of World War II had gained support from the Los Angeles Board of Supervisors. His proposal, nicknamed the "Evans Plan," was officially called "A Los Angeles World's Fair of Victory, Peace and Progress: A Celebration for All Nations."

The idea was to convene a postwar event spread across the city. A flight exposition would debut at Los Angeles International Airport (LAX), then very new; a maritime and naval display would showcase Long Beach Harbor; a petroleum show would rise atop oil-rich Signal Hill; a Motion Picture Museum would grace Hollywood; tourists would be led along the factory floor at Lockheed, home of the P-38; and a yacht harbor would be dug at Playa del Rey. What's more, the plan said, all this activity would spur completion of the region's freeways and put returning soldiers to work.

Among the new monuments and buildings would be a Statue of Peace, to be erected on an artificial island off Long Beach. Rivaling the Statue of Liberty in size, the towering figure was a woman draped in a gown that might have been sketched by costume designer Edith Head, holding the globe in an upraised hand and clutching the county seal to her ample breast. A White House of the Pacific, to be built on the bluffs of Palos Verdes, offered a strange facsimile of the presidential residence in Washington.

The true agenda, however, was a program of slum clearance. Downtown's "blighted area," a.k.a. Bunker Hill, would be demolished and replaced by a glistening neoclassical fortress. A pair of soaring colonnades, ringed by Mexican fan palms, squared off around a reflecting pool out of which rose a slender victory column. Towering over the assembly was an even larger pile, with still taller columns, intended to prove that Los Angeles was now bestride the world—and proud of it.

The Los Angeles Chamber of Commerce haughtily dismissed the proposition. "The Chamber's view...is that we have a war to win. It is doubtful that [fairs] have a useful economic purpose. They are carnival in their spirit and their actuality and they do little to assist in the permanent building of a community." The Board of Supervisors, however, warmly embraced the fair, appointing Evans to head a Los Angeles County World's Fair Commission.

Soon after, Evans and Donald R. Warren, a civil engineer who had helped oversee construction of the San Francisco-Oakland Bay Bridge, showed the county chiefs a drawing of the fair's new centerpiece. The Tower of Civilization, 150 feet in diameter and soaring 1,290 feet, would be the tallest structure in the world. Winding around the needle-thin shaft would be the Path of the Ages, a three-mile-long helix leading to an observatory for paying guests. The long, circular climb, Warren stated, exemplified the development of civilization: "As man travels over the 'Path of the Ages,' higher and higher becomes his civilization,

→ Helical walkway encircles 1,290-foot tower.

TRYLON & PERISPHERE
EIFFEL TOWER
TOWER OF CIVILIZATION
EMPIRE STATE BUILDING
CITY HALL LOS ANGELES
COMPARATIVE DIMENSIONS
DONALD R. WARREN CO
ENGINEERS
LOS ANGELES
H SAYLOR 45
COPYRIGHTED · AUGUST · 28 · 1945
BY · DONALD · R · WARREN · CO
PROPOSED
TOWER · OF · CIVILIZATION
Los Angeles World's Fair

←←
Re-created White House at Palos Verdes

←
Statue of Peace in Long Beach Harbor

→
Presentation book shows movie museum and culture hall.

and with his civilization comes a clearer and broader scope of vision."

The base of the tower would house a museum containing relics of the past and wonders of the present, while high in the clouds, the tip of the tower would project laserlike beams of light, aimed at the firmament above and the horizon below.

As the war wound down, money failed to materialize. The county instead approved a few modest activities to celebrate the state centennial, ending Evans's dream. The idea of a world's fair would have to wait another 15 years, when Long Beach proclaimed it would hold one in the late 1960s.

• MUSEUM OF MOTION PICTURE ARTS AND SCIENCES

To be erected in Hollywood and to house historical "props" and costumes of the motion picture industry. A "Hall of Fame" for motion picture immortals will also be contained in the structure as well as a pre-view theatre and a studio so constructed as to afford a public view of the making of a picture. A television broadcast station will also be included.

• MUNICIPAL AUDITORIUM AND HALL OF CULTURE

To be erected in the Civic Center and to serve as the permanent home for all of the cultural activities of this area. Also to be used for the larger conventions.

SB

WALT DISNEY COMPANY
DISNEYLAND, BURBANK

1952

A fair, an exhibition, a playground, a community center, a museum of living facts, and a showplace of beauty and magic...not intended as a commercial venture.

Walt Disney

Since the 1920s, Walt Disney had toyed with the idea of creating a new type of amusement park based loosely on his animated stories. Families could escape everyday life, not to mention the unsavory carnivals that dominated Los Angeles at the time, with their sketchy games, rickety rides, and illicit shows. A trip to Europe to see Copenhagen's Tivoli Gardens provided the final flood of inspiration, putting Disney in planning mode for what he would call Disneyland.

He presented his initial plan—much smaller than the wonderland built in Anaheim in 1955—to the Burbank City Council in 1952. It was to be located on a 16-acre parcel abutting Riverside Drive and Buena Vista Street, just blocks from Disney's new studios.

Drawn up by Disney and his artists, the $1.5-million proposal, given tentative approval by Burbank city officials, showed many similarities to the final Disneyland, including rudimentary versions of Town Hall, Main Street, Frontierland, Tomorrowland (where visitors could ride a spaceship or a submarine), Fantasyland, and Adventureland. The largest layout was a lagoon, plied by a Mississippi Steamboat and containing Bird Island, which featured a glowing lighthouse and a bird sanctuary. Sinuous landscapes and flowing creeks would lead visitors to an Old Town, evocative of the Wild West, a large carousel, a fairground, a canal, and a meandering automobile course. A railroad would navigate the entire property and connect with adjacent Griffith Park. Disney planners, however, hadn't figured out how to place a large Bavarian castle at the end of a classic American Main Street, as they would in Anaheim.

"Disneyland will be something of a fair, an exhibition, a playground, a community center, a museum of living facts, and a showplace of beauty and magic," Disney informed the *Burbank Daily Review*. He also told the paper that Disneyland was "not intended as a commercial venture."

But the city didn't buy into Disney's vision. "We don't want the carny atmosphere in Burbank," said one council member. So Disney looked to Anaheim, where the company built a $9-million park on 160 acres, and Burbank missed out on one of the richest financial deals for any city in history.

→ Map of original Disneyland, just across Riverside Drive from Walt Disney's studios. Red notes, likely by Disney himself, call out attractions like "Granny's Farm," "Stage Coach Route," and "Mississippi Steamboat."

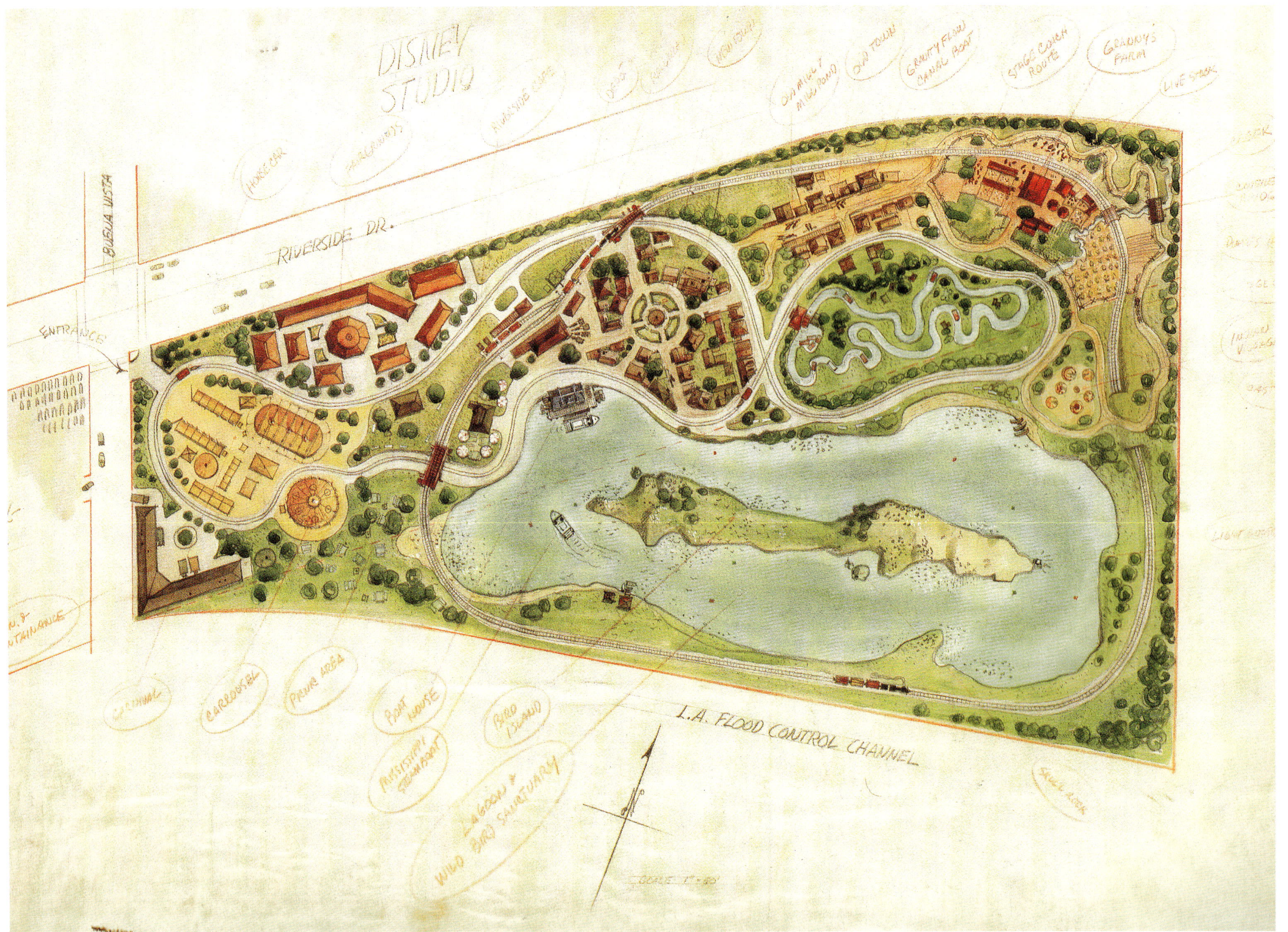
DISNEY STUDIO
RIVERSIDE DR.
ENTRANCE
L.A. FLOOD CONTROL CHANNEL
CARROUSEL
PICNIC AREA
BOAT HOUSE
BIRD ISLAND
LAGOON & WILD BIRD SANCTUARY
GRANNY'S FARM
STAGE COACH ROUTE
OLD TOWN

SB

W. L. COUVERLY
INTERNATIONAL MARKETLAND

1959

International Marketland is an episode in time, a new and shining time, for this ancient world of ours, where the cold war is thawing, and peace is no longer an uneasy thing.

Shopping Center Management Company

At International Marketland, proposed for the city of Orange, the great monuments of the past would meet what, presumably, would be the great monuments of the future. A presentation brochure for the project showed a concourse of pebbled concrete arrayed with replicas of the Leaning Tower of Pisa, the Pyramid of Cheops, the Parthenon, the castellated towers of ancient Babylon, a Jewish temple, and a Moorish mosque with minarets. Surrounding the old was the new: a "Transportorium," a "Multitorium," and a succession of thin-shell-concrete pavilions. Moving sidewalks would connect them all.

"International Marketland is an episode in time, a new and shining time, for this ancient world of ours, where the cold war is thawing, and peace is no longer an uneasy thing. It is the threshold of a truly Golden Age, for all people—a glistening era," the project's economic consultant, Shopping Center Management Company, noted.

A hundred different countries, the owners boasted, could own a hundred different shops, filled with music and laughter. "What we plan to have here is something of a perpetual world's fair," the developer, Charles F. Camarata, told the press in August 1959.

Each precinct of the $15-million scheme was to receive its own architectural treatment. The Market of Many Countries, for instance, would have no posts or interior walls but instead floating roofs suspended from massive arches. The outer translucent walls would swing up to be awnings on hot days and down to provide shelter in "inclement weather." The Foreign Department Store, by contrast, would be housed in a 300-foot-diameter dome replicating the Northern Hemisphere, made of elongated, hexagonal plastic panels. This, too, was translucent. The Contemporary Stores, meanwhile, were studies in "modern architectural progress in their varied roof structures—hyperbolic, vaulted, folded plane, A-frame and flat." The "Transportorium," to imply movement, looked like a cogged gear in a car's transmission.

And so it went, culminating in a 40-story International Hotel, whose conceit was triangular cantilevered balconies with commanding views of "the tableland of Orange County."

Marketland was, above all, a developer's marketing scheme. Located in the crook of the Garden Grove and Santa Ana freeways, it was just a few miles from Disneyland and Fashion Square. The mall was aimed at the march of suburbia into a landscape rich with orange groves then being uprooted. "Growth is thrusting southward at an unprecedented speed," the developers proclaimed, and they were planning to take every advantage of the great shift. "Its advantages of freeway access and a solid backlog of local spendable dollars...(and) its proximity to Disneyland... should make it a merchandising success and a profitable development."

When Camarata announced the project, he declined to say who his backers were. He apparently never found any, because formal foreclosure proceedings were initiated against him and his partners by the former owners of the land. Soon, the shaky team

→ Entryway reveals replicas of architectural monuments from around the world.

NAL
MARKETLAND

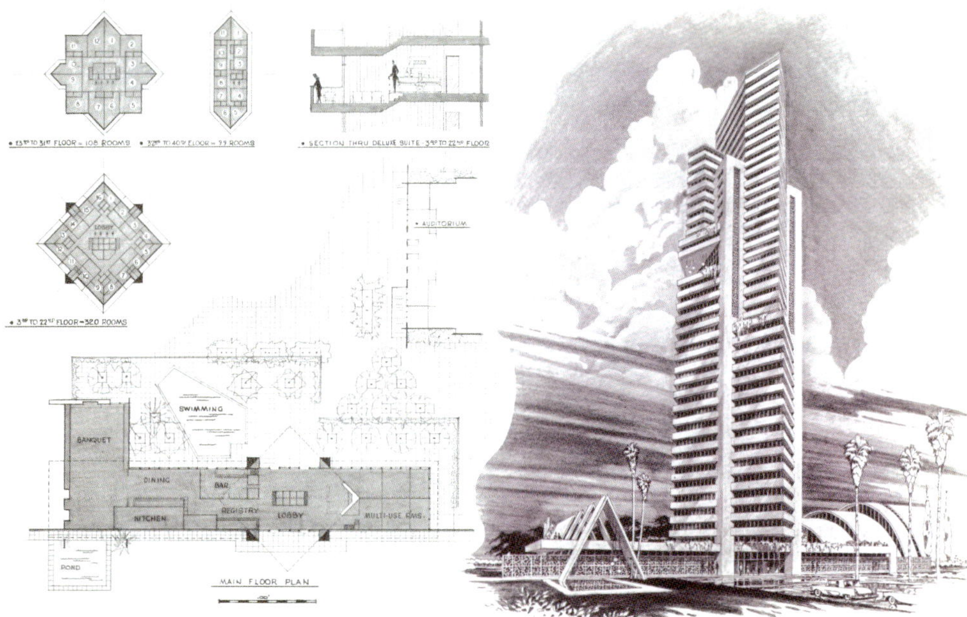

was in bankruptcy. By 1962, the county was in negotiations with the University of California, Irvine, to put its medical facility on 10 of the acres owned by Marketland. In March 1962, the Orange County Board of Supervisors voted to purchase the property, sealing Marketland's fate. No plastic hemisphere would ever emerge. In its place would stand the ever-growing UC Irvine Medical Center.

←←
Translucent plastic Northern Hemisphere dome

←
Hotel floor plan and elevation

↙
Views of thin-shell-concrete roofs bent, folded, and curved

→
Orange County site with undeveloped acreage

SB

BRUCE BUSHMAN
BIBLE STORYLAND

1960

The impact this park will make on people of all ages will be tremendous. The Bible and all its wonders will literally spring into life.

Donald F. Duncan

Bible Storyland was the brainchild of former Disneyland executive Mat Winecoff. A savvy promoter, he'd been approached by a Roman Catholic priest interested in sprucing up his parish yard with an amusement re-creating the Bible story. Winecoff abandoned the priest and instead enlisted actor Jack Haley—a devout Catholic who played the Tin Man in *The Wizard of Oz*—and Donald F. Duncan, the yo-yo manufacturer, to back a $15-million, 60-acre, ride-packed park on Route 66 in Rancho Cucamonga.

Built in the shape of a heart "symbolic of God's love for humanity," Storyland would be subdivided into fanciful versions of the Garden of Eden, Rome, Babylon, Israel, Egypt, and Ur. Bruce Bushman, who had helped design Disneyland, offered drawings inspired by the architectural wonders of the ancient world, including the Tower of Babel, King Solomon's Temple, the Colossus at Rhodes, the Circus Maximus in Rome, and the Ziggurat of Ur. The layout matched the Disneyland blueprint, but with names and imagery drawn from not only the Bible but also classical mythology and pre-Christian relics.

Appropriately, the developers unveiled these plans in Hollywood at the Brown Derby. "The impact this park will make on people of all ages will be tremendous," Duncan told reporters. "The Bible and all its wonders will literally spring into life."

Visitors would travel by camel caravan through the Valley of the Kings and by donkey on the road from Nazareth to Jerusalem. Glass-bottom boats floating on the Dead Sea would offer a glimpse, through the depths, of the ruined twin cities of Sodom and Gomorrah. The way to Heaven was via gold litter, drawn by three cherubs through clouds, stardust, satellites, and comets to the pearly gates. "Signposts along this ethereal way point to alternate routes and to Purgatory. It will be no surprise to Angelenos," the public was told, "that one sign reads 'Los Angeles City Limits.'"

The journey to Hades across the River Styx was "a dark, tingling encounter with monsters, devils cooling off in showers of steam, festering volcanoes, and sulphurous fire fountains. And there, too, is the ingratiating host of this lugubrious place—Lucifer himself."

Elsewhere in the park, Christians could turn the tables and take a bite out of lionburgers, sold at one of the fast-food stands, and teens could aim at a 10-foot giant in the David and Goliath slingshot gallery.

Intended as a spectacle, and as proof that Walt Disney held no monopoly on wooing tourists and thrill seekers alike, the promoters seriously misjudged the local mood. Within weeks of Winecoff's press conference, clergy from around the region were howling. Reverend Francis E. Bloy, bishop of the Episcopal Diocese of Los Angeles, denounced the enterprise as a "blasphemous use of Holy Scriptures for the purpose of an amusement park....The prospectus seriously distorts the sacred history of both Christians and Jews and holds it up to ridicule." Soon, developers dropped the word "Bible" and renamed the project Storyland, but this did little to save it from certain damnation.

→ A Christian-mythological amusement park

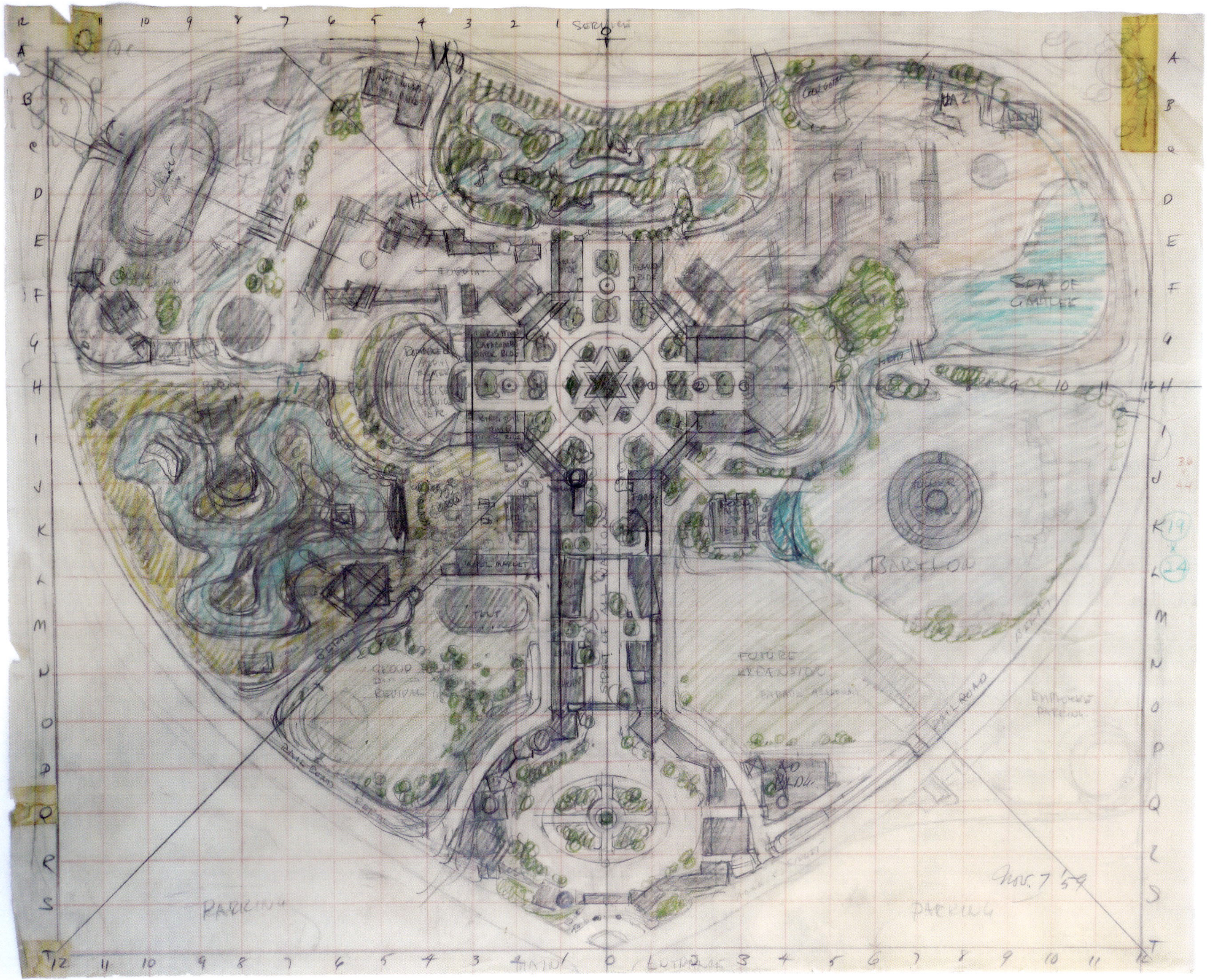

←← Hanging Gardens restaurant

← Bruce Bushman drawings of Great Pyramids, Gate of Rameses II, and Arch of Constantine

→ Ancient Greek theater planted in the Holy Land

THEATRE of DIONYSUS
BUSHMAN
H/C
BIBLE STORYLAND
408

SB

CHARLES LUCKMAN LONG BEACH WORLD'S FAIR

1963–64

The fair will make use of water in all forms. Canals will replace paved streets.

Charles Luckman

A true indicator of the megasized aspirations of 1960s Los Angeles, the Long Beach World's Fair of 1967-68 would have comprised a mind-warping combination of architecture, engineering, and urban planning.

Organizers planned to build the fair, which they heralded as a testament to man's genius, on what would have been the world's largest man-made pier, a two-mile-long stretch consisting of 33 million cubic yards of fill and 3 million tons of rock dredged from the ocean floor.

Total construction was budgeted at $400 million, funded by ticket sales, concessions, and, most important, a raid on Tidelands Oil revenues. The fair gained approval from the U.S. Congress, which presumably bought the attendance estimate of between 45 million and 50 million visitors over two years.

Planned by Charles Luckman beginning in 1963, the fair's main attraction would be the Monument to Freedom, a gigantic structure rising from the ocean on an island and holding aloft the glowing Torch of Freedom. Offsetting the fire, water cascading from the top of the monument would represent "man, in his eternal quest for freedom, cleansed of the ignorance and prejudices that hamper the search."

The fair's organizing theme was the sea, inspired by its Pacific Ocean locale. Designers envisioned "the dream of a modern Venice at last to be realized in California."

"The fair will make use of water in all forms. Canals will replace paved streets. Lagoons will be used for floating displays, regattas, water sports, jets, fountains and spectacles. Canal boats will carry visitors, supplies, and fire fighting equipment to all parts of the fair," said the Luckman proposal.

Back on dry land, exhibition pavilions, a stadium, and an impressive array of amusements would revolve around a central campanile, rising 400 feet in the air and equipped with a giant elevator to ferry 350 passengers at a time to an unimpeded view. The fair would also have a "floating exhibit" area and an underwater zone with a simulated submerged city. To provide access to the fair, the Automobile Association of Southern California proposed not only a new highway but also the use of hydrofoils and "overhead rapid transit" including a monorail.

Despite its idealistic themes, the fair began to unravel as leaders fought off charges of corruption. In the meantime, the mindboggling scope overwhelmed the budget. Luckman pulled out in 1964, and board members swiftly followed suit. The Del Webb Corporation, a vital sponsor, withdrew, and Long Beach soon terminated its agreement to host the fair. Los Angeles began to investigate an alternative fair in Studio City, but that plan never materialized.

→ Abundant attractions at world's largest pier

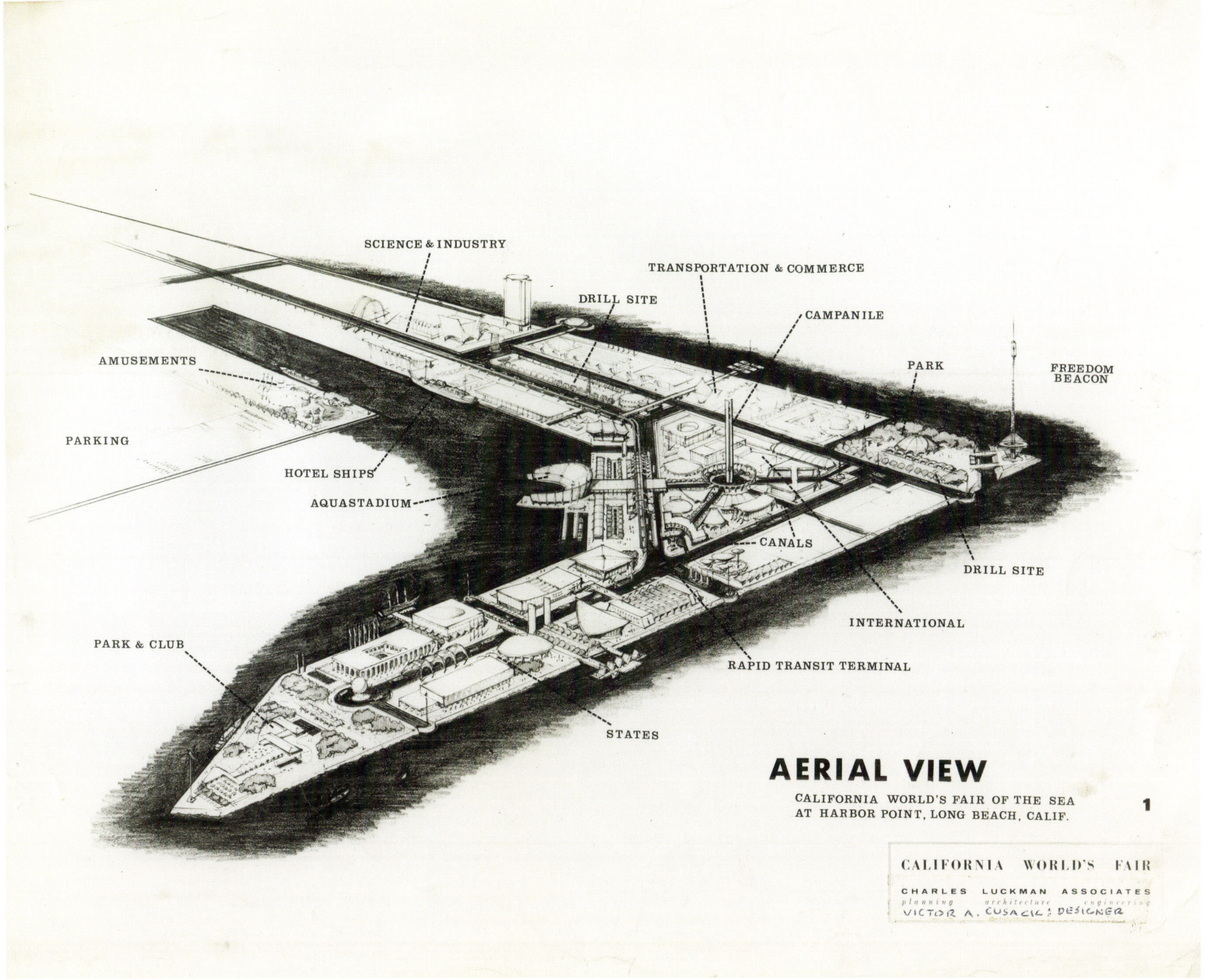
SCIENCE & INDUSTRY
TRANSPORTATION & COMMERCE
DRILL SITE
CAMPANILE
AMUSEMENTS
PARK
FREEDOM BEACON
PARKING
HOTEL SHIPS
AQUASTADIUM
CANALS
DRILL SITE
INTERNATIONAL
PARK & CLUB
RAPID TRANSIT TERMINAL
STATES
AERIAL VIEW
CALIFORNIA WORLD'S FAIR OF THE SEA
AT HARBOR POINT, LONG BEACH, CALIF.
1
CALIFORNIA WORLD'S FAIR
CHARLES LUCKMAN ASSOCIATES
planning architecture engineering
VICTOR A. CUSACK : DESIGNER

THE THEME OF THE CALIFORNIA WORLD'S FAIR IS **THE SEA**

THE SYMBOL OF MAN'S NEW USES OF THE SEA IS THE SITE ITSELF: ON THE SEA AND CREATED FROM THE SEA, THE SITE EXEMPLIFIES THE POSSIBILITY OF CREATING NEW SPACE FOR LIVING ON A CROWDED PLANET.

EXHIBITS AT THE FAIR WILL EXPLORE THE WHOLE RANGE OF ACTIVITIES CONNECTED WITH OCEANOGRAPHY, SALT WATER CONVERSION, THE SEA AS A SOURCE OF FOOD AND RECREATION, SHIPPING AND TRAVEL BY SEA ETC.

DESIGN CONCEPT OF THE FAIR WILL REPRESENT THE FRUITION OF THE DREAM OF A MODERN VENICE AT LAST TO BE REALIZED IN CALIFORNIA. THE FAIR WILL MAKE USE OF WATER IN ALL FORMS. CANALS WILL REPLACE PAVED STREETS. LAGOONS WILL BE USED FOR FLOATING DISPLAYS, REGATTAS, WATER SPORTS, JETS, FOUNTAINS & SPECTACLES. CANAL BOATS WILL CARRY VISITORS, SUPPLIES, FIRE-FIGHTING EQUIPMENT, TO ALL PARTS OF THE FAIR. BUILDINGS WILL BE CONSTRUCTED ON PILES TO AVOID PROBLEMS & DELAYS INVOLVED IN SETTLEMENT OF SAND-FILL.

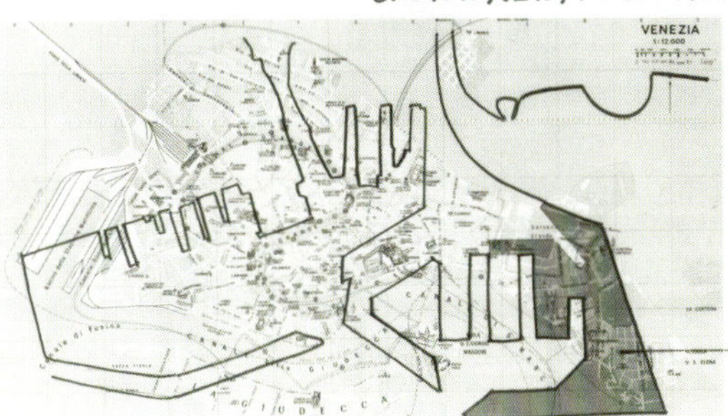

1

CALIFORNIA WORLD'S FAIR
CHARLES LUCKMAN ASSOCIATES
VICTOR A. CUSACK: DESIGNER

← Luckman's explanation of world's fair theme

↙ Map of Long Beach Harbor, with fair pier superimposed

→ Revised site plan, with detail of canal, barges, boats, and gondolas

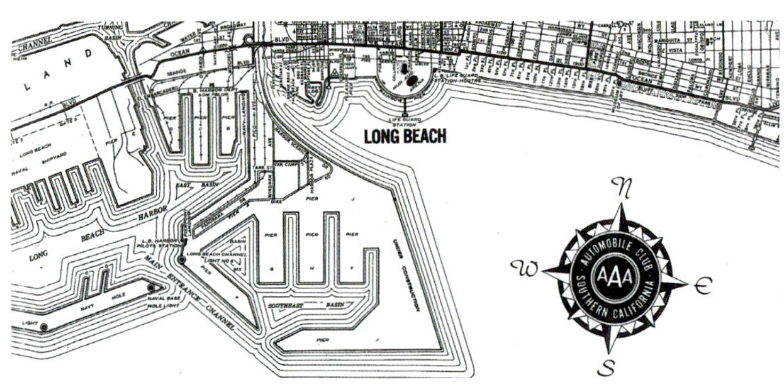

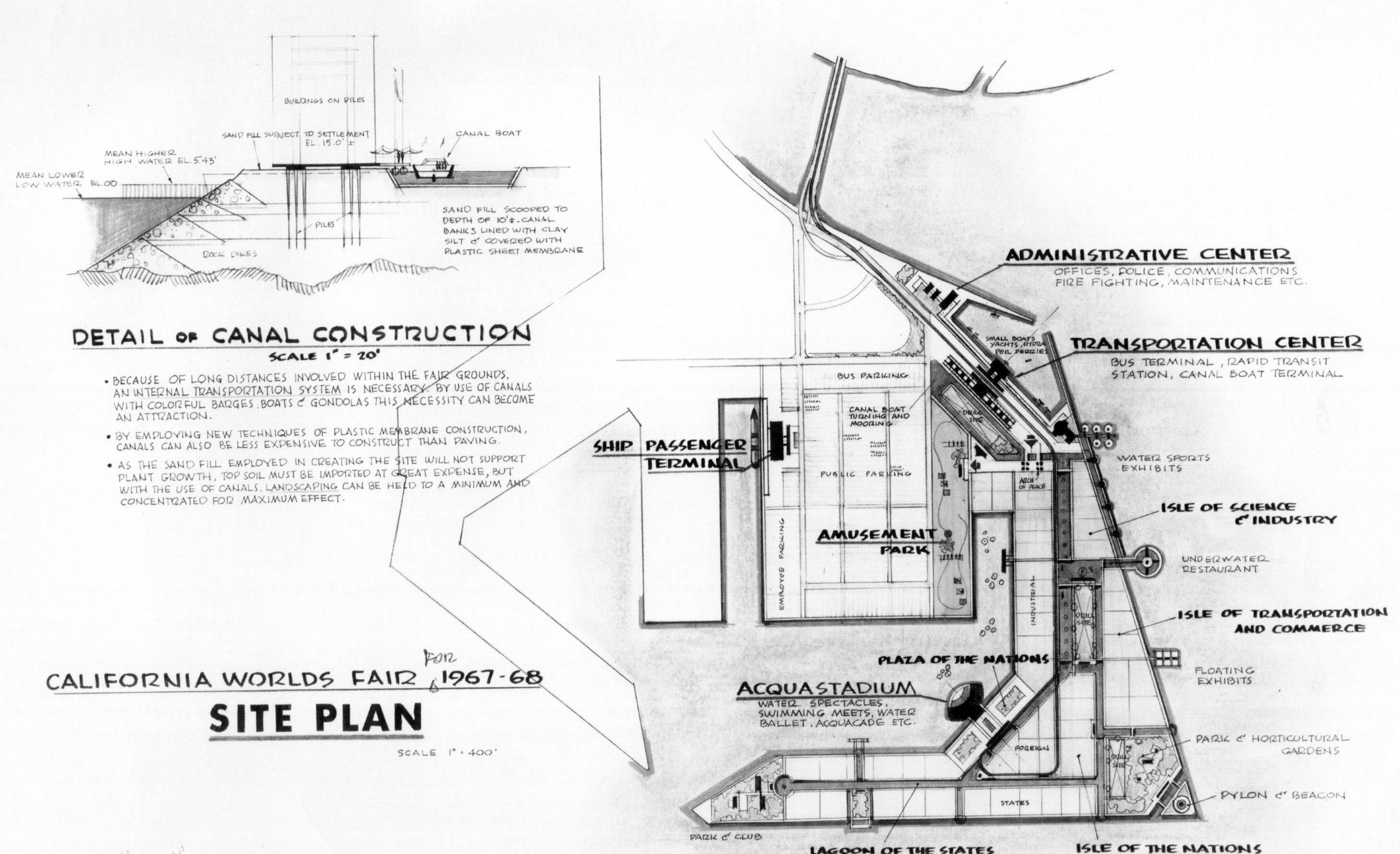

BUILDINGS ON PILES
SAND FILL SUBJECT TO SETTLEMENT EL. 15.0' ±
CANAL BOAT
MEAN HIGHER HIGH WATER EL. 5.43'
MEAN LOWER LOW WATER EL. .00
SAND FILL SCOOPED TO DEPTH OF 10'±. CANAL BANKS LINED WITH CLAY SILT & COVERED WITH PLASTIC SHEET MEMBRANE
PILES
ROCK DIKES
DETAIL OF CANAL CONSTRUCTION
SCALE 1" = 20'
• BECAUSE OF LONG DISTANCES INVOLVED WITHIN THE FAIR GROUNDS, AN INTERNAL TRANSPORTATION SYSTEM IS NECESSARY. BY USE OF CANALS WITH COLORFUL BARGES, BOATS & GONDOLAS THIS NECESSITY CAN BECOME AN ATTRACTION.
• BY EMPLOYING NEW TECHNIQUES OF PLASTIC MEMBRANE CONSTRUCTION, CANALS CAN ALSO BE LESS EXPENSIVE TO CONSTRUCT THAN PAVING.
• AS THE SAND FILL EMPLOYED IN CREATING THE SITE WILL NOT SUPPORT PLANT GROWTH, TOP SOIL MUST BE IMPORTED AT GREAT EXPENSE, BUT WITH THE USE OF CANALS, LANDSCAPING CAN BE HELD TO A MINIMUM AND CONCENTRATED FOR MAXIMUM EFFECT.
CALIFORNIA WORLDS FAIR FOR 1967-68
SITE PLAN
SCALE 1" = 400'
ADMINISTRATIVE CENTER
OFFICES, POLICE, COMMUNICATIONS FIRE FIGHTING, MAINTENANCE ETC.
SMALL BOATS YACHTS, HYDRA FOIL FERRIES
TRANSPORTATION CENTER
BUS TERMINAL, RAPID TRANSIT STATION, CANAL BOAT TERMINAL
BUS PARKING
CANAL BOAT TURNING AND MOORING
SHIP PASSENGER TERMINAL
PUBLIC PARKING
ARCH OF PEACE
WATER SPORTS EXHIBITS
ISLE OF SCIENCE & INDUSTRY
AMUSEMENT PARK
EMPLOYEE PARKING
INDUSTRIAL
UNDERWATER RESTAURANT
ISLE OF TRANSPORTATION AND COMMERCE
PLAZA OF THE NATIONS
FLOATING EXHIBITS
ACQUASTADIUM
WATER SPECTACLES, SWIMMING MEETS, WATER BALLET, AQUACADE ETC.
FOREIGN
PARK & HORTICULTURAL GARDENS
PYLON & BEACON
STATES
PARK & CLUB
LAGOON OF THE STATES
ISLE OF THE NATIONS
1
CALIFORNIA WORLD'S FAIR
CHARLES LUCKMAN ASSOCIATES
planning architecture engineering
VICTOR A. CUSACK : DESIGNER

43. Proposed Worlds Fair, Long Beach (3 photocopies)

DT

ASYMPTOTE
STEEL CLOUD

1988

It's the dream of every visionary architect to build clouds.

Hani Rashid

Asymptote, a firm headed by architects Hani Rashid and Lise Anne Couture, won an international competition to design the Los Angeles West Coast Gateway, a monument to celebrate Pacific Rim immigration to the United States. Chosen from a field of 150 entries, the construct was hailed by *Los Angeles Times* writer Scott Harris as "a bold, innovative, horizontal icon for a bold, innovative, horizontal city." At last, proponents said, Los Angeles would have a landmark befitting its civic character, its own Eiffel Tower or Statue of Liberty.

The architects described their idea for the Gateway as a "living monument, accommodating galleries, libraries, theaters, cinemas, parks and plazas intersected by the fluid, transient spaces of the city." Rhetoric aside, the "Steel Cloud" was an eight-lane-wide bridge over the 101 Freeway downtown. Suspended from Alameda to Broadway—an otherwise virtual dead zone—the metallic bricolage of steel struts and girders would have allowed people to cross from El Pueblo State Historic Park, opposite Union Station, into the city's center. Sixteen-hundred feet long, and rising to nearly the height of the tenth floor of City Hall, the tangled structure would have chartered a chunk of the skyline.

The entrance elevator outside Olvera Street would lift people into a Museum of Time, where U.S. history would unfold within its containerized walls. Moving west, visitors would encounter a computerized library of genealogy, an international foods store, and administrative offices. Farther west, they would find a Park of Peace and Unity, two aquariums (one for the Pacific, another for the Atlantic), two theaters, a fine arts gallery, a sculpture garden, and an immigration museum.

Throughout, this high-tech machine was tuned to the key of rush-hour life. The exterior, clad in LED screens, would flash messages and images at motorists and pedestrians. And a Musical Forest would synthesize the rushing sounds of cars into music—doubtless set to a very slow tempo.

"I was looking at these incredible clouds," said Rashid, after winning the commission. "The sun was setting, turning the clouds to shades of gold and red, pink and purple. It's the dream of every visionary architect to build clouds."

Los Angeles County Metropolitan Transportation Authority board member Nick Patsaouras, who convened the competition and chose the site above the 101 Freeway, wanted to push the limits of the city's artistic tolerance. He got what he asked for. Steel Cloud received immediate ridicule. Critics scoffed at what some

↗ Electronic billboard, parallel to 101 Freeway, flashes messages to drivers.

→ Sixteen-hundred feet long and 10 stories high, with aquariums, library, museum, theaters, and cinemas

called a “giant metal grasshopper.” “It’s stressful just to look at the drawings. It’s getting stranger as it unveils itself,” then-city councilwoman Gloria Molina told the *Times*. “I mean, tanks of fish? Liquid crystal display screens? Take a sound of the freeway and turn it into music?”

The $33-million price tag was also dismissed as preposterously low. Permission from the state’s highway agency for air rights—Steel Cloud might interfere with future plans to double-deck the freeway—was not forthcoming. With not a penny raised and even less political backing, Steel Cloud remained a model in the Carthay Circle offices of Victor Gruen Associates.
The proposal lived on, however, spurring similar bridge ideas—like Morphosis’s 101 Pedestrian Bridge, the “Ponte Vecchio” mixed-use pedestrian walkway, and parks capping freeways—that, although inspired, were also flops.

←
Morphosis's 101 Pedestrian Bridge offered a similar solution to that freeway's neighborhood balkanization.

→
Plans for the "Ponte Vecchio," a mixed-use concourse traversing the 101 Freeway between Main and Los Angeles streets, proposed by Arquitectura and the city of Los Angeles

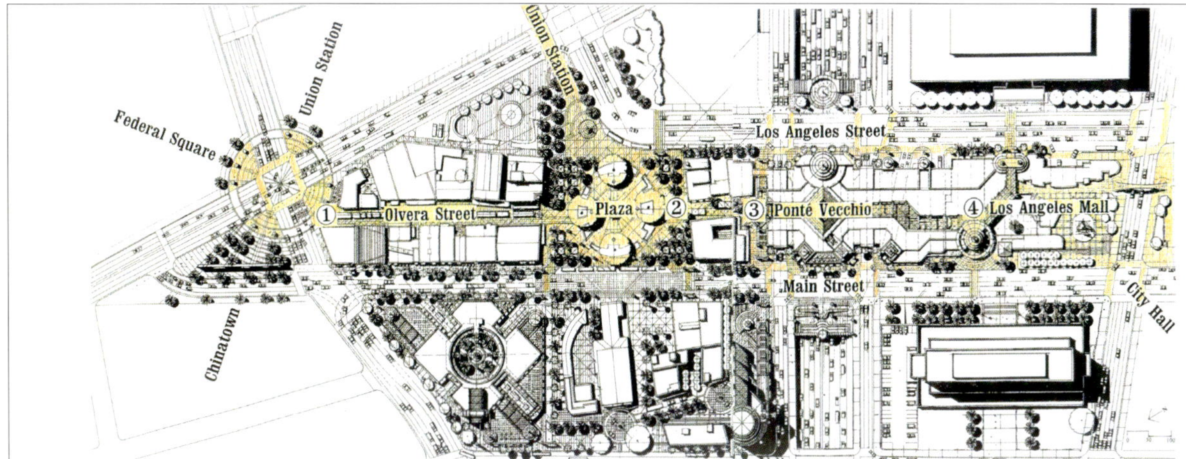

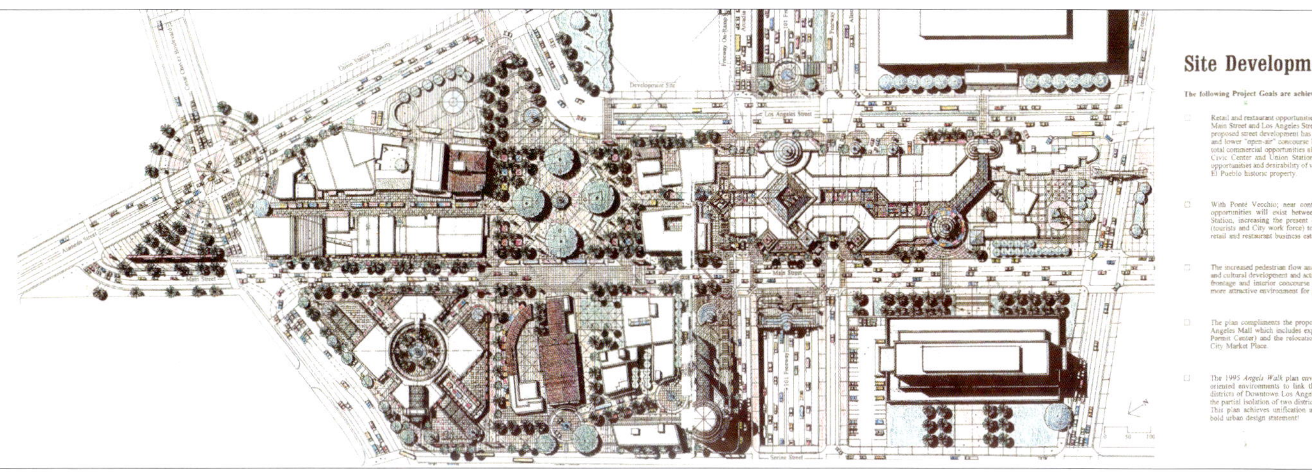

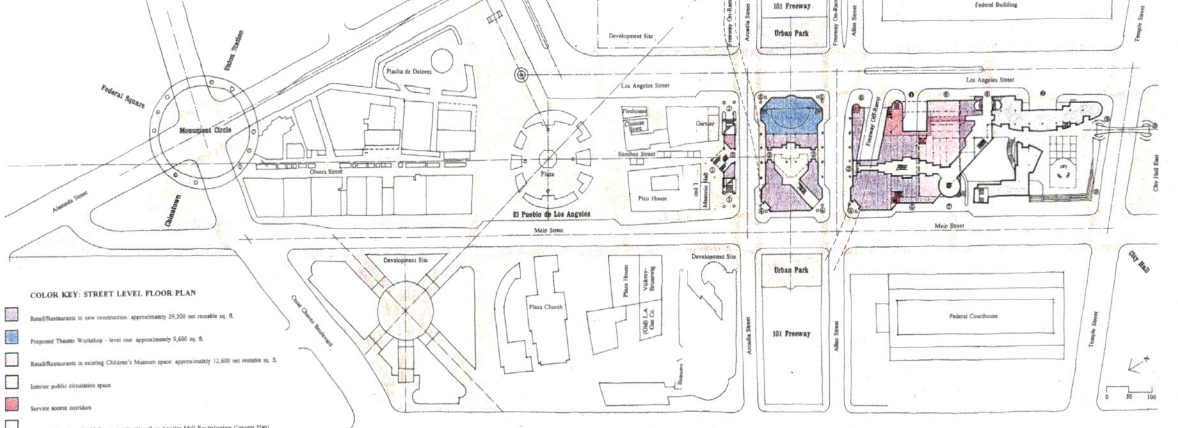

HAMID OMRANI
BEVERLY HILLS
2000

2000

Hamid Omrani, an Iranian immigrant who has designed more "Persian Palaces" than perhaps any other southland architect, conceived Beverly Hills 2000 in response to the desultory condition of the intersection of Wilshire and Santa Monica boulevards. One of the region's most significant crossroads, it is marred by large flat patches of unbroken ground on the former Southern Pacific Railroad right-of-way. The stretch consists of parking lots and incessant traffic. Omrani's vision, which unknowingly echoed Aurele Vermeulen's Archway Plan of 1922, sought to convert the corner into a massive monument consecrated to the Seven Arts.

Omrani planned a 23-story, circular version of the palace at Persepolis, the ancient capital that was near present-day Shiraz, in Iran. A glass-enclosed museum was held aloft on seven Doric columns, each 8-foot-diameter fluted shaft referring to one of the realms of the Liberal Arts—which, in the fifth century, were formalized in the Western canon as the Trivium ("the three roads") and the Quadrivium ("the four roads"). Omrani adapted the metaphor in concrete. As cars sped beneath the elevated structure, pedestrians could enter from elevated walkways connecting the monument to the Beverly Hilton Hotel and to shops on Little Santa Monica and Wilshire.

Spreading from this nucleus would be miles of raised promenades, placed down the spines of the alleys that run behind the expensive storefronts of downtown Beverly Hills. The ambitious scheme was intended to double the land values on streets like Rodeo Drive while giving each street its own identity. Sculpture, Music, Painting, Dance, and so on. Omrani described the promenades as both a money-making boon and "a safe haven for pedestrians and bicyclists."

The mid-street roundabout, he declared, "will be better than the Etoile, in Paris. Why? Because you can walk right into it on top. It can be Beverly Hills's landmark." Proposed amid a backlash against the alleged ostentation of Persian Palaces, the project has repeatedly been tabled by the city's planning commission. Columns and elaborate capitals, it seems, have reached a point of saturation in the embattled halls of the city's bureaucracy.

→ Drawing of triumphal colonnade at the intersection of Wilshire and Santa Monica boulevards

MC

LEO A. DALY
REPTILE AND INSECT HOUSE, LOS ANGELES ZOO

2002

It was intended to be an architectural chameleon both unique and mysterious.

Leo A. Daly

In 2002, the city hired architects Leo A. Daly to design a $25-million Rainforest of the Americas and Reptile and Insect Interpretative Center for the frequently ignored Los Angeles Zoo. Voters had allocated $47.6 million for zoo improvements four years earlier. Daly proposed a serpentine building with no straight lines, inspired by the forms of snakes and insects. The windowless structure would have a sinuous zinc skin that fluidly transitioned from concave to convex. The 9,000-square-foot structure, located between the Aviary, Butterfly Pavilion, and Treetops Terrace, would vary in height from 20 to 50 feet, and its curving exterior would be covered in green metal scales in keeping with its surroundings and reptile motif.

Inside, a spiral ramp would lead visitors past large, freestanding, glass-fronted exhibitions of reptiles and insects from around the globe. Each of the natural settings—desert, island, chaparral, temperate, and rain forest—would have its own biomorphic enclosure. Natural light would pour through translucent elliptical skylights, changing the interior mood during the course of the day.

The structure as a whole was designed to mimic a reptile or insect: The zinc exterior was the skin; the metal framework the skeleton; the living creatures on display within, the organs; the pathway through the building, the cardiovascular system. “In shifting sunlight, the scales produce fluctuating patterns of shimmer and shadow,” the architects said of the building’s snakelike epidermis. It was intended to be “an architectural chameleon both unique and mysterious.”

The zoo’s board of directors deemed the biomorphic form too radical and never had the courage to pursue the project past the design phase. Added to which, the zoo fell into a fiscal crisis and, despite the bond money, dropped the plan in favor of a featureless stucco box.

→ Building’s surface is curved, green, and smooth, like a coiled snake.

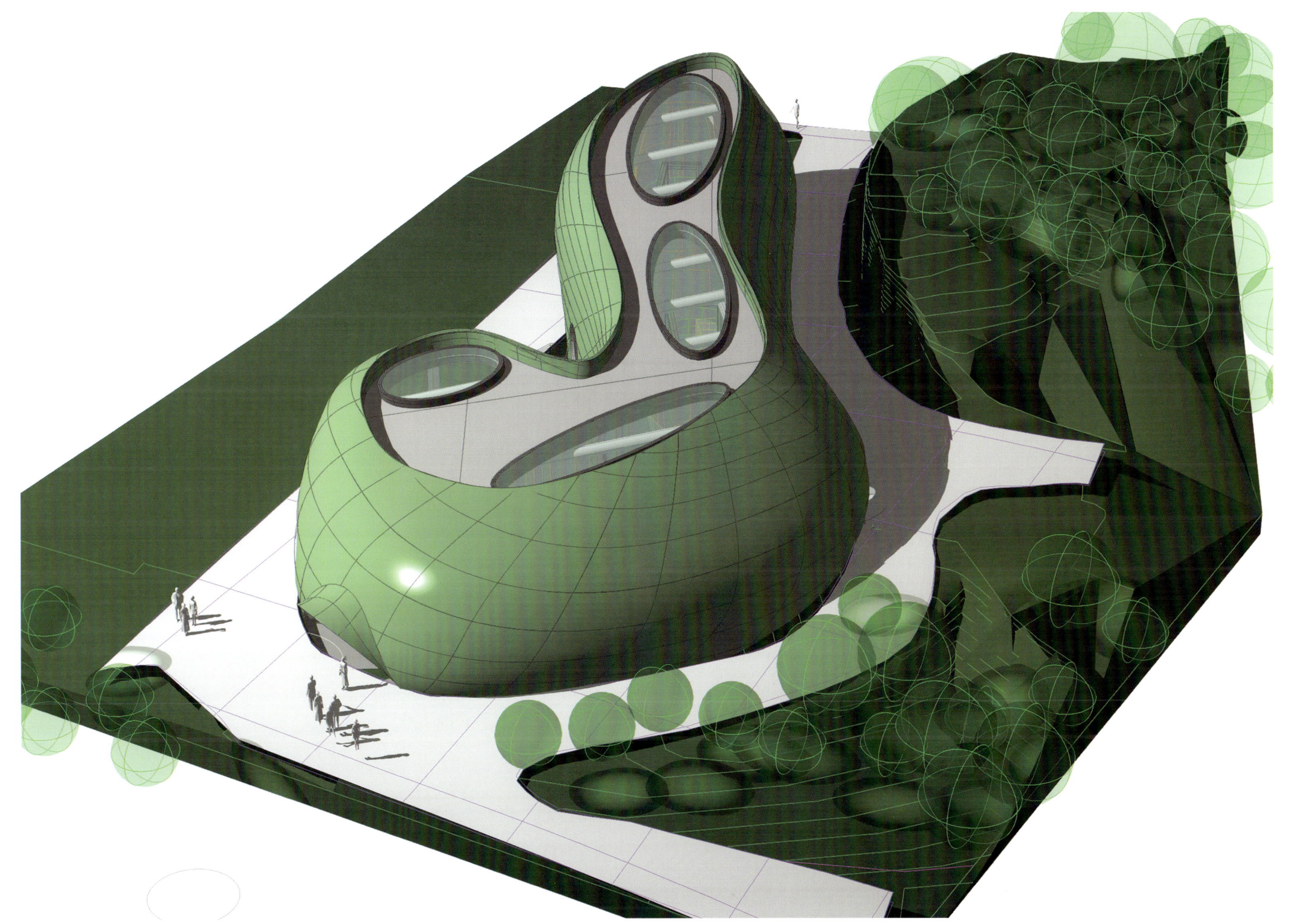

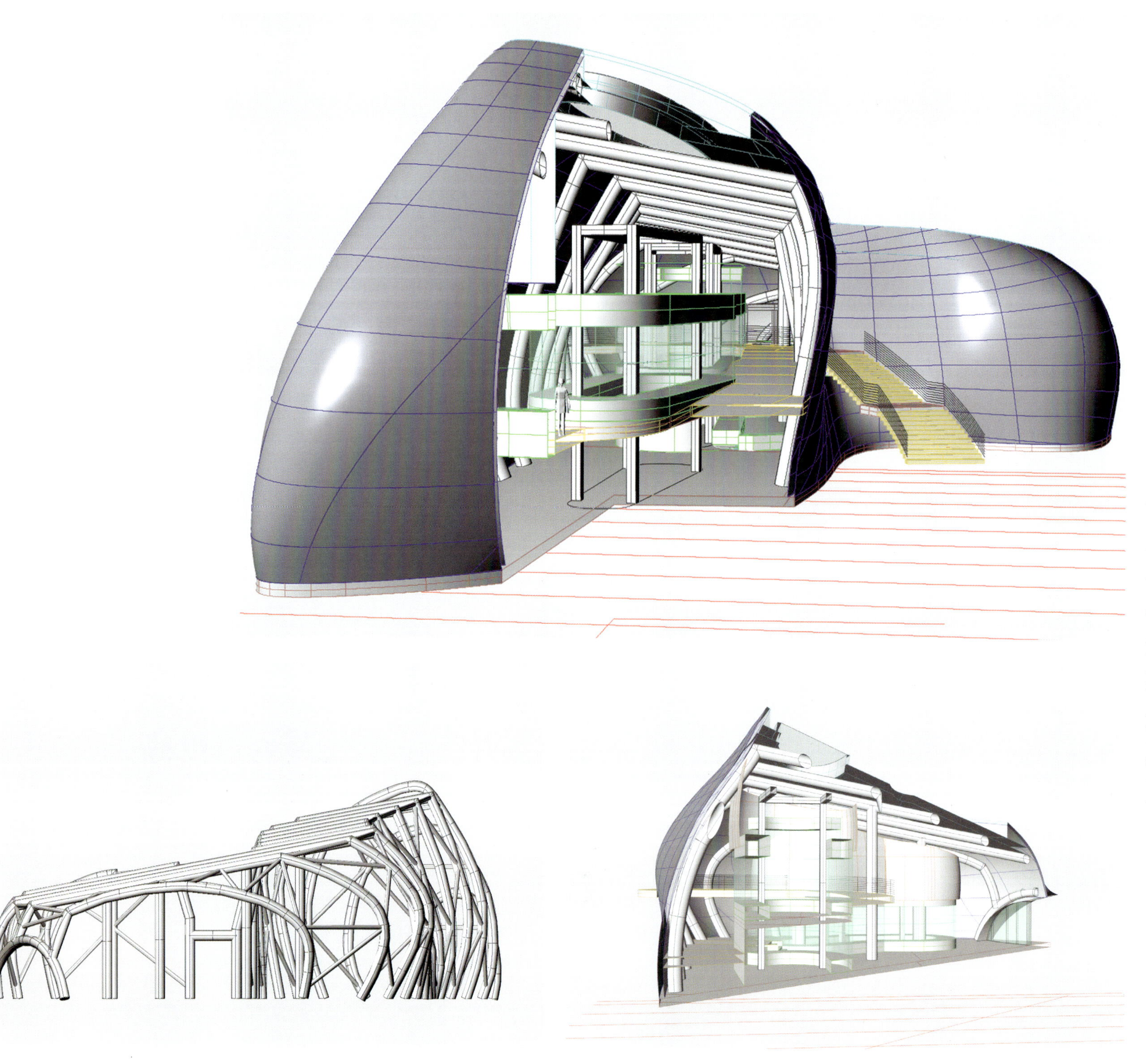

←
Cutaway shows interior spiral ramp.

↙↙
Tubular metal framework suggests a skeleton.

↙
Glass display cases reference internal organs.

→
Building looks like a living organism, even from above.

↘
Zinc scales reflect light and resemble reptile skin.

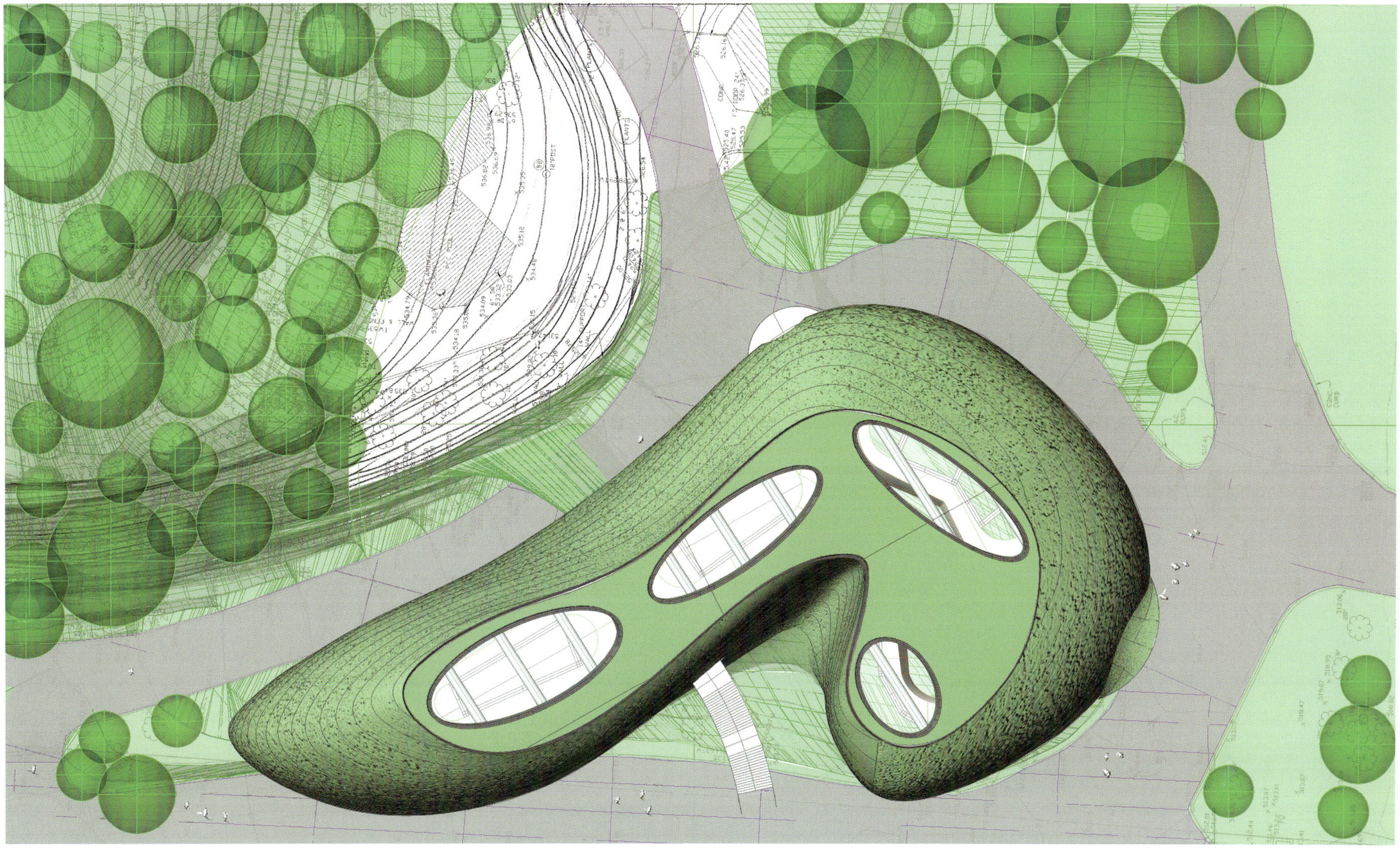

101
308
304
134
101
300
290
5
110
405
SANTA MONICA BLVD
101
296
312
10
WILSHIRE BLVD
306
10
N
E
S
1
LA
110
292

PARKS & PLAZAS

MC

VARIOUS UNNAMED LANDSCAPE ARCHITECTS
HOLLYWOOD STRIP PARK

1924

The most logical and advantageous plan for Hollywood.

Board of Parks Commissioners

One of the earliest examples of the expanding city's intense need for unified park space, and of its equally potent exploitation of eminent domain, was an early plan proposed by the Hollywood Chamber of Commerce to create a string of block-wide parks extending from Sanborn Junction, in Silver Lake, to La Brea Avenue, in Hollywood.

The belt would have run east-west for three miles through a city that had virtually no green space outside of the gargantuan but largely inaccessible wilderness of Griffith Park Traversed by meandering paths and drives, the collection of green spaces was intended to become what the *Los Angeles Times* deemed "one of California's greatest attractions to tourists." The removal of about 1,200 homes was permitted under the city's Park and Playground Act, passed back in 1909.

The $7-million park, the *Times* pointed out, sprang from a desire "to provide greater park facilities for the rapidly growing community before that growth has reached the stage of congestion of all available sites." Proponents also wanted a chance to add to the "natural scenic beauty of California that of the super beauty of landscaped, wide-spaced boulevards."

The scheme received enthusiastic backing from the Los Angeles City Council and the city's Board of Parks Commissioners, which called it "the most logical and advantageous plan for Hollywood."

But while officials cheered the idea, residents in the wrecking ball's path were incensed, as were their neighbors. Those spared from demolition would have been left to pick up the tab, a hefty assessment of $200. Others worried that the park would divide Hollywood into north and south, and that the park's budget could easily swell to triple its early estimates.

The South Hollywood Improvement Association spearheaded the initial opposition. Soon, a new organization emerged—the Central Hollywood Protective League—solely to stop the park. The plan, noted the *Times*, was bringing on "intercine discord, which threatens to disrupt commercial and social unity in Hollywood." One newspaper photo featured livid residents holding torches.

At a meeting of the chamber of commerce on July 15, 1924, not one but two resolutions were put forth to declare that "the park-strip plan be tabled until public demand should revive it." That never happened.

→ Newspaper graphic of three-mile-long series of parks divided by intersecting streets

Boulevard Plan That Threatens to Disrupt Film City

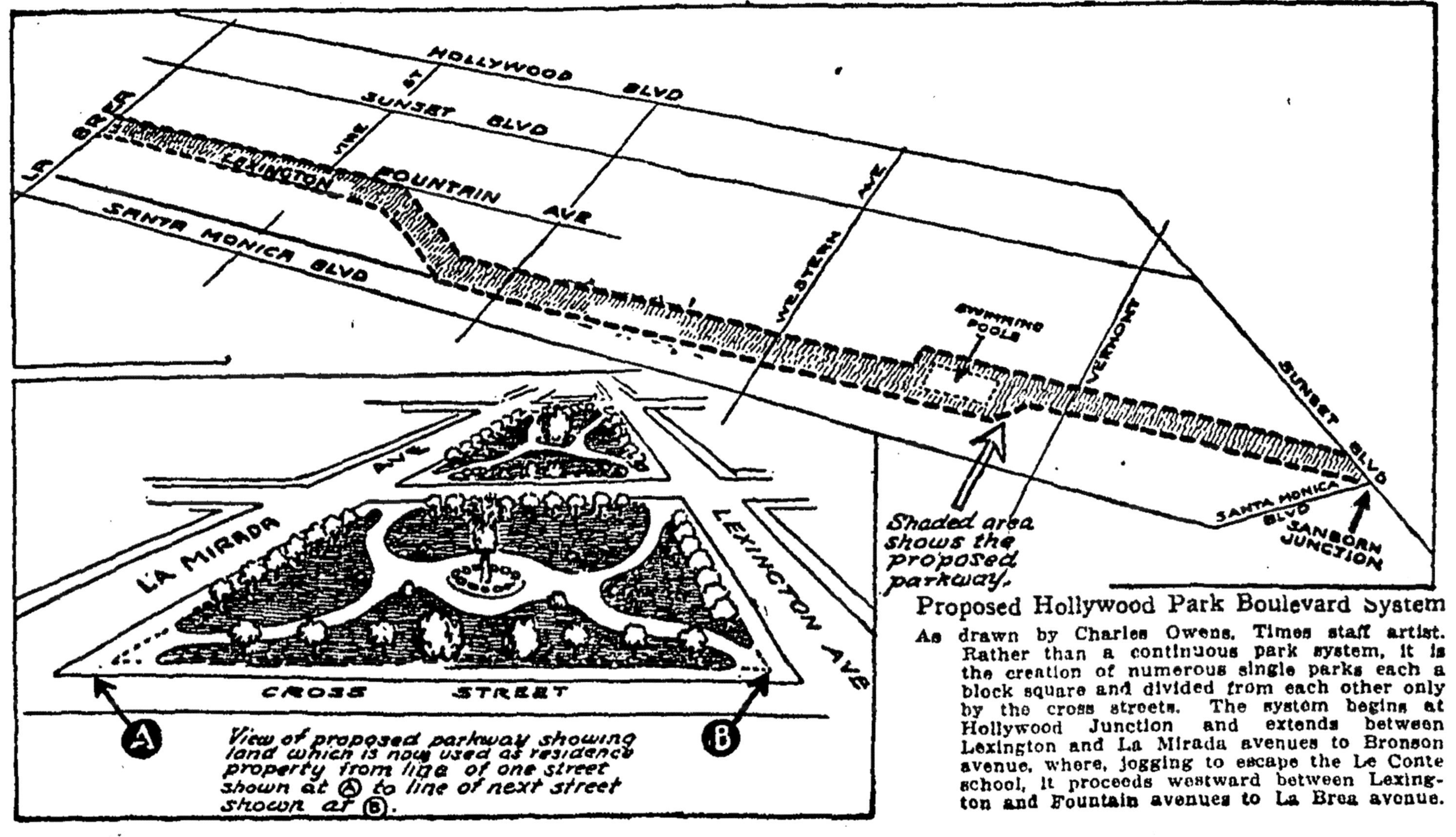

Proposed Hollywood Park Boulevard System

As drawn by Charles Owens, Times staff artist. Rather than a continuous park system, it is the creation of numerous single parks each a block square and divided from each other only by the cross streets. The system begins at Hollywood Junction and extends between Lexington and La Mirada avenues to Bronson avenue, where, jogging to escape the Le Conte school, it proceeds westward between Lexington and Fountain avenues to La Brea avenue.

OLMSTED BROTHERS AND BARTHOLOMEW
PARKS, PLAYGROUNDS, AND BEACHES FOR THE LOS ANGELES REGION

1930

Parks, Playgrounds, and Beaches for the Los Angeles Region is the city's most significant alternative blueprint—and its biggest missed opportunity. Issued in 1930, the 178-page report was the culmination of three years of legwork and deliberation by Olmsted Brothers of Brookline, Massachusetts, the heirs of famed landscape architect Frederick Law Olmsted, and Harland Bartholomew, of St. Louis. A self-appointed "citizen's committee" tied to the Los Angeles Chamber of Commerce had paid Olmsted and Bartholomew $80,000 to come up with a plan to remedy what was already an obvious crisis. Los Angeles, a city promoted into existence as an idyll of boundless natural beauty, was about to "strangle itself" with haphazard speculative development. The team had already authored the city's Major Traffic Street Plan in 1924, thus the veteran urban planners were considered the "brightest minds" to wrestle with the dilemma of open space.

What worried the chamber was that barely 1 percent of the Los Angeles region was dedicated to public parks or beaches, the lowest ratio of public to private land in the country. By one account, there was half an inch of public beach per resident.

Scathing, clear-eyed, and unflinching, the Olmsted-Bartholomew report diagnosed the present and sketched the future. If "the sharp practice of ruthless promoters" continued, it declared, "urban growth will fill in one after another of the open spaces...[leaving people] shut off from any considerable area of open land."

Olmsted and Bartholomew gathered up "the hills and sightly eminences" in Los Angeles and wove them into the fabric of "the expanding structure of the city." They wanted to build 71,000 acres of small parks within roughly a half-mile walking distance of every household and scatter another 92,000 acres of larger parks throughout the basin. They mapped out 95 parks linked within a 440-mile necklace of "pleasureway parks"—the traces of which can be seen today on double-wide streets like Crenshaw Boulevard. They also proposed that nearly the entire coastline, from Malibu to Long Beach, be purchased and held, largely undeveloped, in the public trust.

Opposition congealed on many fronts. To implement the plan, the city needed to create a plenary parks authority, which might have ignited a power tussle. Higher property taxes to fund the project, listed at $224 million, were certain to offend the formidable Taxpayer's Commission. Putting the plan on the ballot might also have trumped a $220-million bond act to bring Colorado River water to Los Angeles County. And, in the greatest roadblock of all, the plan's radical reordering of public and

→ An all-encompassing plan: urban parks and parkways in green; regional reserves in red

LANCASTER
PALMDALE
ANGELES
NATIONAL FOREST
SAUGUS
NEWHALL
Chatsworth
GLENDALE
POMONA
SANTA MONICA
OCEAN PARK
VENICE
LOS ANGELES
WHITTIER
NORWALK
EL SEGUNDO
MANHATTAN BEACH
HERMOSA
REDONDO
LONG BEACH
LOS ANGELES HARBOR
ORANGE CO.
25 MILES
30 MILES

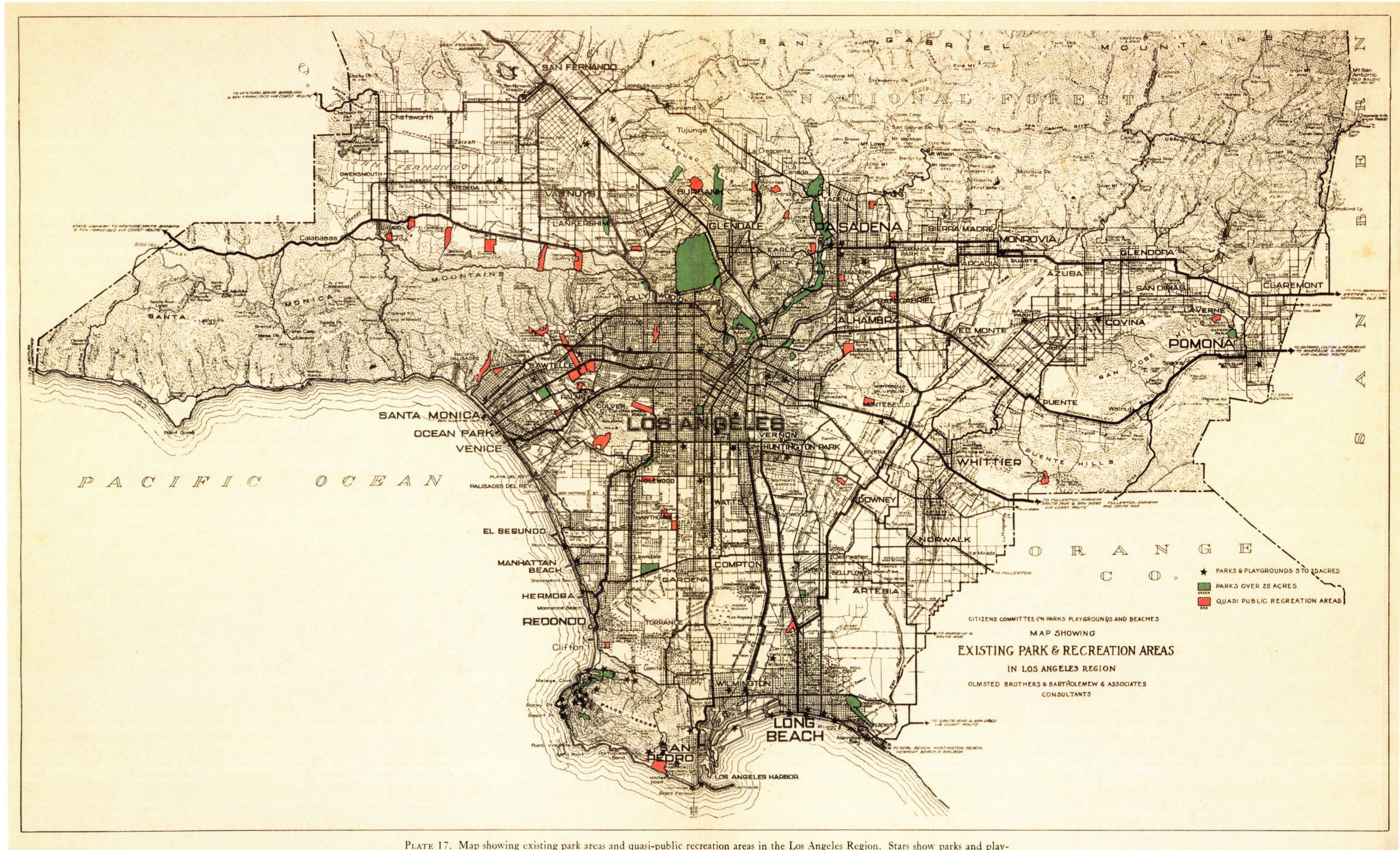

PLATE 17. Map showing existing park areas and quasi-public recreation areas in the Los Angeles Region. Stars show parks and playgrounds over five but under twenty-five acres in area. Green shows park areas over twenty-five acres in extent. Red shows quasi-public golf and country club areas not on public lands. (*Base map by courtesy of Automobile Club of Southern California.*)

←
Map shows city's lack of parks and recreation areas at the time.

→
Typical parkway landscape

private space, and its potential to halt unremitting land speculation, were anathema to the very cadre of city elites who'd commissioned the report in the first place.

[118] Parks, Playgrounds and Beaches for the Los Angeles Region

The chamber of commerce hushed up the report on the very day it was published. Remanded to the silent shelves of libraries and universities, "Parks, Playgrounds, and Beaches" remained an underground classic until 2000, when historians Greg Hise and William Deverell republished it in their book *Eden by Design*. The report's heroic recommendations remain, however, largely unfulfilled, and Los Angeles maintains its status as one of the most park-starved regions in the world.

BILL FAIN
LOS ANGELES GREENWAY CONCEPT

1993

More than 60 years after Olmsted and Bartholomew's plan to create a coordinated park plan for the city fell on deaf ears, architect Bill Fain proposed his Los Angeles Greenway Concept, using preexisting infrastructure—transit lines, bikeways, rivers, rail rights-of-way, and powerline easements—as sites for future public green spaces. The plan would save the city from having to occupy new space for parks: Streets wouldn't be replaced, they would be embedded with long swaths of green trails; the Los Angeles River would be filled with water and plants, becoming a vital part of the city. The remodeling not only would help provide much-needed places for recreation, a respite from concrete, and a home to community, but also would add the "layering and patina" that the city sorely lacked, as Fain put it. The new parks would be closely connected to schools, libraries, senior centers, and other community buildings. One set of parks, Fain argued, would beget another; parks would grow out of parks. The plan never gained traction with city officials,

although it did receive several awards and was exhibited in 1996 in the show *Urban Revisions* at the Museum of Contemporary Art.

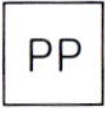

SAMUEL LUNDEN, HARRY SIMS BENT, HENRY WYLDE, AND OTHERS

HANCOCK PARK

1927
1936
1941
1948
1962

From the day in 1916 that oilman G. Allan Hancock deeded the La Brea Tar Pits to Los Angeles County, the oozing trap for Ice Age animals and Pleistocene beasts was a trouble spot. Hancock was explicit that a park be created not for recreation but as a home to a museum for the study of the fossils mired in the asphalt. So for generations, the directors of the County Museum—located in Exposition Park, four and a half miles to the southeast—attempted to fulfill Hancock's injunction. Each effort, it seemed, became engulfed in the tar.

The first proposal, floated in 1927 by leaders of the Los Angeles County Museum of History, Science, and Art, envisioned a footbridge over the largest pit, known as the "lake." Part of a plan to restore the landscape to its prehistoric past, the Beaux-Arts span, presumably constructed out of concrete, would extend about 150 feet and serve as the 23-acre park's formal gateway from Wilshire Boulevard. Dominating the bridge would be a sculpture of a nude goddess, draped lasciviously over a rocky pillar and being pecked at by a teratorn, a giant bird of prey. Despite having been cast in large-scale plaster models, the bridge failed to gain traction.

Another part of the landscape plan was a Pleistocene zoo. Sculptor Joseph Leland Roop shaped its fighting saber-toothed tigers—which grace the park even today—but few of the more than dozen mastodon, elephant, camel, horse, bison, and wolf groupings were ever cast. Roop died shortly after he received the commission.

A decade later, in March 1936, attorney Walter D. Holsinger tried to persuade the county to approve an elaborate Fine Arts Center, consisting of an opera house, an art gallery, a motion-picture museum, schools of music and art, a theater of drama and dance, and an exhibition of prehistoric fossils. Its $15-million budget was exorbitant, and the Depression-wracked county instead turned to the WPA to sponsor a project to create at the tar pits a park modeled on its Pleistocene past. This plan also failed.

Next up—and consigned to a similarly swift death—was architect Samuel Lunden's La Brea Pits Museum. At the behest of the Los Angeles County Board of Supervisors in 1941, Lunden submitted a low-slung, Streamline Moderne building with a glass observation overlook. The plan also called for slicing through the tar to install a stairway to a deep basement where visitors could see the geologic striations as they descended through layers of bones. The modest, graceful $50,000 building had been approved when a county official in charge of prioritizing wartime materials arrived from Washington with news of restrictions on steel, halting the plan for good.

In 1948, Harry Sims Bent, the partner of artist and architect Millard Sheets, was hired to provide a master plan, which called for a museum, a Pleistocene zoo with plaster-cast animals, and an Ice Age botanical garden. Bent's scheme was only partially executed. Three years into the process, the county hired landscape architect Ralph Cornell to rethink the park,

→ Henry Wilde's towering cyclorama dome near the "lake"

RANCHO LA BREA PIT MUSEUM
FOR THE
COUNTY OF LOS ANGELES
Samuel E. Lunden, Architect

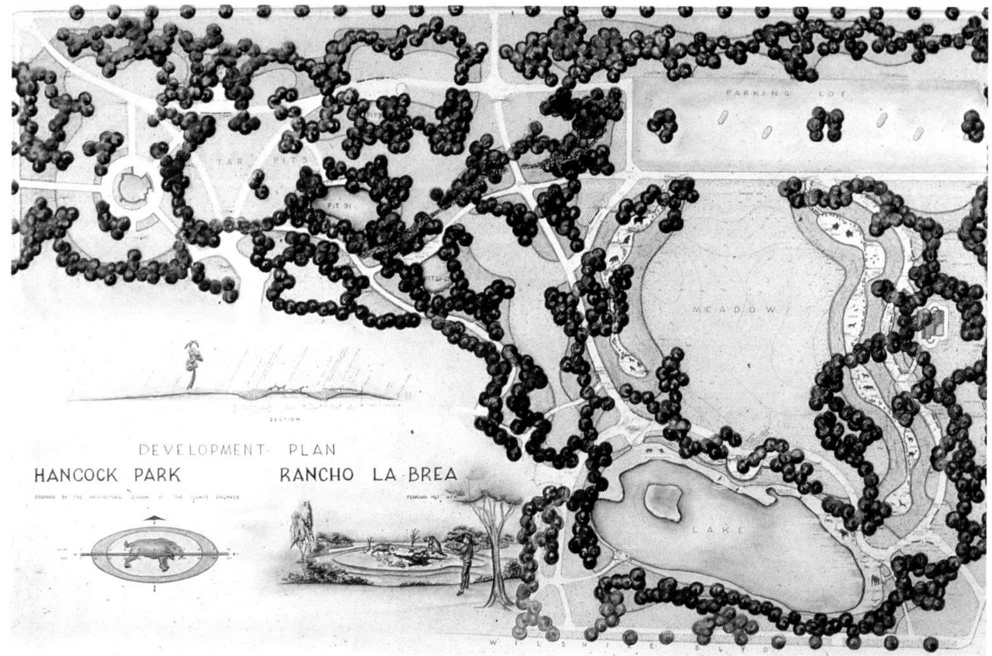

overgrown and muddy after years of neglect during and after World War II. Cornell's watercolor rendering of his "primitive" plantings clearly shows the "zoo," which yet again never materialized—although the Observation Pit was finally built and still stands.

A few years later, in 1962, the most dramatic museum proposal emerged from the mind of Henry Wylde, chief of exhibitions at the County Museum. Wylde sketched a 60-foot-high cyclorama that would have measured 120 feet around, painted with a diorama bringing to life the hothouse world of prehistoric Los Angeles. Museumgoers would board a huge basket and be lifted, by a hydraulic piston, four stories into a heavenly dome.

As usual, there was no money. Appeals to Hancock, who was sitting on millions from his real estate and oil holdings, were rejected. It was not until philanthropist George C. Page gave the county $3 million and commissioned Pasadena architects Thornton and Fagan that a museum devoted to the tar pits' fossil deposits was finally funded. The Page Museum opened in 1977, ending a 50-year curse on Hancock Park.

←←
Samuel Lunden's modest Art Deco structure, with tar pit inside

←
Pleistocene plants and animals line the meadow and tar seep.

↙
A close encounter with Ice Age Los Angeles

→
Section and plan views of cyclorama, with hydraulic basket lift

↘
Modernist museum from 1967 without cyclorama

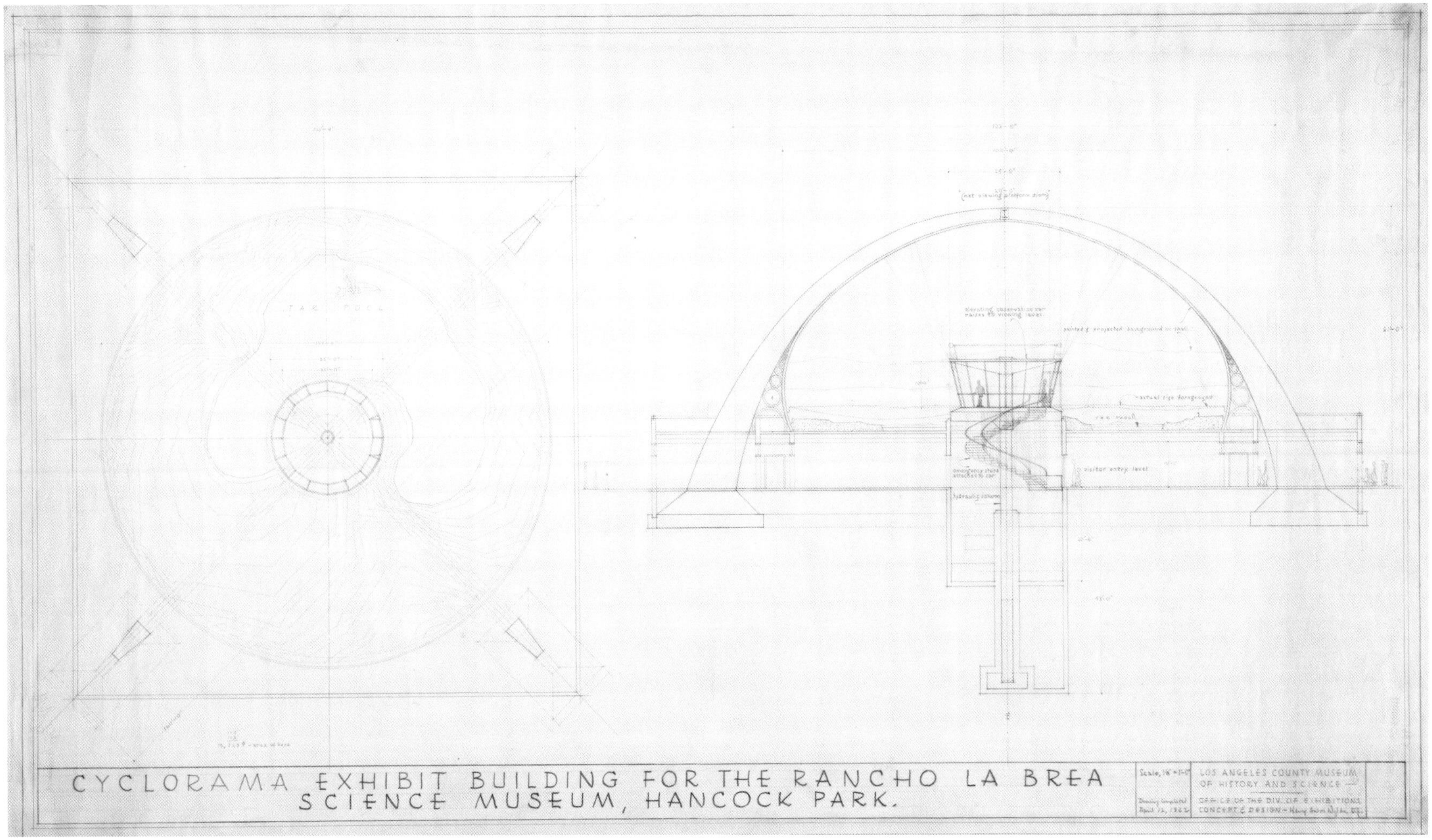

CYCLORAMA EXHIBIT BUILDING FOR THE RANCHO LA BREA
SCIENCE MUSEUM, HANCOCK PARK.
LOS ANGELES COUNTY MUSEUM OF HISTORY AND SCIENCE
OFFICE OF THE DIV. OF EXHIBITIONS

RANCHO LA BREA MUSEUM

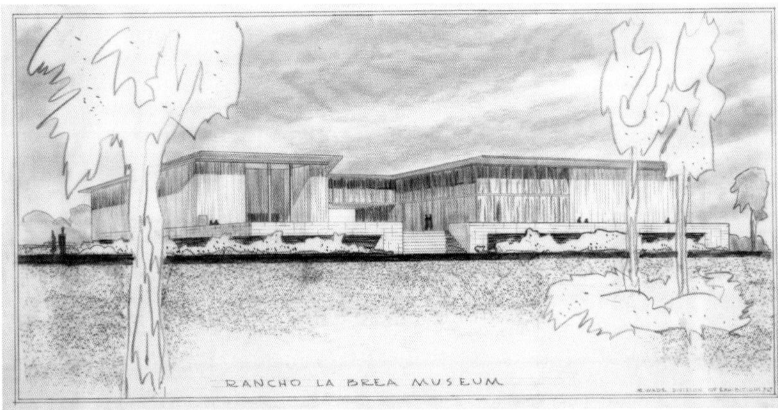

PP

MC

ROBERT ALEXANDER AND CHARLES LUCKMAN GRIFFITH PARK AERIAL TRAMWAY AND HOLLYWOOD HALL OF FAME

1968

Mount Hollywood with a lobotomy.

Art Seidenbaum

Mining millionaire Col. Griffith J. Griffith not only gave Los Angeles 4,000 acres, named Griffith Park in his honor; he also willed the city money to build the Greek Theater and the Griffith Observatory. Yet this $1.5-million bequest was not so simple. His original idea was to put the observatory at the 1,640-foot peak of Mount Hollywood, to be made accessible via funicular. But such an undertaking meant shaving 60 feet off the mountaintop—an unrealistic plan that led two decades later to the observatory being built downslope, on Mount Hollywood's south-facing ledge.

That left the slightly higher elevation of Mount Hollywood a coveted target for developers. In 1942, Griffith's heirs proposed a revolving restaurant for the site, approved by the city's Recreation and Parks Commission. Robert Alexander drew up the plans, Richard Neutra made a promotional sketch, and preliminary work began. Then, World War II, followed by the Korean War, halted the work.

In rapid succession, ideas for the summit came and went between 1954 and 1965. In 1956, Griffith Observatory director Dinsmore Alter wanted to put a 36-inch telescope above an observation deck and coffee shop. In 1959, Alexander proposed a space museum called Griffith Starland, but it was quashed by Griffith's only child, Van Griffith, because it might glorify war. Another Alexander design, the Observatorium, would have had a four-story revolving restaurant, half underground, half above. This, too, died, burdened by a $200,000 price tag.

Shortly after, radio station owner Cliff Gill started peddling a development he called Alpine Village, a 21-story hotel on a four-and-a-half-acre site near the Pilgrimage Theater in the Cahuenga Pass. The round tower looked like a slim version of Welton Becket's iconic Capitol Records building. A town of cube-shaped dwellings would cover the hillside behind the 500-room hotel. A three-stage tramway would first lift passengers 1,000 feet to—what else?—a revolving restaurant overlooking Lake Hollywood. From there, riders would board a gondola and soar over the Hollywood Reservoir, then transfer to the last leg, a mile-long ride ascending 800 feet to Mount Lee, where Gill would erect his Alpine Village. The parks commission voted in favor of the $15-million undertaking, but that's as far as it got.

Gill came back a little more than a year later with an even more brazen, and controversial, idea. Now, partnered with RKO and Don Fedderman (producer of *My Three Sons* and *The Lawrence Welk Show*), he unveiled the Hollywood Hall of Fame. With architect Charles Luckman in his employ, he asked park

→ Mount Hollywood crowned with star-shaped museum

commissioners to sanction a 35,000-square-foot, star-shaped museum, facing a six-acre plaza surrounded by battlements. Once again, there would be an aerial tram, this one travelling 8,900 feet from the Los Angeles Zoo and once again, a revolving restaurant—this time, with a buffet but no alcohol. Gill declared that the $6.3-million Hall of Fame would “achieve international significance.”

The plan required taking 57 feet off the mountaintop, which *Los Angeles Times* columnist Art Seidenbaum denounced as “Mount Hollywood with a lobotomy.” Still, mayor Sam Yorty got behind it, as did the Hollywood Chamber of Commerce. Opposition, led by local conservationists, residents, and councilman Art Snyder—who said the development would “deface the skyline of the city for blatantly commercial purposes”—undid the project. On January 9, 1969, the city’s parks commission voted three to two against Gill’s hilltop fortress. Commission president A. E. England angrily marched out of the hearing room, shouting, “It’s going to be built.” It never was.

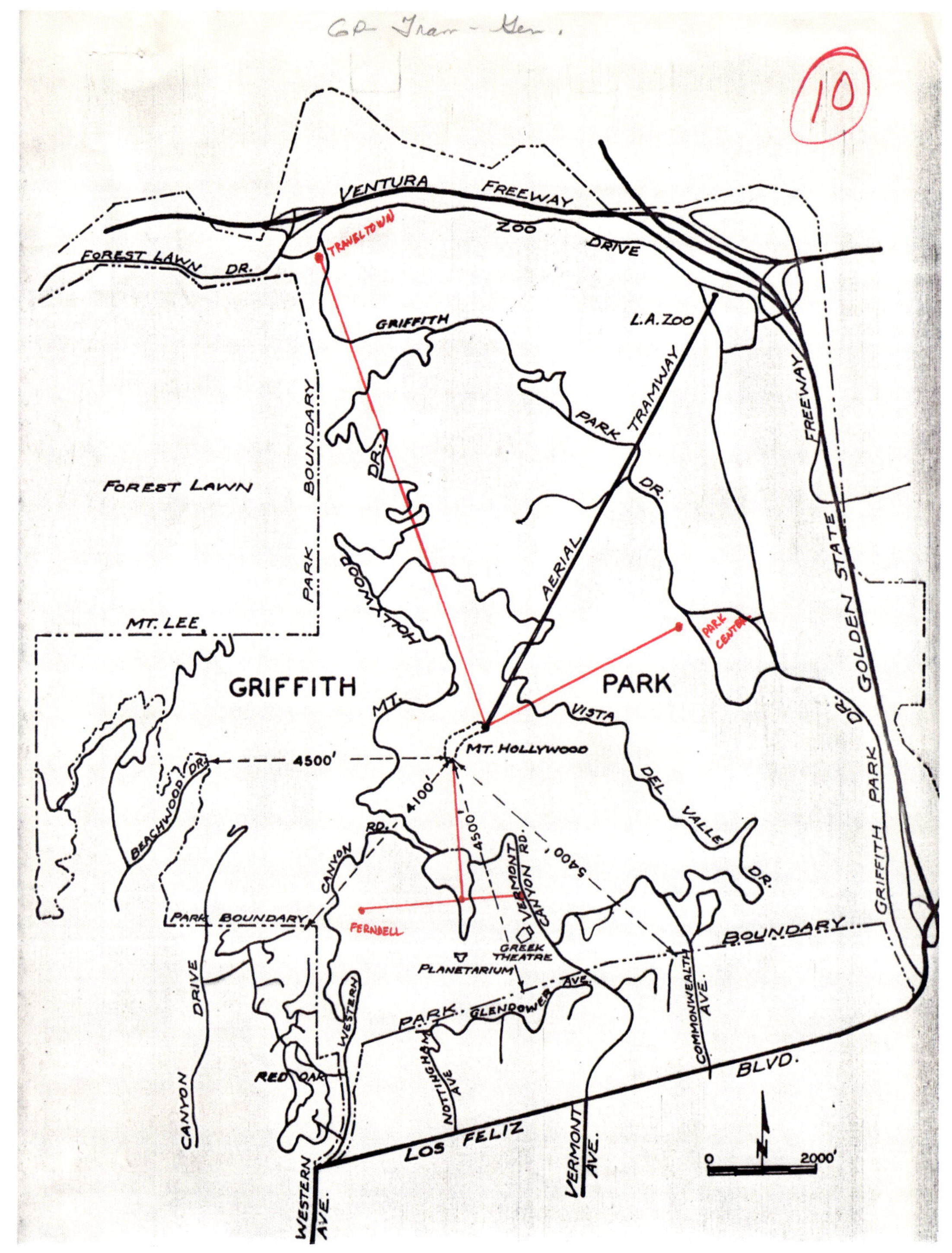

←
Aerial tram routes through Griffith Park

→
Luckman's flat-topped trams and revolving restaurants above the Griffith Park Observatory

→→
In Cahuenga Pass, a Capitol Records doppelgänger

→
Arrival station in a competing plan

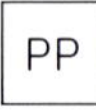

SB

FRANK GEHRY AND LAURENCE HALPRIN
ARTS PARK L.A.

1978

The best elements of a fair and a school.

Frank Gehry and Laurence Halprin

Ever since assembly-line homes first began plopping down in the San Fernando Valley, Los Angeles has tried to inject its less-refined backyard with a dose of “culture.”

Among the more ambitious attempts was the 1978 Arts Park L.A. Presented by the San Fernando Valley Arts Council, the proposal called for an 80-acre outdoor performing and visual arts facility located in the Sepulveda Dam Basin, at the intersection of the Ventura and San Diego freeways.

Designed to provide “the best elements of a fair and a school,” the park—a hilly expanse surrounding a 20-acre lake—would have incorporated a 2,500-seat theater, studios, classrooms, exhibition areas, and a 10-story observation tower.

Simple wooden buildings would be covered with pastel-hued stucco or metal. The theater, a basic box with a lean-to roof, would be raised on stilts and edged with a snaking array of solar panels supported by a steel superstructure. An “art factory” housing classrooms, workshops, and studios would have a rainbow-shaped solar collector on its roof. Bizarre as it sounds, the observation tower, wrapped in steel fencing, would be crowned with a giant pineapple sculpture, an idea that Gehry said came to him in a dream.

The organizers raised $40,000 from the National Endowment for the Arts and the city, but the project never gained enough community support or money to move forward.

→
Solar panels, 20-acre lake, paths on stilts, and pineapple atop observation tower

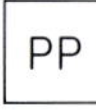

DT

SITE
PERSHING SQUARE GREEN CARPET

1985

New York firm SITE beat out 200 designers in a 1985 competition to redesign Pershing Square, located in the middle of the city's once-thriving cultural and business district. The park, which began in the nineteenth century as a shaded Spanish zocalo, had endured through the 1940s as the city's equivalent of Speakers Corner in London's Hyde Park. But the addition of an underground parking lot, in 1952, lifted the plaza up and destroyed its connection to the city, leaving a blight.

Working under the newly created Pershing Square Management Association, SITE proposed Green Carpet, an undulating, gridded space meant to be a microcosm of Los Angeles, from its dense urban core to its hillsides and its suburbs. The plaza would be flat in the center, with waves of concrete emanating outward, and contain gazebos, kiosks, a restaurant, a performance space, and shade-providing trellises.

The city's powerful downtown commercial establishment did not support the plan. Pershing Square was considered marginal to its favored development, Bunker Hill, a hub of glassy office and cultural buildings to the northwest. And with a price tag estimated at more than $20 million, Green Carpet was deemed too expensive. About a decade later, Ricardo Legorreta and Laurie Olin's competition-winning scheme for the park, a forbidding jumble of giant pastel forms and barren concrete expanses, went ahead, the latest "improvement" to the square that once bore the name Central Park.

↗
Model of proposed park

↗↗
Green Carpet terrain mimics city's hills and valleys.

→
Leafy canopy extends across a lively plaza.

HODGETTS + FUNG, MORPHOSIS, MARK MACK, AND TOD WILLIAMS BILLIE TSIEN ARCHITECTS WEST SIDE ARTS PARK, SEPULVEDA BASIN

1989

Sculptural, kinetic pieces emerging from the Earth to begin to reveal what lies below.

Morphosis

For nearly a decade, business and civic leaders in the San Fernando Valley pushed for the creation of a cultural mecca inside the Sepulveda Dam Basin. After several false starts, including Frank Gehry's Arts Park L.A., the Valley Cultural Foundation held a competition for design teams, and the jury selected a $50-million center proposed by Hodgetts + Fung, Morphosis, Mark Mack, and Tod Williams Billie Tsien.

Nestled among 60 acres of rolling hills would have been Hodgetts + Fung's branch of the Natural History Museum, with an open-air amphitheater; Morphosis's 1,800-seat proscenium theater and 500-seat black-box theater; Mark Mack's children's art center; and Tod Williams Billie Tsien's two-story Arts Park Center, pierced by a central silo containing expansive exhibition spaces.

The tower and roof of Morphosis's subterranean theater would have jutted above ground in a cacophony of grids, fins, and an elevated "skywalk," which the firm called "thrusting circulation bars." Morphosis set out to create a field punctuated by solids and voids, "sculptural, kinetic pieces emerging from the Earth to begin to reveal what lies below."

The museum, by Hodgetts + Fung, would have featured a 560-foot-long winged roof, ascending from an underground exhibition grotto. To create a kind of performance glen, Hodgetts conceived a rammed-earth amphitheater whose stage hovered over a man-made waterfront. Nearby, an experimental farm and irrigated orange groves would recall the region's not-so-distant past.

Mark Mack's Children's Center for the Arts was a string of simple, brightly colored umbrella-like buildings, linked by a gently curving wooden boardwalk. Each building took on a unique form—a shed, a cylinder, a tower—with a front door facing the boardwalk and a back door opening onto the landscape. Running down the middle of the boardwalk was a man-made "arbor," suggesting a wilderness where a child might run amok.

As soon as the plan was announced, it came under attack. Sheila Murphy, the project manager for the U.S. Army Corps of Engineers, the federal agency that controlled the site, declared: "They don't have the option to be as bold or avant-garde as they want because this isn't their land." *Los Angeles Times* urban-affairs critic Sam Hall Kaplan weighed in, saying the idea of "building...precious architectural objects floating in a park somewhere...as if they were cultural cathedrals" defied urban reality. The existing street grid was where the complex needed to go.

The design scheme had been financed by private donations and a grant from the National Endowment for the Arts. No other money was found and, under the weight of a Sierra Club lawsuit, the park collapsed.

→
Morphosis's "skywalk" emerges from underground theater.

CC
LEVEL +19 +22

←
Models and sketch of Hodgetts + Fung's rammed-earth amphitheater and winged museum

↗
Two views of Morphosis's theater model

→→
Mark Mack's Children's Center for the Arts

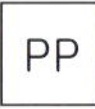

DT

HARGREAVES AND MICHAEL MALTZAN ARCHITECTURE / MORPHOSIS AND FIELD OPERATIONS
CORNFIELDS PARK

2006

Let's do something interesting with this. We definitely won't win it.

James Corner to Thom Mayne

California State Parks held a competition in 2006 to develop the Cornfields, a 32-acre former industrial parcel wedged between Chinatown, the Los Angeles River, and Elysian Park.

Several teams submitted proposals, but the one that made the biggest splash was from Morphosis and landscape firm Field Operations. Their plan called for "a grand land swap," in which Dodger Stadium, located in Elysian Park's Chavez Ravine, would be relocated to the east end of the Cornfields site, freeing up 265 acres in the park to build a new mixed-use neighborhood for up to 25,000 people. Not stopping there, the team called for the construction of a large elevated deck north of the Cornfields site, connecting to Elysian Park and creating 1,000 acres of parkland. The design would have almost doubled the amount of green space in the area, forming a reserve nearly one and a half times larger than New York's Central Park.

Morphosis principal Thom Mayne called the idea a vital piece of "connective tissue" for the city. He later remembered Field Operations founder James Corner telling him: "Let's do something interesting with this. We definitely won't win it."

The megapark would contain forests, gardens, a championship golf course, an observatory, walking paths, and just about everything else a nature lover could ask for. It would extend all the way to the Los Angeles River, with a luxuriant riverside path for bikers and walkers.

But the wining entry, while not as transformative, was infinitely more doable. It belonged to Hargreaves and Michael Maltzan. Their multiuse park was inspired largely by the site's past. In its earliest days, the area was home to some of the city's first Native Americans, drawn by the river and its nutrient-rich soil. Later, the site became the city's industrial center, housing its most important train depot. The banana-shaped plot got its nickname not because, as some mistakenly believe, corn was cultivated there but because kernels from overstuffed train cars sprouted on the barren flats. Either way, the depot was known for a long time as the Ellis Island of Los Angeles, a place where masses of Hispanic and Asian immigrants arrived, many of them working in the immediate area after settling down.

Hargreaves, Maltzan, and their team of experts—including archaeologists and cultural anthropologists—created a design that reflected this layered history. Buildings were to include a Welcome Station visitors' center inspired by the old train depot, an ecology center focused on environmental exhibits, and a restaurant. The park itself would consist of a 15-acre field flanked by a fountain-filled plaza on its southern side and nature-oriented wetlands and gardens connecting to the Los Angeles River on its northern tip.

Within the lawn, Hargreaves established a framework of paths, following the traces of switching-rail lines, and designed play areas and a performance stage, called the Turntable, on the spot where train cars once rotated at the rail's end.

Reflecting a trend in many of L.A.'s unbuilt projects, the Hargreaves-Maltzan plan tried to connect the park with the

→ Pedestrian bridge connecting Hargreaves and Maltzan's scheme to North Broadway

rest of the city, this time via four pedestrian bridges—three linked to Chinatown, and a wide, landscaped span reaching to Elysian Park.

The project hummed along until a California budget crisis in 2009 forced its abandonment. A “temporary” park eventually took shape on the land and is still being completed by state parks employees. Much needed, it nonetheless lacks the energy and passion of the competition proposals.

↖↖
Hargreaves and Maltzan's site plan

↖
Bridge corner with glass-clad lookout spot

←
Three views of Welcome Center, which evokes old train depot.

↙
Visitors interact with folding structures and bridges.

→
New Dodger Stadium in the flats just north of downtown

→→
Chavez Ravine make-over, with massive high-rise residential towers and wide open parks

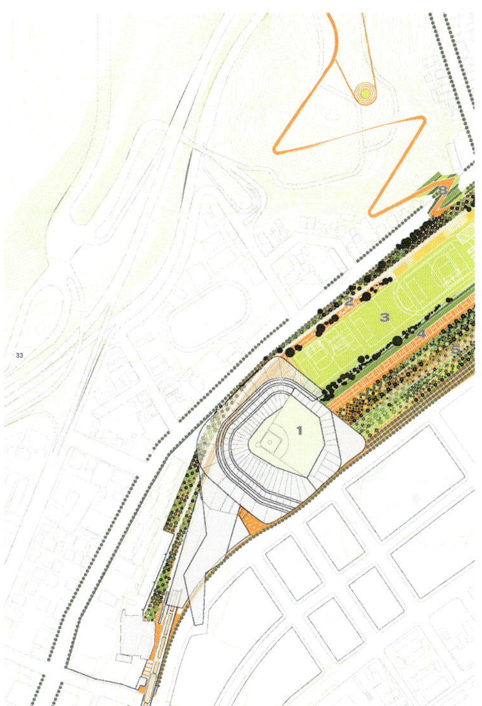

101
134
101
328
5
110
318
405
SANTA MONICA BLVD
101
WILSHIRE BLVD
10
356
360
346
364
350
10
N
E
S
1
LA
110
320
322
330
334
336
340
362
370

TR

LA WS MC DT SB

8 1 2 4 0

TRANSIT PLANS

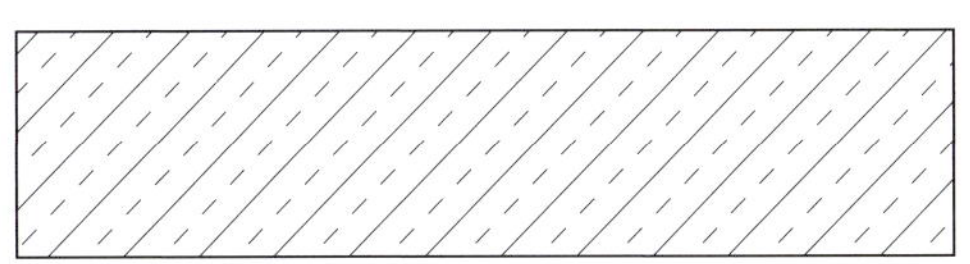

HORACE M. DOBBINS
DOBBINS CYCLEWAY

1900

On New Year's Day, 1900, a crowd of a thousand gathered as Horace M. Dobbins opened his Cycleway, intended as the first leg of a private bicycle freeway linking Pasadena to Los Angeles. The elevated track extended just one and a quarter miles, from Pasadena's newly completed Hotel Green to its biggest tourist hotel, the Raymond. But the Cycleway would never make it past the Pasadena city limits.

Dobbins, who served a two-year stint as Pasadena's mayor and was the prosperous son of the man who built the Washington Monument, had purchased a six-mile right-of-way along the Arroyo Seco. His plan was to tunnel through Elysian Park hills—where, in 1939, highway builders bored the Figueroa Tunnels used today for traffic on the Pasadena Freeway—and build a bridge for cyclers to cross the Los Angeles River into the historic plaza downtown.

The wooden track, made of Oregon pine paved smooth with tar and sand, ranged from 3 to 50 feet off the ground and was wide enough to accommodate four bikes abreast. Incandescent lights, then a novelty, were slated at 300-foot intervals. The terminal stations, described as "Moorish in design," would be equipped with rental and repair shops, so riders could grab a bike at one end and deposit it at the other. The heavy wire railings were painted green to blend into the surrounding hills.

Halfway along the proposed route, near present-day Highland Park, Dobbins was going to build Merlemont, a 200-foot-long casino whose wide veranda would afford commanding views of the San Gabriel Mountains and downtown. The private lair offered cyclists a broad plaza with fountains and was an arboretum of tropical and semitropical plants.

But cycling—a nationwide fad in the Gay Nineties, with Southern California boasting more bikes than anywhere in the world—was soon surpassed by trolleys and eventually by motoring. Dobbins's Cycleway was abandoned, part of it sold to Pasadena to build its City Hall

Dobbins's dream lay buried—much of it under the concrete of the Arroyo Seco Parkway—for nearly 100 years until Dennis Crowley, an avid cyclist, discovered photographs of the Cycleway and in 1995 began a campaign to complete it. Crowley's track would be elevated in spots but on level ground for most of its eight miles. The price tag was between $20 million and $30 million, equal to the cost of a quarter-mile of the proposed extension of the Long Beach Freeway through nearby South Pasadena, yet too expensive for transportation planners who had only $4 million a year earmarked for bicycles. Crowley died of a heart attack in July 2008, his vision, like Dobbins's a century before, unrealized.

↗ Incomplete Cycleway in 1900, view north

↗↗ View south, toward Arroyo Seco

→ Tollbooth, with Hotel Green in background

→→ Dobbins in his Oldsmobile

KELKER, DE LEUW AND COMPANY MASS TRANSIT PLAN

1925

Responding to a new city charter calling for a "comprehensive elevated railway and subway plan," the Los Angeles City Council hired transportation consultants Kelker, De Leuw and Company. R. F. Kelker and Charles De Leuw, authors of the Chicago Rapid Transit Plan, were preeminent in their field. Their report, completed in April 1925 at a cost of $40,000, presented a strategy to undo the existing mess of snarled streetcars. The city, they said, needed to spend the next five years constructing 153 miles of underground, elevated, and surface railway. The cost: $133,385,000. Subway lines would radiate from a central station beneath Pershing Square, traveling through downtown, into Hollywood and across Third Street. The line along Wilshire Boulevard would stretch as far as Beverly Hills, where an elevated would become a streetcar to Santa Monica—the very same Wilshire Bouelvard route the city is still trying to complete via subway today.

Kelker, De Leuw foresaw a city of 3 million inhabitants spreading into the rural San Fernando and San Gabriel valleys, Venice Beach, and the bluffs of San Pedro. Over its entire projected lifetime (well beyond its intial five years), the plan called for 41 miles of subway and 241 miles of elevated and surface track to be laid, with express trains running through the most congested parts of town. Stations would be placed anywhere between a quarter-mile and a mile apart. Altogether, this was the most exhaustive proposal of the prewar era. And in a forward-looking concept, the report urged the city to buy empty land near future subway stations so it could reap the added value of public transportation—the very mechanism today's planners use to create transit-oriented development.

A year after it was issued, the report was foiled by a public wary of clattering, ugly els. Voters in a 1926 straw poll rejected a transit terminal whose linchpin was elevated rail.

→ Existing rapid transit in black; proposed in red

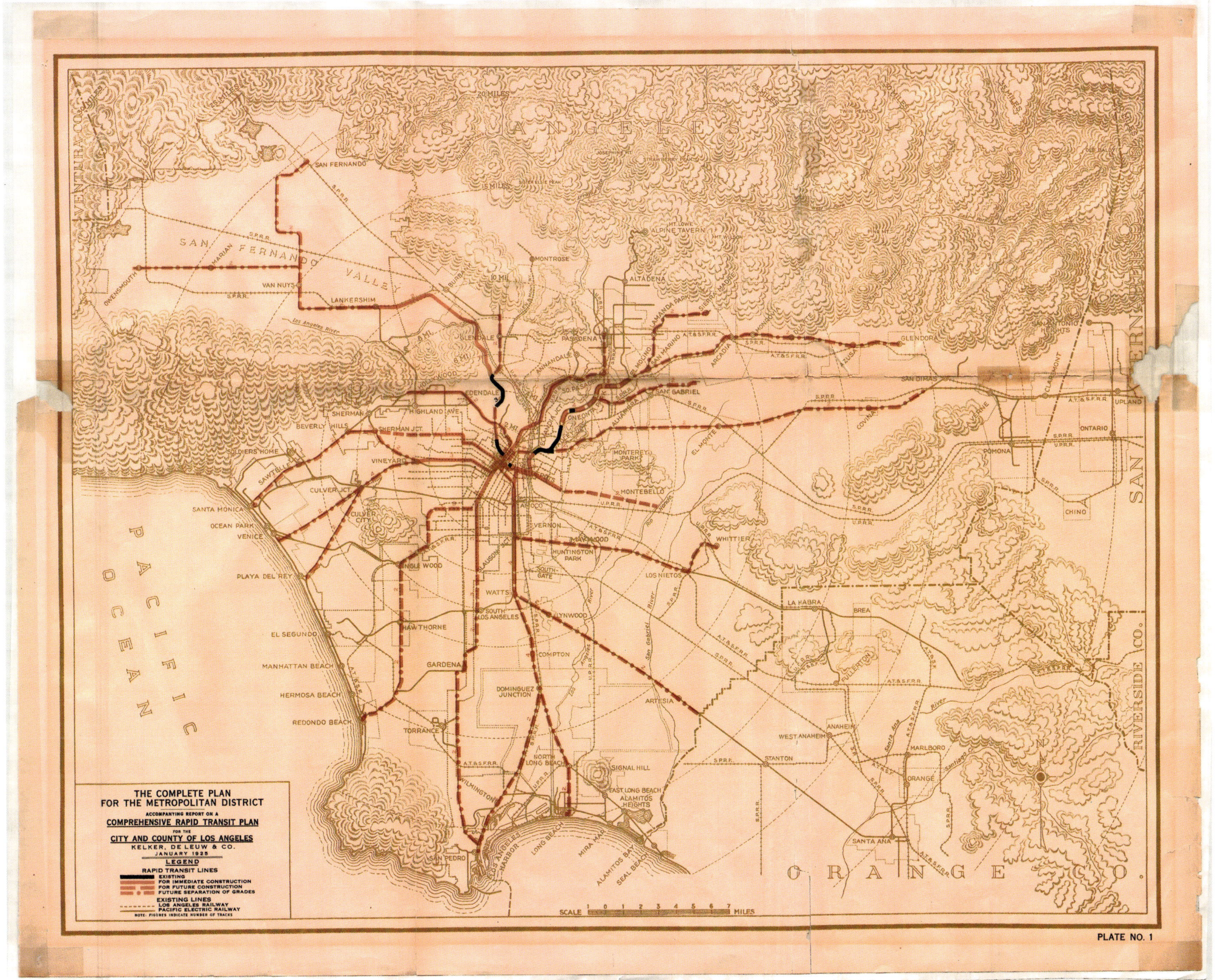
THE COMPLETE PLAN
FOR THE METROPOLITAN DISTRICT
ACCOMPANYING REPORT ON A
COMPREHENSIVE RAPID TRANSIT PLAN
FOR THE
CITY AND COUNTY OF LOS ANGELES
KELKER, DE LEUW & CO.
JANUARY 1925
LEGEND
RAPID TRANSIT LINES
EXISTING
FOR IMMEDIATE CONSTRUCTION
FOR FUTURE CONSTRUCTION
FUTURE SEPARATION OF GRADES
EXISTING LINES
LOS ANGELES RAILWAY
PACIFIC ELECTRIC RAILWAY
NOTE: FIGURES INDICATE NUMBER OF TRACKS
PLATE NO. 1
SAN FERNANDO
SAN FERNANDO VALLE
VAN NUYS
LANKERSHIM
OWENSMOUTH
MARIAN
MONTROSE
ALTADENA
PASADENA
GLENDALE
GLENDORA
SAN DIMAS
CLAREMONT
UPLAND
ONTARIO
POMONA
CHINO
SAN GABRIEL
EL MONTE
COVINA
ARCADIA
MONTEREY PARK
MONTEBELLO
WHITTIER
LOS NIETOS
LA HABRA
BREA
FULLERTON
ANAHEIM
WEST ANAHEIM
STANTON
ORANGE
SANTA ANA
MARLBORO
HIGHLAND AVE.
SHERMAN
SHERMAN JCT.
BEVERLY HILLS
SAWTELLE
VINEYARD
CULVER JCT.
CULVER CITY
SANTA MONICA
OCEAN PARK
VENICE
PLAYA DEL REY
INGLEWOOD
HAWTHORNE
EL SEGUNDO
MANHATTAN BEACH
HERMOSA BEACH
REDONDO BEACH
GARDENA
TORRANCE
DOMINGUEZ JUNCTION
COMPTON
LYNWOOD
WATTS
SOUTH LOS ANGELES
SOUTH GATE
HUNTINGTON PARK
VERNON
MAYWOOD
ARTESIA
NORTH LONG BEACH
SIGNAL HILL
EAST LONG BEACH
ALAMITOS HEIGHTS
LONG BEACH
WILMINGTON
SAN PEDRO
LOS ANGELES HARBOR
ALAMITOS BAY
SEAL BEACH
PACIFIC OCEAN
ORANGE CO.
RIVERSIDE CO.
SCALE MILES

LA

SUBWAYS AND ELEVATED RAIL

1933
1939
1945
1959–62
1964

The Los Angeles population explosion of the 1920s made subways seem like an imperative, certainly among successive waves of urban planners. Study after study mapped out underground lines, usually along the same major thoroughfares.

After the Kelker, De Leuw plan failed, Donald Baker's 1933 Rapid Transit System for Los Angeles, California proposed a less costly version: roughly $37 million in improvements to the city's existing rail facilities, including new grade separations, elevated tracks, and a downtown subway. Those changes stalled when federal grants and city bonds failed to materialize. Next, the 1939 "Transit Program for the Los Angeles Metropolitan Area," published by the city's Transportation Engineering Board, recommended trenching one route westward beneath Wilshire Boulevard and another along Broadway, the spine of downtown. Immediately after the war, in 1945, a team of consultants, including De Leuw, called for rapid-rail and bus transit along several of the city's emerging freeways and for a new subway along Broadway.

But any subway—or any type of mass transit, for that matter—was fatally hamstrung by lack of a funding mechanism. There were no state tax write-offs, no bond issues, no federal subsidies. The fare box was the only source of revenue, and that source became limited as automobile ownership grew and use of public transport declined.

By the late 1950s, downtown traffic crawled and the idea of a subway again gained currency. Studies done between 1959 and 1962 conceived of "Four Corridors"—Wilshire, San Bernardino, Long Beach, and Reseda—where mass transit would entice people out of their vehicles. There was only one glitch: Local transit officials had no authority to float the bonds to pay for any of the routes.

In 1961, subway ambitions were trimmed to a run from El Monte, in the San Gabriel Valley, through downtown to Century City, a plan dubbed the Backbone Route. To make the idea publicly and, perhaps fiscally, palatable, the 12 miles of subway along Wilshire would double as an atomic fallout shelter. This was the cold war (with the Cuban missile crisis just months away). Schools still conducted drop drills, and nuclear brinksmanship was government policy. Preliminary engineering and design for the route, including extensive soil testing and construction evaluation, was undertaken. The Metropolitan Transit Authority (ancestor of today's METRO) held public groundbreaking ceremonies downtown and in Beverly Hills in 1962, even though no funding was available to rev the steam shovels.

→ Proposed downtown station

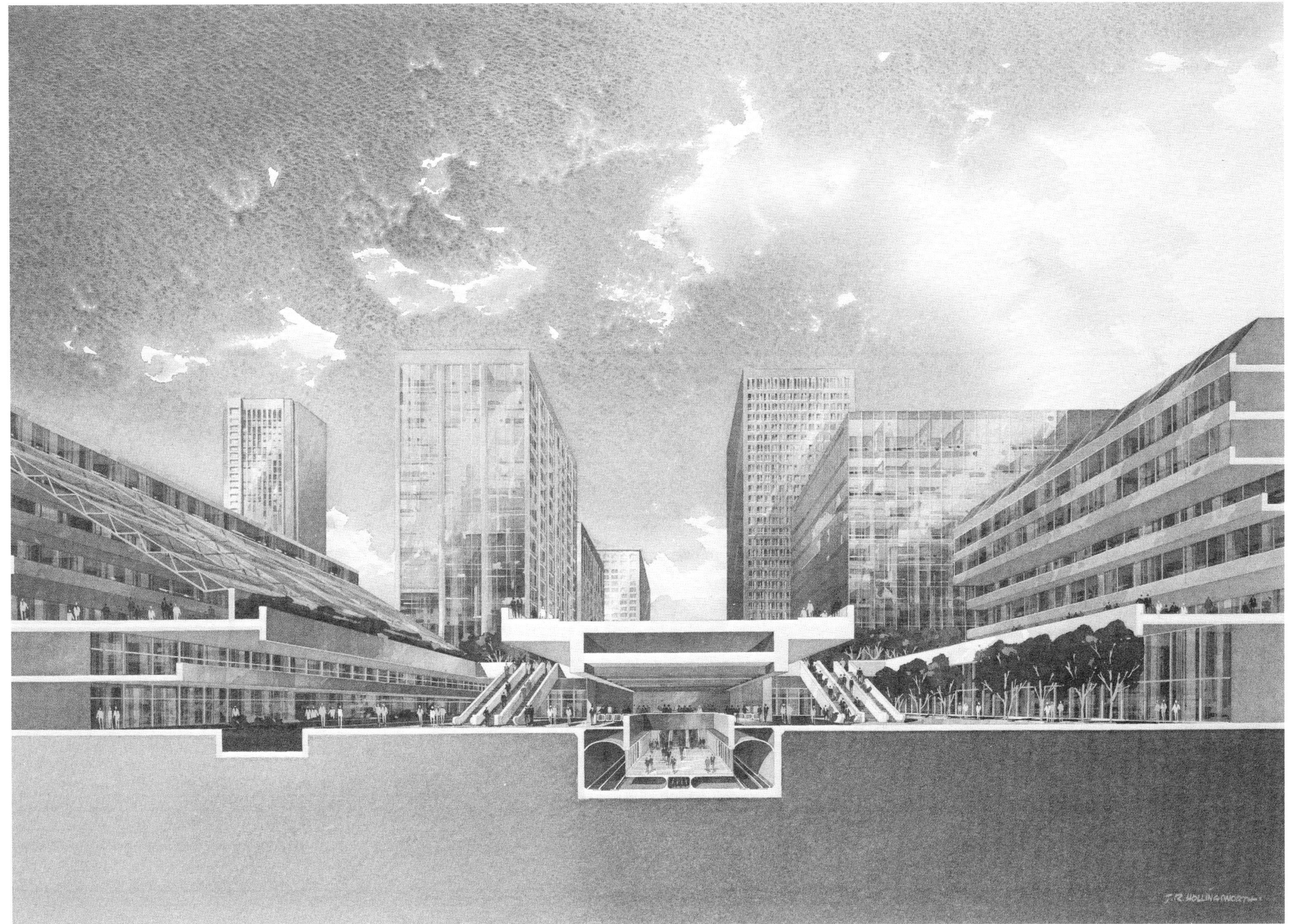
T.R. HOLLINGWORTH

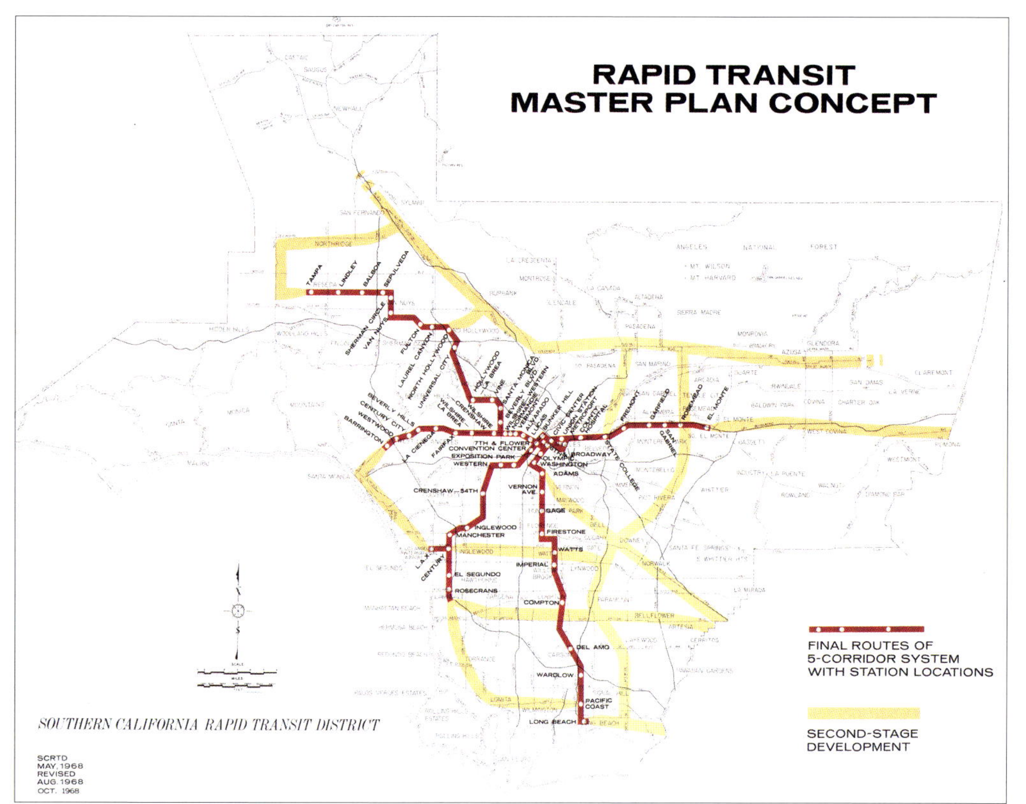

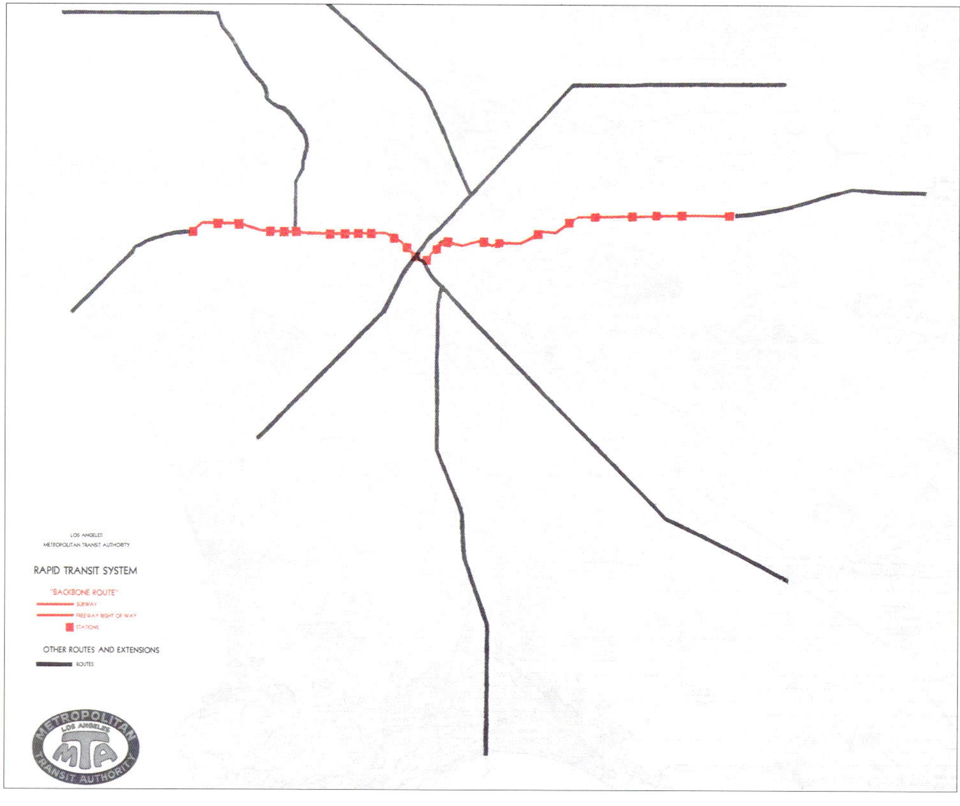

↖
Southern California Rapid Transit District Master Plan, 1968

↑
Metropolitan Transit Authority's "Backbone Route"

→
Rendering of proposed elevated station

Finally, in 1964, relenting after nearly four decades of pleas for financial resources, the state legislature created the Southern California Rapid Transit District (RTD), with the right to hold referendums on bond issues and tax increases and the power to exercise eminent domain. During the next 15 years, waving exquisite artists' renderings (which now included not four but five corridors), the RTD went to the voters three times and failed on each attempt. Not until the federal spigot opened did ground break, in 1986, for the Red Line, from downtown to Hollywood. Subway construction at last became a reality for Los Angeles.

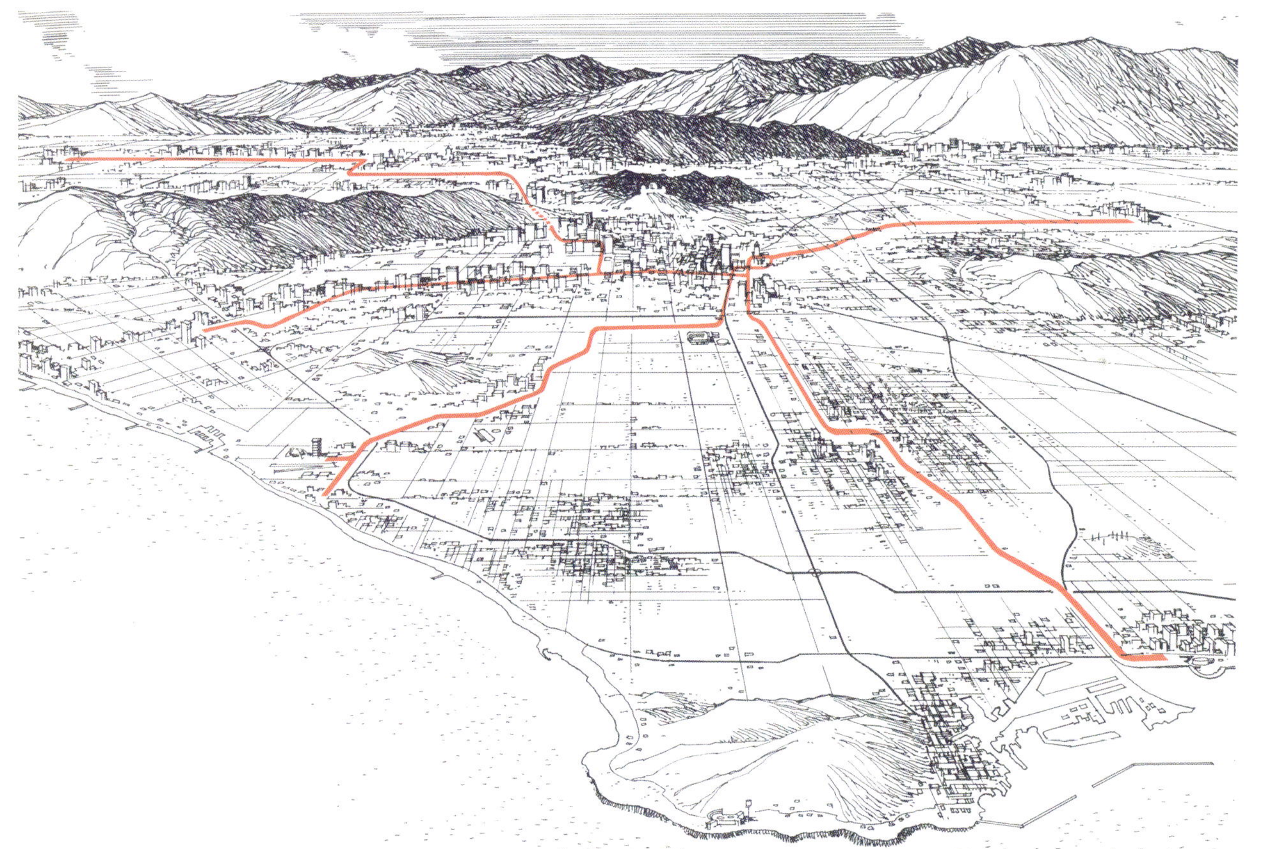

↔
Maps and sketches from Southern California Rapid Transit District's 1968 Five Corridor System, by DMJM and Kaiser Engineers

MC

TEGART AND WEBB HOLLYWOOD HILLS TUNNEL

1927–30

The hills dividing the Los Angeles Basin from the San Fernando Valley were no obstacle to a group of dreamers in the late 1920s. In 1927, the self-proclaimed Griffith Park Intercity Tunnels Association hired engineers Tegart and Webb, and in 1930, they proposed a $2.5-million stretch of tunnels connecting Bronson Canyon, on the north edge of Hollywood, with Riverside Drive in Burbank.

The City Planning Commission that same year approved the tunnel “without specifying any change.”

The project, originating at Canyon Drive, would have consisted of two parallel 20-foot-wide shafts, divided into three successive sections to overcome the problem of ventilating a longer tunnel. The first leg would measure 3,580 feet. Two shorter runs would measure 1,800 feet and 1,200 feet, boring through hills near Western, Normandie, and Vermont avenues.

“Having for some time suffered inconvenience in travels back and forth from the San Fernando Valley to the Central Section of Los Angeles in the form of a mountain barrier which necessitated long detours, [I] undertook to find a more direct route through the Hollywood Hills,” Harold M. Tegart wrote.

Proponents said the tunnels would carry 46,000 cars a day through the mountains. In addition to connecting to Riverside Drive, the ultimate goal was to reach the planned Whitnall “Super” Highway, stretching from the Valley to the shore at Malibu. In the end, the state deemed both the tunnel and the highway too expensive to build.

→ Tunnel entrance

→→ Red line traces tunnel route.

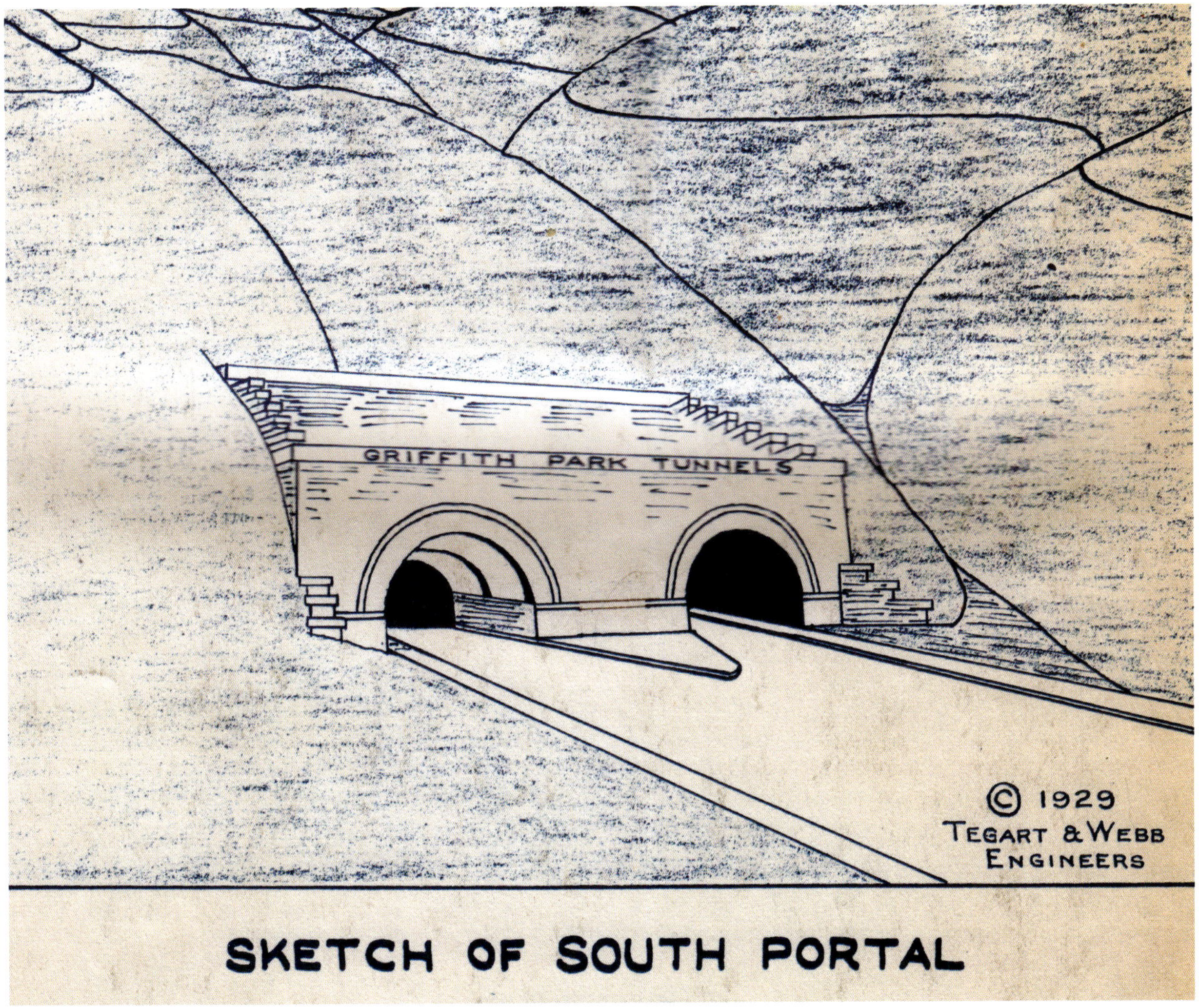

GRIFFITH PARK TUNNELS
© 1929
TEGART & WEBB
ENGINEERS
SKETCH OF SOUTH PORTAL

VERDUGO
MOUNTAINS
BURBANK
GLENDALE
EAGLE
ROCK
VICTORY
GRIFFITH
PARK
PROPOSED TUNNELS
ELYSIAN PARK
RIVERSIDE DRIVE
SAN FERNANDO BLVD.
SUNSET
HOLLYWOOD
VAN NESS AVE
ROSSMORE ST.
WESTERN
VERMONT
HIGHLAND
LA BREA
WILSHIRE
SANTA MONICA
SHERMAN
BEVERLY
HILLS
CRENSHAW BLVD.
CAHUENGA
LANKERSHIM
LAUREL CANYON
PICO
VENICE

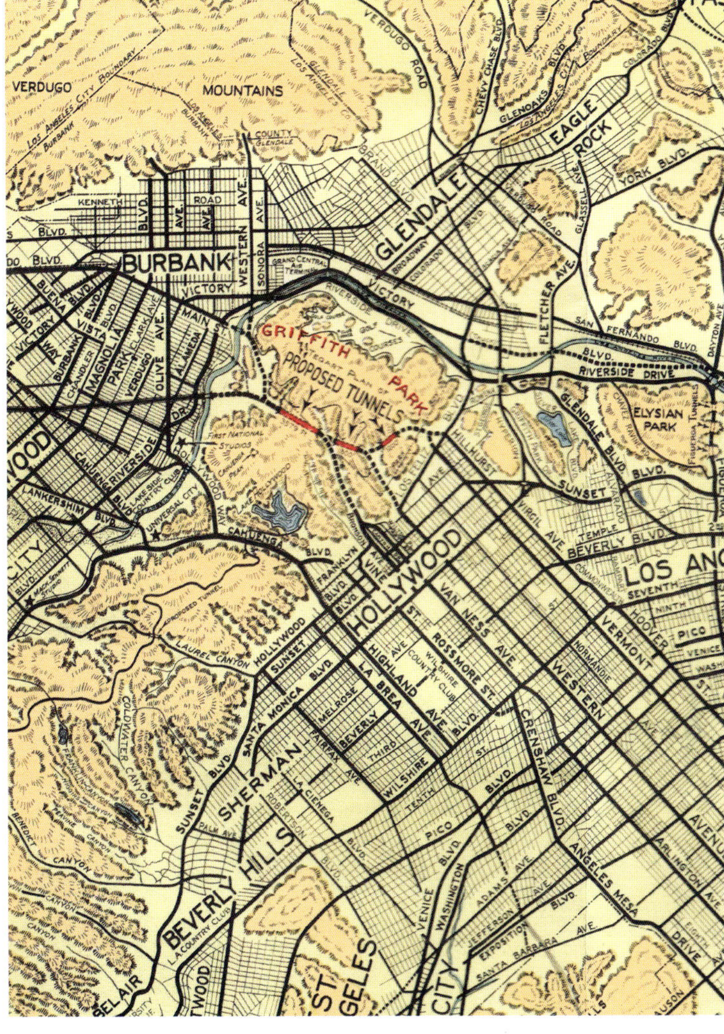

TR

LA

FREEWAYS

1920s-60s

Long before construction started, in March 1938, on the city's first freeway, the Arroyo Seco Parkway, local planners and engineers were dreaming of spanning time and space with a ribbon of concrete highways. The first well-articulated notion of a separate elevated or sunken motorway to speed traffic surfaced in 1924, when engineer William Hudson suggested that Los Angeles might adopt a "continuous elevated highway with approach ramps" to solve its nascent traffic woes. By 1937, the Automobile Club of Southern California issued its "Traffic Study," promoting a comprehensive freeway system expanding from downtown to Santa Monica, San Pedro, San Fernando, Anaheim, and San Gabriel. The study portrayed 120-foot-wide roadways banded by greenbelts twice as wide and proposed "motorway buildings" bridging the roadbeds.

This Arcadian view never emerged. What did was a vision of the region girded and encircled by freeways. One early portrayal, a county master plan for 1941 titled "Major Highways Ultimate Development," shows a dense grid of regular lines from Palmdale to Palos Verdes, and from Santa Monica to Riverside, etched by diagonals to speed the flow of cars. In 1949, the Automobile Club mapped out a parkway system with dozens of roads. Many would become the now-familiar matrix of freeways. Others would be relegated to wish lists.

Highway building, however, was mostly a local affair, which meant schemes were largely starved for money and support. Not until the state legislature passed the Collier-Burns Highway Act of 1947, followed by the federal National System of Interstate and Defense Highways, in 1956, did freeway building begin in earnest. In 1959, California approved the definitive Expressway System master plan for Los Angeles, Orange, and Ventura counties, imposing a weave of freeways for metropolitan L.A. that, had it been completed, would have left no commuter more than four miles away from an on-ramp. Slated for completion in 1980, the plan had ambitions scaled for an empire: A total of 1,557 miles of road would have been paved. Just a small sample: Every canyon cutting through the Santa Monica Mountains, from downtown to the county line, at Ventura, would have been cleared by earthmovers and graded into a multilane speedway.

The state department of highways, later renamed the California Department of Transportation, or Caltrans, would build only about half of this massive network. The era of freeway construction was short-lived, lasting roughly 20 years (there were exceptions, of course). Paid for with a gas tax designed as a perpetual-motion mechanism—more freeways meant more drivers, which meant more gas tax revenue, which meant more freeways—the invention, like all such devices, failed. The tax couldn't keep up with inflated construction costs, escalated by the expenses of landscaping, environmental remediation, compensation to displaced businesses and homeowners, and protracted legal battles opposing key routes. Every project was an uphill climb. Although hardly impoverished, Caltrans felt the fiscal and political squeeze. In the late 1960s, the legislature started to delete routes, converting dotted lines on maps into never-built freeways.

→ Highway routes of 1958 snake their way through the region.

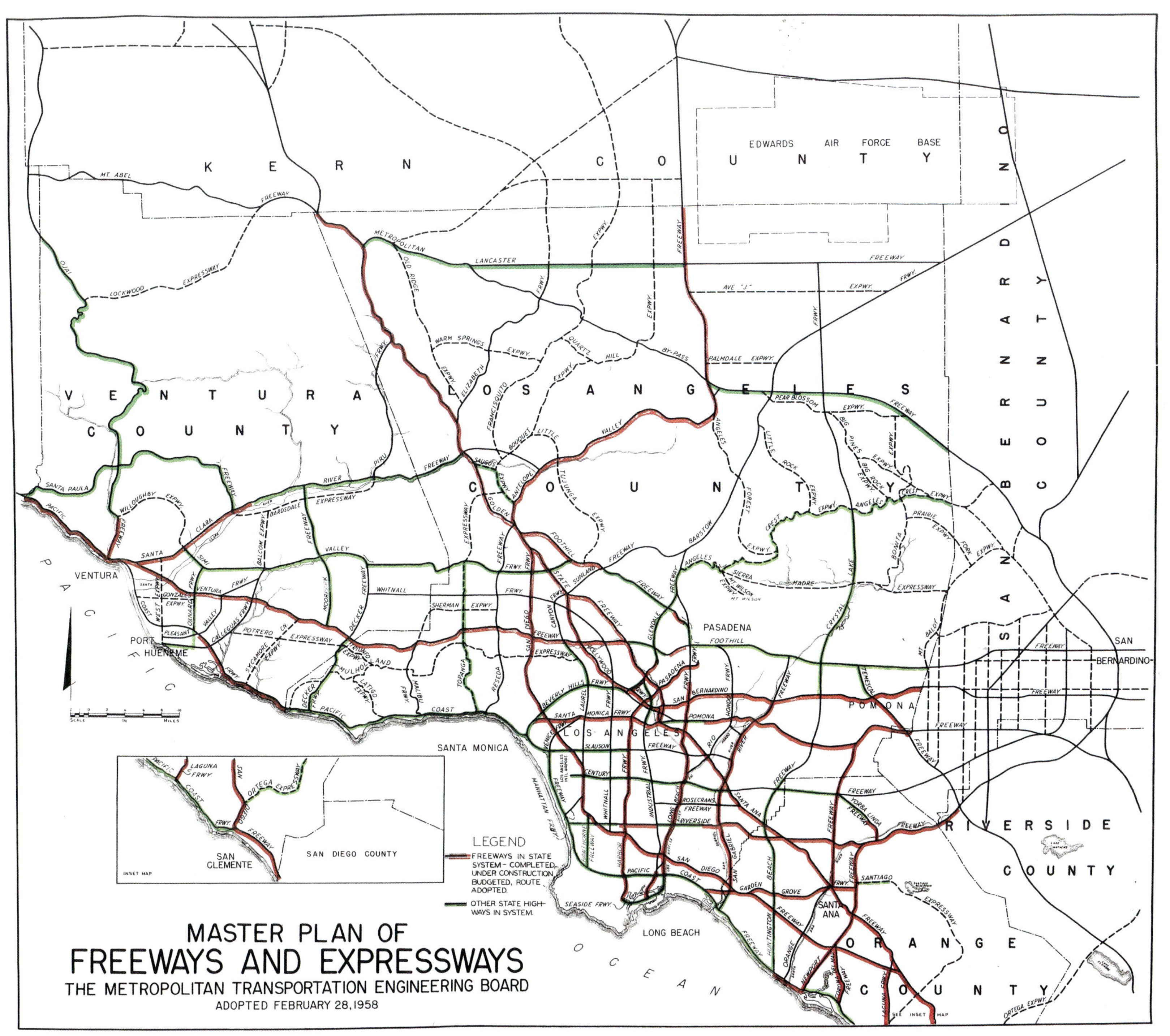
MASTER PLAN OF
FREEWAYS AND EXPRESSWAYS
THE METROPOLITAN TRANSPORTATION ENGINEERING BOARD
ADOPTED FEBRUARY 28, 1958
LEGEND
FREEWAYS IN STATE SYSTEM - COMPLETED, UNDER CONSTRUCTION, BUDGETED, ROUTE ADOPTED.
OTHER STATE HIGHWAYS IN SYSTEM.
KERN COUNTY
VENTURA COUNTY
LOS ANGELES COUNTY
SAN BERNARDINO COUNTY
RIVERSIDE COUNTY
ORANGE COUNTY
SAN DIEGO COUNTY
PACIFIC OCEAN
EDWARDS AIR FORCE BASE
VENTURA
PORT HUENEME
SANTA MONICA
LOS ANGELES
PASADENA
POMONA
SAN BERNARDINO
LONG BEACH
SANTA ANA
SAN CLEMENTE
INSET MAP

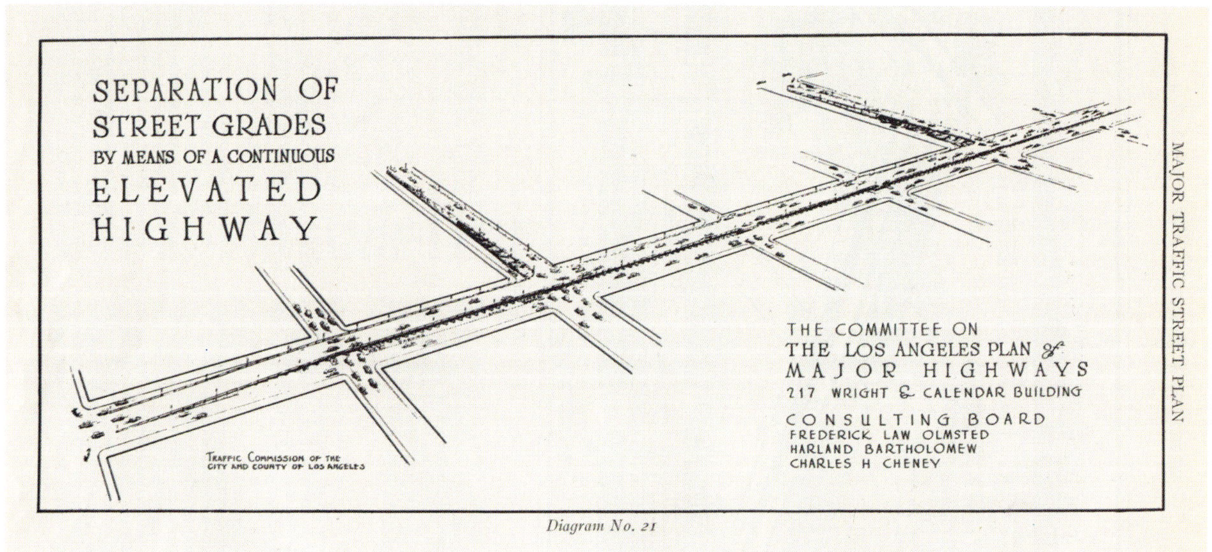

Diagram No. 21

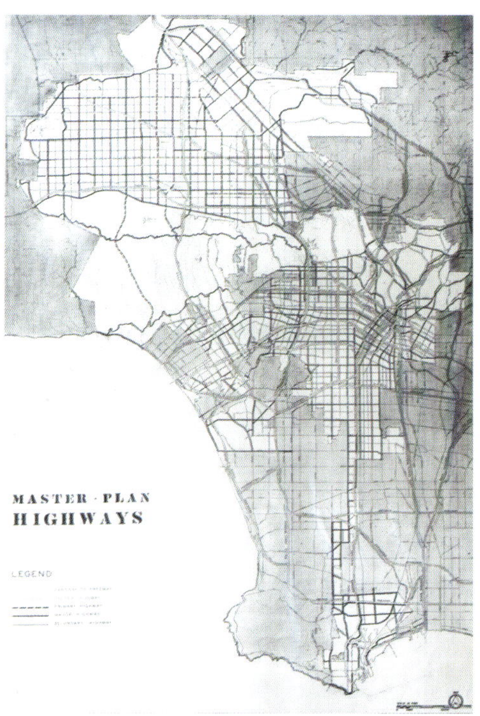

↖
Olmsted, Bartholomew, and traffic engineer Charles Cheney envision freeway in 1924.

←←
Dense freeway grid on 1947 map

←
Plan from 1968 puts every driver within four miles of a freeway entrance.

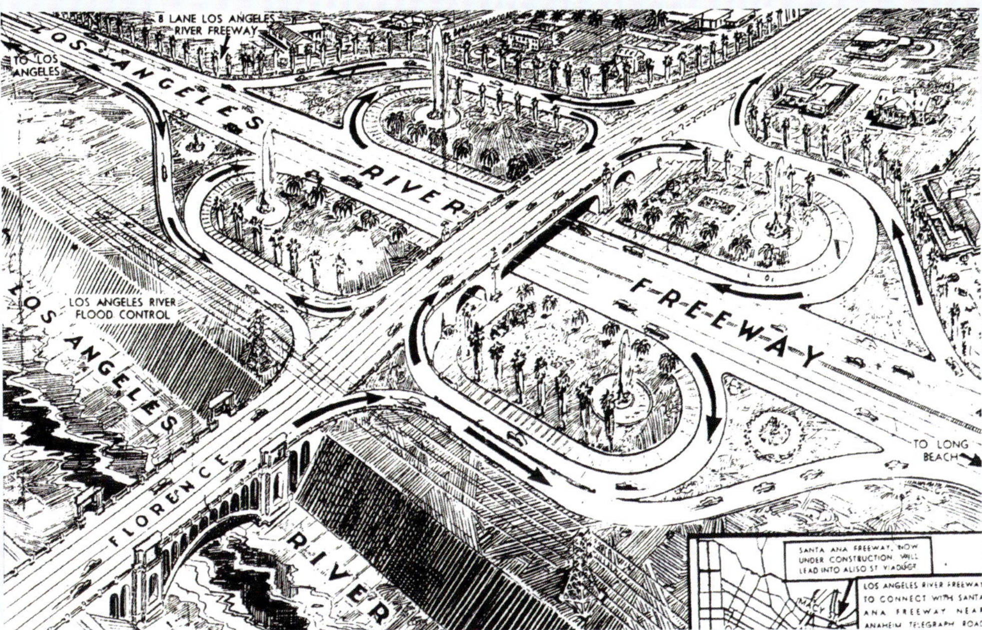

OLMSTED BROTHERS AND BARTHOLOMEW AND CHARLES H. CHENEY
LOS ANGELES RIVER FREEWAY

1924

The Los Angeles River has tempted traffic planners since the Arroyo Seco Parkway was dreamed up in 1897. Ironically, it was the same landscape architects and road engineers—Olmsted Brothers, Harland Bartholomew, and their colleague Charles H. Cheney, who first said the Los Angeles River should be used as a freeway. Six years before calling for parkways beneath arbors of willows and sycamores to be built along the river—their vision of a "lost future," to use critic Mike Davis's phrase—they proposed a more hardened River Truck Speedway. The riverbed through downtown would become a paved roadway, permitting trucks to avoid the mess of railway crossings and traffic in the city center. "It would be submerged by flood waters so rarely and for such short periods as not materially to impair its usefulness," the 1924 Major Traffic Street Plan stated.

This piece of the plan was never implemented, although the idea retained currency. Following the worst flooding in Los Angeles history, in 1938, the U.S. Army Corps of Engineers began to channelize and cement the riverbed. This offered new temptations. The river channel was considered an inexpensive and ready-made transportation corridor throughout the 1940s and 1950s and again in the 1970s—studies that were rejected because the federal government opposed using their flood control system for a traffic route and because postwar freeways ended up running parallel to the river, seemingly obviating the need.

The idea resurfaced in 1989. State assemblyman Richard Katz, who represented suburban Sylmar, suggested reconfiguring the riverbed to relieve freeway congestion. For a tenth of the cost of building a subway, Katz argued, carpool lanes could be carved into the river bottom. Ten-foot-high walls would protect motorists on most rainy days; on potential flood days, the lanes could be closed. Katz calculated that, accounting for severe storms, the riverbed freeway would be open 300 days a year. Using existing infrastructure, the 40-mile run would begin in the San Fernando Valley and end in Long Beach. Trees, bikeways, and pocket parks would be added to create a greenbelt along the riverbanks. "Before my proposal is dismissed as silly or unrealistic," Katz wrote in the *Los Angeles Times*, "I challenge anyone to come up with workable methods to stop the trend of traffic congestion before it stops us."

"Over our dead bodies," declared Lewis MacAdams, founder of Friends of the Los Angeles River (FoLAR).

Katz persuaded the L.A. County Transportation Commission to fork over $100,000 to study the idea. But resurrecting it had unintended consequences. Mayor Tom Bradley, heeding the call of FoLAR, pledged during his fifth-term inaugural speech to make the river "an oasis of beauty and opportunity." He created the Los Angeles River Task Force, and by August 1990, a state assembly committee had approved $500,000 to fund a master plan for restoring the river's natural ecosystem.

In March 1991, the transportation commission's study reported the riverbed speedway could reduce gridlock on local freeways by 20 percent. HOV lanes would cost $700 million; truck lanes in the river, $365 million. By the time the report was issued, however, FoLAR had won the more important war for public opinion. River restoration, rather than a river freeway, would continue to hold the imagination for at least a generation to come.

SELECTED FREEWAYS

1930s-60s

BEVERLY HILLS FREEWAY

First known as the Santa Monica Freeway, this proposed nine-mile, 10-lane route would have peeled off from the 101 Freeway near Vermont Avenue. Spliced between Melrose Avenue and Santa Monica Boulevard, it would run through West Hollywood, Beverly Hills, and Century City, finally joining the 405 near Sepulveda Boulevard. The city of Beverly Hills shut it down, but not before then-governor Ronald Reagan made three rescue attempts, authorizing extensive investigation of tunneling underground. The legislature canceled the freeway in 1975.

LAUREL CANYON FREEWAY

The Laurel Canyon Freeway would take drivers from Sunland, north of Burbank, where the 101 Freeway would melt into the 5 Freeway, all the way south to Los Angeles International Airport (LAX). It would not only churn up the hillsides of Laurel Canyon, one of the city's fabled bohemian neighborhoods, but also wipe out nearly the entire length of La Cienega Boulevard.

RESEDA FREEWAY

The Reseda Freeway was to carve its way through the west edge of the San Fernando Valley, proceeding south down Reseda Boulevard and through the Santa Monica Mountains to intersect with the proposed Pacific Coast Highway, a.k.a. Highway 1. In the late 1920s, Valley Chamber of Commerce members were boasting about a "Reseda to the Sea" route winding through Temescal Canyon to the PCH. In the 1950s, the state's highway builders adopted the plan. In the 1960s, the Los Angeles City Council voted to study the feasibility of building it as a toll road, but the idea died. The construction of Palisades High School—sitting on the freeway's centerline—effectively finished off the route, although it continued to show up on freeway-builders' maps of planned construction for years to come.

SLAUSON FREEWAY

The Slauson Freeway was meant to cross southern Los Angeles and northern Orange counties, beginning at the beach, continuing through Culver City, Inglewood, Huntington Park, Maywood, Pico Rivera, and Santa Fe Springs, and ending at the Riverside Freeway in Anaheim. It never happened. Neighborhood opposition reduced it to the 90 Freeway, a spur off the 405 running shy of Marina del Rey. The city of Yorba Linda, in Orange County, never gave up on the route, widening a city street along its proposed length and renaming it the Richard M. Nixon Parkway.

WHITNALL FREEWAY

One of the craziest lines on any freeway map, the Whitnall was a horseshoe bending north, south, east, and west from Malibu through the San Fernando Valley, down into Hollywood and then onto Hawthorne, well south of LAX. In all, it was a 47-mile journey, named for L.A.'s first city planner, Gordon Whitnall (a Socialist who might well have opposed the freeway). But with much of the route through the Valley ceded to city utility power-line rights-of-way, the freeway became too expensive to build.

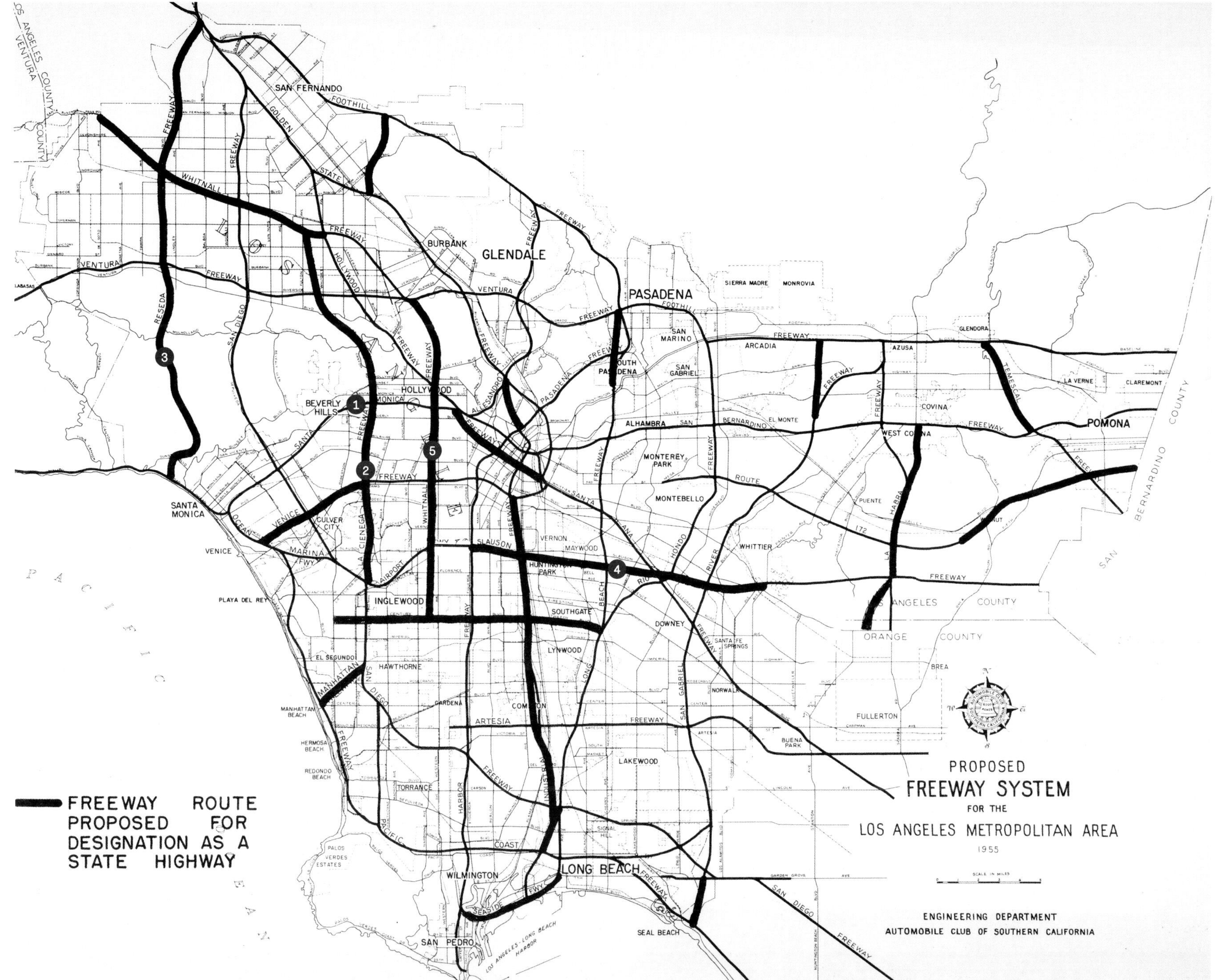

→ Automobile Club of Southern California's 1955 proposed freeway system

LA

JOSEPH B. STRAUSS
AIRTRAM SYSTEM

1936

The speed of the airplane, the comfort and quiet of the automobile.

Joseph B. Strauss

Among the solutions offered to relieve Los Angeles traffic congestion was engineer Joseph B. Strauss's Airtram System. Reaching to all corners of the city, his concept promised to bring elevated rail—strongly opposed for its noise and visual pollution—to a more sophisticated level. Famous as the chief engineer on the Golden Gate Bridge, Strauss had an instant audience when he peddled his invention, a hybrid of futuristic bravura and hard-nosed practicality. "It is not an elevated railway nor a subway nor a surface system nor a monorail," he said. "As its name implies, it is a form of aerial transit which operates on a fixed airway, thus insuring the positive automatic safety not otherwise attainable in aerial transportation."

In reality, the Airtram looked a lot like a monorail. Long, narrow fuselages—some resembling rockets and others, trolley cars—would be suspended from multiwheel conveyors running on an overhead track, much like the moving racks at a dry cleaner. In one version, the track would be welded to steel posts rising from the sidewalk. In another, the track would be strung along a single row of columns with an opening, shaped like the eye of a needle, at the top to permit the cars to pass through.

Strauss, in hawking his system in L.A. and San Francisco, claimed his Airtram promised "the speed of the airplane, the comfort and quiet of the automobile" and the pleasure of "riding in ease in the sunshine and air." Los Angeles would become a more beautiful place: no more trolleys, with their bumpy tracks, clattering cars, and maze of wires. Using cushioning devices, silent drive motors, and noiseless breaks, the aluminum alloy Airtram cars would glide effortlessly from station to station 33 feet above the ground. Strauss claimed his smooth-running trams, rolling on ball bearings, would achieve speeds of 60 miles per hour, at a time when Pacific Electric's cars trundled along at an average of 11 miles per hour. Travel times from downtown Los Angeles would be 10 minutes to Pasadena, 15 to Burbank, 18 to Santa Monica, and 20 to Long Beach.

→ A cross between a streetcar and a monorail

Real estate developer George D. Rowan, at the time a member of the Los Angeles Junior Chamber of Commerce traffic committee, took up the cause of the Airtram idea and authored a four-page mimeographed pamphlet—*Need for a Rapid Transit System in Los Angeles*—to help promote the scheme. But after Strauss died, in 1938, Rowan gave up his quixotic pursuit and the Airtram transit solution came to a standstill.

THE AIRTRAM SYSTEM

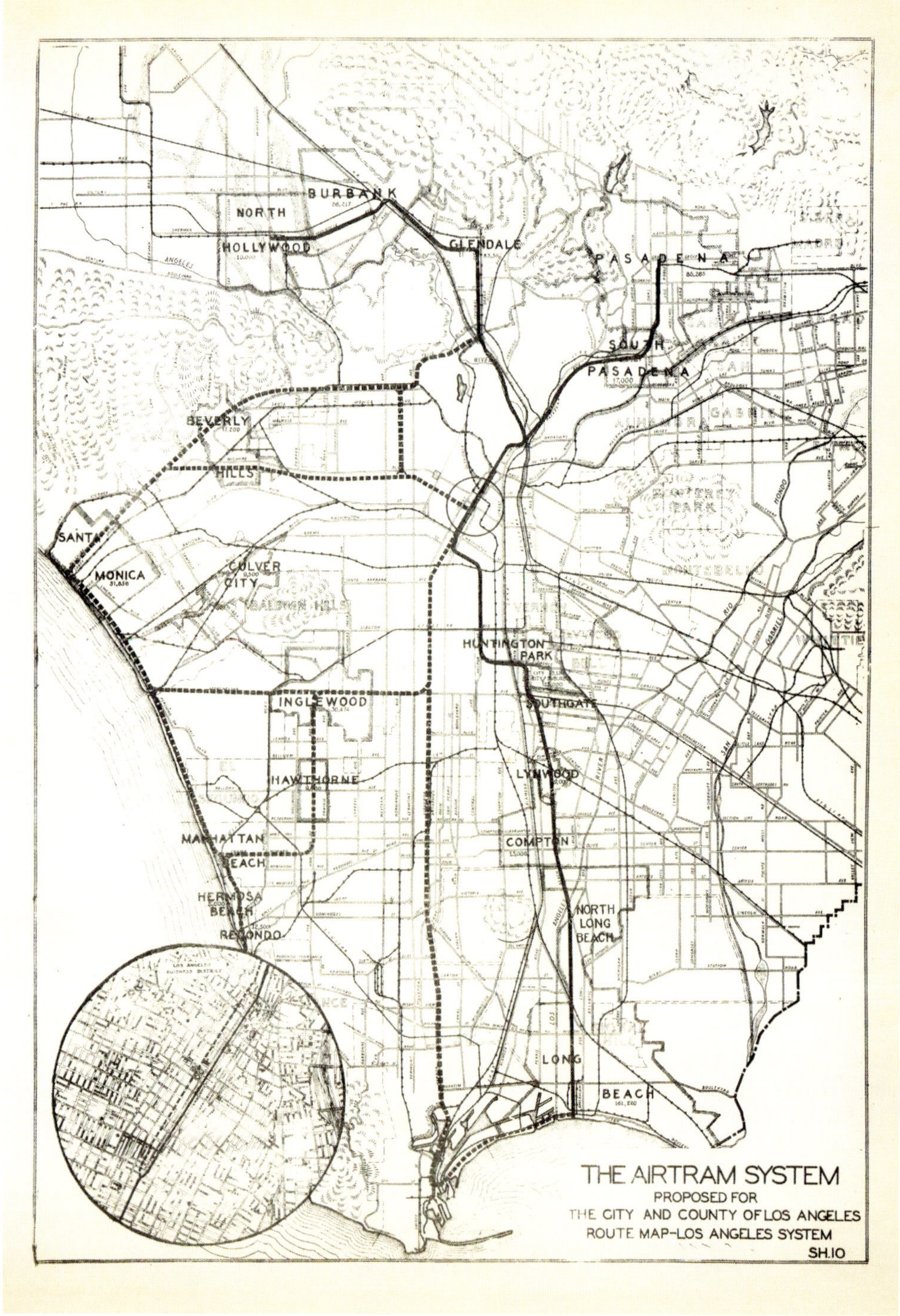

← Routes from North Hollywood to Long Beach

→ Airtram travels through arcades cut into buildings.

→→ Towers spaced 120 feet apart; tracks 26 feet wide

↘↘ Track hangs from cables like a suspension bridge.

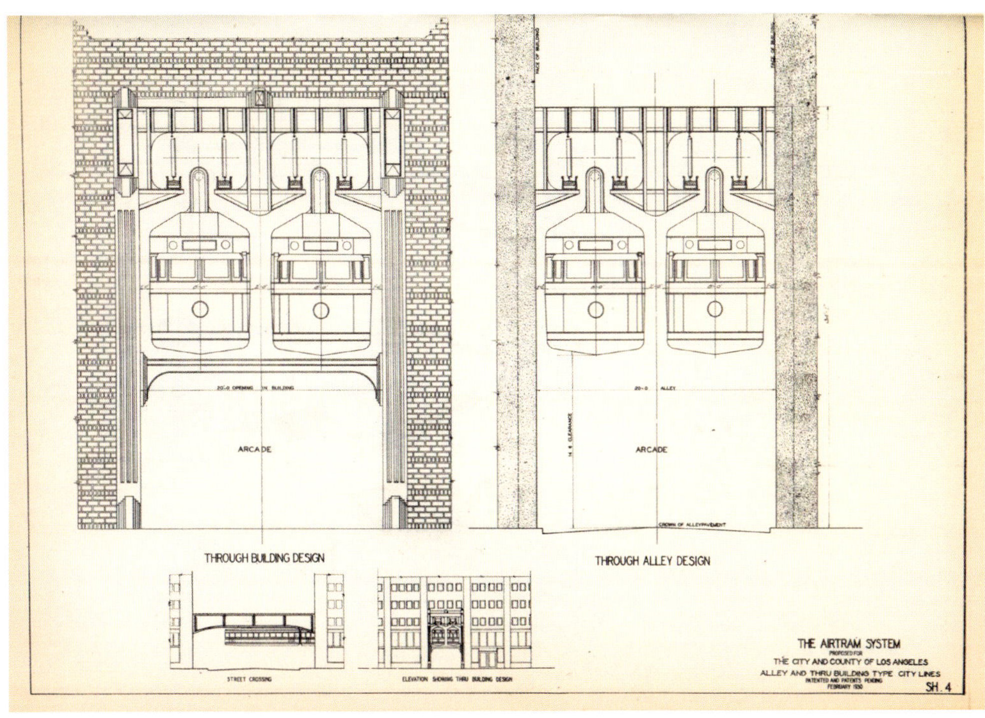
THROUGH BUILDING DESIGN
THROUGH ALLEY DESIGN
ARCADE
ARCADE
STREET CROSSING
THE AIRTRAM SYSTEM
THE CITY AND COUNTY OF LOS ANGELES
ALLEY AND THRU BUILDING TYPE CITY LINES
SH. 4

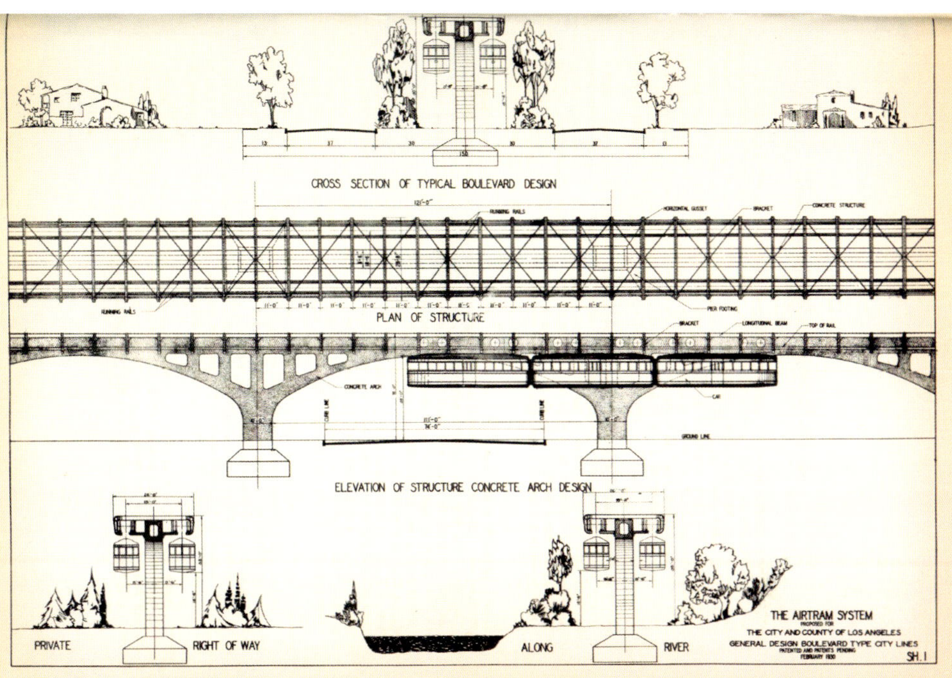
CROSS SECTION OF TYPICAL BOULEVARD DESIGN
PLAN OF STRUCTURE
ELEVATION OF STRUCTURE CONCRETE ARCH DESIGN
PRIVATE
RIGHT OF WAY
ALONG
RIVER
THE AIRTRAM SYSTEM
THE CITY AND COUNTY OF LOS ANGELES
GENERAL DESIGN BOULEVARD TYPE CITY LINES
SH. 1

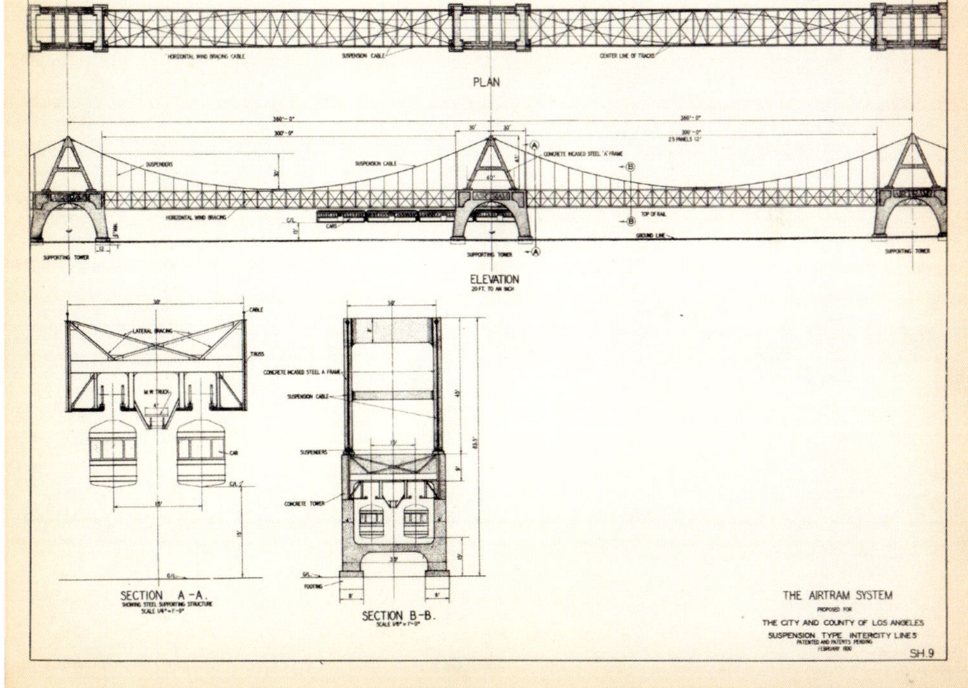
PLAN
ELEVATION
SECTION A-A.
SECTION B-B.
THE AIRTRAM SYSTEM
THE CITY AND COUNTY OF LOS ANGELES
SUSPENSION TYPE INTERCITY LINES
SH. 9

LA

COVERDALE AND COLPITTS, GOODELL, AND ALWEG MONORAILS

1953
1963

We've got to have mass transportation and... the people are about ready for it—traffic is already making them nervous wrecks.

William Parker

In 1953, the state legislature ordered the Los Angeles Metropolitan Transit Authority to study a monorail system to extend from the San Fernando Valley to Long Beach via downtown Los Angeles. Officials mandated a route that would run within a four-mile-wide swath on either side of the Los Angeles River. The study, carried out by George W. Burger of the New England engineering firm Coverdale and Colpitts, presented a monorail suspended from a single track attached to 30-foot-tall T-shaped columns.

Using existing bus routes and old rights-of-way abandoned by the city's once-extensive light-rail system, the comprehensive elevated monorail network would have been the world's fastest urban-transit system, whizzing by at up to 60 miles per hour. For two miles downtown, the track would dive underground.

"There is not now in any city in the world any suburban or interurban service operating at the overall speed contemplated for this line," Coverdale and Colpitts said.

The entire 45-mile run, with station stops of 20 seconds each, was supposed to take a bit more than an hour. A park-and-ride ethos was embraced: Large lots would allow passengers to park their cars and walk to a station. Coverdale and Colpitts estimated that the monorail would draw 230,000 riders per day. The promise was to reduce travel times to about half of what they were via private automobile.

"This type of high-speed transportation might do for the area what Pacific Electric Railway did fifty years ago," Burger said. The price tag was $165 million; in five years, Burger asserted, the trains would be up and running. In a truly unrealistic prognostication, he said the monorail might even become "self-supporting which in itself is a novelty in a rapid-transit system."

Even with the backing of the city's powerful and vocal chief of police, William Parker, the plan never got the necessary votes in the state legislature. Parker nevertheless pleaded with state senators: "We are deluged by a sea of automobiles that will destroy our economy. We've got to have mass transportation and I should say the people are about ready for it—traffic is already making them nervous wrecks."

A decade later, the monorail lobby was back with renewed vigor and new routes. Two firms battled with similar bids to provide the city with a "free" monorail in exchange for the next 40 years of fare-box revenues—and perpetual ownership of the rights-of-way.

In June 1963, German manufacturer Alweg, best known for its Disneyland monorail, presented a $187.5-million, 43-mile system spread among three routes fanning out from downtown: Valley, San Bernardino, and Wilshire. Sleek cars, nearly identical to the company's monorail at the 1962 Seattle World's Fair, would run on smooth-rolling rubber tires straddling a cast-concrete beam. "A monorail system goes together almost like an Erector Set," an Alweg official told *Popular Mechanics* that year.

→ Goodell's monorail resembled a Cadillac.

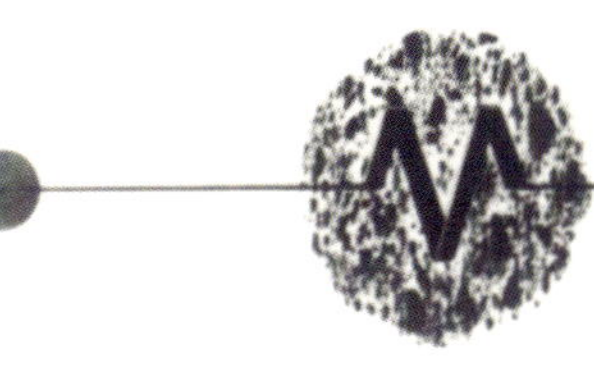

MONORAIL COACH

BY MITCHELL GOODELL MONORAIL ·

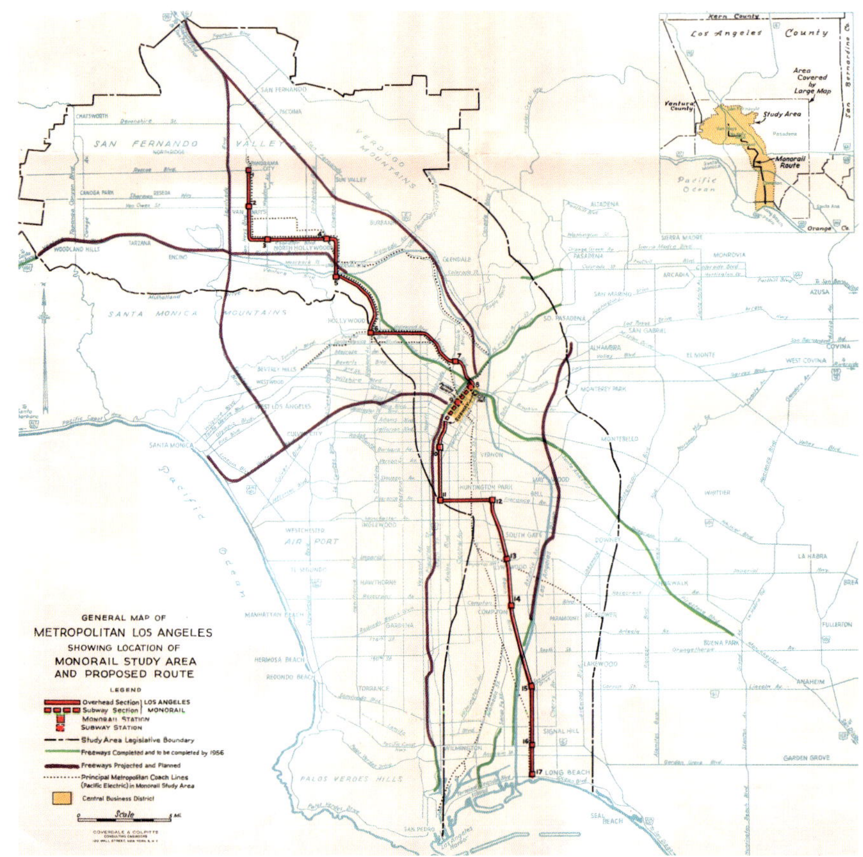

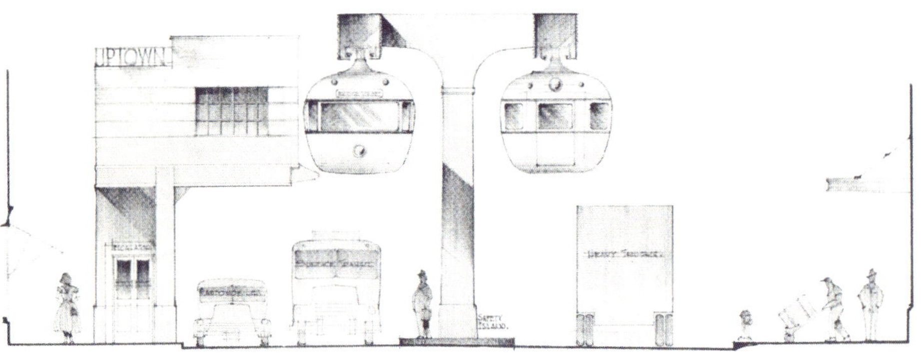

SUSPENDED MONORAIL SYSTEM
SPLIT-RAIL TYPE

Within days, Houston entrepreneur Murel Goodell countered that he would build a 60-mile system for $214 million. His proposal—a dangling pod replete with *Jetsons*-like fins, capable of going 90 miles per hour—followed the same route as Alweg's but added a 17-mile branch to deliver passengers from downtown to LAX in 12 minutes. He had backing from Wall Street financiers Paine, Webber, Jackson and Curtis and claimed that for an additional $124 million, he'd build a 12.3-mile-long subway with 16 stations along Wilshire Boulevard through Beverly Hills as part of the operation.

Each company said that its system would cost about one-fifth the price of a subway. One mile of track, Alweg claimed, could be built every 20 days. Goodell said his line could go up at a rate of a mile a week.

The ultimate irony, in light of its present-day opposition to tunneling, was that the city of Beverly Hills rejected the elevated monorail and demanded that a subway be dug down Wilshire Boulevard. This held up the entire proposal, and political chaos ensued. In September 1963, a frustrated county Board of Supervisors threw up its hands and issued a moratorium on all further transit meetings, threatening to disband the MTA and reorganize it under new leadership. Besides, MTA board chairman A. J. Eyraud had always favored conventional subway and trolley cars, with steel flanged wheels running on two rails. Monorails, he said, were like "buying a Volkswagen when you need a Cadillac."

←←
Coverdale and Colpitts's proposed route

←
Street traffic flows beneath modern transportation system.

→
Coverdale and Colpitts system zips through residential neighbor-hood, 1953.

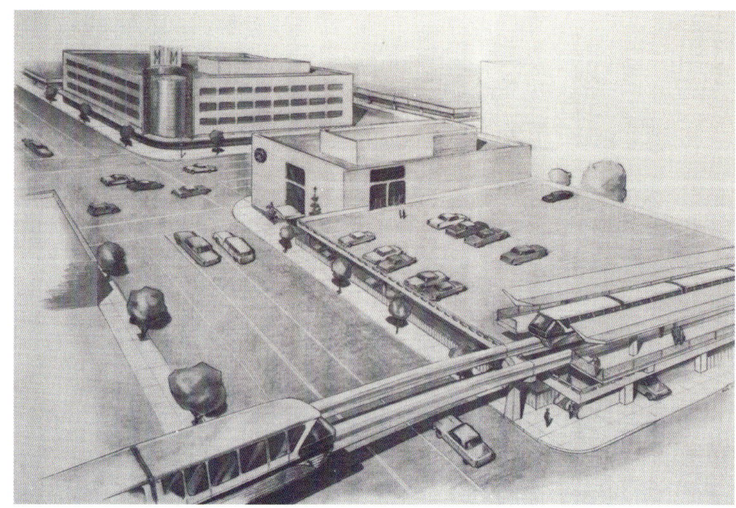

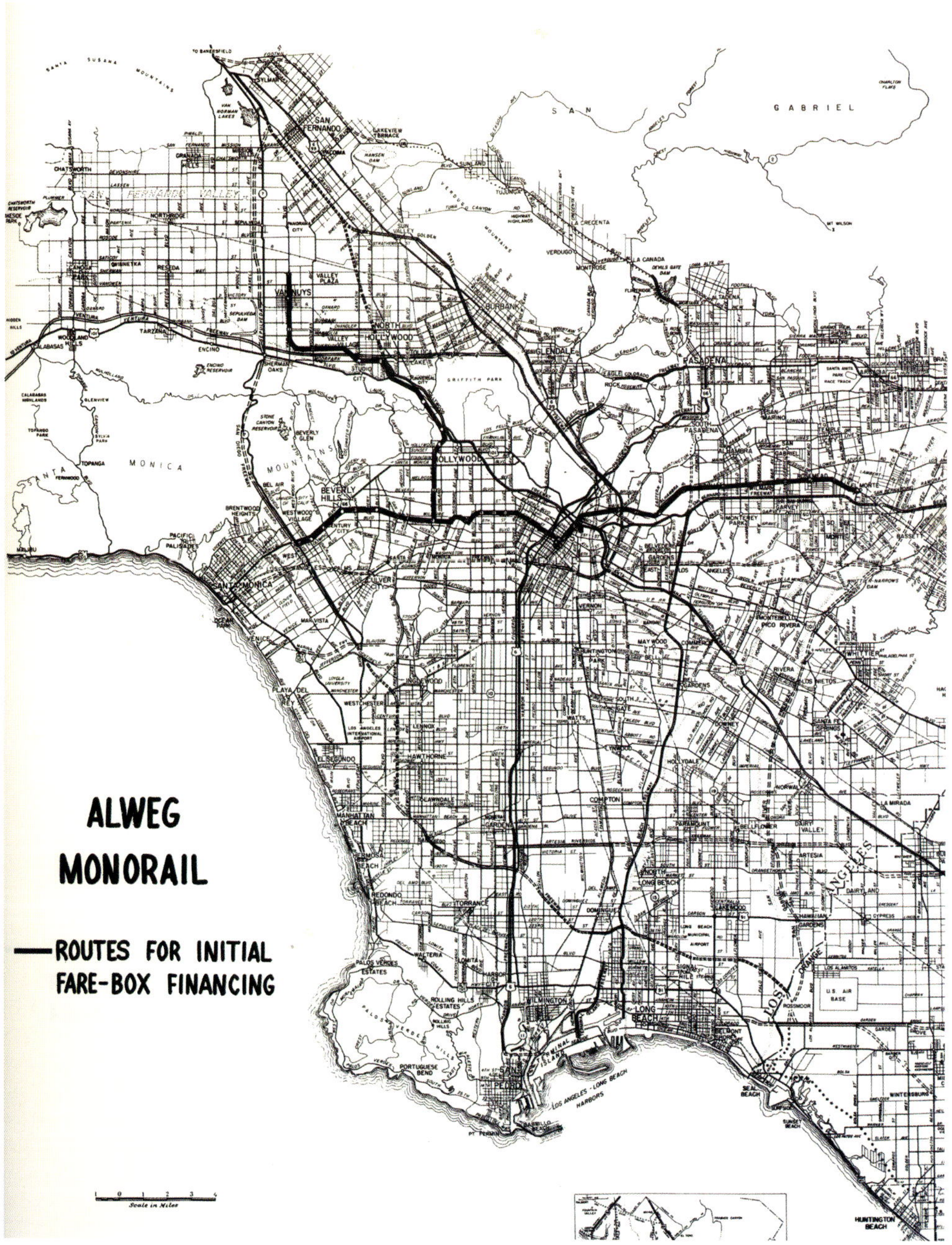

←←
Monorail cruises down Eighth Street, a block from May Company building.

←
Map of Alweg's system from San Fernando Valley to Long Beach

ALWEG MONORAIL

— ROUTES FOR INITIAL FARE-BOX FINANCING

JOSEPH W. FAWKES
FAWKES FOLLY

ca. 1910

Joseph Fawkes was an apricot grower with inspiration, and a patent to go with it. A gadfly with a waxed mustache, Fawkes tooled around turn-of-the-century Burbank in a horse-drawn carriage trailed by a pair of Dalmatians. He dabbled in oil painting and poetry and invented an electric sign that paid him handsome royalties. His new invention was a 50-foot-long, 2,000-pound monorail, shaped like a torpedo and powered by an airplane propeller. He named the car Pegasus and built a quarter-mile run through his orchard. The monorail was suspended, said Fawkes, on “ordinary trolley wire” tensioned between steel towers. Fawkes boasted that his “aerial sparrow” could move a mile a minute, and that it would dispatch its cargo of 56 passengers from Burbank to Los Angeles in less than 15 minutes. During a three-day fiesta, over the July 4, 1912, holiday, Fawkes lit fireworks and gave away free dinners and rides. “Back me and with this setup I can glide straight over Mount Hollywood if they won’t let me go along the river,” he declared. “Once we build a line into Los Angeles it’ll revolutionize interurban travel. I can cross creeks and arroyos without bridges. It’ll be a gold mine in ten years.” It seems no one enjoyed riding the monorail; the exposed propeller blew gusts of wind at passengers. The track and the car sat unused on his property until the early 1920s, gradually rusting away until its skeleton was scrapped. Today, the 5 Freeway runs right past the site of L.A.’s first monorail.

FLETCHER E. FELTS
FELTS MONORAIL

1909

Los Angeles inventor Fletcher E. Felts, who held patents for an airless car tire and a wing-flapping airplane, also weighed in with a monorail. In 1909, he received a patent for an Elevated Suspended-Track Automotor-Railway, which he boasted would achieve speeds of 100 miles per hour. He planned to run the torpedo-shaped monorail between Pasadena and Los Angeles, moving along an elevated track supported by steel towers that looked like Erector Set centurions guarding the empty space below. The main route would have begun in Eagle Rock and proceeded through canyons in both Mount Washington and Elysian Park, terminating downtown. An alternative called for towers both on city streets and in the bed of the Arroyo Seco. The entire trip, supporters claimed, would cut the travel time between Los Angeles and Pasadena to eight minutes. Felts, who said he could “put a girdle round about the earth in 40 minutes,” had an even bigger vision for his elevated, which he said ought to connect Los Angeles to San Francisco. Declaring speeds could easily be increased to 150 miles per hour, he planned a running time of three hours, 39 minutes, including stops in Santa Barbara, San Luis Obispo, Paso Robles, and San Jose. The idea never got off the ground.

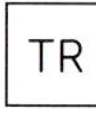

DT

SAMUEL LUNDEN
CARVEYOR

1956

The Carveyor is the best thing man has yet been able to devise for moving people quickly and efficiently over short distances in highly congested areas.

Robert F. Mercer

The Carveyor was the first of what would become many entries in the city's people-mover category. It was a joint venture between Stephens-Adamson Manufacturing Company, which in 1950 introduced the first airport moving sidewalks, and Goodyear Rubber Company. Samuel Lunden, a powerhouse Los Angeles architect with deep social and political connections, was reading a transit magazine and saw a short article about a "carveyor," an automated rail system intended to connect New York City's Pennsylvania and Grand Central stations. That night, he sketched his own version for Los Angeles, elevating it above sidewalks on new, strengthened lampposts. His idea was to run east-west and north-south loops through the center of downtown. The next morning, Lunden called Stephens-Adamson's local chief and they began to collaborate.

Unveiled in early 1956, Lunden's version involved a conveyor belt upon which strings of six-passenger pods swept silently about the town. Passengers would hop on and off the cars from moving sidewalks, synchronized at one and a half miles per hour. Once the cars left the stations, they'd speed up to 15 miles per hour. Pods would leave stations every three seconds, toting 14,000 passengers per hour. The four loops, each one and a half miles long, would cost a total of $8.8 million. Users would leave their automobiles at the edge of downtown in huge parking lots, thus relieving central city traffic.

In the late fifties, Lunden went around Los Angeles giving talks to civic organizations and showing hand-colored, large-scale drawings of his "waitless" Carveyor. He added new routes, from Union Station to Dodger Stadium, and an elevated loop within LAX, years before the airport got its double-decker roadway. In 1960, the Los Angeles Airport Commission declined to fund Lunden's concept.

More than a decade later, Goodyear was still promoting the plan but found no takers. "The Carveyor is the best thing man has yet been able to devise for moving people quickly and efficiently over short distances in highly congested areas," Robert F. Mercer, head of the company's Industrial Products division, told the *Los Angeles Times*. The Carveyor found no takers, but people movers remained alive in the city's master transit plans for years to come.

→ Lone pedestrian walks beneath "Overhead Carveyor Structure."

OVERHEAD CARVEYOR STRUCTURE
LUNDEN, HAYWARD & O'CONNOR
Architects
November 1955
JOB 364 P-9

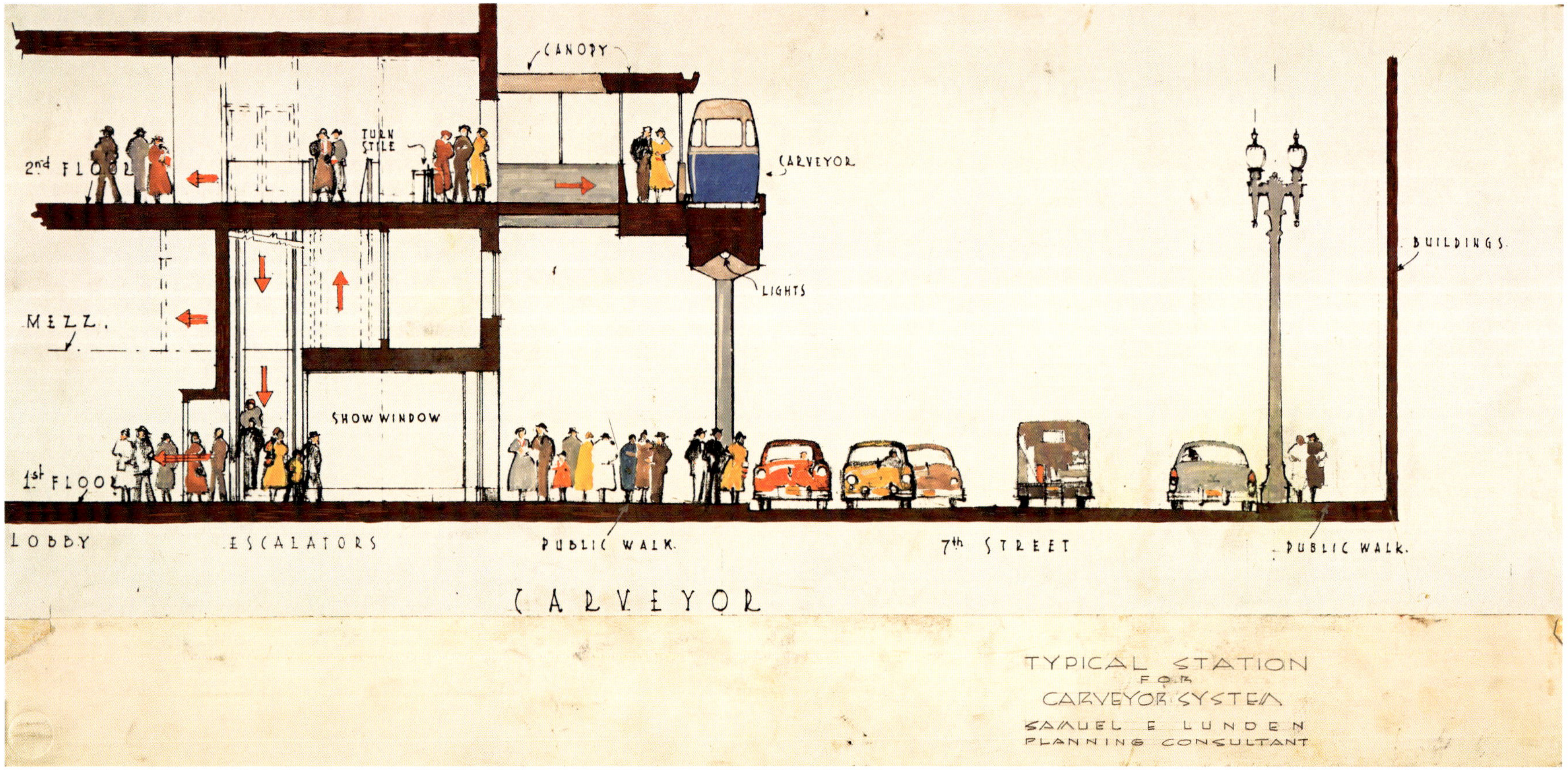

←
Business bustles with addition of second-floor entrances.

↙
A car-free Broadway in downtown Los Angeles

→
Carveyor shuttle to LAX

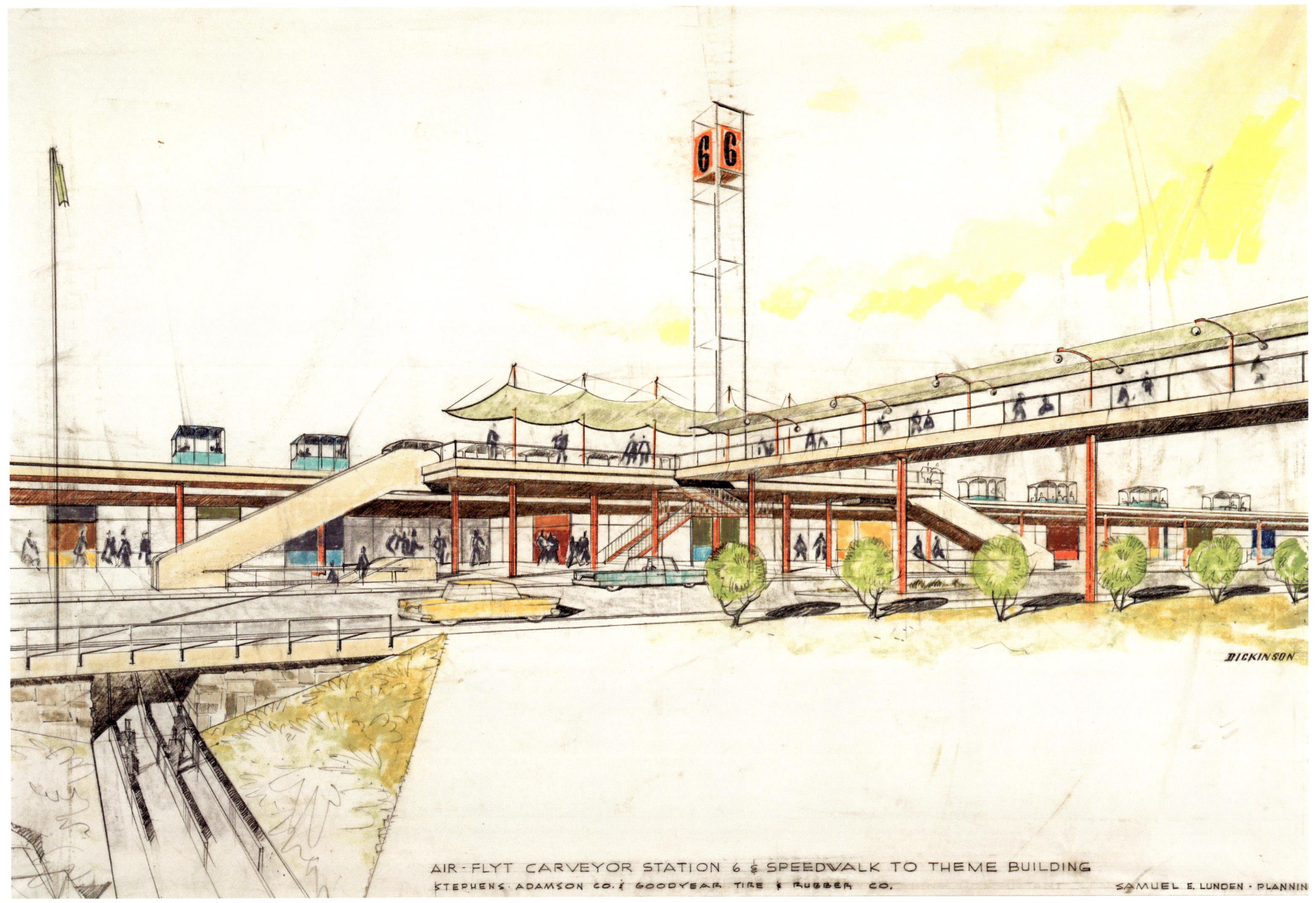
66
DICKINSON
AIR-FLYT CARVEYOR STATION 6 & SPEEDWALK TO THEME BUILDING
STEPHENS ADAMSON CO. & GOODYEAR TIRE & RUBBER CO.
SAMUEL E. LUNDEN · PLANNIN

JOHN DRESCHER AND MOFFAT AND NICHOL
SANTA MONICA OFFSHORE FREEWAY

1965

Beginning in the early 1960s, Santa Monica planners seriously considered the idea of an offshore freeway running along six miles of the bay from Santa Monica to Malibu. The proposal for a $600-million causeway, connecting the 10 Freeway to the Pacific Coast Highway, originated with highway engineers but was adopted by visionary millionaire John Drescher. He dreamed up a 30,000-foot-long chain of small man-made islands—similar to the Florida Keys—with residences for 29,000 people, marinas, and amenities for boating and other activities. Down the middle of this artificial archipelago would run the multilane, 200-foot-wide Sunset Seaway. Before Drescher was done, he would hook the state legislature and local officials on the idea.

The main purpose of the Seaway, Drescher and his allies said, was to provide an alternative to a planned—and, ultimately, shelved—double-decker coastal freeway, which some feared would be too narrow to avoid traffic jams but large enough to shred Palisades Park into a series of on- and off-ramps.

The city paid $30,000 for a feasibility study, which recommended building the 1,200-foot-wide offshore landmass using infill from quarries on Catalina Island. If barges couldn't haul the necessary 97 million cubic yards of rock the 22 miles from Catalina, the coastal mountains could be dynamited and terraced, with the bonus of creating new land for subdivisions. The project, connected to the shore via several bridges, was estimated to take 10 years to construct, and Santa Monica's Causeway Freeway Commission planned to sell rights-of-way and developable parcels.

Up for discussion as part of the causeway was a gondola to connect the marina to the proposed Third Street Mall (today's Promenade). The aerial tram, like those in the Swiss Alps, would hoist passengers from the shoreline to the shopping district, crossing the PCH and the sheer, 100-foot-tall palisades in fast-moving pods. The overheated planners gleefully reported: "The possible higher costs (of the causeway) will be amortized many times over in the years to come by the vast amount of land

→ Freeway, man-made islands, and new marina enclose Santa Monica Bay.

The Causeway

AN UNUSUAL FUTURE

conserved and by the unmeasurable shopping and tourist revenues drawn into the city because of such a unique solution!"

Drescher and his architects, Victor Gruen, labeled the scheme a "bold and exciting concept," moving traffic away from the beachfront and the palisades area. They acknowledged its undoubted effects on the beach and surf but saw a silver lining: "This should not be considered a negative aspect, however, since quiet waters would afford a different type of swimming activity appealing to an entirely different group of beach users."

Such patronizing attitudes were a clarion call to inland hill dwellers and beach bums alike. Having enlisted actor James Arness, who played TV lawman Matt Dillon on *Gunsmoke*, opponents launched a Save Our Beach campaign. The city establishment, led by the *Santa Monica Lookout* along with the city council and chamber of commerce, faced a rebellion whose petition garnered 50,000 signatures and landed on the governor's desk.

Bowing to budget shortages and citizen upheaval, governor Edmund G. "Pat" Brown vetoed the causeway in September 1965. The Causeway Freeway Commission was disbanded in 1966. "The ghost of this white elephant," the *Lookout* reported in 2003, "continued to stalk City Hall until the 70s, when a scale model of the project, sitting in the planning office, mysteriously disappeared."

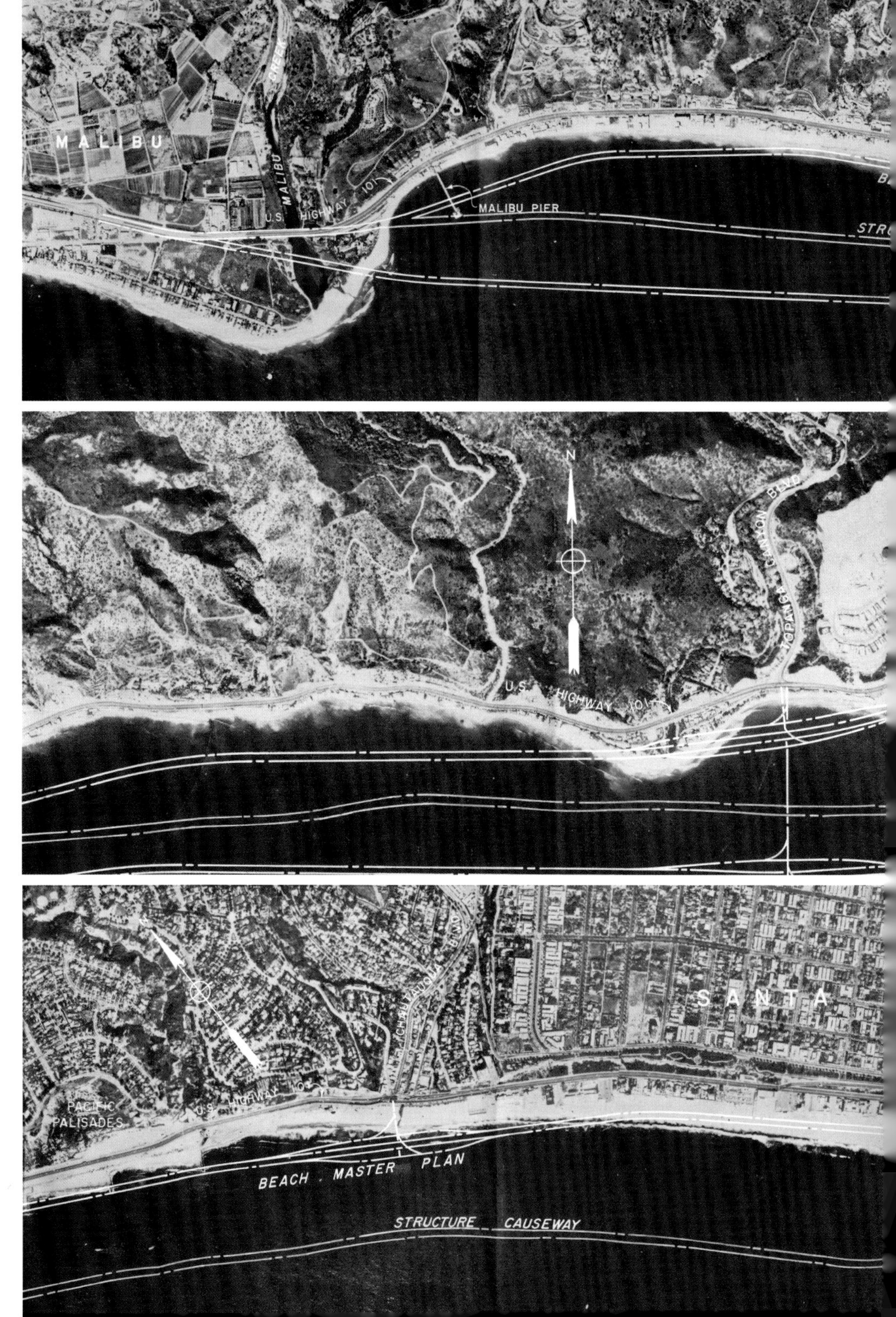

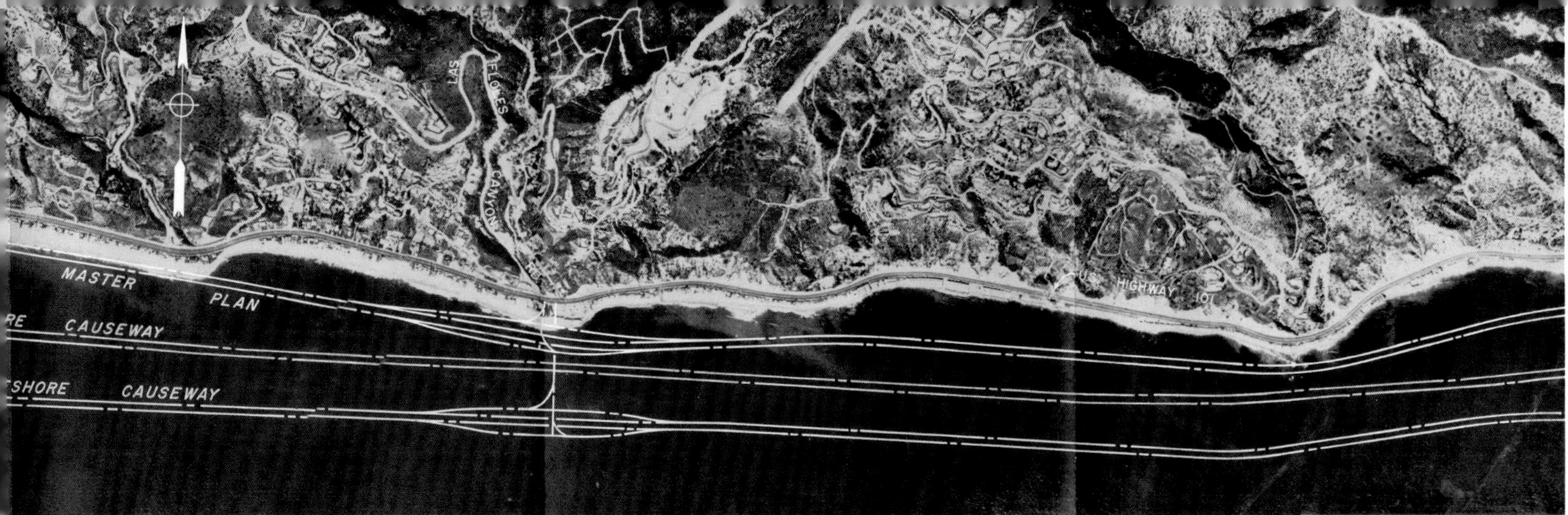
MASTER
PLAN
CAUSEWAY
SHORE
CAUSEWAY
U.S. HIGHWAY 101

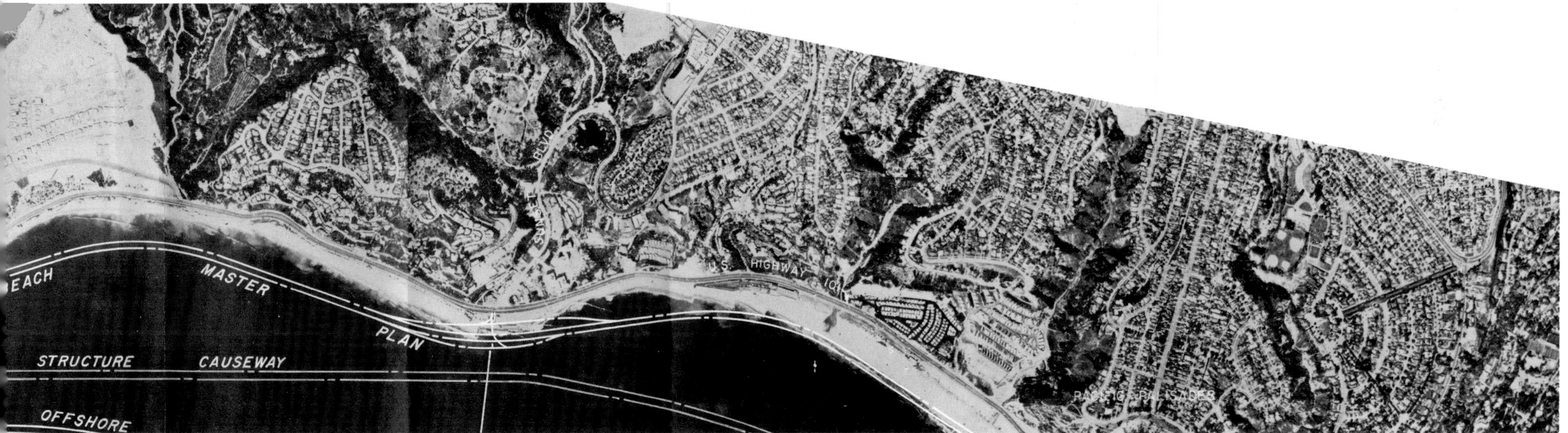
EACH
MASTER
PLAN
STRUCTURE
CAUSEWAY
OFFSHORE
U.S. HIGHWAY 101

MONICA
HIGHWAY 101
SANTA MONICA PIER

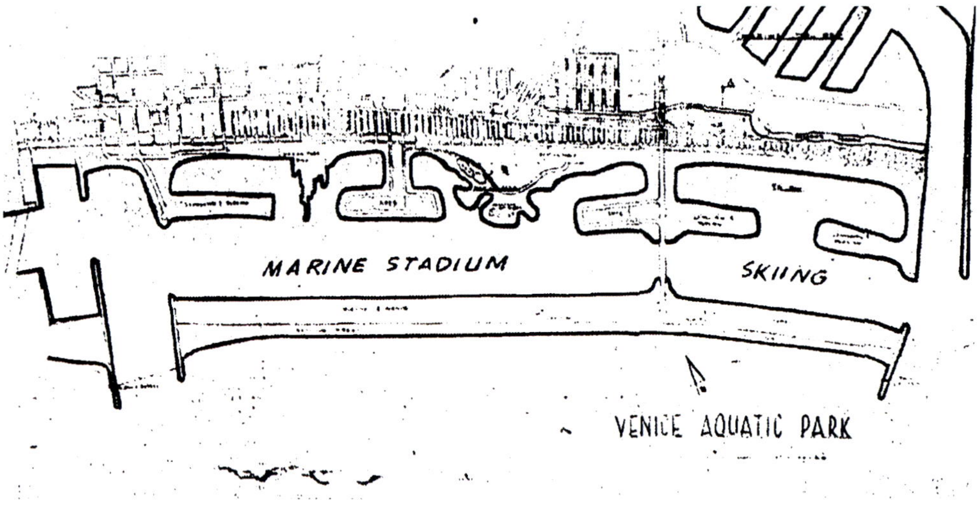

MOFFAT AND NICHOL
VENICE AQUATIC PARK

1961

The city of Los Angeles's vast shoreline development plan, honed throughout the '50s and '60s, aimed to add hundreds of acres of recreation and development to an area that for years had grown in random, piecemeal fashion. While not as huge as the neighboring offshore freeway, one of the largest elements of the city's plan was put forward by the Marina Peninsula Property Owners Association. It called for a $20 million aquatic park linking Santa Monica to Marina del Rey, three miles south. A man-made island would parallel the existing shoreline, creating the park's quieter lagoon.

The parkway would create a marine "stadium," made up of stands stretching for two miles, overlooking a boat-racing course and a water ski area. The initial scheme, drawn up by Moffat and Nichol, who were also the engineers of the Santa Monica offshore freeway, would handle 20,000 bathers and 18,000 boats. The plan, though, was completely dependent on the causeway. Both projects fizzled when the offshore freeway was shot down.

(Preceding spread) State transportation department routing maps superimposed on aerial photograph of coastline

↓

Santa Monica's new man-made islands

→

Map of land-sea connections

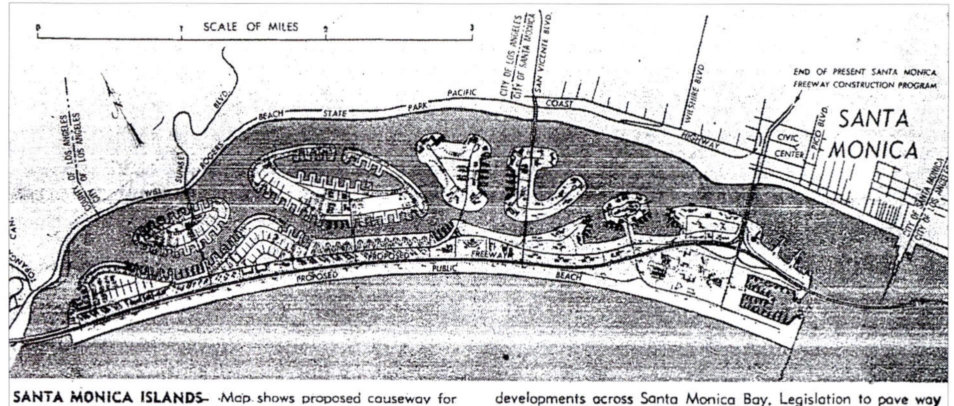

SANTA MONICA ISLANDS— Map shows proposed causeway for the Pacific Coast Freeway and "island" residential and commercial developments across Santa Monica Bay. Legislation to pave way for $600 million project is to be introduced soon in Sacramento.

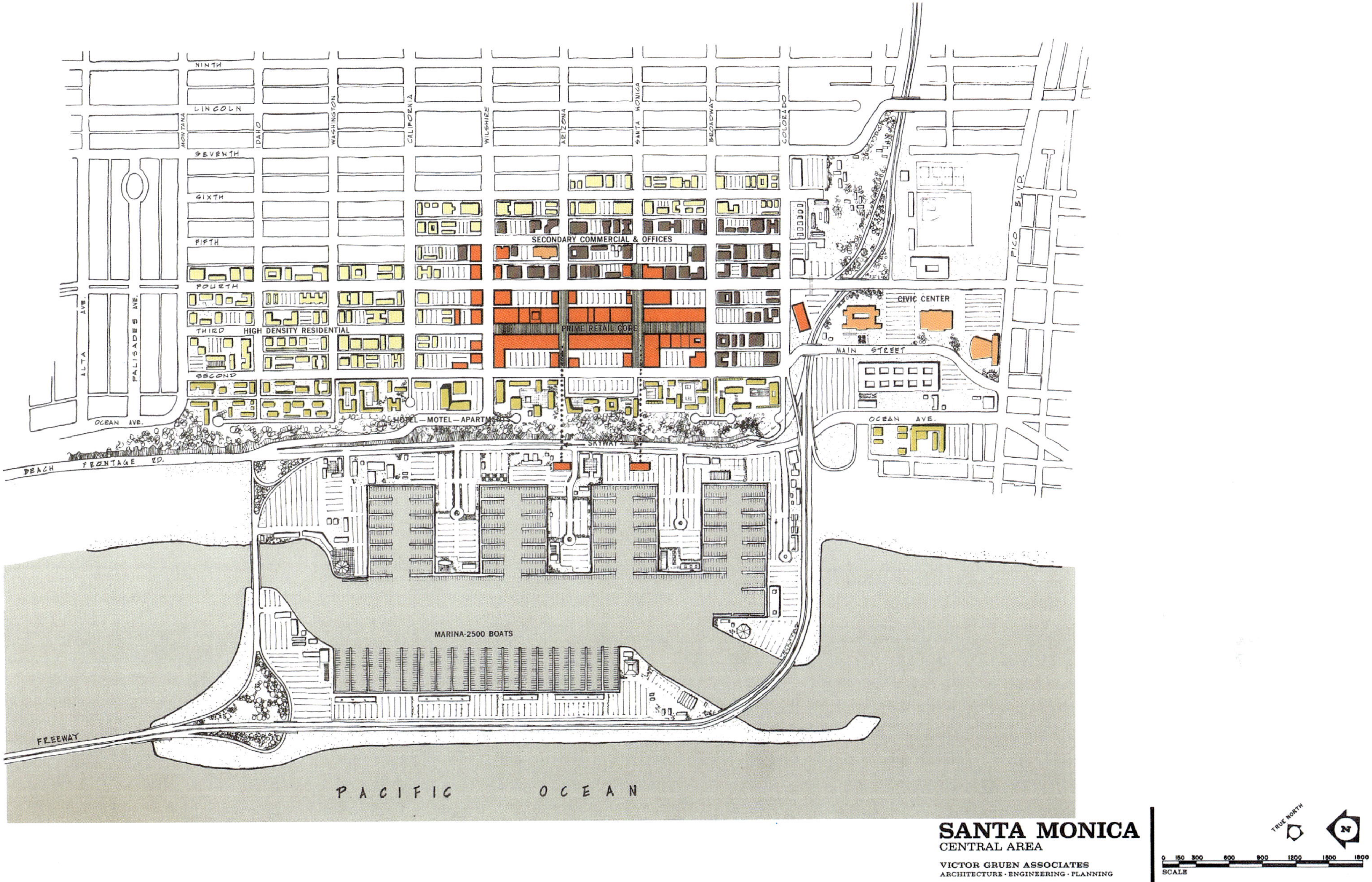

NINTH
LINCOLN
SEVENTH
SIXTH
FIFTH
FOURTH
THIRD
SECOND
MONTANA
IDAHO
WASHINGTON
CALIFORNIA
WILSHIRE
ARIZONA
SANTA MONICA
BROADWAY
COLORADO
ALTA AVE.
PALISADES AVE.
OCEAN AVE.
PICO BLVD.
MAIN STREET
SECONDARY COMMERCIAL & OFFICES
PRIME RETAIL CORE
HIGH DENSITY RESIDENTIAL
CIVIC CENTER
HOTEL—MOTEL—APARTMENTS
SKYWAY
BEACH FRONTAGE RD.
MARINA-2500 BOATS
FREEWAY
PACIFIC OCEAN

SANTA MONICA
CENTRAL AREA

VICTOR GRUEN ASSOCIATES
ARCHITECTURE · ENGINEERING · PLANNING

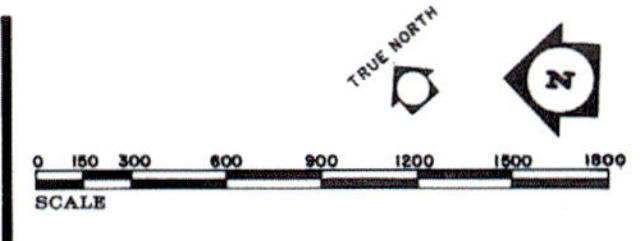

27 ILLUSTRATIVE PLAN FOR COMPREHENSIVE DEVELOPMENT

TR

DT

A. C. MARTIN
METROPORT

1965

A decade after the failure of its Union Station Transportation Center, A. C. Martin was at it again in the same location. The firm proposed—on behalf of Los Angeles World Airports, the authority that owns LAX—the City Airline Passenger Terminal, familiarly known as Metroport. This multistory parking structure, above the railroad tracks behind Union Station, would double as an airport transit hub. Its massive rooftop platform would be L shaped, with the longer arm used as a runway for aircraft, then in development, that could perform vertical takeoffs and landings. The shorter section was reserved for very large jet-powered, heavy-lift copters.

A major focus of the project was on “sky lounges,” or helicopter-ferried buses, which would attach to the underside of a Sikorsky Skycrane, like suckerfish glued to the skin of a shark, and could carry 23 passengers at a time between downtown and LAX.

Concrete bridges linked the half-mile-long terminal to Union Station. Beneath the parking lot, at street level, a sleek, semicircular plaza would serve as the portal to an elevated high-speed railway. Dubbed the Skyrail, the express would make just one stop, at Seventh and Flower streets, before heading to the airport.

In 1967, the Los Angeles City Council condemned a 13-acre site next to Union Station to make way for the project. This was a first step in duplicating the Metroport throughout the region, with helicopter transports making short hops to Beverly Hills, Hollywood, the San Fernando and Antelope valleys, Pomona, and Orange County. The new-fangled Harrier jets, meanwhile, would fly to cities within a 500-mile radius, relieving airport traffic to and from San Francisco, Sacramento, and San Diego.

But the concept of flying buses and vertical-lift planes lost momentum sometime after 1969, when the Los Angeles County Board of Supervisors raised concerns over the noise impact on the recently completed, county-owned Los Angeles Music Center. Proponents admitted the disruptions would be unavoidably bad. The end seemed nigh, but the city’s airport commission was reluctant to write an obituary. As late as 1975, its annual report still touted the plan. Despite such optimism, to this day, no form of high-speed transit goes directly into LAX.

→ All transit modes accommodated

METROPORT STATION

N325Y

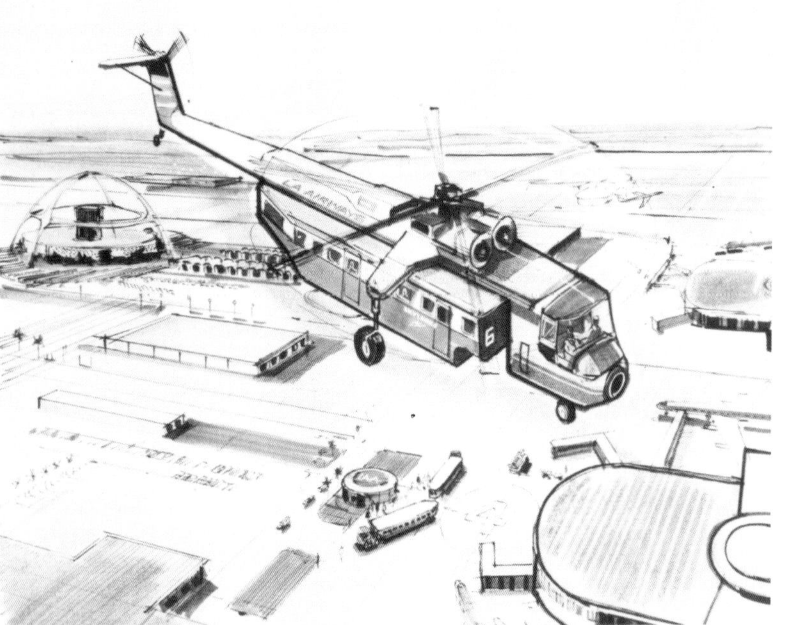

SIKORSKY S-64

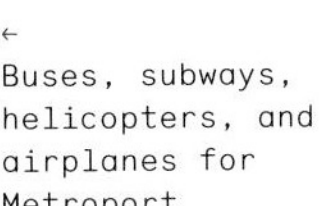

← Buses, subways, helicopters, and airplanes for Metroport

→ Raised pathways connect Metroport to Union Station.

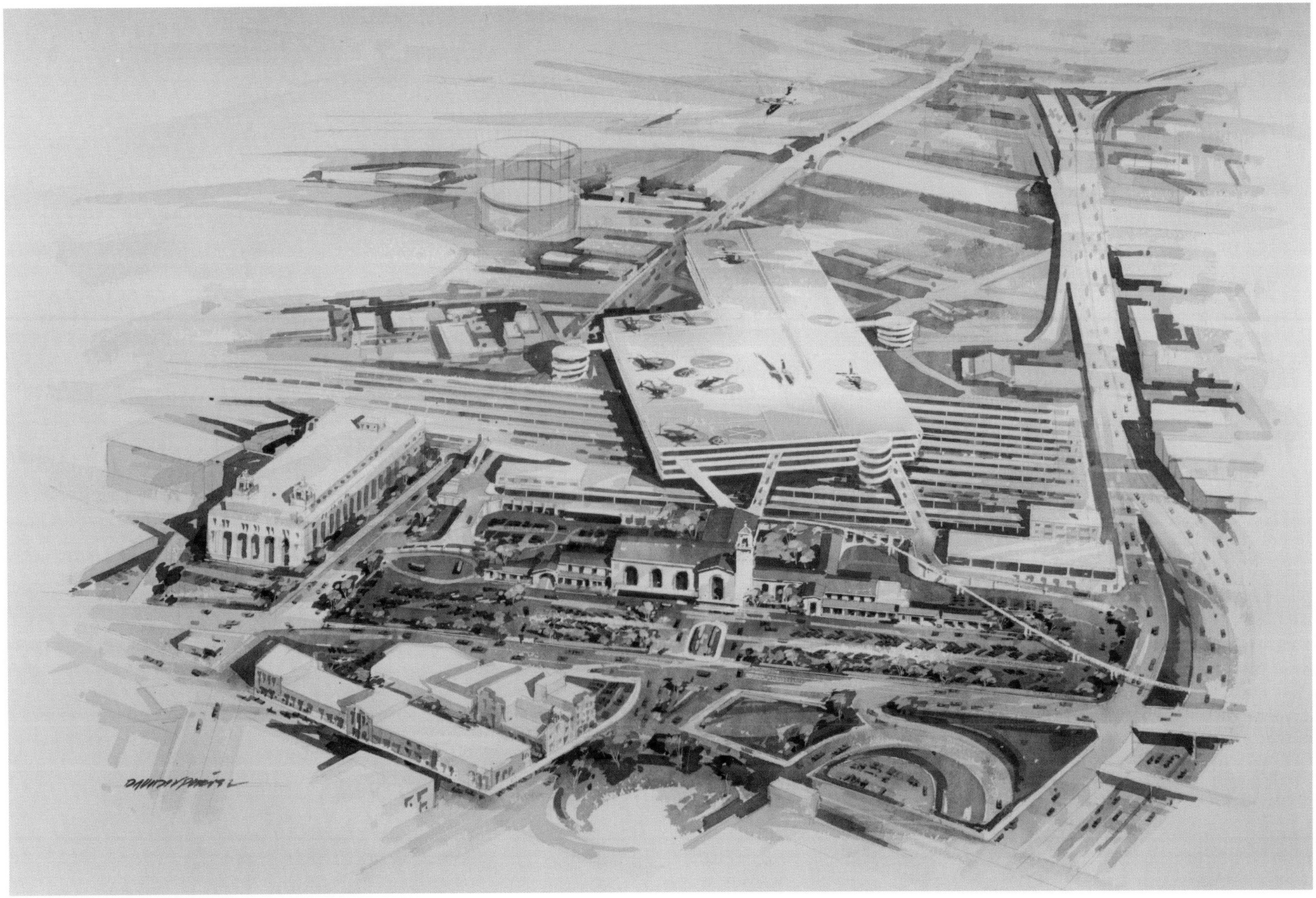

DT

CALVIN HAMILTON
PEDWAY

1971

Legendary city planner Calvin Hamilton, like all his predecessors and successors, confronted the eternal downtown tension between pedestrians and drivers. "These conflicts," Hamilton wrote, "create congestion, frustration, and potential danger." In late 1971, he sent the City Planning Commission his Central City Elevated Pedway Plan, an addendum, of sorts, to a much larger downtown blueprint being developed at the time by the consulting team of Wallace, McHarg, Roberts and Todd.

Hamilton wanted to get pedestrians out of the way of cars, and vice versa, by providing a landscaped walkway 17 feet in the air. The immediate plan was to build the first elevated sidewalk midblock between Figueroa and Flower streets, linking Atlantic Richfield Plaza on the north to Broadway Plaza on the south. A second Pedway would extend east-west, conceivably on Seventh Street.

Hamilton's idea was to create a well-designed pedestrian mall, incorporating a wide variety of pavement textures and colors. Its layout would have meeting areas, miniplazas, vending machines, low-key lighting, clear directional aids, places to rest, and spots to take in the view. Users would access second-story paths via stairs and escalators leading to a realm planted with ample trees and shrubbery. All this would cost around $27 per square foot; a single bridge span could cost $100,000. It would take about a year and a half to complete.

The city planner's idea borrowed heavily from a 1946 program presented by Plant Engineering Company, whose inspiration was the elevated sidewalks at the 1939 Chicago World's Fair City of Tomorrow. Hamilton's latter-day Pedway was incorporated into the Wallace, McHarg plan in 1972, but only a short section around the Bonaventure Hotel became reality. No others were built.

→ Hand-drawn downtown map. Thick lines show elevated sidewalk.

→→ Diagram of foot traffic separated from car traffic

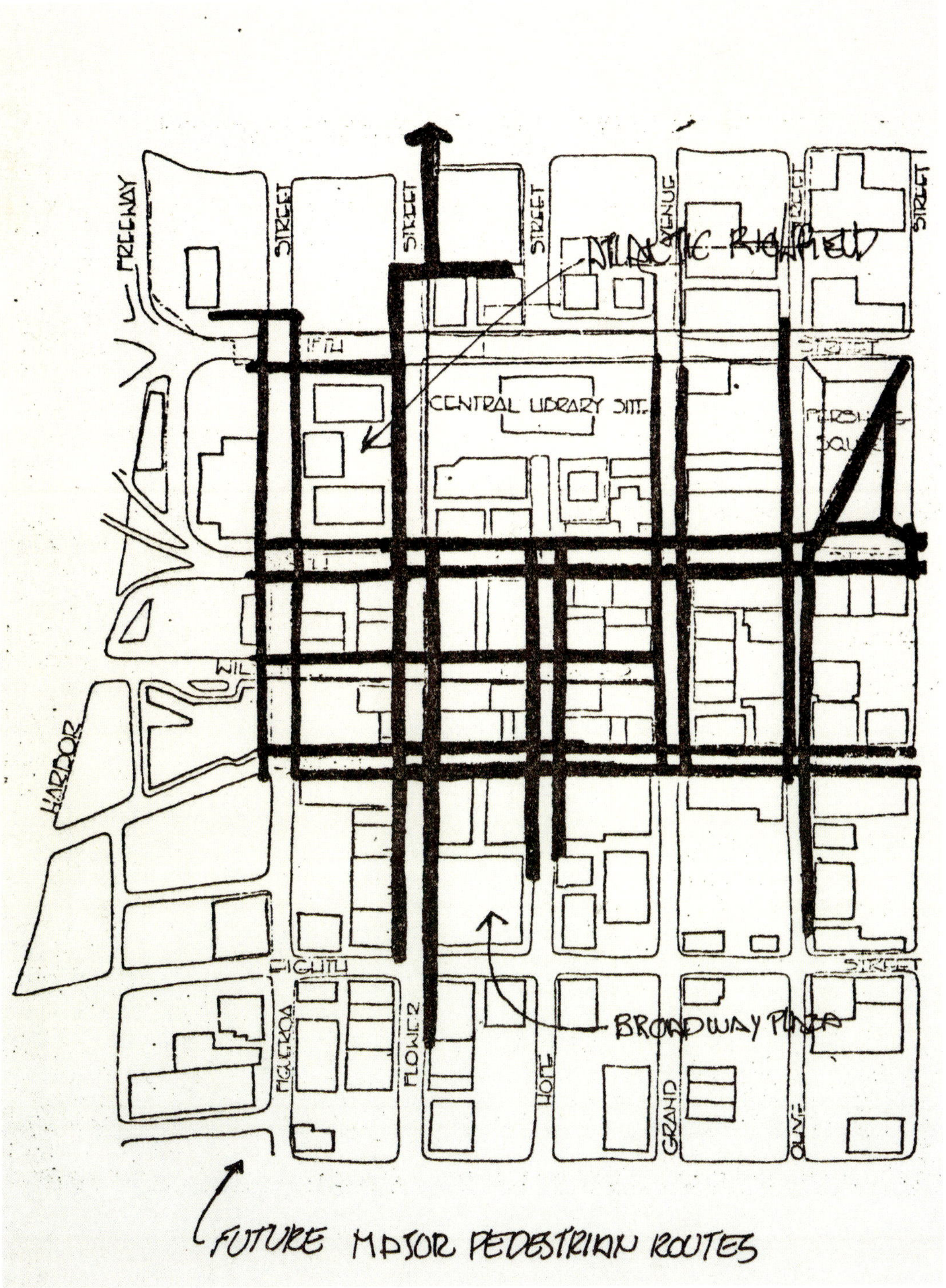
FREEWAY
STREET
STREET
STREET
AVENUE
STREET
STREET
ATLANTIC-RICHFIELD
FIFTH
STREET
CENTRAL LIBRARY SITE
PERSHING
SQUARE
WIL
HARDOR
EIGHTH
STREET
FIGUEROA
FLOWER
HOPE
GRAND
OLIVE
BROADWAY PLAZA
FUTURE MAJOR PEDESTRIAN ROUTES

RAY KAPPE
AUTOMATED VEHICLE

1970s

Ray Kappe, known in Southern California for his residential designs, was also deeply involved with city and transit planning. He developed, among other things, a park plan for Santa Monica and revitalization schemes for Inglewood and Watts.

The architect found himself particularly taken with L.A.'s transportation challenges. While he helped local leaders develop one of several people-mover proposals for downtown, with sleek, glass-canopied stations, he didn't believe that rail transport was the only answer for mobility throughout the spreading metropolis. He offered a plan in which the city's freeways would be traversed by a fleet of small, electric-powered, automated cars. These single-seaters, controlled by computer or radar, would, he claimed, increase freeway capacity as much as ten-fold. The tiny vehicles would also free up precious residential space, replacing driveways and garages with narrow, sidewalk-adjacent storage lots, hidden behind leafy trellises. Kappe was perfecting this scenario 30 years before Google announced its nascent fleet of self-guided cars.

He also posited, far ahead of his time, a "video communication system which could eliminate a large portion of the present automobile trips" through teleconferencing—the equivalent of today's online shopping. Perhaps taking his plans a little too far into the world of Ray Bradbury, Kappe suggested replacing trucking with "goods moved through tubes in capsules." Once his system was in place, Kappe foresaw transportation becoming merely recreational and social. That day, as evidenced by tightening traffic gridlock, is still far in the future.

→ Electric minicars free up urban space reclaimed from driveways and garages.

DT

PEOPLE MOVERS

1970s

With 13 stations less than four blocks apart, a healthy frog probably could jump the distance from station to station and get there just as fast.

Ernani Bernardi

The people mover, a concept with roots reaching back to the 1950s, was a permanent item on the Los Angeles Community Redevelopment Agency's agenda for more than a decade. The idea gained currency in 1969, when the federal government started a bidding war among cities anxious for a subsidy to create fully automated, elevated trams that would provide short hops within a metropolitan downtown. The federal money was intended to kick-start a transit layout that could be copied by any city. By 1976, Los Angeles was one of six finalists, and it seemed the federal Urban Mass Transportation Administration would provide 80 percent of the $175 million needed to build a system connecting Union Station, at the northern edge of downtown, to the Convention Center, at the southern.

Sixty automatically operated cars, riding on air cushions or rubber tires, would silently travel the 2.96-mile route. For 25 cents, riders could get on and off at one of 13 stops, including Little Tokyo, Civic Center, Pershing Square, Central Library, and several along the Figueroa corridor.

Concrete troughs called "guideways" would be lifted two to three stories above the street, held aloft on slender concrete pylons and supported in some places by large horizontal beams stretching from sidewalk to sidewalk. In some places, the tracks would come to within 10 feet of the windows of buildings. In others, twin "guideways" would run down the middle of streets and avenues, with 100-foot-long stations occupying large swaths of air space. One short stretch would pierce a tunnel through Bunker Hill.

→ Plaza brought to life by short-hop transit

The plan seemed a lock. Mayor Tom Bradley staked his election on a vow to bring mass transit to his city with the officially titled People Mover. The city council gave its approval. Architects and transit designers weighed in with their own visions. The chamber of commerce and Central City Association pledged to underwrite operating costs. And, the 417-page "Environmental Impact Statement" from the Community Redevelopment Agency (CRA) concluded that the elevated transit would provide "a unifying visual element to an area of downtown which presently does not possess a strong identity."

Critics, from the NAACP to the Los Angeles Conservancy, attacked the People Mover as an urban blight. They denounced it as a "$200 million boondoggle" that would divert precious money from the development of comprehensive public transit. They derided the CRA's claim that it would attract 72,400 riders a day by 1990, when the city's minibus traveling a nearly identical route only carried 6,000. They pointed out that, in any case,

PLAZA
RTD

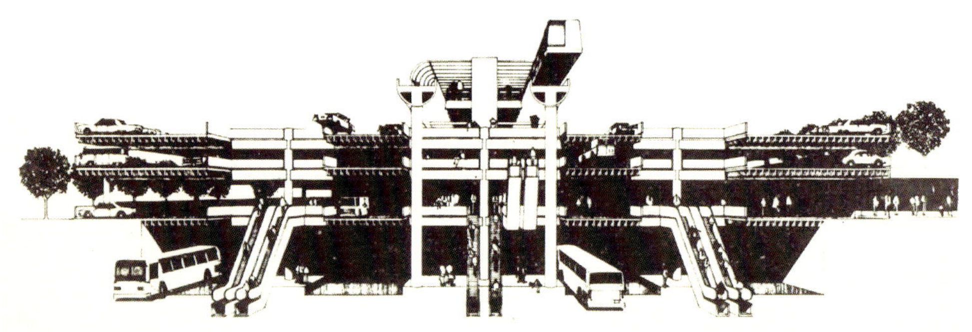

most of the central city's bus traffic was east of the proposed route, on Broadway, not near Figueroa Street. And they skewered the aesthetics of the project, describing the aerial cars as "intimidating and intrusive concrete dinosaurs" that "would plunge large portions of downtown into perpetual shadows." City councilman Ernani Bernardi joined the chorus. It's "a computerized Toonerville Trolley," he chortled, adding that "with 13 stations less than four blocks apart, a healthy frog probably could jump the distance from station to station and get there just as fast."

Even after Cleveland, Houston, and St. Paul dropped out of the federal program, Los Angeles persisted. Delays added to escalating costs—the figure jumped to more than $250 million—and finally an unlikely ally emerged to side with preservationists and the NAACP against the city's power elite. Newly elected President Ronald Reagan simply pulled the plug. Without the federal subsidy, the People Mover was finished.

Remnants of the project remain. Foundations of a few towers on Bunker Hill contain parts of the tunnel. And the World Trade Center, at Third and Figueroa, embraces an orphaned station site in the form of an oddly placed courtyard.

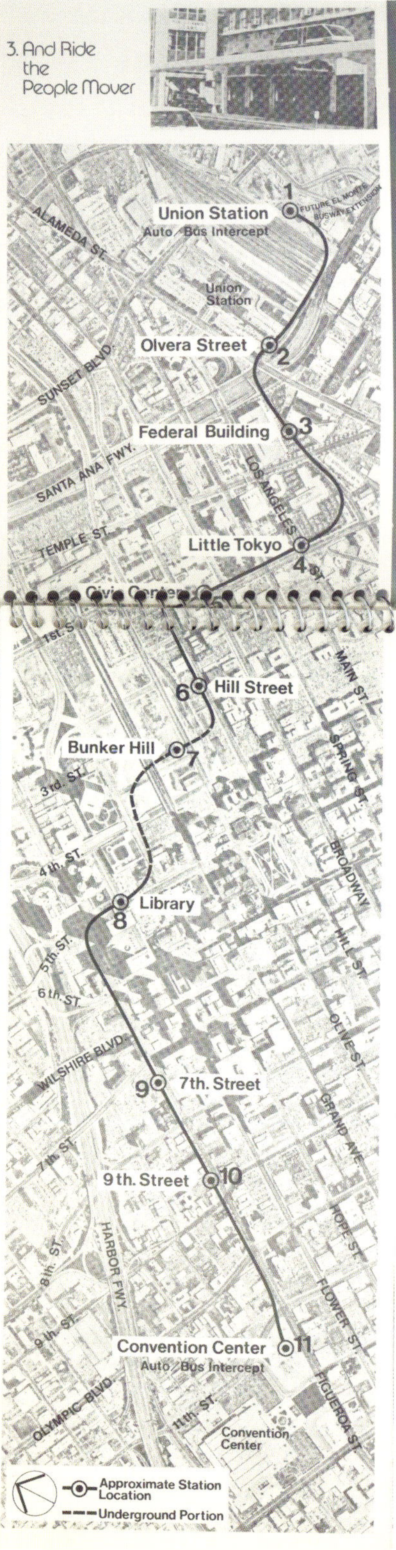

SOME TYPES OF PEOPLE MOVER VEHICLES UNDER CONSIDERATION

FIGURE 4-25A

FIGURE 4-25D

FIGURE 4-25B

FIGURE 4-25C

←←
People Mover station merges with parking.

←
Route map, from Union Station to Convention Center

↙↙
Ray Kappe, sketch of People Mover station hovering above Figueroa Street

→
Different People Movers under consideration

5th St
BANK AMERICA

← Gliding above Figueroa Street, Bonaventure Hotel in background

→ Ray Kappe's station

LA

AIR CUSHION AND MAGLEV TRAINS

1970s-2012

The dream of hurtling along by rail between LAX and regional airports began in the 1970s with a $300,000 federal grant to study an air cushion train.

Powered by whisper-quiet, pollution-free electric motors, "tracked air cushion vehicles"—or TACVs—would hover over elevated U-shaped guideways, achieving speeds of up to 150 miles per hour. Phase one involved a 16.3-mile run from LAX to the Sepulveda Dam in the San Fernando Valley. Using the right-of-way down the middle of the San Diego Freeway, the train would make the trip in 10 minutes, 35 seconds.

Set for completion in 1973, this was to be the first leg of a proposed link to Palmdale Airport, 66 miles away. LAX transit planners were also contemplating TACV connections to other far-flung regional airports. That idea fizzled during the 1973 oil crisis, ridiculed because the TACV would have carried just 6,000 passengers a day, a tenth of what a simple bus line could do at a fraction of the cost.

During the next two decades, a new technology emerged. Magnetic levitation, as its name implies, uses magnets to propel trains at high speeds without wheels, axles, or bearings. By the 1990s, the government was pouring millions of dollars into Maglev research, and transit wonks once again saw a futuristic, sleek-bodied train speeding from LAX to Palmdale—this time, going 300 miles per hour.

That concept was halted when, in the summer of 1990, the state's highway division rejected Maglev in favor of building more freeways through Orange and San Diego counties.

A decade later, L.A.'s biggest planning agency, the Southern California Association of Governments, revived the idea. In 2002, it proposed a Maglev from Ontario Airport to West Los Angeles. The 56-mile run would take 29 minutes. The cost would be $5.5 billion; the opening date, 2018.

But Maglev plans—including one from Anaheim to Las Vegas and another from Irvine to Palmdale—lost support when Congress earmarked funds for high-speed rail, a less costly, more efficient solution. Federal money evaporated, and Maglevs disappeared, perhaps for good, from planning documents in 2012.

→
Proposed Maglev line between Las Vegas and Orange County

CN
California-Nevada
Super Speed Train
Commisson

ACKNOWLEDGMENTS

2013

LA

To AJS and PGG. Thank you for providing the inspiration and always making the road less rocky.
Greg

To Kellsy, for your love, patience, and inspiration.
Sam

This book, and an accompanying exhibition, began in a warehouse deep in the San Fernando Valley. That storage facility contains models owned by the Getty Research Institute, among them a number of examples of designs meant for Los Angeles but never built. In the fall of 2009, the Getty approached Tibbie Dunbar, director of the A+D Architecture and Design Museum > Los Angeles. The Getty's architecture curators, Wim de Witt and Christopher Alexander, asked if she would be interested in putting together a show based on the unbuilt project models in the Getty's storehouse. In turn, Tibbie lassoed Brooke Hodge, who had recently joined the museum's board, and, as they say, one thing led to another. A wily Tibbie drafted us to work on an exhibition slated to be a simple look at schemes that stalled between 1980 and 2001.

Nothing is ever as simple as it seems, but we first must thank Tibbie for luring us in. To Frances Anderton, Greg owes a special debt, since it was she who recommended that he join forces with Sam. Our fascination with the never built expanded to include more than a century of works, but we could not have begun this journey without the aid of Wim and Christopher. Their support went beyond offering clues; they have been and continue to be our scouts and guides.

Soon Laura Ng joined, almost at the very beginning, and it was her willingness to go firm by firm in a never-ending search for never builts that became the foundation of this work. Laura also tirelessly combed archives to turn rumors into facts, hints into actual drawings. For providing further indispensable investigations and support we'd like to thank Kate DeFronzo, Carren Jao, Sarah Lane, Stephanie Marracco, and Annie Park.

At the onset, we consulted a small group of savants whose knowledge of the city and its deep historical and spatial recesses helped draw our roadmap. They are: Edward Cella, William Deverell, Alan Hess, Greg Hise, Dana Huff, Dana Hutt, Scott Johnson, Edward Lifson, David Martin, John McIntyre, Jim Heimann, Chris Nichols, Merry Norris, Simon Pastucha, Kevin Roderick, Bill Roschen, Dan Rosenfeld, Roger Sherman, Deborah Sussman, D. J. Waldie, Michael Webb, Douglas Woods, and John Wyka.

No one can write about architecture in postwar Los Angeles without turning to the work of UCLA historian Tom Hines. Tom's work points back to the librarians, archivists, and architecture devotees who are the silent guardians of our city's heritage. The excitement they demonstrated, and the willingness to peel away from the demands of their daily work to pull out documents and records and renderings that no one had thought to view in years, if ever, is a testimony to their abiding faith in the meaning of the past to inform the present and guide the future. Thanks to Fred Barker and Paul Soifer at the Los Angeles Department of Water and Power; Erin Chase and Alan Jutzi of the Huntington Library's architectural collection; the always helpful Bert Rinderle and John Sullivan, also at the Huntington; Glen Creason and the librarians at the Los Angeles Public Library; Simon Elliot and Genie Guerard of the UCLA Library Special Collections; UCLA archivist Charlotte Brown; Michael Holland, master of the vaults at the Los Angeles City Archives; the Natural History Museum's chief historian Cathy McNassor; independent historian Tom Sitton; Dace Taube, curator at the USC Doheny Memorial Library; the librarians at the Seaver Center for Western History Research; Kenneth Bicknell, Matthew Barrett, and Denise Villegas at the Dorothy Peyton Gray Transportation Library; Janet Coles, peerless map-finder at the Caltrans library; Janet Abrams and Julia Dawson, Canadian Centre for Architecture; Patrick Prescott, Burbank City Planning; Jocelyn Gibbs and Melinda Gandara, Architecture and Design Collection at UCSB; Sarah Sherman and the archivists at the Getty Research Institute; Daniel Paul, Anthony Lumsden expert; Ethel Pattison, Flight Path Learning Center; Matthew Roth at AAA of Southern California; Margo Stipe, Frank Lloyd Wright Foundation; Scott Taylor, CalArts; Richard Adkins and Mary Mallory of Hollywood Heritage; Steve Vaught, independent Hollywood expert; Nat Gale, with the L.A. mayor's office; Jessica Varner, independent researcher; Richard Koshalek, director of the Hirshhorn Museum; Kenneth Caldwell, A. Quincy Jones enthusiast; David Doherty, historian; Mike Eberts, historian of Griffith Park; John Enright, Konrad Wachsmann aficionado; Adam Arenson, historian and Millard Sheets buff; Jessica Gambling, LACMA archivist; independent archivist Harvey Jordan and filmmaker Stephanie Hubbard; and Laura Verlaque of the Pasadena Historical Society.

Special thanks to family members and former employees of architects no longer living: Helena Arahuete, Bruce Becket, John Caldwell, Ena Dubnoff, Chris Georgesco, Mike Jones, Gloria Koenig, John Lumsden, Dion Neutra, Stephen Quick, John Staude, and Eric Lloyd Wright.

Without the dedicated staffers at architectural firms around the globe, neither facts nor images would have been forthcoming. Our list, no doubt partial, must include: Donna Clandening, Danielle Cornwell, Ryan Davis, John Grant, Holly Hampton, Cynthia Kallmeyer, Brigitte Kouo, Jen Lathrop, Denise Lee, Alan Lewis, Meaghan Lloyd, Julie Maniere, Eric McNevin, Nicole Meyer, Christine Noblejas, James O'Connor, Matt Parent, Joyce Shin, Dana Smith, Legier Stahl, Andrea Tzvetkov, Julia van den Hout, and Talitha van Dijk.

A special IOU to George Helfand of Luna Imaging and Gary Krakower of ARC printing for turning originals into digital reproductions for all to see.

And, of course, to the architects and planners whose work appears in these pages and inspired us to keep digging.

A final thank you to Eric Heiman of Volume Inc., our dedicated designer, who understood the feel of the book from the first; to Anne Thompson, who tirelessly sifted the text to near perfection; and, not least, to Diana Murphy of Metropolis Books, who fell in love with *Never Built* and moved heaven and earth to make the book a reality, unlike the projects it depicts.

SELECTED BIBLIOGRAPHY

Eric Avila, *Popular Culture in the Age of White Flight: Fear and Fantasy in Suburban Los Angeles* (Berkeley: University of California Press, 2006)

Jeremiah B. C. Axelrod, *Inventing Autopia* (Berkeley: University of California Press, 2009)

Jean-François Bédard, ed., *Cities of Artificial Excavation* (Montreal: Canadian Centre for Architecture/New York: Rizzoli, 1994)

Willy Boesiger, ed., *Richard Neutra: 1950–60, Buildings and Projects* (London: Thames and Hudson, 1964)

David Brodsly, *L.A. Freeway: An Appreciative Essay* (Berkeley: University of California Press, 1981)

Michael Broggie, *Walt Disney's Railroad Story* (Pasadena: Pentrex, 1997)

Cory Buckner, *A. Quincy Jones* (London: Phaidon, 2002)

John and Laree Caughey, *Los Angeles: Biography of a City* (Berkeley: University of California Press, 1976)

Glen Creason, *Los Angeles in Maps* (New York: Rizzoli, 2010)

Cynthia Davidson, ed., *Tracing Eisenman* (New York: Rizzoli, 2006)

David G. De Long, *Frank Lloyd Wright and the Living City* (Milan: Skira, 1998)

Stephen Dobney, *Barton Myers* (Tokyo: Books Nippan, 1994)

Mike Eberts, *Griffith Park: A Centennial History* (Los Angeles: Historical Society of Southern California, 1996)

Robert M. Fogelson, *The Fragmented Metropolis* (Berkeley: University of California Press, 1967)

William Fulton, *The Reluctant Metropolis: The Politics of Urban Growth in Los Angeles* (Baltimore: Johns Hopkins University Press, 2001)

David Gebhard, *Robert Stacy-Judd: Maya Architecture and the Creation of a New Style* (Santa Barbara: Capra, 1993)

———, *Schindler* (London: Thames and Hudson, 1971)

David Gebhard and Harriette Von Breton, *Lloyd Wright, Architect: 20th Century Architecture in an Organic Exhibition* (Santa Monica: Hennessey and Ingalls, 1998)

David Gebhard and Robert Winter, *An Architectural Guidebook to Los Angeles* (Salt Lake City: Gibbs Smith, 2003)

———, *A Guide to Architecture in Los Angeles and Southern California* (Santa Barbara: Peregrine Smith, 1977)

Ralph Hancock, *Fabulous Boulevard* (New York: Funk and Wagnalls, 1949)

Thomas S. Hines, *Architecture of the Sun: Los Angeles Modernism, 1900–1970* (New York: Rizzoli, 2010)

———, *Richard Neutra and the Search for Modern Architecture* (New York, Rizzoli, 2005)

William Dudley Hunt, *Total Design: Architecture of Welton Becket and Associates* (New York: McGraw-Hill, 1971)

Lloyd Wright Drawings (Tokyo: GA Gallery, 1986)

Richard Longstreth, *City Center to Regional Mall: Architecture, the Automobile, and Retailing in Los Angeles, 1920–1950* (Cambridge, Mass.: MIT Press, 1997)

———, *The Drive-In, the Supermarket, and the Transformation of Commercial Space in Los Angeles, 1914–1941* (Cambridge, Mass.: MIT Press, 1999)

Karal Ann Marling, *Designing Disney's Theme Parks: The Architecture of Reassurance* (New York: Flammarion, 1997)

Casey C. M. Mathewson, *Frank O. Gehry: Selected Works, 1969 to Today* (Richmond Hill, Ontario: Firefly Books, 2007)

William Alexander McClung, *Landscapes of Desire: Anglo Mythologies of Los Angeles* (Berkeley: University of California Press, 2000)

Esther McCoy, *Richard Neutra* (New York, George Braziller, 1960)

Cathy McNassor, *Los Angeles's La Brea Tar Pits and Hancock Park* (Charleston, S.C.: Arcadia, 2011)

Kimberli Meyer and Susan Morgan, *Sympathetic Seeing: Esther McCoy and the Heart of American Modernist Architecture and Design* (West Hollywood: MAK Center for Art and Architecture/Nürnberg: Verlag für Moderne Kunst, 2011)

Doyce B. Nunis, Jr., ed., *Los Angeles and Its Environs in the Twentieth Century* (Los Angeles: Ward Ritchie, 1973)

Laurie Olin, *Transforming the Common Place: Selections from Laurie Olin's Sketchbooks* (New York: Princeton Architectural Press, 1997)

Nicholas Olsberg, ed., *Between Earth and Heaven: The Architecture of John Lautner* (New York: Rizzoli, 2008)

John Pastier, *Cesar Pelli* (New York: Whitney Library of Design, 1980)

Daniel Paul, "The Aesthetics of Efficiency: Contexts and the Early Development of Late-Modern Glass Skin Architecture" (master's thesis, California State University, Northridge, 2004)

Bruce Brooks Pfeiffer, *Frank Lloyd Wright Designs: The Sketches, Plans and Drawings* (New York: Rizzoli, 2011)

Dale Pitt and Leonard Pitt, *Los Angeles A to Z: An Encyclopedia of the City and County* (Berkeley: University of California Press, 1997)

Terence Riley, ed., *Frank Lloyd Wright, Architect* (New York: The Museum of Modern Art, 1994)

Matthew William Roth, "Concrete Utopia: The Development of Roads and Freeways in Los Angeles, 1910–1950" (Ph.D. diss., University of Southern California, 2007)

Allen J. Scott and Edward W. Soja, eds., *The City: Los Angeles and Urban Theory at the End of the Twentieth Century* (Berkeley: University of California Press, 1996)

Paula A. Scott, *Santa Monica: A History on the Edge* (Charleston, S.C.: Arcadia, 2004)

Meryle Seacrest, *Frank Lloyd Wright: A Biography* (New York: Knopf, 1992)

Charles Seims, *Trolley Days in Pasadena* (San Marino: Golden West Books, 1982)

Alison Sky and Michelle Stone, *Unbuilt America: Forgotten Architecture in the United States from Thomas Jefferson to the Space Age* (New York: McGraw-Hill, 1977)

Elizabeth A. T. Smith, *Case Study Houses: The Complete CSH Program 1945–1966* (New York: Taschen, 2002)

Kathryn Smith, *Frank Lloyd Wright, Hollyhock House and Olive Hill: Buildings and Projects for Aline Barnsdall* (New York: Rizzoli, 1992)

Jeffrey Stanton, *Santa Monica Pier: A History from 1875 to 1990* (Los Angeles: Donahue, 1990)

———, *Venice California: "Coney Island of the Pacific"* (Los Angeles: Donahue, 1993)

Maggie Valentine, *The Show Starts on the Sidewalk* (New Haven: Yale University Press, 1994)

Alan Weintraub, *Lloyd Wright: The Architecture of Frank Lloyd Wright Jr.* (New York: Abrams, 1998)

Frank Lloyd Wright, *The Living City* (New York: Horizon, 1958)

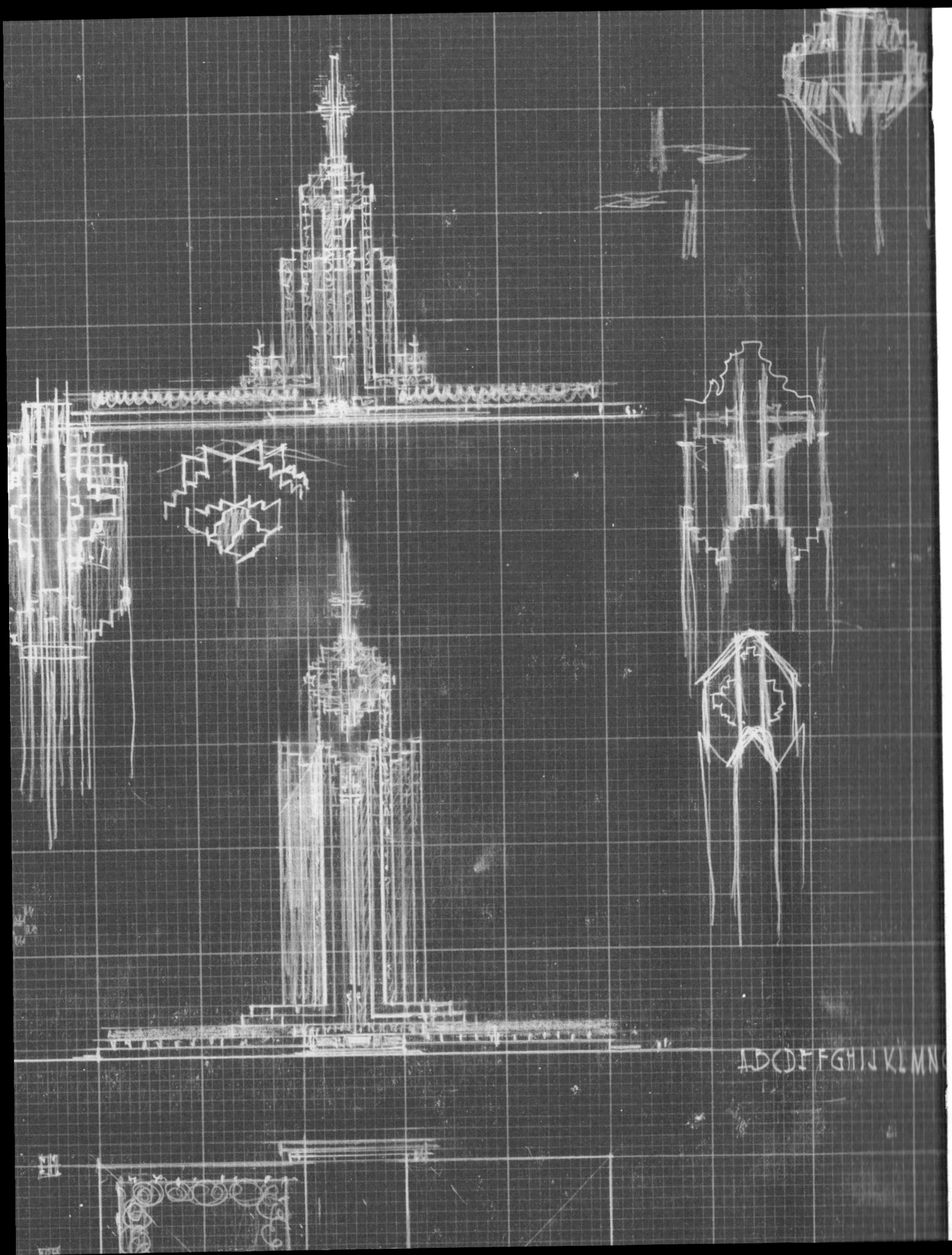

Project director: Diana Murphy
Copy-editor: Anne Thompson
Design: Volume Inc., San Francisco
Separations and printing: Asia One, Hong Kong

Library of Congress Cataloging-in-Publication Data is available upon request.
ISBN 978-1-935202-96-7

Metropolis Books
ARTBOOK | D.A.P.
155 Sixth Avenue, 2nd floor
New York, NY 10013
tel 212 627 1999
fax 212 627 9484
www.artbook.com
www.metropolisbooks.com

Illustration Credits

A. C. Martin, 28, 34L, 171, 249R; AECOM, 41B; Akademie der Künste, Berlin, Konrad-Wachsmann-Archiv, 187; Altoon Partners, 38T; Architecture and Design Collection, Art Design & Architecture Museum, UC Santa Barbara, 25R, 27, 142, 143, 146, 147, 149, 156, 157, 275–77; Asymptote Architecture, 279; Atelier Christian de Portzamparc, 235–37; Ateliers Jean Nouvel, 239–41; B+U, 242, 243; Barton Myers Associates, 125, 126, 129–31, 196B, 197, 244; Böhm and Partners, 127LC; Burbank Public Library, 21 BL; California Institute of the Arts, 97R; California Public Utilities Commission, *Report on Railroad Grade Crossing Elimination and Passenger and Freight Terminals in Los Angeles: California Railroad Commission, Engineering Department / Richard Sachse, Chief Engineer* (Sacramento: Railroad Commission of the State of California, 1920), 18T; Caltrans Transportation Library and History Center, 331, 332B, 352, 353; Canadian Centre for Architecture, 200, 201; Chris Nichols, 267–69; City of Santa Monica, 351; Coop Himmelb(l)au, 225; courtesy Cory Buckner, 18R; Culver City Planning Division, 31R; courtesy Dion Neutra, 76–79; Doug Suisman Urban Design, 133; Edward Cella Gallery/ Carlos Diniz Archive, 30, 107, 172, 173L, 185; EE&K/UNStudio, 39; Eric Owen Moss Architects, 229–31; courtesy Eric Lloyd Wright, 65–69, 151–55, back endsheet; Escher GuneWardena Architecture, 37; (fer) Studio, 45, 137R; Frank Lloyd Wright Foundation, 53, 54L, 56, 57, 59–62, 165–67; Gehry Partners, 40, 211, 305; Getty Research Institute, Los Angeles, 99–101, 182, 183; Glen Creason, 333; Gruen Associates, 169, 355; Hamid Omrani, 283; Hans Hollein, 127T; Hargreaves Associates, 313, 314; Harvey Jordan, 271–73; Harry Wolf, 33R; Hodgetts + Fung Design and Architecture, 310; Hollywood Heritage Museum, 21BR, 179, 180B, 181; Huntington Library, San Marino, CA, 22, 180T, 261–63, 293, 294, 295L, 335, 337–39, 347–49; JAHN, 33L, 203, 204, 205TL and BR; Jerde Partnership, 38B; John Friedman Alice Kimm Architects, 226, 227; John Lautner Archive, Research Library, Getty Research Institute, Los Angeles, California, 29L, 91–95, 189–91; John Lumsden, 103–5, 192, 193; Johnson Fain, 135B, 206, 207L, 251, 295R; Kanner Architects, 248; Kohn Pedersen Fox, 250; Koning Eizenberg Architecture, 42; LAX Flight Path Learning Center, 81–85, 358, 359; Lehrer Architects, 35; Leo A. Daly Architecture, 285–87; Library of Congress, 54R, 55; Lorcan O'Herlihy Architects, 44; Los Angeles City Archives, 21TL, 257–59, 301–3, 329; Los Angeles City Planning Department, 111–13, 115–17, 361; Los Angeles County Metropolitan Transportation Authority Research Library and Archive, 281, 321, 323–27, 332B, 341–44, 357, 365TL and R, 367–69; Los Angeles Department of Water and Power, 32; Los Angeles Times, 21TR, 31L, 49, 97L, 145, 205TR, 255, 291, 354; Mark Mack Architects, 311BR; Meyer and Allen, 41T; Mia Lehrer + Associates, 43; Michael Graves and Associates, 209; Michael Maltzan Associates, 313, 314; courtesy Mike Jones, 175–77; Moore Ruble Yudell Architects, 135T, 136, 213; Morphosis Architects, 17, 233, 280, 309, 311L and TR, 315; Natural History Museum of Los Angeles County, 297–99; NBBJ, 245, 247L; OMA, 36, 215, 216, 217L; Parsons Corporation, 371; Pasadena Museum of History, 319; Ray Kappe, 363, 366BL; Richard Keating, 223, 247R, 249L; Robert Mangurian, 199; Rockwell Group, 246; Samuel Wacht, 109; Seaver Center for Western History Research, 24; SITE Architecture, Art & Design, 307; Southern California Library for Social Studies and Research, 75; SPF:architects, 217R; Steven Holl Architects, 219–21; Steve Vaught, 26L; Sterling Architects, 127BL; Studio Daniel Libeskind, 251; Sussman-Prejza, 119–22, 123L; The Walt Disney Company, 265; Time Warner Inc., 345R; Todd Stevens, 73; UCLA Charles E. Young Research Library Department of Special Collections, 18L, 26R, 51, 65–69, 76–79, 141, 151–55, 161–63, 175–77; UCLA University Archives, 71, 72; University of Southern California, on behalf of the USC Special Collections, 87–89, 123R, 127R, 195, 196T, 207R, 332L, 345L; X-TEN Architecture, 37L

Goodell Monorail

Goodell Monorail

ABCDEFGHIJKLMNO